T0224389

Lecture Notes in Computer Science 6054

Commenced Publication in 1973
Founding and Former Series Editors:
Gerhard Goos, Juris Hartmanis, and Jan van Leeuwen

Editorial Board

David Hutchison
  Lancaster University, UK
Takeo Kanade
  Carnegie Mellon University, Pittsburgh, PA, USA
Josef Kittler
  University of Surrey, Guildford, UK
Jon M. Kleinberg
  Cornell University, Ithaca, NY, USA
Alfred Kobsa
  University of California, Irvine, CA, USA
Friedemann Mattern
  ETH Zurich, Switzerland
John C. Mitchell
  Stanford University, CA, USA
Moni Naor
  Weizmann Institute of Science, Rehovot, Israel
Oscar Nierstrasz
  University of Bern, Switzerland
C. Pandu Rangan
  Indian Institute of Technology, Madras, India
Bernhard Steffen
  TU Dortmund University, Germany
Madhu Sudan
  Microsoft Research, Cambridge, MA, USA
Demetri Terzopoulos
  University of California, Los Angeles, CA, USA
Doug Tygar
  University of California, Berkeley, CA, USA
Gerhard Weikum
  Max Planck Institute for Informatics, Saarbruecken, Germany

Radu Sion   Reza Curtmola   Sven Dietrich
Aggelos Kiayias   Josep M. Miret
Kazue Sako   Francesc Sebé (Eds.)

Financial Cryptography and Data Security

FC 2010 Workshops, RLCPS, WECSR, and WLC 2010
Tenerife, Canary Islands, Spain, January 25-28, 2010
Revised Selected Papers

 Springer

Volume Editors

Radu Sion
Stony Brook University, Stony Brook, NY, USA
E-mail: sion@cs.stonybrook.edu

Reza Curtmola
New Jersey Institute of Technology, Newark, NJ, USA
E-mail: crix@njit.edu

Sven Dietrich
Stevens Institute of Technology, Hoboken, NJ, USA
E-mail: spock@cs.stevens.edu

Aggelos Kiayias
University of Connecticut, Storrs, CT, USA
E-mail: aggelos@cse.uconn.edu

Josep M. Miret
Francesc Sebé
Universidad de Lleida, Spain
E-mail: {miret, fsebe}@matematica.udl.cat

Kazue Sako
NEC Central Research Labs
Kawasaki, Japan
E-mail: k-sako@ab.jp.nec.com

CR Subject Classification (1998): C.2, K.4.4, K.6.5, D.4.6, E.3, J.1

LNCS Sublibrary: SL 4 – Security and Cryptology

ISSN   0302-9743
ISBN-10   3-662-52003-1 Springer Berlin Heidelberg New York
ISBN-13   978-3-662-52003-1 Springer Berlin Heidelberg New York
DOI 10.1007/978-3-642-14992-4

This work is subject to copyright. All rights are reserved, whether the whole or part of the material is
concerned, specifically the rights of translation, reprinting, re-use of illustrations, recitation, broadcasting,
reproduction on microfilms or in any other way, and storage in data banks. Duplication of this publication
or parts thereof is permitted only under the provisions of the German Copyright Law of September 9, 1965,
in its current version, and permission for use must always be obtained from Springer. Violations are liable
to prosecution under the German Copyright Law.

springer.com

© IFCA/Springer-Verlag Berlin Heidelberg 2010
Softcover re-print of the Hardcover 1st edition 2010

Typesetting: Camera-ready by author, data conversion by Scientific Publishing Services, Chennai, India
Printed on acid-free paper   06/3180

Preface

This volume contains the workshop proceedings of the accompanying workshops of the 14th Financial Cryptograpy and Data Security International Conference 2010, held on Tenerife, Canary Islands, Spain, January 25-28, 2010.

Financial Cryptography and Data Security is a major international forum for research, advanced development, education, exploration, and debate regarding information assurance, with a specific focus on commercial contexts. The conference covers all aspects of securing transactions and systems and especially encourages original work focusing on both fundamental and applied real-world deployments on all aspects surrounding commerce security.

Three workshops were co-located with FC 2010: the Workshop on Real-Life Cryptographic Protocols and Standardization (RLCPS), the Workshop on Ethics in Computer Security Research (WECSR), and the Workshop on Lightweight Cryptography for Resource-Constrained Devices (WLC).

Intimate and colorful by tradition, the high-quality program was not the only attraction of FC. In the past, FC conferences have been held in highly research-synergistic locations such as Tobago, Anguilla, Dominica, Key West, Guadelupe, Bermuda, the Grand Cayman, and Cozumel Mexico. 2010 was the first year that the conference was held on European soil, in the Spanish Canary Islands, in Atlantic waters, a few miles across Morocco. Over 100 researchers from more than 20 countries were in attendance.

FC 2010 Organizers

Workshop Organization

Workshop on Lightweight Cryptography for Resource-Constrained Devices (WLC)
Chairs: Josep M. Miret and Francesc Sebé, Universitat de Lleida

Program Committee

Carlo Blundo   Josep Domingo-Ferrer
Jordi Castellà-Roca   Javier Herranz
Vanesa Daza

We also appreciate the assistance in evaluating the quality of submitted papers provided by the additional referees:

Arnau Erola   Carla Ràfols
Albert Fernández-Mir   Michal Sramka
Bo Qin   Arnau Vives-Guasch

Workshop on Real-Life Cryptographic Protocols and Standardization (RLCPS)
Chairs: Aggelos Kiayias, University of Connecticut, and Kazue Sako, NEC

Program Committee

N. Asokan   Nokia
Hongxia JinIBM   Almaden
Aggelos Kiayias   University of Connecticut
Helger Lipmaa   Cybernetica AS
Sandra Marcello   Thales
David Naccache   ENS
Kaisa Nyberg   TKK and Nokia
Satoshi Obana   NEC
Pascal Paillier   Gemalto and CryptoExperts
Ahmad-Reza Sadeghi   Ruhr University Bochum
Kazue Sako   NEC
Moti Yung   Google and Columbia University

Workshop on Ethics in Computer Security Research (WECSR)
Chair: Sven Dietrich, Stevens Institute of Technology

Program Committee

Michael Bailey	University of Michigan
Elizabeth Buchanan	University of Wisconsin-Milwaukee
Aaron Burstein	UC Berkeley
Michael Collins	RedJack
Marc Dacier	Symantec Research
George Danezis	Microsoft Research
Dorothy Denning	Naval Postgraduate School
Roger Dingledine	The Tor Project
Toralv Dirro	McAfee
David Dittrich	University of Washington
Engin Kirda	EURECOM
Howard Lipson	CERT
John McHugh	Dalhousie University
Vern Paxson	ICIR
Angela Sasse	University College London

Table of Contents

WLC Preface 1
  Josep M. Miret and Francesc Sebé

Hummingbird: Ultra-Lightweight Cryptography for
Resource-Constrained Devices 3
  *Daniel Engels, Xinxin Fan, Guang Gong, Honggang Hu, and
  Eric M. Smith*

Lighten Encryption Schemes for Secure and Private RFID Systems 19
  Sébastien Canard, Iwen Coisel, and Jonathan Etrog

Analysis and Improvement of a Pseudorandom Number Generator for
EPC Gen2 Tags 34
  J. Melia-Segui, J. Garcia-Alfaro, and J. Herrera-Joancomarti

A Note on a Fatal Error of Optimized LFC Private Information
Retrieval Scheme and Its Corrected Results 47
  Jin Tamura, Kazukuni Kobara, Hanane Fathi, and Hideki Imai

Reliable Food Traceability Using RFID Tagging 57
  Guillermo Azuara, José L. Salazar, José L. Tornos, and Joan J. Piles

Lightweight Cryptography and DPA Countermeasures: A Survey 68
  Amir Moradi and Axel Poschmann

Securing the Use of RFID-Enabled Banknotes 80
  Santi Martínez, Concepció Roig, and Magda Valls

Increasing Privacy Threats in the Cyberspace: The Case of Italian
E-Passports 94
  *Vincenzo Auletta, Carlo Blundo, Angelo De Caro,
  Emiliano De Cristofaro, Giuseppe Persiano, and
  Ivan Visconti*

RLCPS Preface 105
  Aggelos Kiayias and Kazue Sako

SPAKE: A Single-Party Public-Key Authenticated Key Exchange
Protocol for Contact-Less Applications 107
  *Jean-Sébastien Coron, Aline Gouget, Pascal Paillier, and
  Karine Villegas*

A Secure and Privacy-Preserving Targeted Ad-System 123
  Elli Androulaki and Steven M. Bellovin

Cryptographic Cloud Storage   136
   Seny Kamara and Kristin Lauter

Extending IPsec for Efficient Remote Attestation   150
   Ahmad-Reza Sadeghi and Steffen Schulz

Open Mobile Alliance Secure Content Exchange: Introducing Key
Management Constructs and Protocols for Compromise-Resilient
Easing of DRM Restrictions   166
   David William Kravitz

How to Evaluate the Security of Real-Life Cryptographic Protocols?
The Cases of ISO/IEC 29128 and CRYPTREC   182
   Shin'ichiro Matsuo, Kunihiko Miyazaki, Akira Otsuka, and
   David Basin

WECSR Preface   195
   Sven Dietrich

Preaching What We Practice: Teaching Ethical Decision-Making to
Computer Security Professionals (Keynote Talk)   197
   Kenneth R. Fleischmann

A Case Study on Measuring Statistical Data in the Tor Anonymity
Network   203
   Karsten Loesing, Steven J. Murdoch, and Roger Dingledine

A Case Study in Ethical Decision Making Regarding Remote Mitigation
of Botnets   216
   David Dittrich, Felix Leder, and Tillmann Werner

Ethical Proactive Threat Research (Position Paper)   231
   John Aycock and John Sullins

A Framework for Understanding and Applying Ethical Principles in
Network and Security Research (Position Paper)   240
   Erin Kenneally, Michael Bailey, and Douglas Maughan

Ethical Concerns in Computer Security and Privacy Research Involving
Human Subjects (Panel)   247
   Lorrie Faith Cranor

Ethical Guidelines for Computer Security Researchers:
"Be Reasonable" (Panel)   250
   Len Sassaman

Author Index   257

WLC Preface

Low-cost devices are the key component of several applications: RFID tags permit an automated supply chain management while smart cards are a secure means of storing cryptographic keys required for remote and secure authentication in e-commerce and e-government applications. These devices must be cheap in order to permit their cost-effective massive manufacturing and deployment. Unfortunately, their low cost limits their computational power. Other devices such as nodes of sensor networks suffer from an additional constraint, namely, their limited battery life. Secure applications designed for these devices cannot make use of classical cryptographic primitives designed for full-fledged computers.

The International Workshop on Lightweight Cryptography for Resource-Constrained Devices (WLC 2010) is a forum for the presentation and discussion of current research on different topics related to low-cost cryptography, from cipher design to implementation details.

In this first edition, we received 13 papers from which the Program Committee selected the best 8 to be presented at the workshop. We are very grateful to the members of the Program Committee: Carlo Blundo, Jordi Castellà-Roca, Vanesa Daza, Josep Domingo-Ferrer and Javier Herranz. We also appreciate the assistance in evaluating the quality of submitted papers provided by the additional referees: Arnau Erola, Albert Fernández-Mir, Bo Qin, Carla Ràfols, Michal Sramka and Arnau Vives-Guasch.

We would also thank the organizers of the Financial Cryptography and Data Security conference in its 2010 edition for allocating the workshop with their conference. Special thanks go to the General Chair Pino Caballero-Gil, the Local Chair Candelaria Hernández-Goya and the Program Chair Radu Sion.

February 2010

Josep M. Miret
Francesc Sebé

Hummingbird: Ultra-Lightweight Cryptography for Resource-Constrained Devices

Daniel Engels[2], Xinxin Fan[1], Guang Gong[1],
Honggang Hu[1], and Eric M. Smith[2]

[1] Department of Electrical and Computer Engineering
University of Waterloo
Waterloo, Ontario, N2L 3G1, Canada
{x5fan,h7hu,ggong}@uwaterloo.ca
[2] Revere Security Corporation
4500 Westgrove Drive, Suite 335, Addison, TX 75001, USA
eric.smith@reveresecurity.com

Abstract. Due to the tight cost and constrained resources of high-volume consumer devices such as RFID tags, smart cards and wireless sensor nodes, it is desirable to employ lightweight and specialized cryptographic primitives for many security applications. Motivated by the design of the well-known Enigma machine, we present a novel ultra-lightweight cryptographic algorithm, referred to as Hummingbird, for resource-constrained devices in this paper. Hummingbird can provide the designed security with small block size and is resistant to the most common attacks such as linear and differential cryptanalysis. Furthermore, we also present efficient software implementation of Hummingbird on the 8-bit microcontroller ATmega128L from Atmel and the 16-bit microcontroller MSP430 from Texas Instruments, respectively. Our experimental results show that after a system initialization phase Hummingbird can achieve up to 147 and 4.7 times faster throughput for a size-optimized and a speed-optimized implementations, respectively, when compared to the state-of-the-art ultra-lightweight block cipher PRESENT [10] on the similar platforms.

Keywords: Constrained devices, lightweight cryptographic primitive, security analysis, efficient implementation.

1 Introduction

With the advent of pervasive computing, various smart devices such as RFID tags, smart cards, and wireless sensor nodes are penetrating into and impacting people's life at a staggering rate and in significant ways. Their applications range from access control and supply-chain management to home automation and healthcare. Since a multitude of applications involve processing of sensitive personal information like health or biomedical data, the increasing demand for integrating cryptographic functions into embedded applications has risen. However, these pervasive smart devices usually have extremely constrained resources

R. Sion et al. (Eds.): FC 2010 Workshops, LNCS 6054, pp. 3–18, 2010.
© IFCA/Springer-Verlag Berlin Heidelberg 2010

in terms of computational capabilities, memory, and power supply. Hence, classical cryptographic primitives designed for full-fledged computers might not be suited for resource-constrained smart devices. For instance, the popular 1024-bit RSA algorithm cannot be implemented on RFID tags due to their harsh constrains with respect to gate count and power consumption. Moreover, the tight cost constrains inherent in mass deployments of smart devices also bring forward impending requirements for designing new cryptographic primitives that can perform strong authentication and encryption, and provide other security functionalities for ultralow-power applications in the era of pervasive computing. This emerging research area is usually referred to as *lightweight cryptography*.

The key issue of designing lightweight cryptographic algorithms is to deal with the trade-off among *security*, *cost*, and *performance* [29]. A host of lightweight cryptographic primitives that particularly target resource-constrained smart devices have been published in the past few years and we will focus on lightweight symmetric ciphers in this paper. All the previous proposals can be roughly divided into the following three categories. The first category consists of highly optimized and compact hardware implementations for standardized block ciphers such as AES [17,18,19] and IDEA [23], whereas the proposals in the second category involve slight modifications of a classical block cipher like DES [26] for lightweight applications. Finally, the third category features new low-cost designs, including lightweight block ciphers HIGHT [21], mCrypton [22], SEA [32], PRESENT [10] and KATAN and KTANTAN [11], as well as lightweight stream ciphers Grain [20] and Trivium [12]. Moreover, the design and implementation of lightweight asymmetric ciphers is also an ongoing research direction and a good survey about lightweight cryptography implementations can be found in [14].

Motivated by the design of the well-known Enigma machine, we present a novel ultra-lightweight cryptographic algorithm in this paper, referred to as Hummingbird[1], which is originally designed by Engels, Schweitzer and Smith, for resource-constrained devices like RFID tags and wireless sensor nodes. Hummingbird has a *hybrid structure* of block cipher and stream cipher and was developed with both lightweight software and lightweight hardware implementations for constrained devices in mind. The hybrid model can provide the designed security with small block size and is therefore expected to meet the stringent response time and power consumption requirements for a large variety of embedded applications. Moreover, we also implement Hummingbird on the 8-bit microcontroller ATmega128L from Atmel and the 16-bit microcontroller MSP430 from Texas Instrument (TI), which are the most popular processors used in wireless sensor network platforms because of their low power design, multiple sensor interfaces, and widely available development tools[2]. Our experimental results show that after a system initialization phase Hummingbird can achieve up to 147 and 4.7 times faster throughput than that of the ultra-lightweight block cipher PRESENT [10] for a size-optimized and a speed-optimized implementations,

---

[1] Hummingbird algorithm is first reported in [15] as a technical report of Center for Applied Cryptographic Research (CACR), University of Waterloo.

[2] The implementation of Hummingbird on a 4-bit microcontroller can be found in [16].

respectively. Due to space limitations, the compact hardware implementation of Hummingbird will be discussed in a separate work.

This paper is organized as follows. Section 2 presents the specification and the design rationale of Hummingbird. In Section 3, we give the security analysis of Hummingbird against common attacks such as differential and linear cryptanalysis. Section 4 treats efficient software implementation of Hummingbird across a range of wireless sensor network processors. Finally, Section 5 concludes this contribution.

2   The **Hummingbird** Cryptographic Algorithm

Different from existing (ultra-)lightweight cryptographic primitives which are either block ciphers or stream ciphers, Hummingbird is an elegant combination of the above two cipher structures with 16-bit block size, 256-bit key size, and 80-bit internal state. The size of the key and the internal state of Hummingbird provide a security level which is adequate for many embedded applications. For clarity, we use the notation listed in Table 1 in the algorithm description. A top-level structure of the Hummingbird cryptographic algorithm is shown in Figure 1.

Table 1. Notation

PT_i	the i-th plaintext block, $i = 1, 2, \ldots, n$
CT_i	the i-th ciphertext block, $i = 1, 2, \ldots, n$
K	the 256-bit secret key
$\mathbf{E}_K(\cdot)$	the encryption function of Hummingbird with 256-bit secret key K
$\mathbf{D}_K(\cdot)$	the decryption function of Hummingbird with 256-bit secret key K
k_i	the 64-bit subkey used in the i-th block cipher, $i = 1, 2, 3, 4$, such that $K = k_1 \| k_2 \| k_3 \| k_4$
$E_{k_i}(\cdot)$	a block cipher encryption algorithm with 16-bit input, 64-bit key k_i, and 16-bit output, i.e., $E_{k_i} : \{0,1\}^{16} \times \{0,1\}^{64} \to \{0,1\}^{16}, i = 1, 2, 3, 4$
$D_{k_i}(\cdot)$	a block cipher decryption algorithm with 16-bit input, 64-bit key k_i, and 16-bit output, i.e., $D_{k_i} : \{0,1\}^{16} \times \{0,1\}^{64} \to \{0,1\}^{16}, i = 1, 2, 3, 4$
RSi	the i-th 16-bit internal state register, $i = 1, 2, 3, 4$
LFSR	a 16-stage Linear Feedback Shift Register with the characteristic polynomial $f(x) = x^{16} + x^{15} + x^{12} + x^{10} + x^7 + x^3 + 1$
$\boxplus$	modulo 2^{16} addition operator
$\boxminus$	modulo 2^{16} subtraction operator
$\oplus$	exclusive-or (XOR) operator
$m \lll l$	left circular shift operator, which rotates all bits of m to the left by l bits, as if the left and the right ends of m were joined.
$K_j^{(i)}$	the j-th 16-bit key used in the i-th block cipher, $j = 1, 2, 3, 4$, such that $k_i = K_1^{(i)} \| K_2^{(i)} \| K_3^{(i)} \| K_4^{(i)}$
S_i	the i-th 4-bit to 4-bit S-box used in the block cipher, $S_i : \mathbb{F}_2^4 \to \mathbb{F}_2^4, i = 1, 2, 3, 4$
NONCE_i	the i-th nonce which is a 16-bit random number, $i = 1, 2, 3, 4$
IV	the 64-bit initial vector, such that $IV = \mathsf{NONCE}_1 \| \mathsf{NONCE}_2 \| \mathsf{NONCE}_3 \| \mathsf{NONCE}_4$

2.1   Encryption/Decryption and Initialization

The overall structure of the Hummingbird encryption algorithm (see Figure 1(a)) consists of four 16-bit block ciphers $E_{k_1}, E_{k_2}, E_{k_3}$ and E_{k_4}, four 16-bit internal

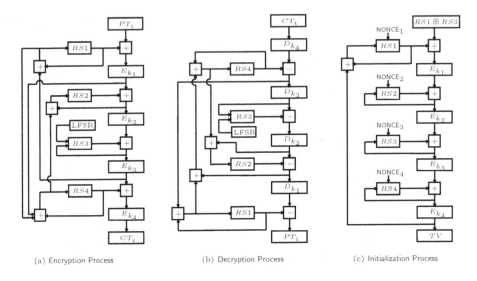

(a) Encryption Process   (b) Decryption Process   (c) Initialization Process

Fig. 1. A Top-Level Description of the Hummingbird Cryptographic Algorithm

state registers $RS1, RS2, RS3$ and $RS4$, and a 16-stage LFSR. The 256-bit secret key K is divided into four 64-bit subkeys k_1, k_2, k_3 and k_4 which are used in the four block ciphers, respectively. A 16-bit plaintext block PT_i is encrypted by first executing a modulo 2^{16} addition of PT_i and the content of the first internal state register $RS1$. The result of the addition is then encrypted by the first block cipher E_{k_1}. This procedure is repeated in a similar manner for another three times and the output of E_{k_4} is the corresponding ciphertext CT_i. Furthermore, the states of the four internal state registers will also be updated in an unpredictable way based on their current states, the outputs of the first three block ciphers, and the state of the LFSR. The decryption process (see Figure 1(b)) follows the similar pattern as the encryption. When using Hummingbird in practice, four 16-bit random nonce NONCE_i are first chosen to initialize the four internal state registers RSi ($i = 1, 2, 3, 4$), respectively, followed by four consecutive encryptions on the message $RS1 \boxplus RS3$ by Hummingbird running in the initialization mode (see Figure 1(c)). The final 16-bit ciphertext TV is used to initialize the LFSR. Moreover, the 13th bit of the LFSR is always set to prevent a zero register. The LFSR is also stepped once before it is used to update the internal state register $RS3$. The exact encryption/decryption and initialization procedure as well as the internal state updating of Hummingbird are illustrated in Table 2.

2.2   16-Bit Block Cipher

Four identical 16-bit block ciphers are employed in a consecutive manner in the Hummingbird encryption scheme. The 16-bit block cipher is a typical substitution-permutation (SP) network with 16-bit block size and 64-bit key as shown in

Table 2. Encryption/Decryption and Initialization of Hummingbird

Encryption Process	Decryption Process	Initialization Process (Four Rounds Encryption)
$V12_t = E_{k_1}(PT_i \boxplus RS1_t)$	$V34_t = D_{k_4}(CT_i) \boxminus RS4_t$	$V12_t = E_{k_1}((RS1_t \boxplus RS3_t) \boxplus RS1_t)$
$V23_t = E_{k_2}(V12_t \boxplus RS2_t)$	$V23_t = D_{k_3}(V34_t) \boxminus RS3_t$	$V23_t = E_{k_2}(V12_t \boxplus RS2_t)$
$V34_t = E_{k_3}(V23_t \boxplus RS3_t)$	$V12_t = D_{k_2}(V23_t) \boxminus RS2_t$	$V34_t = E_{k_3}(V23_t \boxplus RS3_t)$
$CT_i = E_{k_4}(V34_t \boxplus RS4_t)$	$PT_i = D_{k_1}(V12_t) \boxminus RS1_t$	$TV = E_{k_4}(V34_t \boxplus RS4_t)$
Internal State Updating		
$\text{LFSR}_{t+1} \leftarrow \text{LFSR}_t$		
$RS1_{t+1} = RS1_t \boxplus V34_t$		$RS1_{t+1} = RS1_t \boxplus TV_t$
$RS3_{t+1} = RS3_t \boxplus V23_t \boxplus \text{LFSR}_{t+1}$		$RS2_{t+1} = RS2_t \boxplus V12_t$
$RS4_{t+1} = RS4_t \boxplus V12_t \boxplus RS1_{t+1}$		$RS3_{t+1} = RS3_t \boxplus V23_t$
$RS2_{t+1} = RS2_t \boxplus V12_t \boxplus RS4_{t+1}$		$RS4_{t+1} = RS4_t \boxplus V34_t$

Figure 2. It consists of four regular rounds and a final round that only includes the key mixing and the S-box substitution steps. The 64-bit subkey k_i is split into four 16-bit round keys $K_1^{(i)}, K_2^{(i)}, K_3^{(i)}$ and $K_4^{(i)}$ which are used in the four regular rounds, respectively. Moreover, the final round utilizes two keys $K_5^{(i)}$ and $K_6^{(i)}$ directly derived from the four round keys (see Figure 2). Like any other SP network, one regular round comprises of three stages: a key mixing step, a substitution layer, and a permutation layer. For the key mixing, a simple exclusive-OR operation is used in this 16-bit block cipher for efficient implementation in both software and hardware. The substitution layer is composed of 4 Serpent-type S-boxes [1] with 4-bit inputs and 4-bit outputs, having additional properties whose selecting criteria is described in the appendix of [15]. According to the nine criteria presented in [15], we select four S-boxes, the action of which in hexadecimal notation is described in Figure 2. The permutation layer in this 16-bit block cipher is given by the linear transform $L : \{0,1\}^{16} \to \{0,1\}^{16}$ defined as follows:

$$L(m) = m \oplus (m \lll 6) \oplus (m \lll 10),$$

where $m = (m_0, m_1, \cdots, m_{15})$ is a 16-bit data block.

Remark 1. To further reduce the consumption of the memory, area and power of Hummingbird in both software and hardware implementations, four S-boxes used in Hummingbird can be replaced by a single S-box, which is repeated four times in the 16-bit block cipher. The compact version of Hummingbird can achieve the same security level as the original Hummingbird and will be implemented on wireless sensor nodes in this paper.

2.3 Design Rationale of Hummingbird

The design of the Hummingbird cryptographic algorithm is motivated by the well-known Enigma machine[3] and takes into account both security and effi-

---

[3] In Enigma machine each rotor has 26 contacts, whereas in Hummingbird each virtual rotor (i.e., a 16-bit block cipher) has $2^{16} = 65536$ contacts.

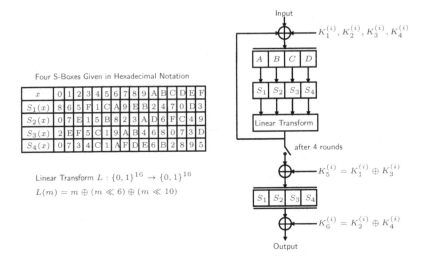

Fig. 2. The Structure of the Block Cipher in the Hummingbird Cryptographic Algorithm

ciency simultaneously. The encryption/decryption process of Hummingbird can be viewed as the continuous running of a rotor machine, where four small block ciphers act as four virtual rotors which perform permutations on 16-bit words. The salient characteristics of Hummingbird lies in implementing extraordinarily large virtual rotors with custom block ciphers and using successively changing internal states to step each virtual rotor in various and unpredictable ways. Besides a novel cipher structure, Hummingbird is also designed to protect against the most common attacks such as linear and differential cryptanalysis, which will be discussed in detail in Section 3. Moreover, extremely simple arithmetic and logic operations are extensively employed in Hummingbird, which make it well-suited for resource-constrained environments.

3 Security Analysis of the **Hummingbird** Cryptographic Algorithm

In this section, we analyze the security of the Hummingbird cryptographic algorithm by showing that it is resistant to the most common attacks to block ciphers and stream ciphers including birthday attack, differential and linear cryptanalysis, etc. Note that Hummingbird has a hybrid mode of block cipher and stream cipher (This is the reason that the analysis in [10] can not be employed directly here.), which can be considered as a finite state machine with the internal state $(RS1, RS2, RS3, RS4, \text{LFSR})$. However, the value of LFSR does not depend on those of $RS1$, $RS2$, $RS3$, and $RS4$. The purpose of using the LFSR is to guarantee the period of the internal state is at least 2^{16}.

A. *Birthday Attack on the Initialization.* For a fixed key, one may want to find two identical internal states $(RS1, RS2, RS3, RS4, \text{LFSR})$ initialized by two different IVs using the birthday attack. However, if we fix the key in the initialization procedure of the Hummingbird encryption scheme, the mapping $(RS1_t, RS2_t, RS3_t, RS4_t) \rightarrow (RS1_{t+1}, RS2_{t+1}, RS3_{t+1}, RS4_{t+1})$ is one-to-one. Hence the birthday attack does not work in this case.

B. *Differential Cryptanalysis.* Let $\mathbf{E}_K(x)$ denote the encryption function of Hummingbird with 256-bit key K. Recall that $E_k(x)$, defined in Section 2, denotes the 16-bit block cipher encryption used in Hummingbird with 64-bit key k. Then $\mathbf{E}_K(x)$ is the composition of four $E_k(x)$. For a function $F(x)$ from $\mathbb{F}_2^m$ to $\mathbb{F}_2^m$, the differential between $F(x)$ and $F(x + a)$, where $+$ is the bit-wise addition, is denoted by $D_F(a, b)$ and defined as follows.

$$D_F(a, b) = |\{x \mid F(x) + F(x + a) = b, \ x \in \mathbb{F}_2^m\}|.$$

For many keys, we have computed the differentials of both $\mathbf{E}_K(x)$ and $E_k(x)$. Note that from Section 2, we know that there are five rounds in $E_k(x)$. We list the differential $D_{E_k}(a, b)$ for each round in the following Table 3 (a). For substantially large amount of initial vectors IV and keys K, the differentials for both $E_k(x)$ and $\mathbf{E}_K(x)$ satisfy the following inequalities.

$$\max_{a,b\in\mathbb{F}_2^{16}, a\neq0} \{D_{E_k}(a, b)\} \leq 20, \text{ and } \max_{a,b\in\mathbb{F}_2^{16}, a\neq0} \{D_{\mathbf{E}_K}(a, b)\} \leq 20.$$

In other words, the differential of $\mathbf{E}_K(x)$ has the same upper bound as $E_k(x)$, the block cipher component in $\mathbf{E}_K$. We also tested the reduced version of Hummingbird for more instances of different pairs of (IV, K). From those experimental results, in general, the standard differential cryptanalysis method is not applicable to Hummingbird with practical time complexity.

C. *Linear Cryptanalysis.* For the linear cryptanalysis of $\mathbf{E}_K(x)$, we need to consider $|\hat{\mathbf{E}}_K(a, b)|$, the absolute value of the Walsh transform of $\mathbf{E}_K(x)$, where

$$\hat{\mathbf{E}}_K(a, b) = \sum_{x\in\mathbb{F}_2^{16}} (-1)^{\langle a, \mathbf{E}_K(x)\rangle + \langle b, x\rangle}, \ a, b \in \mathbb{F}_2^{16}, a \neq 0$$

Table 3. Differential and Linear Properties of the 16-bit Block Cipher

(a) Differential Properties

# of Rounds	$\max_{a\neq0,b} D_{E_k}(a,b)$
0	16384
1	1024
2	98
3	20
4	20

(b) Linear Properties

$wt(a)$	$wt(b)$	Constant c
1	1	4.703125
1	2	4.359375
1	3	4.500000
2	1	4.390625
2	2	4.281250
2	3	4.828125
3	1	4.968750
3	2	4.718750
3	3	4.781250

where $\langle x, y \rangle$ is the inner product of two binary vectors x and y (see Appendix for the detail). Unlike the case for the differential of $\mathbf{E}_K(x)$ or $E_k(x)$, we cannot perform an exhaustive computation for $|\hat{\mathbf{E}}_K(a, b)|$ for all $a, b \in \mathbb{F}_2^{16}, a \neq 0$, since there are around 2^{48} instances for (a, b, x) that need to be verified for a pair of fixed IV and key K. For some fixed pairs of (IV, K), we have computed random subsets of (a, b) with size around 2^{20}. Those experimental results show that $|\hat{\mathbf{E}}_K(a, b)| \leq c \cdot \sqrt{2^{16}}$, where $c \leq 4.96875$. We list some data in Table 3 (b). We also conducted the experiments for an 8-bit version of the Hummingbird encryption scheme which means that all the rotors $RS_i, i = 1, 2, 3, 4$ and LFSR contain only 8 bits. The Walsh transform of this reduced version of Hummingbird is bounded by $5 \cdot \sqrt{2^8}$ for many pairs of IV and key. This is the supporting evidence (albeit weak) that the absolute value of the Walsh transform of Hummingbird encryption function could be bounded by the square root of 2^{16} multiplying by a constant. Hence, Hummingbird seems to be resistant to linear cryptanalysis attack with practical time complexity.

D. *Structural Attack.* The Hummingbird encryption scheme may be viewed as a certain operation mode of a block cipher. For example, the ciphertext can be viewed as the internal state of a block cipher in CBC mode. In [4,5], Biham investigated some operation modes of block ciphers. He found that many triple modes are not as secure as one expected. In [6], Biham and Knudsen broke the ANSI X9.52 CBCM Mode. However, the internal state transition in Hummingbird encryption scheme is much more complicated than those studied by [4,5,6]. Hence, those attacks cannot be simply applied to the Hummingbird encryption scheme. In [33], by choosing IV, Wagner presented some new attacks on some modes proposed by Biham. Because IV initialization is used in the Hummingbird encryption scheme, Wagner's attacks are not applicable.

E. *Algebraic Attack.* For the Hummingbird encryption scheme, the degree of each S-box in the block cipher $E_k(x)$ is maximized. Moreover, each block cipher $E_k(x)$ consists of five rounds. Thus, there are totally 20 rounds for the Hummingbird encryption scheme, i.e., $\mathbf{E}_K(x)$. Furthermore, the internal state transition involves modulo 2^{16} operation. Hence it is hard to apply efficient linearization techniques for algebraic attacks to Hummingbird.

F. *Cube Attack.* The success probability of cube attack is high if the degree of the internal state transition function in a stream cipher is low. For example, the degree of internal state transition function of Trivium grows slowly [13]. However, for the Hummingbird encryption scheme, the degree of the internal state transition function is very high. In addition, Hummingbird encryption scheme has a hybrid mode of block cipher and stream cipher. We have tested both the 16-bit block cipher $E_k(x)$ used in the Hummingbird encryption scheme and the Hummingbird encryption function $\mathbf{E}_K(x)$. We note that no linear equations of key bits can be used in the way as suggested in [13].

G. *Slide and Related-Key Attack.* Both slide attacks [8,9] and related-key attacks [3] need to exploit the weakness of key scheduling. However, there is no key scheduling in Hummingbird. In particular, the subkeys used in four small block ciphers are independent. In addition, the four rotors affect the output of each small block cipher in a nonlinear way. Hence, both slide attacks [8] and related-key attacks cannot be applied to the Hummingbird.

H. Interpolation and Higher Order Differential Attack. Interpolation and higher order differential attacks [24,25] can be applied to block ciphers with the low algebraic degree. As we discussed before for algebraic attack, the algebraic degree of the Hummingbird encryption is high. Hence it is difficult to apply interpolation and higher order differential attacks to the Hummingbird.

I. Complementation Properties. The DES has the following well-known complementation property, namely that if C is the ciphertext of the plaintext P under key K, then $\overline{C}$ is the ciphertext of $\overline{P}$ under key $\overline{K}$, where $\overline{x}$ is the bitwise complement of x. However, Hummingbird does not have this weakness due to the presence of the carry propagation resulting from four rotors.

4 Efficient Implementation of **Hummingbird** on Low-Power Microcontrollers

In this section, we present software implementation results of the compact version of Hummingbird (i.e., a single 4×4 S-box S_1 is used four times in the 16-bit block cipher) on two microcontrollers ATmega128L and MSP430, which are the processors used for the wireless sensor nodes MICAz and TELOSB/TMote Sky, respectively. We also provide two implementation variants for each platform, one of which is optimized for **code size** and the other for **speed**. Moreover, two variants can perform both encryption and decryption.

4.1   8-Bit Microcontroller **ATmega128L** and Development Tools

The ATmega128L from Atmel is a low-power 8-bit microcontroller based on the AVR enhanced RISC architecture. The processor is equipped with 133 powerful and highly-optimized instructions and most of them can be executed with one clock cycle. Moreover, ATmega128L comes with 128 KBytes of In-System Self-Programmable Flash, 4 KBytes EEPROM and 8 KBytes Internal SRAM. Optionally it can handle up to 64 KBytes of external memory space. Its clock frequency can run from 0 to 8 MHz and the power supplies can go from 2.7 to 5.5 V. In addition, at a frequency of 4 MHz with a power supply of 5 V the ATmega128L microcontroller draws 5.5 mA current when active, 2.5 mA in Idle Mode and less than 15 μA in Power-down Mode.

In order to implement and test the performance of Hummingbird on the target platform, we use a combination of the integrated development environment AVR Studio 4.17 [2] from Atmel and the open-source WinAVR-20090313 tool kit [34] for our purpose. While AVR Studio is used as an editor and a simulator, the WinAVR provides a GNU GCC compiler with the according libraries and a linker.

4.2   16-Bit Microcontroller **MSP430** and Development Tools

Our second target microcontroller is a 16-bit MSP430F1611 from Texas Instrument, which is different in many ways from the Atmel chip. The MSP430F1611 microcontroller has a traditional *von-Neumann* architecture and all special function registers (SFRs), peripherals, RAM, and Flash/ROM share the same address space. Moreover, it comes with 48 KBytes Flash memory and 10 KBytes RAM. The clock frequency of the MSP430F1611 ranges from 0 to 8 MHz and the power supplies can go from 1.8 to 3.6 V. In particular, the MSP430F1611 microcontroller features the ultralow power consumption. At a frequency of 1 MHz and a voltage supply of 2.2 V the chip draws 200 μA current in Active Mode, 0.7 μA in Real-time Clock Mode, and 0.1 μA in Off Mode (RAM Retention). Although the instruction set of the MSP430F1611 only contains 27 instructions, 7 different addressing modes provide great flexibility in data manipulation.

We use CrossWorks for MSP430 Version 2 from Rowley Associates [31] to implement and simulate Hummingbird on the target platform. The CrossWorks for MSP430 bundles an ANSI C compiler, macro assembler, linker/locator, libraries, core simulator, flash downloader, JTAG debugger, and an integrated development environment CrossStudio. Different optimization levels can be set to generate codes with either smallest size or fastest speed.

4.3   Size Optimized Implementation

Note that the final round of the 16-bit block cipher in Hummingbird requires two derived round keys $K_5^{(i)} = K_1^{(i)} \oplus K_3^{(i)}$ and $K_6^{(i)} = K_2^{(i)} \oplus K_4^{(i)}$ (see Figure 2). For a size optimized implementation it is wise to calculate the above two keys $K_5^{(i)}$ and $K_6^{(i)}$ on-the-fly, which can save the storage requirements by 16 bytes. Moreover, the single S-box is implemented as a byte array with 16 elements, in which the lower half of a byte is used to store the value of the Hummingbird S-box and the higher half of a byte is padded with zeros. The S-box look-up of 16-bit block is conducted sequentially and 4 bits are processed each time. To generate the code with minimal size, we set the optimization level to be "OPT = s" for GCC compiler in WinAVR-20090313 and choose "Minimize Size" as the optimization strategy in CrossStudio, respectively.

Performance Results. Table 4 summarizes the memory consumption and cycle count of two lightweight ciphers Hummingbird and PRESENT on 8-bit and 16-bit microcontrollers for the size optimized implementation.

From Table 4 we note that the code size of Hummingbird is about 13% and 69% smaller than that of PRESENT on the 8-bit and 16-bit microcontrollers,

Table 4. Memory Consumption and Cycle Count Comparison (Size Optimized Implementation)

Cipher	Key Size [bit]	Block Size [bit]	8-bit/16-bit Microcontroller	Flash Size [bytes]	Hex Code Size [Kbytes]	SRAM Size [bytes]	Init. [cycles]	Enc. [cycles/ block]	Dec. [cycles/ block]
Hummingbird	256	16	ATmega128L	1,308	3.68	0	14,735	3,664	3,868
			MSP430F1611	1,064	2.95	0	9,667	2,414	2,650
PRESENT [29]	80	64	ATmega163	1,474	--	32	--	646,166	634,614
			C167CR	--	9.67	--	--	1,442,556	1,332,062

respectively. In addition, Hummingbird needs a relatively long initialization process when compared to the block cipher PRESENT because of the hybrid structure of block cipher and stream cipher adopted in Hummingbird. However, after an initialization procedure, Hummingbird encryption algorithm can achieve the throughput of 17.5 Kbps and 26.5 Kbps at a frequency of 4 MHz on the 8-bit and 16-bit microcontrollers, respectively. Under the same settings, the throughput of Hummingbird decryption algorithm can amount to 16.5 Kbps and 24.2 Kbps, respectively. Therefore, for the size optimized implementation, the throughput of Hummingbird is about 40 and 148 times faster than that of PRESENT on the target 8-bit and 16-bit platforms, respectively. Considering the cost of the initialization phase in Hummingbird, we compare the overall performance of Hummingbird and PRESENT for encrypting and decrypting messages with different length in the following Table 5.

Table 5. Overall Performance Comparison at 4 MHz (Size Optimized Implementation)

(a) Encryption Performance Comparison

Message Length	Microcontroller Word Length [bit]	PRESENT [29] Encryption [ms]	Hummingbird Encryption [ms]	Performance Improvement
64-bit	8	161.54	7.35	95.5%
	16	360.64	4.83	98.7%
128-bit	8	323.08	11.01	96.6%
	16	721.28	7.24	98.9%
192-bit	8	484.62	14.68	96.9%
	16	1,081.92	9.66	99.1%

(b) Decryption Performance Comparison

Message Length	Microcontroller Word Length [bit]	PRESENT [29] Decryption [ms]	Hummingbird Decryption [ms]	Performance Improvement
64-bit	8	158.65	7.55	95.2%
	16	333.02	5.07	98.5%
128-bit	8	317.31	11.42	96.4%
	16	666.03	7.72	98.8%
192-bit	8	475.96	15.29	96.8%
	16	999.05	10.37	98.9%

For the size optimized implementation, Table 5 shows that one can achieve around 95% ∼ 99% performance improvements when using Hummingbird instead of PRESENT to encrypt or decrypt message blocks with length 64-bit, 128-bit, and 192-bit.

4.4   Speed Optimized Implementation

For a speed optimized implementation, we precompute and store all required round keys $K_5^{(i)}$ and $K_6^{(i)}$ (see Figure 2) in an array and this precomputation procedure requires additional 16 bytes of data memory and has to done once when a new key is used. Furthermore, in order to accelerate the implementation of S-box layer in Hummingbird, we use a more efficient technique that combines two identical 4×4 S-boxes $S(x)$'s to form a larger 8×8 S-box $S_{8 \times 8}(x)$ such that $S_{8 \times 8}(x_1 \| x_2) = S(x_1) \| S(x_2)$, where x_1 and x_2 are 4-bit inputs to the two 4×4 S-boxes $S(x)$'s, respectively. Using the S-box $S_{8 \times 8}(x)$ significantly reduces the time for the S-box loop-up at the cost of 512 bytes of data memory (Note that both $S_{8 \times 8}(x)$ and $S_{8 \times 8}^{-1}(x)$ have 256 entries of each 1 byte). To generate the code with maximal speed, we set the optimization level to be "OPT = 3" for GCC compiler in WinAVR-20090313 and choose "Maximize Speed" as the optimization strategy in CrossStudio, respectively.

Performance Results. Table 6 summarizes the memory consumption and cycle count of two lightweight ciphers Hummingbird and PRESENT on 8-bit and 16-bit microcontrollers for the speed optimized implementation.

Table 6. Memory Consumption and Cycle Count Comparison (Speed Optimized Implementation)

Cipher	Key Size [bit]	Block Size [bit]	8-bit/16-bit Microcontroller	Flash Size [bytes]	Hex Code Size [Kbytes]	SRAM Size [bytes]	Init. [cycles]	Enc. [cycles/ block]	Dec. [cycles/ block]
Hummingbird	256	16	ATmega128L	10,918	30.5	0	8,182	1,399	1,635
			MSP430F1611	1,360	3.76	0	4,824	1,220	1,461
PRESENT [29]	80	64	ATmega163	2,398	–	528	–	9,595	9,820
			C167CR	–	92.2	–	–	19,464	33,354

From Table 6 we note that the code size of Hummingbird is about 78% larger and 96% smaller than that of PRESENT on the 8-bit and 16-bit microcontrollers, respectively. The main reason is that the -O3 option of the GCC compiler aggressively optimizes for speed by unrolling all loops in the code, which drastically increase the size of the code. Assuming that the microcontrollers operate at the frequency of 4 MHz, Hummingbird encryption algorithm can achieve the throughput of 45.7 Kbps and 52.5 Kbps on the 8-bit and 16-bit microcontrollers, respectively, which is about 0.7 and 2.5 times faster than that of PRESENT on the similar platforms. Base on the same assumption, the throughput of Hummingbird decryption algorithm can amount to 39.1 Kbps and 43.8 Kbps on the 8-bit and 16-bit microcontrollers, respectively, which is around 0.5 and 4.7 times faster than that of PRESENT on the similar platforms. Combining the overhead of the initialization phase in Hummingbird, we compare the overall performance of Hummingbird and PRESENT for encrypting and decrypting messages with different length in the following Table 7 for the speed optimized implementation.

For the speed optimized implementation, Table 7 shows that on 8-bit microcontrollers Hummingbird encryption is about 28.9% slower than PRESENT encryption when the message length is 64 bits. Furthermore, Hummingbird decryption is about 33.2% and 7.5% slower than PRESENT decryption for messages

Table 7. Overall Performance Comparison at 4 MHz (Speed Optimized Implementation)

(a) Encryption Performance Comparison

Message Length	Microcontroller Word Length [bit]	PRESENT [29] Encryption [ms]	Hummingbird Encryption [ms]	Performance Improvement
64-bit	8	2.40	3.38	-28.9%
	16	4.87	2.43	50.1%
128-bit	8	4.80	4.72	1.7%
	16	9.68	3.65	62.3%
192-bit	8	7.20	6.06	15.8%
	16	14.61	4.87	66.7%

(b) Decryption Performance Comparison

Message Length	Microcontroller Word Length [bit]	PRESENT [29] Decryption [ms]	Hummingbird Decryption [ms]	Performance Improvement
64-bit	8	2.46	3.68	-33.2%
	16	8.34	2.67	67.9%
128-bit	8	4.92	5.32	-7.5%
	16	16.68	4.13	75.2%
192-bit	8	7.38	6.95	5.8%
	16	25.02	5.59	77.6%

with length 64-bit and 128-bit, respectively. The main reason is that Hummingbird has a hybrid structure which involves a relatively long initialization process when compared to the block cipher PRESENT. However, on 16-bit microcontrollers Hummingbird is consistently faster (around 50% ∼ 78% performance improvements are achieved) than PRESENT for different message blocks in our experiment because the size (i.e., 16 bits) of the block and the internal state registers is perfectly suited to the architecture of 16-bit microcontrollers.

5   Encryption Mode and Concluding Remarks

In this paper we present a novel ultra-lightweight cryptographic algorithm, Hummingbird, which is a combination of block cipher and stream cipher. There are two modes related to Hummingbird as follows: (a) **Enigma Mode**: this is the mode where Hummingbird is used as a word-based cipher (16-bit word) where the plaintext is transitioned through a series of rotors. The ciphertext is dependent on the plaintext; (b) **Stream Mode**: this is the mode of Hummingbird where two values in the internal state ($RS1 \boxplus RS3$) are fed into the input of Hummingbird. The output is a keystream that is XOR'ed with plaintext. The hybrid structure adopted in Hummingbird can provide the designed security with small block size which is expected to meet the stringent response time and power consumption requirements in a large variety of embedded applications. We show that Hummingbird seems to be resistant to the most common attacks to block ciphers and stream ciphers including birthday attacks, differential and linear cryptanalysis, structure attacks, algebraic attacks, cube attacks, etc. Moreover, efficient software implementations of Hummingbird on 8-bit and 16-bit microcontrollers are also presented. When compared to the ultra-lightweight block cipher PRESENT implemented on similar platforms, our experimental results show that after a system initialization procedure Hummingbird can achieve up to 147 and 4.7 times faster throughput for a size-optimized and a speed-optimized implementations, respectively.

Acknowledgement

This work is supported by NSERC Strategic Grant. The authors would like to thank the two anonymous reviewers for their insightful comments.

References

1. Anderson, R., Biham, E., Knudsen, L.: Serpent: A Proposal for the Advanced Encryption Standard, http://www.cl.cam.ac.uk/~rja14/Papers/serpent.pdf
2. Atmel. AVR Studio 4.17, http://www.atmel.com/dyn/Products/tools_card.asp?tool_id=2725
3. Biham, E.: New Types of Cryptanalytic Attacks Using Related Keys. J. of Cryptology 7, 229–246 (1994)
4. Biham, E.: Cryptanalysis of Multiple Modes of Operation. J. Cryptology 11(1), 45–58 (1998)
5. Biham, E.: Cryptanalysis of Triple Modes of Operation. J. Cryptology 12(3), 161–184 (1999)
6. Biham, E., Knudsen, L.R.: Cryptanalysis of the ANSI X9.52 CBCM Mode. J. Cryptology 15(1), 47–59 (2002)
7. Biham, E., Shamir, A.: Differential Cryptanalysis of the Data Encryption Standard. Springer, New York (1993)
8. Biryukov, A., Wagner, D.: Slide Attacks. In: Knudsen, L.R. (ed.) FSE 1999. LNCS, vol. 1636, pp. 245–259. Springer, Heidelberg (1999)
9. Biryukov, A., Wagner, D.: Advanced Slide Attacks. In: Preneel, B. (ed.) EUROCRYPT 2000. LNCS, vol. 1807, pp. 589–606. Springer, Heidelberg (2000)
10. Bogdanov, A., Knudsen, L.R., Leander, G., Paar, C., Poschmann, A., Robshaw, M.J.B., Seurin, Y., Vikkelsoe, C.: PRESENT: An Ultra-Lightweight Block Cipher. In: Paillier, P., Verbauwhede, I. (eds.) CHES 2007. LNCS, vol. 4727, pp. 450–466. Springer, Heidelberg (2007)
11. De Cannière, C., Dunkelman, O., Knežević, M.: KATAN and KTANTAN A Family of Small and Efficient Hardware-Oriented Block Ciphers. In: Clavier, C., Gaj, K. (eds.) CHES 2009. LNCS, vol. 5747, pp. 272–288. Springer, Heidelberg (2009)
12. De Cannière, C., Preneel, B.: Trivium – A Stream Cipher Construction Inspired by Block Cipher Design Principles. ECRYPT Stream Cipher (2005), http://www.ecrypt.eu.org/stream/papersdir/2006/021.pdf
13. Dinur, I., Shamir, A.: Cube Attacks on Tweakable Black Box Polynomials. In: Joux, A. (ed.) EUROCRYPT 2009. LNCS, vol. 5479, pp. 278–299. Springer, Heidelberg (2010)

14. Eisenbarth, T., Kumar, S., Paar, C., Poschmann, A., Uhsadel, L.: A Survey of Lightweight-Cryptography Implementations. IEEE Design & Test of Computers 24(6), 522–533 (2007)
15. Engels, D., Fan, X., Gong, G., Hu, H., Smith, E.M.: Ultra-Lightweight Cryptography for Low-Cost RFID Tags: Hummingbird Algorithm and Protocol, Centre for Applied Cryptographic Research (CACR) Technical Reports, CACR 2009-29, http://www.cacr.math.uwaterloo.ca/techreports/2009/cacr2009-29.pdf
16. Fan, X., Hu, H., Gong, G., Smith, E.M., Engels, D.: Lightweight Implementation of Hummingbird Cryptographic Algorithm on 4-Bit Microcontroller. In: The 1st International Workshop on RFID Security and Cryptography 2009 (RISC 2009), pp. 838–844 (2009)
17. Feldhofer, M., Dominikus, S., Wolkerstorfer, J.: Strong Authentication for RFID Systems Using the AES Algorithm. In: Joye, M., Quisquater, J.-J. (eds.) CHES 2004. LNCS, vol. 3156, pp. 357–370. Springer, Heidelberg (2004)
18. Feldhofer, M., Wolkerstorfer, J., Rijmen, V.: AES Implementation on a Grain of Sand. IEE Proceedings Information Security 15(1), 13–20 (2005)
19. Hämäläinen, P., Alho, T., Hännikäinen, M., Hämäläinen, T.D.: Design and Implementation of Low-Area and Low-Power AES Encryption Hardware Core. In: The 9th EUROMICRO Conference on Digital System Design: Architectures, Methods and Tools - DSD 2006, pp. 577–583. IEEE Computer Society, Los Alamitos (2006)
20. Hell, M., Johansson, T., Meier, W.: Grain: A Stream Cipher for Constrained Environments. International Journal of Wireless and Mobile Computing 2(1), 86–93 (2007)
21. Hong, D., Sung, J., Hong, S., Lim, J., Lee, S., Koo, B.S., Lee, C., Chang, D., Lee, J., Jeong, K., Kim, H., Chee, S.: HIGHT: A New Block Cipher Suitable for Low-Resource Device. In: Goubin, L., Matsui, M. (eds.) CHES 2006. LNCS, vol. 4249, pp. 46–59. Springer, Heidelberg (2006)
22. Lim, C., Korkishko, T.: mCrypton - A Lightweight Block Cipher for Security of Low-cost RFID Tags and Sensors. In: Song, J.-S., Kwon, T., Yung, M. (eds.) WISA 2005. LNCS, vol. 3786, pp. 243–258. Springer, Heidelberg (2006)
23. Liu, D., Yang, Y., Wang, J., Min, H.: A Mutual Authentication Protocol for RFID Using IDEA, Auto-ID Labs White Paper, WP-HARDWARE-048 (March 2009), http://www.autoidlabs.org/uploads/media/AUTOIDLABS-WP-HARDWARE-048.pdf
24. Jakobsen, T., Knudsen, L.: The Interpolation Attack on Block Ciphers. In: Biham, E. (ed.) FSE 1997. LNCS, vol. 1267, pp. 28–40. Springer, Heidelberg (1997)
25. Lai, X.: Higher Order Derivatives and Differential Cryptanalysis. In: Proceedings of Symposium on Communication, Coding and Cryptography, in honor of James L. Massey on the occasion of his 60'th birthday (1994)
26. Leander, G., Paar, C., Poschmann, A., Schramm, K.: New Lightweight DES Variants. In: Biryukov, A. (ed.) FSE 2007. LNCS, vol. 4593, pp. 196–210. Springer, Heidelberg (2007)
27. Leander, G., Poschmann, A.: On the Classification of 4 Bit S-Boxes. In: Carlet, C., Sunar, B. (eds.) WAIFI 2007. LNCS, vol. 4547, pp. 159–176. Springer, Heidelberg (2007)
28. Matsui, M.: Linear Cryptanalysis Method for DES Cipher. In: Helleseth, T. (ed.) EUROCRYPT 1993. LNCS, vol. 765, pp. 386–397. Springer, Heidelberg (1994)
29. Poschmann, A.: Lightweight Cryptography - Cryptographic Engineering for a Pervasive World, Ph.D. Thesis, Department of Electrical Engineering and Information Sciences, Ruhr-Universitäet Bochum, Bochum, Germany (2009)

30. Rolfes, C., Poschmann, A., Leander, G., Paar, C.: Ultra-Lightweight Implementations for Smart Devices-Security for 1000 Gate Equivalents. In: Grimaud, G., Standaert, F.-X. (eds.) CARDIS 2008. LNCS, vol. 5189, pp. 89–103. Springer, Heidelberg (2008)
31. Rowley Associates. CrossWorks for MSP430,
    http://www.rowley.co.uk/msp430/index.htm.
32. Standaert, F.-X., Piret, G., Gershenfeld, N., Quisquater, J.-J.: SEA: A Scalable Encryption Algorithm for Small Embedded Applications. In: Domingo-Ferrer, J., Posegga, J., Schreckling, D. (eds.) CARDIS 2006. LNCS, vol. 3928, pp. 222–236. Springer, Heidelberg (2006)
33. Wagner, D.: Cryptanalysis of Some Recently-Proposed Multiple Modes of Operation. In: Vaudenay, S. (ed.) FSE 1998. LNCS, vol. 1372, pp. 254–269. Springer, Heidelberg (1998)
34. WinAVR. Suite of Executable, Open Source Software Development Tools for the Atmel AVR Series of RISC Microprocessors Hosted on the Windows Platform,
    http://winavr.sourceforge.net/
35. Youssef, A., Gong, G.: On the Interpolation Attacks on Block Ciphers. In: Schneier, B. (ed.) FSE 2000. LNCS, vol. 1978, pp. 109–120. Springer, Heidelberg (2001)

Lighten Encryption Schemes for Secure and Private RFID Systems⋆

Sébastien Canard[1], Iwen Coisel[2], and Jonathan Etrog[3]

[1] Orange Labs, 42 rue des Coutures, BP6234, F-14066 Caen Cedex, France
[2] UCL, Place du Levant, 3, B-1348 Louvain-la-Neuve, Belgium
[3] Orange Labs, 38-40 rue du Général Leclerc, F-92794 Issy les Moulineaux, France

Abstract. We provide several concrete implementations of a generic method given by Vaudenay to construct secure privacy-preserving RFID authentication and identification systems. More precisely, we give the first instantiation of the Vaudenay's result by using the IND-CCA secure DHAES cryptosystem. Next we argue that weaker cryptosystems can also be used by recalling the WIPR RFID system and giving a new protocol based on the El Gamal encryption scheme. After that, we introduce a new generic construction based on the use of any IND-CPA secure public key cryptosystem together with a MAC scheme and describe a possibility using the Hash El Gamal cryptosystem. We finally compare all these schemes, both in terms of implementation and security, proving that, nowadays the DHAES and our Hash El Gamal based solutions appear as the most promising schemes.

1 Introduction

RFID (Radio-Frequency IDentification) technology appeared a while ago but it only spread into a very large number of applications recently, because of both technical improvements and dramatic cost decrease. RFID tags usually broadcast a unique identifier over the air whenever they are powered on, as for Electronic Product Code (EPC) tags with long range used in supply chains, but also for most short range (ISO 14443/15693) tags regardless of theoretically broader abilities. This behavior raises many concerns on privacy and active research has recently been done on this subject.

Many use cases for tags thus require authentication, identification and privacy. For instance, if the tag is embedded into a passport, it is desirable that the latter be authenticated and identified by immigration officials while counterfeited passports should be detected. Moreover, other entities should not be able to trace all RFID tag's movements.

⋆ This work has been financially supported by the French Agence Nationale de la Recherche under the RFID-AP project while 2nd author was working at Orange Labs.

R. Sion et al. (Eds.): FC 2010 Workshops, LNCS 6054, pp. 19–33, 2010.
© IFCA/Springer-Verlag Berlin Heidelberg 2010

1.1   Related Work

Many privacy-friendly RFID authentication constructions already exist in the literature. Some of them are symmetric-based constructions [19,17,10] and some others [24,20,15,18,4] are designed using asymmetric cryptography, on which we will focus in this paper.

As an example, Batina *et al.* [4] prove that it is possible to embed elliptic curve cryptography, but their scheme does not include the privacy properties. The GPS authentication family, based on the initial work of Girault and Poupard-Stern , also fits the RFID setting, as stated by Girault and Lefranc [15]. A practical implementation is moreover given in [18]. But, again, the proposed scheme does not provide the privacy properties we need. An attempt has been made in [9]. However the efficiency of this scheme is bad as the reader has to perform an exhaustive search in the database and computes lots of modular exponentiations in order to identify a tag.

Recently, Vaudenay proposes in [24] a generic privacy-preserving authentication and identification scheme based on any encryption scheme with undistinguishability property against adaptive chosen-cipher attack (IND-CCA). He proves that if the cryptosystem is IND-CCA, the scheme is secure and private. However, no practical instantiation is given by Vaudenay and thus, it only remains a theoretical scheme.

One such concrete instantiation, named WIPR, has afterward been proposed in [20] using the Rabin encryption scheme. Oren and Feldhofer consequently provide a concrete hardware implementation of the Vaudenay's proposal. However, as the Rabin cryptosystem is only IND-CPA and since there is no security proof in [20], it remains some work to do on privacy-preserving RFID identification schemes based on public key cryptosystems.

1.2   Our Contributions

In this paper, we focus on the generic construction from Vaudenay [24] based on the use of a public key cryptosystem and we go further by making the following contributions.

1. We give in Section 2 the first concrete instantiation of the Vaudenay's result by using the IND-CCA secure cryptosystem DHAES.
2. We next notice in Section 3 that the IND-CCA property is only reached by a few public key cryptosystems that can be embedded into an RFID tag and consequently, we argue that a weaker cryptosystem can also be used. More precisely, we introduce the "constant fixed non malleability".
3. Next, in Section 5, we give a new generic construction based on the use of an IND-CPA secure public key cryptosystem (undistinguishability against chosen plaintext attack) together with a MAC scheme. We next give an example of a concrete implementation of this construction.
4. Finally, we make an implementation comparison between all the above instantiations in Section 6.

2   RFID Systems

In the following, we study protocols where the reader interacts with a tag in order to authenticate and identify it by retrieving the corresponding identifier ID, while protecting the privacy of the tag owner against all other readers.

An RFID authentication scheme, denoted S is composed of the following procedures, where λ is a security parameter.

- SETUP(1^λ) is a probabilistic algorithm which outputs the parameters param of the system, generates a private/public key pair (rsk, rpk) for the reader and initialized the database $DB_\mathcal{R}$ to the empty set.
- TKEYGEN(1^λ, param, ID, rpk) is a probabilistic algorithm which returns a tag-dependent key set tk$[ID]$. (ID, tk$[ID]$) is added in $DB_\mathcal{R}$ containing the whole set of legitimate tags.
- IDENT is an interactive protocol between the reader $\mathcal{R}$ taking as inputs 1^λ, param, rsk, rpk and $DB_\mathcal{R}$, and a tag $\mathcal{T}$ with identifier ID taking as inputs 1^λ, param, tk$[ID]$, rpk and eventually ID. At the end of the protocol, the reader either accepts the tag and outputs its identifier ID or rejects it and outputs $\perp$.

2.1   Usual Security Properties

Before introducing the security properties required for an RFID identification system, it is necessary to first define the adversary by giving him access to some oracles. Next, we will show that an RFID identification system should provide two main security properties.

Oracles. We consider that there is only one valid reader $\mathcal{R}$ in the system. However, as we will see below, the adversary will play the role of dishonest readers to interact with a tag and we assume that the tag does not know *a priori* if it is interacting with $\mathcal{R}$ or the adversary $\mathcal{A}$. We assume that $\mathcal{A}$ is always given 1^λ, param and rpk that are initially generated.

- We first assume that there are no tag at the beginning of one experiment and we give to $\mathcal{A}$ an oracle to introduce new tags.
- Vaudenay has been the first to introduce the concept of "future correlations", that is the possibility for an adversary against privacy to recognize a tag she has previously corrupted. For this purpose, he introduces the concept of free and drawn tags. More precisely, the adversary can only interact with tags that are sufficiently close to her without having access to other existing ones. Thus, drawn tags are the ones within "visual contact" to the adversary so that she can communicate with them using a temporary pseudonym while free tags are all the other tags. At the creation of a new tag, this tag has the status free and, at any time, the adversary is able to draw some tags or to free specific tags.

- As a consequence, the adversary is only able to interact with tags by using the pseudonyms. To simplify notation, we denote by tk[t] the secret key of the tag with pseudonym t, which is equal to the secret key tk[ID] of the underlying identifier ID of this tag. At the creation of a new tag, this tag has the status legitimate. Next, $\mathcal{A}$ is able to corrupt tags by using a specific oracle.
- Finally, the adversary can be *passive* by running the whole protocol IDENT between a valid tag and the valid reader, or *active* by participating in an IDENT protocol, stopping at any step the identification protocol, deleting or modifying some requests or responses.   .

Finally, Vaudenay gives the following classification for an adversary which is said *weak* if she has no access to the corruption oracle; *forward* if, after a corruption query, she can next only make corruption queries; *destructive* if she cannot use anymore a corrupted pseudonym t; *strong* if she has no limit on the oracles. An adversary is moreover said *narrow* if she is not able to obtain the result of an identification.

Correctness. The first security property, the correctness (also known as the completeness property) says that a legitimate tag is always accepted in the IDENT protocol. A formal definition can be found in [12]. Note that in some cases, it is necessary to define a strong correctness, where the aim of the active adversary is to make rejected a legitimate tag [10], but this is not our case in this paper.

Soundness. The second property is the soundness one. It states that a fake tag cannot be accepted by the system. One formal definition, called the strong soundness, is described in [12] where the adversary can corrupt tags.

Privacy. The scheme has to preserve the privacy of a tag in its previous authentications, even if an adversary compromises it and outputs its internal data: this is what is called forward-privacy.

In fact, several attempts have been done concerning the design of a privacy model for RFID systems. Le *et al.* adopt in [17] a specific approach to the formalization of protocol security based on the Universal Composability (UC) framework. Some other proposals are based on a different concept, introduced by Avoine [2] in the RFID setting, where privacy is formalized by the ability for the adversary to distinguish two known tags. This model was refined by Juels and Weis [16]. However, none of these models permit the adversary against privacy to make future correlations (that is the target tags cannot have been corrupted by the adversary). This case is taken into account in Vaudenay's model [24], which is very elegant and complete. However, this model is very hard to handle and only few papers have used it so far.

Our aim in this paper is not to give a new privacy model for RFID systems but, in the following, we only give some arguments on what is behind the "privacy property" according to Vaudenay's model. In a nutshell, the goal is to prove that for a given experiment, the success probability of an adversary, which interacts with the system through oracles, is undistinguishable of a "blinded" adversary, which interacts with a simulated system controlled by a simulator, which does not know anything about secret values. If those success probabilities are undistinguishable, it means that there are no privacy loss through the communication channel. In other words, the adversary make no effective use of the messages as their simulation (without using the secret values) leads to the same probability of success.

Contrary to previous models, as for example the Juels-Weis model, this model is more complete as the success of the adversary is not limited to linking two conversations of a same tag. However, a too much powerful adversary will be able to win against every scheme. Consequently, it is not possible to prove the strong privacy property (for a non-narrow adversary) for any scheme, as it has been proven by Vaudenay in his article [24].

3 Privacy of RFID Systems and IND-CCA Cryptosystems

In this section, we recall the result of Vaudenay which says that the narrow-strong (which corresponds to the strong privacy for a narrow adversary) and the forward privacy can be obtained using any public key cryptosystem[1].

3.1 The Generic Construction from Vaudenay

We first recall the notion of public key cryptosystems and what does IND-CCA and IND-CPA say. We next give the generic construction of [24].

Public Key Cryptosystem. Let a public-key encryption scheme $\mathcal{E} = (\text{KeyGen}, \text{Enc}, \text{Dec})$ such that:

- KeyGen is a probabilistic key generation algorithm which on input the security parameter 1^λ outputs the encryption public key epk and the corresponding decryption secret key esk,
- Enc is a probabilistic encryption algorithm which on input a message m and the public key epk outputs the corresponding ciphertext c,
- Dec is a deterministic decryption algorithm which on input a ciphertext c and the decryption secret key esk outputs a plaintext m.

The correctness of the scheme is defined as $\text{Dec}(\text{Enc}(m, \text{epk}), \text{esk}) = m$. Moreover, an encryption scheme should also be secure in the sense that it should not be possible for an adversary to learn any information about the plaintext m underlying a challenge ciphertext c. Such scheme is said to have the indistinguishability (IND) property.

---

[1] Note that Vaudenay has proved in [24] that, in the model he has defined, the strong privacy cannot be reached by an RFID identification system, and thus do not consider that case.

We then consider three different attacks for the adversary.

- Under *chosen-plaintext attack* (CPA), the adversary can obtain ciphertexts of plaintexts of her choice, using the public key.
- Under *non-adaptive chosen-cipher attack* (CCA1), the adversary gets, in addition to the public key, access to an oracle for the decryption function. The adversary may use this decryption function only for a period of time before receiving the challenge ciphertext c.
- Under *adaptive chosen-cipher attack* (CCA2) the adversary again gets, in addition to the public key, access to an oracle for the decryption function, but this time she may use this decryption function even on ciphertexts chosen after obtaining the challenge ciphertext c, the only restriction being that the adversary may not ask for the decryption of c itself.

Note that the notion of IND-CCA usually refers to the IND-CCA2 property while the IND-CCA1 is rarely used in practice. We utilize this notation in the following.

Proposed Construction. Using a public key cryptosystem $\mathcal{E}$ such as defined above, Vaudenay introduces the following RFID identification scheme, also depicted in Figure 1. In this scheme and in all the following ones in this paper, the reader key pair (rsk, rpk) corresponds to the public key cryptosystem key pair (esk, epk). Moreover, let tk be the λ-bit key of a tag, which is known by both the tag and the reader. In [24], Vaudenay proves that if the cryptosystem is IND-CPA, then the identification scheme is narrow-strong private and if the cryptosystem is IND-CCA2, the scheme is further secure and forward private. We do not recall the security proof in this paper.

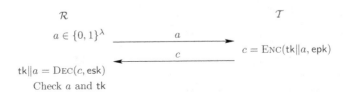

Fig. 1. Vaudenay's protocol

3.2   A Very Practical Instantiation: The DHAES Case

The DHAES has been introduced in [1] by Abdalla, Bellare and Rogaway and has been submitted to the IEEE P1363a standard. Its aim is to propose a method to encrypt strings using the Diffie-Hellman assumption, since the standard El Gamal encryption scheme has some flaws when regarding the message as a string. It is as efficient as the standard El Gamal encryption but has more and better security properties since it has been proved to have the indistinguishability property against adaptive chosen ciphertext attacks with unlimited access to the decryption oracle (IND-CCA2). It is thus possible to directly use it in the above generic construction to obtain the security of the underlying privacy-preserving RFID identification scheme (see 3.1 and [24]).

Let G be a cyclic group of prime order q. The private key to decrypt a message is $esk \in \mathbb{Z}_q$ and the corresponding public key is $epk = g^{esk}$. The DHAES encryption scheme can be used to obtain and RFID identification scheme as described in Figure 2, where $\mathcal{H}$ is a cryptographically secure hash function.

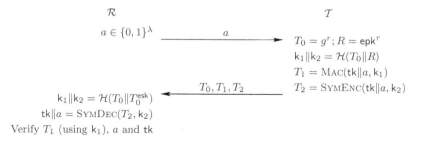

Fig. 2. DHAES based protocol

3.3 The "Constant Fixed Non Malleability" Property

In [5], Bellare *et al.* have shown that the IND-CCA property is equivalent to the NM-CCA one. The Non-Malleability (NM) property formalizes an adversary's inability, given a challenge ciphertext y, to output a different ciphertext y' such that the plaintexts x, x' underlying these two ciphertexts are "meaningfully related" (for example, $x' = x + 1$).

Intuitively, the soundness property of the Vaudenay's generic scheme comes from the non-malleability of the public key cryptosystem while the privacy property comes from the indistinguishability property. But the non-malleability property may be too strong for our purpose and, as we need lightweight computation, this may be not a good choice. In fact, most of existing IND-CCA secure cryptosystems are not relevant in the RFID setting and thus, cannot be used in practice.

However, we can notice that in the Vaudenay's generic construction, the RFID tag does not simply encrypt a message but the concatenation of some secret values tk that are always the same for a particular tag together with some randomness a that are "publicly" known, since they are sent in clear by the reader. We thus introduce the following security definition for encryption schemes.

Definition 1 (Constant Fixed Non Malleability). *A public key encryption scheme verifies the* constant fixed non malleability *if given the encryption public key and having access to an oracle which on input a value a, outputs the encryption of tk∥a, where tk is secret, an adversary is unable to output the encryption of tk∥ã on input ã with non-negligible probability.*

As a conclusion, if we are able to find a public key cryptosystem not necessarily IND-CCA but having the constant fixed non malleability property, then we have the following result on privacy-preserving RFID systems.

Theorem 1. *The Vaudenay's generic construction given in Figure 1 using a constant fixed non malleable encryption scheme is secure and forward private.*

The following sections discuss about the potential existence of a secure and private scheme based on the constant fixed non-malleability of the used public-key cryptosystem.

4   Privacy of RFID Systems and IND-CPA Cryptosystems

The scheme presented in Figure 1 can be instantiated with a public-key cryptosystems which is only IND-CPA. In Vaudenay's article [24], the author claims that such a scheme is narrow-strong private but not necessarily sound (see section 2.1). In this section, we study the case of several existing IND-CPA public-key cryptosystems.

We first show that a construction based on the Hash El Gamal is insecure. We next recall the WIPR construction which is due to Oren and Feldhofer [20] and which falls in the above case. Finally, we introduce our new construction based on the El Gamal encryption scheme.

4.1   The Hash El Gamal Case

The Hash El Gamal encryption scheme [11] consists in computing $T_0 = m \oplus \mathcal{H}(\mathsf{epk}^r)$ and $T_1 = g^r$ for the encryption of the message m.

Using the hash El Gamal encryption scheme in the Vaudenay's construction, it is trivially possible to break the soundness of the resulting scheme. Concretely, from one successful authentication $T_0 = (\mathsf{tk}\|a) \oplus \mathcal{H}(\mathsf{epk}^r)$ and $T_1 = g^r$, one can fake the valid tag by simply computing, on reception of the new random $\tilde{a}$, $\tilde{T}_0 = T_0 \oplus (0 \cdots 0 \| (a \oplus \tilde{a}))$ which is obviously equal to $(\mathsf{tk}\|\tilde{a}) \oplus \mathcal{H}(\mathsf{epk}^r)$. Thus, $(\tilde{T}_0, T_1)$ is a valid authentication of ID under the request $\tilde{a}$. One possibility to avoid this attack is to keep all received successful authentications and checks that the received T_1 has not previously been used. But we do not want the reader to perform so many comparisons and store so much data in its database.

4.2   The Rabin Case

The Rabin cryptosystem [21] is a public key cryptosystem introduced by Rabin whose security is related to the factorization problem. In the RFID setting, this cryptosystem has been used by Shamir to describe a MAC scheme [22]. In [20], Oren and Feldhofer also use this cryptosystem in the design of their privacy-preserving RFID identification scheme named WIPR. Let p and q be two large prime numbers and let $n = pq$. The private key esk is the factorization (p, q) of n and the corresponding public key epk is n. The scheme is described in Figure 3, where BYTEMIX is a publicly known byte-interleaving operation used to ensure that neither the tag nor the reader fully dominates a large element of the plaintext. Moreover, reduction modulo n is replaced by an addition of a multiple of the divisor n.

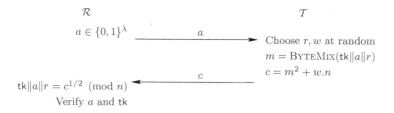

Fig. 3. The WIPR protocol

Security Considerations. As said above, it is well-known that the Rabin cryptosystem is not IND-CCA. The preprocessing step which consists in adding some redundancy permits to overcome some known chosen ciphertext attacks but no security proof can be done. However, it is not possible to prove that the resulting encryption scheme is IND-CCA secure.

Nevertheless, we only need that the scheme verifies the *constant fixed non malleability* property. In [25], the authors show that without a good preprocessing step (*e.g.* a weak BYTEMIX), the scheme is unsecure. They use the preprocessing step SAEP (Simple OAEP) so as to prove the security in a simple model where, unfortunately, strong privacy is not taken into account.

4.3 The El Gamal Case

The El Gamal encryption scheme has been introduced in [14] and is now largely used in many cryptographic papers. The El Gamal encryption scheme can be used either in groups of prime order or in groups of unknown order. In the following, we use a group of prime order.

Description of the System. Let G be a cyclic group of prime order q. The private key to decrypt a message is $\mathsf{esk} \in \mathbb{Z}_q$ and the corresponding public key is $\mathsf{epk} = g^{\mathsf{esk}}$. We next obtain the RFID identification scheme described in Figure 4.

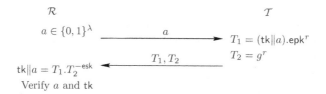

Fig. 4. El Gamal based protocol

Security Considerations. As for the Rabin case, we are unable to provide a proof that the construction based on El Gamal is secure but again, it would seem that this is the case.

In addition to what has been said for the Rabin case, the El Gamal opens a new problem. In fact, we should be careful here that the message $tk\|a$ truly belongs to the right working group. This should be done by using a good preprocessing step. Note however that this may imply some additional computations for the RFID tag. This is for example the case if the implementation is done using elliptic curves [8].

5   Privacy and IND-CPA Cryptosystems + MAC

In this section, we first provide a generic construction of a privacy-preserving RFID identification system which make use of any IND-CPA public key cryptosystem and a MAC function. Next, we provide a practical implementation using the Hash El Gamal encryption scheme.

5.1   Our New Generic Construction

Our generic construction needs a public key cryptosystem and a MAC scheme as defined below.

MAC Function. A cryptographic message authentication code (MAC) is a cryptographic tool used to authenticate a message and belongs to the family of symmetric cryptography. A *MAC scheme* denoted $\mathcal{M}$ is composed of the following procedures: KEYGEN is the key generation algorithm which permits to generate the MAC key denoted k; MAC is the code generation algorithm which accepts as input an arbitrary-length message m and the secret key k and outputs the MAC σ for message m, under the secret key k; VERMAC is the code verification algorithm which takes as input a message m, the secret key k and a message authentication code σ and outputs 1 if $\sigma = \text{MAC}(m, k)$ and 0 otherwise.

To be considered as secure, a MAC scheme should resist to existential forgery under chosen-plaintext attacks (EF-CPA). This means that even if an adversary $\mathcal{A}$ has access to an oracle which possesses the secret key and generates MACs for messages chosen by the adversary, $\mathcal{A}$ is unable to guess the MAC for a message it did not query to the oracle.

Proposed Construction. Let $\mathcal{E}$ be a public-key encryption scheme with the IND-CPA property and a MAC scheme $\mathcal{M}$ such as defined above, we next introduce our new RFID identification scheme in Figure 5, wheree ach tag shares with the reader a unique key denoted tk.

Security Considerations. Assume an adversary able to impersonate an uncorrupted tag. As she has no control over the nonce a chosen by the reader, the returned values will correspond, with a significant probability, to a new message $tk\|a$, which contradict the EF-CPA property of the MAC. Consequently, under the EF-CPA property, our new generic construction is sound.

Regarding the untraceability property, we have to prove that for every adversary $\mathcal{A}$ of this protocol, there exists a blinded adversary $\mathcal{A}^{\mathcal{B}}$ such that whatever

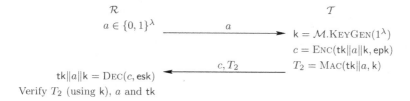

$$\mathcal{R} \qquad\qquad\qquad\qquad\qquad \mathcal{T}$$
$$a \in \{0,1\}^{\lambda}$$
$$\xrightarrow{\qquad\qquad a \qquad\qquad} \quad \mathsf{k} = \mathcal{M}.\textsc{KeyGen}(1^{\lambda})$$
$$c = \textsc{Enc}(\mathsf{tk}\|a\|\mathsf{k}, \mathsf{epk})$$
$$\xleftarrow{\qquad c, T_2 \qquad} \quad T_2 = \textsc{Mac}(\mathsf{tk}\|a, \mathsf{k})$$
$$\mathsf{tk}\|a\|\mathsf{k} = \textsc{Dec}(c, \mathsf{esk})$$
$$\text{Verify } T_2 \text{ (using k)}, \, a \text{ and tk}$$

Fig. 5. Our generic protocol

$\mathcal{A}$ do, $\mathcal{A}^{\mathcal{B}}$ can obtain the same result by interacting with the simulator. The game technique, presented by Shoup is perfectly adapted to obtain this result. The purpose is to replace every interactions with oracles of $\mathcal{A}$ by an answer of the simulator. The success of each game is the experiment that perform the adversary, for example : find a non-trivial link between two pseudonyms. If the difference between the success probabilities of two successive games is negligible, then it follows that the difference between the success probability of the adversary and the one of the blinded adversary is negligible.

We give here some details about this proof. It is possible to replace one by one every plaintexts of the public key cryptography by random messages. As detailed in [23], these operations cannot influenced the success probability of the adversary, otherwise it is possible to exhibit a distinguisher for the IND-CPA experiment. In order to obtain a perfect simulation of all messages exchanged during the experiment, it is also necessary to modify inputs of the MAC function. For this purpose, the MAC scheme must be a pseudo random function, which is also required to avoid attacks as those presented in [6]. This is not restrictive in practice as most of MAC schemes verifies this property. In conclusion, as we use the game technique, the difference between the success probabilities of $\mathcal{A}$ and $\mathcal{A}^{\mathcal{B}}$ is increased by the advantage of an adversary against the IND-CPA property of the encryption scheme plus the advantage of an adversary against the pseudo-random property. As both of these advantages are negligible by definition, the success probability of $\mathcal{A}$ must be negligible which demonstrates the untreacability property of our scheme.

5.2   The Hash El Gamal Case

The Hash El Gamal encryption scheme [11] is a variant of the classical El Gamal encryption scheme which uses a hash function. It allows a compact ciphertext and avoids problems with messages whose orders are not the one of the group.

Description of the System. Let G be a cyclic group of prime order q. The private key to decrypt a message is $\mathsf{esk} \in \mathbb{Z}_q$ and the corresponding public key is $\mathsf{epk} = g^{\mathsf{esk}}$. We thus obtain the RFID identification scheme described in Figure 6.

In a nutshell, we have described an efficient authentication scheme based on an IND-CPA public-key cryptosystem and a MAC scheme. It is sound and private as the DHAES scheme and seems to be efficient. In the next section we

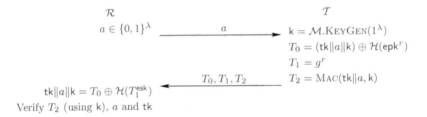

Fig. 6. Hash El Gamal based protocol

give some implementation estimation for all presented schemes. We will then be able to conclude about the relevancy of an authentication scheme based on an IND-CPA public-key cryptosystem.

6 Comparison

It is notoriously difficult to make implementation estimates without going through the implementation process and so, by necessity, our estimates offer a rough guide only. In particular, since there are so many implementation variables (space, power, speed...) and so we have concentrated our efforts on getting an estimate for the space required, using as our data-points established reference points in the literature. Of course power consumption and timing are vital considerations, however our goal has been to give a first-order comparison between the schemes described in this paper. Throughout, we will use *gate equivalents* (GEs) as the unit of comparison. We're aiming for a 80-bit security level which is typically of interest and we will use approximatively 160-bit elliptic curves.

The Case of DHAES. To reach our security model we choose the parameters tk, a, k_1 and k_2 to all be 80-bits in length. We might consider using coupons and pre-computing a set of 320-bit valid coupons of the form $(T_0, k_1 \| k_2)$ where $T_0 = g^r$ and $k_1 \| k_2 = \mathcal{H}(T_0 \| epk^r)$. These would be stored on the tag.

In terms of computational operations, the tag computes SYMENC over a 160-bit input as well as a MAC with a 160-bit input.

An efficient option would probably be to build the symmetric primitives out of a block cipher. One could use AES for SYMENC and a corresponding MAC-construction which could all be done for around 3600 GE [13], though some significant overheads to deal with different modes should be anticipated. A more lightweight possibility would be to use PRESENT [7] to construct both SYMENC and the corresponding MAC. A range of implementations suggests that 1500 GE would be a good estimate for the basic core, with a range of overheads suggesting that 2000-3000 GE could be enough. Finally the last possibility is to store the 160-bit key k_3 generated by a pseudo random generator and k_2 and to don't store k_2 in the tag as a coupon. This means using 400-bit coupons $(T_0, k_1 \| k_3)$. As the exclusive-or on the tag of two 160-bit numbers requires around

400 GE, this increases slightly the number of gates but requires half less PRESENT computations so it appears as the most efficient in term of implementation.

The Case of WIPR. In [20], Oren and Feldhofer propose a hardware implementation of WIPR and obtain a total chip area of 5705 GEs. Note that this implementation does not use elliptic curves and coupons, and so this offers some additional storage and usage advantages over the schemes that do.

The Case of El Gamal. As in the case of DHAES, it is interesting to consider the use of coupons. In this scheme the 320-bit coupons are of the form $(\mathsf{epk}^r, T_2 = g^r)$. However even though we use coupons, the computation that remains on the tag is an elliptic curve addition. Depending on the elliptic curve and the underlying field arithmetic, there are a vast range of different elliptic curve implementations available. The most striking are those of Batina *et al* [3] where we might expect an elliptic curve addition to take a few thousand GEs.

The Case of Hash El Gamal. Again, coupons are likely to make the most efficient implementations. In this scheme, the 480-bit coupons are of the form $(k, \mathcal{H}(\mathsf{epk}^r), T_1 = g^r)$. It is possible to generalize the scheme by replacing the computation of T_0 via the exclusive-or to encryption using any symmetric scheme. However, the use of the exclusive-or would perhaps offer the best implementation opportunities. In this case in term of implementation the situation is like the last possibility for DHAES with the difference than the tag has to store bigger coupons and to perform an exclusive-or between two 240-bit numbers instead of two 160-bit numbers so it requires approximatively 200 GE more.

Summary. While coupons carry a storage and usage cost, they are often the best technique available to make a serious reduction in the cost of an on-tag RFID computation. With these in place, most of the rest of the functionality can be provided using lightweight primitives such as PRESENT. This tend to all lead to roughly the same space cost for the cryptographic operations (except for the case of El Gamal) with a slightly edge for DHAES.

Table 1 sum up the previous comparison of this paper. It is obvious that in terms of security, the DHAES scheme is most promising than the Hash El Gamal scheme as for the same estimation of gate equivalent, security is proven in a better model, the standard one. But in terms of time execution, the the Hash El Gamal scheme seems better since the generation of the key k can be pre-computed while the execution of the hash function cannot.

Table 1. Comparison of schemes in gate equivalents and security proofs

Scheme	DHAES	WIPR	El Gamal	Our scheme
Security proof	standard model	don't exist	don't exist	ROM
GE	≈ 3000	5705	> 5000	≈ 3000

Nevertheless, we have prove in this paper that it is possible to reach the higher security level for an RFID authentication scheme from an IND-CPA encryption scheme. Then, it is may be possible to develop a really performant scheme by using such a scheme.

References

1. Abdalla, M., Bellare, M., Rogaway, P.: DHAES: An Encryption Scheme Based on the Diffie-Hellman Problem. Technical report, UC Davis Computer Science (1998)
2. Avoine, G.: Adversarial Model for Radio Frequency Identification. Cryptology ePrint Archive, Report 2005/049 (2005)
3. Batina, L., Guajardo, J., Kerins, T., Mentens, N., Tuyls, P., Verbauwhede, I.: An Elliptic Curve Processor Suitable for RFID-Tags. In: IACR eprint (2006), http://eprint.iacr.org/2006/227
4. Batina, L., Guajardo, J., Kerins, T., Mentens, N., Tuyls, P., Verbauwhede, I.: Public-Key Cryptography for RFID-Tags. In: PerCom Workshops 2007, pp. 217–222. IEEE Computer Society, Los Alamitos (2007)
5. Bellare, M., Desai, A., Pointcheval, D., Rogaway, P.: Relations Among Notions of Security for Public-Key Encryption Schemes. In: Krawczyk, H. (ed.) CRYPTO 1998. LNCS, vol. 1462, pp. 26–45. Springer, Heidelberg (1998)
6. Bellare, M., Namprempre, C.: Authenticated Encryption: Relations among Notions and Analysis of the Generic Composition Paradigm. In: Okamoto, T. (ed.) ASIACRYPT 2000. LNCS, vol. 1976, pp. 531–545. Springer, Heidelberg (2000)
7. Bogdanov, A., Knudsen, L.R., Leander, G., Paar, C., Poschmann, A., Robshaw, M.J.B., Seurin, Y., Vikkelsoe, C.: PRESENT: An ultra-lightweight block cipher. In: Paillier, P., Verbauwhede, I. (eds.) CHES 2007. LNCS, vol. 4727, pp. 450–466. Springer, Heidelberg (2007)
8. Boyen, X., Martin, L.: Identity-Based Cryptography Standard (IBCS) #1. In: Request for Comments: 5091. IETF (2007)
9. Bringer, J., Chabanne, H., Icart, T.: Efficient Zero-Knowledge Identification Schemes which respect Privacy. In: ACM Symposium on Information, Computer and Communication Security – ASIACCS 2009, Sydney, Australia (March 2009)
10. Canard, S., Coisel, I.: Data Synchronization in Privacy-Preserving RFID Authentication Schemes. In: Proceedings of RFIDSec 2008 (2008)
11. Chevallier-Mames, B., Paillier, P., Pointcheval, D.: Encoding-Free ElGamal Encryption Without Random Oracles. In: Yung, M., Dodis, Y., Kiayias, A., Malkin, T.G. (eds.) PKC 2006. LNCS, vol. 3958, pp. 91–104. Springer, Heidelberg (2006)
12. Damgård, I., Pedersen, M.Ø.: RFID Security: Tradeoffs between Security and Efficiency. In: Malkin, T.G. (ed.) CT-RSA 2008. LNCS, vol. 4964, pp. 318–332. Springer, Heidelberg (2008)
13. Feldhofer, M., Dominikus, S., Wolkerstorfer, J.: Strong Authentication for RFID Systems Using the AES Algorithm. In: Joye, M., Quisquater, J.-J. (eds.) CHES 2004. LNCS, vol. 3156, pp. 357–370. Springer, Heidelberg (2004)
14. Gamal, T.E.: A Public Key Cryptosystem and a Signature Scheme Based on Discrete Logarithms. IEEE Transactions on Information Theory 31(4), 469–472 (1985)
15. Girault, M., Lefranc, D.: Public Key Authentication with One (Online) Single Addition. In: Joye, M., Quisquater, J.-J. (eds.) CHES 2004. LNCS, vol. 3156, pp. 413–427. Springer, Heidelberg (2004)

16. Juels, A., Weis, S.A.: Defining Strong Privacy for RFID. In: PERCOMW 2007, Washington, DC, USA, pp. 342–347. IEEE Computer Society, Los Alamitos (2007)
17. Van Le, T., Burmester, M., de Medeiros, B.: Universally composable and forward-secure RFID authentication and authenticated key exchange. In: ASIACCS 2007, pp. 242–252. ACM, New York (2007)
18. McLoone, M., Robshaw, M.J.B.: Public Key Cryptography and RFID Tags. In: Abe, M. (ed.) CT-RSA 2007. LNCS, vol. 4377, pp. 372–384. Springer, Heidelberg (2006)
19. Ohkubo, M., Suzuki, K., Kinoshita, S.: Cryptographic Approach to "Privacy-Friendly" Tags. In: RFID Privacy Workshop 2003 (2003)
20. Oren, Y., Feldhofer, M.: WIPR - Public Key Identification on Two Grains of Sand. In: Proceedings of RFIDSec 2008 (2008)
21. Rabin, M.O.: Digitalized Signatures and Public-Key Functions as Intractable as Factorization. In: MIT Laboratory for Computer Science. MIT, Cambridge (1979)
22. Shamir, A.: SQUASH - A New MAC with Provable Security Properties for Highly Constrained Devices Such as RFID Tags. In: Nyberg, K. (ed.) FSE 2008. LNCS, vol. 5086, pp. 144–157. Springer, Heidelberg (2008)
23. Shoup, V.: Sequences of Games: a Tool for Taming Complexity in Security Proofs (2004)
24. Vaudenay, S.: On Privacy Models for RFID. In: Kurosawa, K. (ed.) ASIACRYPT 2007. LNCS, vol. 4833, pp. 68–87. Springer, Heidelberg (2007)
25. Wu, J., Stinson, D.: How to Improve Security and Reduce Hardware Demands of the WIPR RFID Protocol. In: IEEE International Conference on RFID – RFID 2009, Orlando, Florida, USA (April 2009)

Analysis and Improvement of a Pseudorandom Number Generator for EPC Gen2 Tags

J. Melia-Segui[1], J. Garcia-Alfaro[1,3], and J. Herrera-Joancomarti[2]

[1] Universitat Oberta de Catalunya,
Rambla Poble Nou 156, 08018 Barcelona - Spain
melia@uoc.edu
[2] Universitat Autònoma de Barcelona,
Edifici Q, Campus de Bellaterra, 08193, Bellaterra - Spain
jherrera@deic.uab.es
[3] Institut Telecom, Telecom Bretagne
02, rue de la Chatagneraie, Cesson-Sevigne 35576 - France
joaquin.garcia-alfaro@acm.org

Abstract. The EPC Gen2 is an international standard that proposes the use of Radio Frequency Identification (RFID) in the supply chain. It is designed to balance cost and functionality. The development of Gen2 tags faces, in fact, several challenging constraints such as cost, compatibility regulations, power consumption, and performance requirements. As a consequence, security on board of Gen2 tags is often minimal. It is, indeed, mainly based on the use of on board pseudorandomness. This pseudorandomness is used to blind the communication between readers and tags; and to acknowledge the proper execution of password-protected operations. Gen2 manufacturers are often reluctant to show the design of their pseudorandom generators. Security through obscurity has always been ineffective. Some open designs have also been proposed. Most of them fail, however, to prove their correctness. We analyze a recent proposal presented in the literature and demonstrate that it is, in fact, insecure. We propose an alternative mechanism that fits the Gen2 constraints and satisfies the security requirements.

1 Introduction

The EPC Gen2 is an international standard that proposes the use of Radio Frequency Identification (RFID) in the supply chain. It is designed to balance cost and functionality. The development of Gen2 tags faces, in fact, several challenging constraints such as cost, compatibility regulations, power consumption, and performance requirements. As a consequence, the computational capabilities of Gen2 tags are very simple. In this sense, the Gen2 specification only considers two basic on board security features: pseudorandom number generators (PRNGs) and password-protected operations. The pseudorandomness offered by on board PRNGs is, indeed, used to protect the password-protected operations. PRNGs are also used as an anti-collision mechanism for inventorying processes [4]; and to acknowledge other Gen2 specific operations (e.g., memory writing, decommission of tags, and self-destruction). PRNGs are, therefore, the crucial components that guarantee Gen2 security.

R. Sion et al. (Eds.): FC 2010 Workshops, LNCS 6054, pp. 34–46, 2010.
© IFCA/Springer-Verlag Berlin Heidelberg 2010

Commercial developments of the Gen2 standard are often reluctant to present the design of their PRNGs. Manufacturers simply refer to testbeds that show the accomplishment of some expected requirements, most of them for compatibility purposes. They fail to offer convincing information about the PRNGs designs [15]. This is mostly security through obscurity, which is always ineffective in security engineering. Vulnerable designs appeared in recent commercial RFID technologies, such as the vulnerable PRNGs used by the cryptosystem of the MIFARE Classic chip [5], confirm this principle. Cryptographic suitable PRNGs designs must, moreover, satisfy unpredictability characteristics. For example, an external adversary who eavesdrops the communication cannot compute the PRNG internal state, even if many outputs of the generator have been observed. The adversary cannot either compute the next sequence, even if many other previous sequences have been observed. If the adversary can observe, or even manipulate, the input samples that are fed by a PRNG, but its internal state is not known, the adversary must not be able to compute the next sequence or the next internal state of the PRNG. Finally, if the adversary has somehow learned the internal state of the PRNG, but the input samples that are fed in cannot be observed, then the adversary should not figure out the internal state of the PRNG after the re-keying operation. Most of these characteristics are, in fact, required by the EPC Gen2 specification [4].

PRNGs designs for highly resource-constrained devices (e.g, Gen2 RFID tags) exist in the literature (e.g., [11,10,1,14,2]). Some of them fail, however, to proof their correctness. We analyze in this paper the approach presented in [2], in which Che *et al.* propose the use of *linear feedback shift registers* (LFSRs) fed by an oscillator-based physical device that transforms thermal noise into *true random* sequences of bits. The authors claim that this approach leads to the construction of cost-effective PRNGs for RFID devices. For example, a Gen2 compatible PRNG can be implemented by using a 16-bit LFSR that is modified on every interrogation by XORing some of the LFSR cells with the random bits of the oscillator-based device. We demonstrate, however, that their approach leads to insecure implementations. We proof that the scheme does not succeed in handling the linearity of LFSRs. We show how an eavesdropper may obtain the feedback polynomial of the LFSR by using very few observations. We propose, moreover, an alternative solution that highly improves the security of the analyzed scheme. Our improvement fits, moreover, the resource constraints of Gen2 devices.

Paper Organization — Section 2 describes the suitability of using LFSRs for the generation of pseudorandom sequences and analyzes the Che *et al.* scheme. Section 3 describes an attack to the scheme. Section 4 introduces an alternative solution. Section 5 surveys some related works.

2   LFSR-Based Pseudorandom Number Generators

A linear feedback shift register (LFSR) is a digital circuit that contains a shift register and a feedback function. The shift register is composed of a sequence of binary cells that share the same clock signal. Each time a bit is needed, the content of the register is shifted one cell, obtaining the most significant bit of the register in the previous state. The feedback function computes a new bit using some bits of the register, obtaining the less significant bit to be filled in the new state of the register. The feedback function of an LFSR is basically an exclusive or logical operation (XOR, denoted as $\oplus$ hereinafter) of some cells content, named *taps*. The period (quantity of different possible states) of an LFSR with n cells is up to $(2^n - 1)$ when taps configuration follows a primitive-polynomial function, with optimum statistical properties, such as:

$$C(x) = 1 + c_1 x^1 + c_2 x^2 + \cdots + c_n x^n \qquad (1)$$

The LFSR can then be determined by this polynomial function. In turn, the sequences of the LFSR can be determined by the polynomial function of the LFSR and the initial state of the register cells (often referred as *seed*).

LFSRs are the most common type of shift registers used in cryptography. They lead to efficient and simple hardware implementations. They have, however, important drawbacks that must be handled. First, the sequences of an LFSR are predictable [9,3]. For example, let $s_{k+1}, s_{k+2}, \cdots, s_{k+2n}$ be a sequence of $2n$ consecutive bits generated from an LFSR. Let $c_n, c_{n-1}, \cdots, c_1$ be the feedback function of the LFSR. Then, the feedback function can be easily computed by solving the following equation system:

$$\begin{bmatrix} s_{k+1} & s_{k+2} & \cdots & s_{k+n} \\ s_{k+2} & s_{k+3} & \cdots & s_{k+n+1} \\ \vdots & \vdots & \ddots & \vdots \\ s_{k+n} & s_{k+n+1} & \cdots & s_{k+2n-1} \end{bmatrix} \begin{bmatrix} c_n \\ c_{n-1} \\ \vdots \\ c_1 \end{bmatrix} = \begin{bmatrix} s_{k+n+1} \\ s_{k+n+2} \\ \vdots \\ s_{k+2n} \end{bmatrix} \qquad (2)$$

By solving Equation (2) we obtain the feedback polynomial coefficients. Therefore, a n-bit (cells) LFSR with period $2^n - 1$ can be determined with only $2n$ values. This linearity must be handled before using LFSRs to build *pseudorandom number generators* (PRNGs). There are several solutions in the literature to decrease the degree of linearity of LFSR-based PRNGs. The use of non-linear filtering and the combination of multiple LFSRs are appropriate examples. Another way of decreasing the linearity degree of LSFR-based PRNGs is the addition of true random bits to the feedback function. This is in fact the strategy proposed by Che *et al.* in [2] for the construction of a cost-effective PRNG for RFID devices. We analyze their proposal in the sequel.

2.1   Che *et al.* Scheme Brief Description

The combination of true random numbers (*trn*) and PRNG techniques are used when *trn* generation throughput is not enough to cover the stream generation requirement. The *trn* is therefore used for replacing some parts of the PRNG stream or as a seed for PRNG initialization. Although *trn* addition can also be applied to LFSRs in PRNG, there are not many references regarding this technique in the literature. This is because *trn* addition to PRNG communication model cannot be applied to a traditional communication scheme where *sender* and *receiver* share k as a key for the PRNG one-time pad transmission/reception, because of the uncertainty of the *trn*. On the other hand, *trn* addition to PRNG is of a great interest for RFID communications where good PRNG are needed for secured communications. Specially in the EPC Gen2 technology, where the usage scenario does not allow the key sharing [4].

Che *et al.* present in [2] a new PRNG for application in RFID tags, improving the poor randomness from the basic PRNGs. This mechanism relies on an oscillator-based

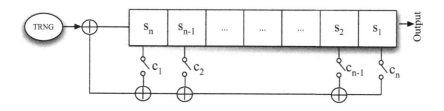

Fig. 1. PRNG scheme based on the Che *et al.* specifications

Truly RNG (TRNG), and exploits the thermal noise of two resistors to modulate the edge of a sampling clock. Authors state the final system prevents potential attackers to perform any effective prediction about the generated sequence (even if the design is known) thanks to the white noise based cryptographic key generation.

After describing its TRNG oscillator-based core, the authors focus on design considerations specially regarding *power consumption* and *output data rates* trade-offs. Knowing the fact that the higher the frequency oscillation of the system, the higher the current (thus also power) consumption, the authors look for system level optimization in order to reduce the power consumption due to the low-power restrictions of RFID.

The optimization proposed by Che *et al.* relies on the combination of the TRNG and a *linear feedback shift register* (LFSR) (cf. Figure 1). Adding an LFSR to the TRNG lets the system reduce the clock frequency proportionally to the number of cells of the LFSR. Specifically, exploiting the initial state of a 16-bit LFSR combined with the addition of the generated truly random number (*trn*) for each cycle ring, allows the system to decrease the clock frequency with a $\frac{1}{16}$ factor.

According to the authors, the addition of only a truly random bit in the cycle ring as a random number seed, the LFSR output sequence will be unpredictable and irreproducible, just like a TRNG. We show in the sequel that this claim is false.

2.2 Predictability of the Scheme

We have detailed above that the main vulnerability of a PRNG based on a linear feedback register comes from its easy predictability due to its linearity properties. We will show that the randomness introduced in the Che *et al.* scheme is not enough to mask the linearity of the scheme.

Following the Che *et al.* scheme (cf. Figure 1) the pseudorandom sequence is produced by an LFSR XORed in its first cell with a *truly* random bit (generated in the oscillator) for each register cycle in order to be unpredictable and irreproducible [2]. The pseudorandom output sequence for an n cell LFSR can be represented as:

$$s_{k+1} \oplus trn_1, s_{k+2} \oplus trn_1, s_{k+3} \oplus trn_1, \ldots s_{k+n} \oplus trn_1,$$

$$s_{k+n+1} \oplus trn_2, \ldots s_{k+2n} \oplus trn_2, s_{k+2n+1} \oplus \ldots$$

Since the LFSR seed is modified with the trn_i bit, the LFSR output will also be modified regarding the trn values. If we assume that the trn_i bits are generated by a true random generator, then the probability that $trn_i = 0$ or $trn_i = 1$ is equal to $p = \frac{1}{2}$.

Then, since the trn_i value is only XORed for each cycle, when two consecutive 0's are generated by the true random generator, $trn_i = trn_{i+1} = 0$, then the $2n$ bits output stream of the system will be exactly the same of the one produced by the LFSR. This situation can represent a threat for the unpredictability of the system, since these $2n$ values can be used to obtain the feedback polynomial of the LFSR.

3 Proposed Attack

Based on the vulnerability sketched in the previous section, we present a detailed attack on the Che *et al.* scheme. Our scenario is composed by a Che *et al.* system that produces pseudorandom bits. Only a part of the pseudorandom output sequence, denoted by s_a, is known to the attacker. The attack will succeed if the attacker can provide the LFSR feedback polynomial. From now on, we denote by $|s_a|$ the length of s_a.

To generalize the attack, we also assume that the attacker cannot determine the first bit of the sequence, that means he has no information if a given s_a sequence, with $|s_a| = 2n$, has been affected by exactly two trn values (that means the attacker finds two exact LFSR periods) or the sequence has been modified by three trn values.

With these constrains, given a sequence, s_a with $|s_a| = 2n$, the probability that s_a has been affected by exactly two trn is $\frac{1}{n}$. Furthermore, the probability that the two trn used in that sequence are exactly zeros is $\frac{1}{4}$. Then, given $|s_a| = 2n$ from a Che *et al.* output sequence if we analyze the system as described in Section 2 we will obtain the correct feedback polynomial with probability $\frac{1}{4n}$. However, in this situation, the attack itself cannot verify the correctness of the resulting polynomial.

Now, assume that $|s_a| = 3n - 1$. If the sequence is divided into n subsequences of length $2n$, we can ensure that one of these subsequences has been affected by exactly two trn. The remainder $n - 1$ subsequences, have been affected by three trn. However, notice that if the three trn are zeros, the n vectors of length $2n$ will give the same feedback polynomial. The probability of such event is $\frac{1}{8}$. Then, Equation 3 provides the probability of success of an attack that analyzes a sequence with $|s_a| = 3n - 1$:

$$P_{success}(3n - 1) = \frac{1}{4}\left(\frac{1}{n}\right) + \frac{1}{8}\left(\frac{n-1}{n}\right) = \frac{n+1}{8n} \qquad (3)$$

Furthermore, in this case where $|s_a| = 3n - 1$ the attack is self-verified since all n vectors will produce the same feedback polynomial, and then, the attacker will be sure to have obtained the correct polynomial.

Notice that $3n - 1$ is the smaller sequence that produces a self verified attack in the sense that n identical feedback vectors are found, providing three consecutive zeros in the true random sequence. Obviously, the probability of success increases with $|s_a|$ since increasing the $|s_a|$ implies that more trn bits affect the sequence and then the probability of finding three consecutive zeros also increases.

Figure 2 shows the probability of success of an attack with s_a length for a particular system with an LFSR of length $n = 16$, like in the Che *et al.* scheme [2] and the EPC Gen2 specifications. Notice that only 160 bits ($10n$) are enough to perform a successful attack with probability higher than 50%, and 464 bits ($29n$) implies more than a 90% of success probability.

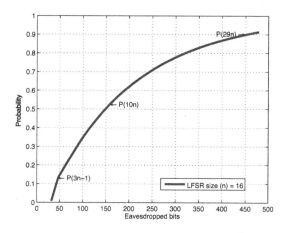

Fig. 2. Reliability on the Che *et al.* attack regarding $|s_a|$

3.1   Attack Implementation

The proposed attack defined above has been implemented to support the theoretical analisys with practical results.

The Che *et al.* scheme has been implemented by strictly following the specifications stated in [2]. The code has several configurable parameters, such as the size of the LFSR, the feedback polynomial, and the seed values. The sequences of true random bits are obtained from [6]. Algorithm 1 provides the pseudocode of the attack.

Ten different test sequences of 341 MB, T_i, have been generated with different *seed* and true random bit sequences. Several experiments have been performed over each generated sequence T_i. Two different analysis have been done. The first one validates that the probability of finding the feedback polynomial matches the one described in Equation 3. In this case, the algorithm takes $|s_a| = 3n - 1$ bits from T_i starting at a random position and tries to attack the system by finding n equal feedback polynomials. The operation is repeated one thousand times for each test sequence T_i. Attack success

---

Algorithm 1. Attack to the Che *et al.* Model
___
1: $count \leftarrow 0$; // *Initialize counter*
2: // *Initialize index i at a random position*
3: // *data_set stores $2^n - 1$ bits of data*
4: **While** $count < size(LFSR)$ **do**
5:      **take** $vector[i .. 2n + i]$ **from** $data\_set$;
6:      **compute** $polynom$ **from** $vector$; // *cf. Equation 2*
7:      **If** $(polynom_{prev.} = polynom)$ **then**
8:          $count \leftarrow count + 1$;
9:      **Else**
10:          $count \leftarrow 0$;
11:      $i \leftarrow i + 1$;
12:      $polynom_{prev.} \leftarrow polynom$;
___

Table 1. Attack success rate for $|s_a| = 3n - 1$

Sequence	T_1	T_2	T_3	T_4	T_5	T_6	T_7	T_8	T_9	T_{10}
% of attack success	0.1320	0.1370	0.1310	0.1260	0.1390	0.1370	0.1290	0.1370	0.1380	0.1280

Table 2. Value of $|s_a|$ for a successful attack in the worst case after 10 tests

Sequence	T_1	T_2	T_3	T_4	T_5	T_6	T_7	T_8	T_9	T_{10}
$|s_a|$	238	254	254	190	510	158	254	286	238	222

rates are reported in Table 1. Notice that they are close to the theoretic value $\frac{(n+1)}{8n}$ with $n = 16 \approx 0,1328$.

The second analysis provides the number of bits that has been needed to achieve a successful attack. Ten different attacks have been performed for every T_i data sequence taking the first bit of s_a at random. Results presented in Table 2 show the number of bits for a successful attack in the worst case, that is the attack that needs a major number of bits. Notice that, although taking the worst case, the number of bits is significantly lower than the whole period $2^{16} - 1$.

4   Proposed PRNG Scheme

We present a new PRNG scheme based also on the use of a LFSR, and perturbed by true random data. Our proposal successfully handles the vulnerabilities found in the Che *et al.* scheme [2]. We show, moreover, that our proposal is compatible with the requirements defined by EPCglobal for designing Gen2 compliant PRNGs [4].

4.1   System Description

Similarly to the Che *et al.* scheme, our proposal relies on a *linear feedback shift registers* LFSR core perturbed by a *true random number* (trn) source. We keep the LFSR core for different reasons. On the one hand, LFSR schemes are very fast and efficient in hardware implementations as well as simple in terms of computational requirements. This makes the use of LFSRs an ideal system for both energy and computational constrained environments. On the other hand, an LFSR follows the same hardware scheme than *cyclic redundancy check* (CRC) functions. These functions are included in the EPC Gen2 standard. Therefore, current EPC Gen2 tags including CRC are able of executing LFSR-based functions in the same hardware.

Different proposals exist to derive true random sequences of bits from the hardware of an RFID tag. Some examples of on-tag *trn* acquisition are, for instance, taking advantage of thermal noise, high frequency sampling or fingerprint data in circuits. Some commercial tags include, moreover, some extra functionalities (e.g., *received signal strength indicator*, RSSI [13]) that can be useful for *trn* addition techniques.

Similarities of our scheme with the one of Che *et al.* end here. In our proposal, randomness is used in a different way in order to truly mask the linearity of the LFSR.

We have seen in the Che *et al.* scheme that using true random data to modify the output of the LFSR is not enough to break the predictability of the LFSR. We take a different approach and we use the *trn* bits to modify the characteristic polynomial of the LFSR rather than the LFSR output. A first idea is to replace the static feedback polynomial

$$C(x) = 1 + c_1 x^1 + c_2 x^2 + \cdots + c_n x^n$$

with a dynamic one, that depends on the true random data

$$C(x) = 1 + (trn_j)x^1 + (trn_{j+1})x^2 + \cdots + (trn_{j+n})x^{n-1} + x^n$$

where only the most significant cell is always switched on to set the function degree to n. However, such an approach does not produce a good pseudorandomness output sequence since not all feedback polynomials randomly generated are primitive. Feedback polynomials of an LFSR must be primitive to guarantee good pseudorandom properties. Using primitive polynomials as feedback polynomials must, therefore, be enforced.

Taking different primitive polynomials as the feedback polynomial of an LFSR has already been used in non-security related scenarios. In [8,17], for instance, the authors call this technique *Multiple-Polynomial* (MP) LFSRs. They apply this technique for *Built-In Self Tests* (BIST) operations. These operations are intended for testing chip designs, generating test vectors and evaluating test responses. The *multiple-polynomial* characteristic means several polynomial configurations are applied to the LFSR, depending on an input parameter. These schemes must guarantee complete fault coverage tests while minimizing test application time, test overhead and data storage [17].

Following these ideas, we build up our PRNG design using an LFSR that is enhanced by a multiple feedback polynomial. Instead of a fixed feedback polynomial, the LFSR uses 2^m different feedback primitive polynomials. A *decoding logic unit* provides, at every LFSR cycle, one of the 2^m primitive polynomials as a feedback polynomial. The selection of each primitive polynomial for every cycle is performed by the true random data source. We present in the sequel the implementation details of our proposal. We discuss the exact parametrization of the system and provide some practical results.

4.2 Implementation Details

We fix the length of the LFSR to $n = 16$. This value offers EPC Gen2 tag compatibility and allows a better comparison with the proposal of Che *et al.* The total number of different feedback polynomials is set to eight (i.e., indexed by three *trn* bits). This value gives an appropriate trade off between computational and system complexity. Although an increase of the number of feedback polynomials leads to a higher number of different primitive polynomials, it also increases the amount and complexity of logial gates onboard of the tag. It is assumed that the price of a given circuit increases by one cent for each extra one thousand gates [12].

The selected polynomials, included in Table 3, are primitive polynomials of degree 16 with the highest number of common elements. From 2,048 possible primitive polynomials, the selected ones have ten common elements and six different ones. With this special selection only six bits are needed to encode all of them. To avoid two consecutive selections of the same feedback polynomial, what would turn into a prediction

Table 3. Feedback polynomials used in our scheme

Primitive polynomials			
$x^{16} + x^{15} +$		$x^{10} + x^9 + x^8 + x^6$	$+ 1$
$x^{16} + x^{15} + x^{14} + x^{12} + x^{10} + x^9$			$+ 1$
$x^{16} + x^{15} + x^{14}$		$+ x^{10} + x^9 + x^8$	$+ 1$
$x^{16} + x^{15} +$		x^9 $+ x^6$	$+ 1$
$x^{16} + x^{15} +$		x^9 $+ x^4$	$+ 1$
$x^{16} + x^{15} +$	x^{12}	$+ x^9 + x^6 + x^4$	$+ 1$
$x^{16} + x^{15} + x^{14} + x^{12}$		$+ x^9 + x^8$	$+ 1$
$x^{16} + x^{15} + x^{14} + x^{12}$		$+ x^9 + x^4$	$+ 1$

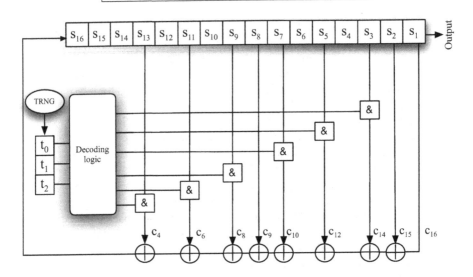

Fig. 3. Gen2 compliant PRNG proposal

vulnerability, a simple rotation is applied to the *decoding logic unit* for the polynomial selection. Regarding this polynomial selection, Figure 3 shows our proposed system with polynomial tap configurations.

4.3 Suitability to the EPC Gen2 Standard

The proposed PRNG system has been implemented in a software simulation in order to check its suitability as a PRNG for EPC Class1 Gen2 standard [4]. The pseudorandom datasets have been obtained from our PRNG using the same initial parameters (seed and *trn* source) than the ones used in Section 3.1. We generated above 3.3 Gb of data, divided in ten test sequences T_i. This amount of data represents 1.5 hours of constant 16-bit numbers transmission, assuming a bit rate of 640 kbps (as it is specified by the EPC Gen2 standard).

Table 4. Successful fulfillment of our proposal to the first requirement of the EPC Gen2 standard

Sequence	T_1	T_2	T_3	T_4	T_5	T_6	T_7	T_8	T_9	T_{10}
Lowest $\frac{p}{2^{16}}$	0.9246	0.9199	0.9082	0.9169	0.9151	0.9217	0.9195	0.9191	0.9184	0.9246
Highest $\frac{p}{2^{16}}$	1.0792	1.0821	1.0850	1.0781	1.0839	1.0832	1.0861	1.0799	1.0869	1.0811

Table 5. Successful fulfillment of our proposal to the third requirement of the EPC Gen2 standard

Sequence	T_1	T_2	T_3	T_4	T_5
Correlation	-0.000046	-0.000005	-0.000038	-0.000023	0.000036

Sequence	T_6	T_7	T_8	T_9	T_{10}
Correlation	-0.000036	0.000000	0.000025	-0.000055	-0.000089

Statistical behaviour — The EPC specification defines three statistical properties that PRNGs on board of Gen2 tags must satisfy:

1. **Probability of a single sequence** — The probability that any random sequence drawn from the PRNG has value j, for any j, shall be bounded by:

$$\frac{0.8}{2^{16}} < P(j) < \frac{1.25}{2^{16}} \tag{4}$$

2. **Probability of simultaneously identical sequences** — For a tag population of up to ten thousand tags, the probability that any of two or more tags simultaneously generate the same sequence of bits shall be less than 0.1%, regardless of when the tags are energized.

3. **Probability of predicting a sequence** — A given sequence drawn from the PRNG 10 ms after the end of the transmission shall not be predictable with a probability greater than 0.025% if the outcomes of prior draws from PRNG, performed under identical conditions, are known.

Regarding the first property, tests over the generated data checked the occurrence of each 16-bit values. The obtained values for the ten test sequences, included in Table 4, show that after almost 200 million of sequences were analyzed, the probability of occurrence of a 16-bit value lies between $\frac{0,90}{2^{16}}$ and $\frac{1,09}{2^{16}}$. Then, our proposed PRNG fulfills the first specification of the EPC Gen2 standard.

The second property for building Gen2 compliant PRNGs enforces that two simultaneous identical sequences must not appear with more that 0.1% for a population up to ten thousand tags. To test this property, ten thousand PRNGs have been initialized with random data in order to simulate a real population of 10,000 tags. The correlation of the ten thousand obtained sequences has been performed. Due to the true random data that uses the proposed system, none of the different systems generate the same sequence.

The third property is related to the probability of prediction, stating that a 16-bit pseudorandom number shall not be predictable with a probability greater than 0.025%, if the outcomes of prior draws from PRNG performed under identical conditions are known. Since our scheme uses a trn input to generate the output sequence, predictability becomes very difficult. To prove further, a serial correlation test has been performed. This test computes the degree of dependence of a n bit output from the previous one. Results, shown in Table 5, are very close to zero which determines good pseudorandomness.

Hardware constrains — Once we have checked the PRNG proposal suitability to Gen2 in terms of statistical behavior, we analyze now some hardware related issues. Specifically, pseudorandom generators for the EPC Gen2 standard are expected to be implemented with a small amount of equivalent logic gates, defined in the literature between 2,000 and 5,000 [16]. The available time for a label operation in real-time is also of major importance. This value will condition the PRNG complexity, regarding the hardware scenario constraints. According to [4], the maximum tag to reader (uplink) data transmission rate is 640 kbps. Some authors place the PRNG execution time between 5 and 10 ms taking as a reference the performance criteria of an RFID system that demands a minimum label reading speed of at least 200 labels per second [16], or 2.2 ms taking as a reference the system clock frequency $f_S = 100$ KHz (that implies a clock cycle of 0.01 ms) by reading 450 tags in one second [14].

Table 6. Logical Gate Equivalence for our Proposed PRNG

Element	Function	Gate count
LFSR16	Register for PRNG output	192
LFSR3	Register for trn storage	36
6 AND	For feedback polynomial selection	15
8 XOR	XOR operations	20
Decoding logic	MUX selection and rotation logic	347
Seed storage	For initialization purposes	24
Control (20%)		127
Total		761

Regarding existing estimations presented in the literature (e.g., [16,14,7]), we approximate the hardware complexity of our approach in 634 logic gates. Adding a 20% of logic gates for control purposes as recommended in [14], the final amount is of 761 logic gates (cf. Table 6). This value perfectly matches the Gen2 requirements, and it has a lower hardware complexity than other low-overhead PRNG proposals for RFID as LAMED or Grain [14,7]. For the time consumption requirement, taking the most restricting criteria that forces the generation of 16-bit sequences in 220 clock cycles (2.2 ms) [14], our proposal remains suitable enough for the generation of sixteen LFSR rotations and feedback polynomial selection.

5 Related Works

Some proposals in the literature propose suitable PRNG designs for Gen2 tags. We specially focus on designs motivated by security purposes. In this sense, Peris-Lopez *et al.* present in [14] a deterministic algorithm that relies on the use of 32-bit keys and pre-established initial states. Similarly, Klimov et al. present in [11] invertible bit transformations of 32 or 64 bits, suitable for PRNG applications. Other authors propose the use of on board physical properties to obtain random data generation. Holcomb *et al.* show in [10] a method to derive random data using the initial state of tag memory. Balachandran *et al.* propose in [1] the extraction of randomness by sampling radio signals. Che *et al.* describe in [2] an hybrid approach that combines the use of Linear Feedback Shift Registers (LFSR) and physical properties to build random sequences. We demonstrated in Section 2 that their approach is not secure, and presented in Section 3 an enhanced version based on a multiple-polynomial LFSR scheme [8,17]. It is worth mentioning that Strüker *et al.* also cite in [18] functional weaknesses of the Che *et al.* scheme. Although, no results nor proofs are given in their paper.

6 Conclusions

We analyzed a *pseudorandom number generator* (PRNG) model for Radio Frequency Identification (RFID) devices, presented by Che *et al.* in [2]. The scheme uses a 16-bit *linear feedback shift register* (LFSR) for the generation of pseudorandom sequences. The LFSR is modified each cycle by XORing the first cell of the LFSR and a *true random* bit. We demonstrated that the proposal is not appropriate for security purposes, since it does not correctly handle the inherent linearity of the LFSR. We then showed empirically the possibility of successfully retrieving the feedback polynomial of the LFSR by using very few observations.

A new scheme has been then proposed. Our model is based on the use of a *multiple-polynomial* LFSR. We analyzed a 16-bit PRNG based on a software simulation of our model. We performed statistical analysis of random sequences generated by our simulation. Results confirm the validity of our technique. A hardware complexity estimation has also been presented. Our estimation successfully meets the requirements of the EPC Gen2 standard.

Acknowledgments. The work has been supported by the Spanish Ministry of Science and Innovation, the FEDER funds under the grants TSI2007-65406-C03-03 E-AEGIS, CONSOLIDER CSD2007-00004 ARES, an IN3-UOC doctoral fellowship, and the IRF project LOCHNESS.

References

1. Balachandran, G., Barnett, R.: A 440nA true random number generator for passive RFID tags. IEEE Transactions on Circuits and Systems I: Regular Papers 55(11), 3723–3732 (2008)

2. Che, W., Deng, H., Tan, X., Wang, J.: A Random Number Generator for Application in RFID Tags. In: Networked RFID Systems and Lightweight Cryptography, ch. 16, pp. 279–287. Springer, Heidelberg (2008)
3. Chen, C.L.: Linear Dependencies in Linear Feedback Shift Registers. IEEE Transactions on Computers C-35(12), 1086–1088 (1986)
4. EPCglobal. EPC radio-frequency identity protocols class-1 generation-2 UHF RFID protocol for communications at 860-960 MHz. Tech. report (2007), http://www.epcglobalinc.org/standards/
5. Garcia, F., Koning, G., Muijrers, R., van Rossum, P., Verdult, R., Wichers, R., Jacobs, B.: Dismantling MIFARE Classic. In: Jajodia, S., Lopez, J. (eds.) ESORICS 2008. LNCS, vol. 5283, pp. 97–114. Springer, Heidelberg (2008)
6. Haahr, M.: True random number service, http://www.random.org
7. Hell, M., Johansson, T., Meier, W.: Grain: a stream cipher for constrained environments. International Journal of Wireless and Mobile Computing 2(1), 86–93 (2007)
8. Hellebrand, S., Rajski, J., Tarnick, S., Venkataraman, S., Courtois, B.: Built-in test for circuits with scan based on reseeding of multiple-polynomial linear feedback shift registers. IEEE Transactions on Computers 44(2), 223–233 (1995)
9. Herlestam, T.: On Functions of Linear Shift Register Sequences. In: Pichler, F. (ed.) EUROCRYPT 1985. LNCS, vol. 219, pp. 119–129. Springer, Heidelberg (1986), doi:10.1007/3-540-39805-8
10. Holcomb, D., Burleson, W., Fu, K.: Initial SRAM state as a fingerprint and source of true random numbers for RFID tags. In: Proceedings of the Conference on RFID Security (July 2007)
11. Klimov, A., Shamir, A.: A New Class of Invertible Mappings. In: Kaliski Jr., B.S., Koç, Ç.K., Paar, C. (eds.) CHES 2002. LNCS, vol. 2523, pp. 470–483. Springer, Heidelberg (2003)
12. Lehtonen, M., Staake, T., Michahelles, F., Fleisch, E.: From Identification to Authentication - A Review of RFID Product Authentication Techniques. In: Networked RFID Systems and Lightweight Cryptography, ch. 9, pp. 169–187. Springer, Heidelberg (November 2007)
13. Motorola. XR Series RFID Readers. Product Guide (2008), https://docs.symbol.com/manuals/SIGN_71773.pdf
14. Peris-Lopez, P., Hernandez-Castro, J., Estevez-Tapiador, J., Ribagorda, A.: LAMED A PRNG for EPC Class-1 Generation-2 RFID specification. Computer Standards & Interfaces (2008)
15. Peris-Lopez, P.: Lightweight Cryptography in Radio Frequency Identification (RFID) Systems. PhD Thesis (2008)
16. Ranasinghe, D., Cole, P.: An Evaluation Framework. In: Networked RFID Systems and Lightweight Cryptography, ch. 8, pp. 157–167. Springer, Heidelberg (November 2007)
17. Rosinger, P., Al-Hashimi, B.M., Nicolici, N.: Dual multiple-polynomial LFSR for low-power mixed-mode BIST. IEE Proceedings on Computers and Digital Techniques 150(4), 209–217 (2003)
18. Strüker, J., Wonnemann, C., Kähmer, M., Gille, D.: Managing the Deactivation Process of EPC Class-1 Generation-2 Tags in Retail Industry. University of Freiburg, Germany (2007), http://www.telematik.uni-freiburg.de

A Note on a Fatal Error of Optimized LFC Private Information Retrieval Scheme and Its Corrected Results

Jin Tamura[1], Kazukuni Kobara[2], Hanane Fathi[3], and Hideki Imai[2]

[1] National Institute of Information and
Communications Technology, Japan
j-tamura@nict.go.jp
[2] National Institute of Advanced
Industrial Science and Technology, Japan
k-kobara@aist.go.jp, h-imai@aist.go.jp
[3] Aalborg University, Denmark
hanane.fathi@hanane.tel

Abstract. A number of lightweight PIR (Private Information Retrieval) schemes have been proposed in recent years. In JWIS2006, Kwon et al. proposed a new scheme (optimized LFCPIR, or OLFCPIR), which aimed at reducing the communication cost of Lipmaa's $O(\log^2 n)$ PIR(LFCPIR) to $O(\log n)$. However in this paper, we point out a fatal error of overflow contained in OLFCPIR and show how the error can be corrected. Finally, we compare with LFCPIR to show that the communication cost of our corrected OLFCPIR is asymptotically the same as the previous LFCPIR.

Keywords: Private Information Retrieval, CPIR, LFCPIR, OLFCPIR[1].

1 Introduction

Nowadays, a large amount of data is computerized and the processing efficiency has also improved. However, such computerization carries with it huge risks of leakage of personal or private information. In today's large databases, such a leakage is even more critical when it concerns for example competitive secret corporate information. This is the case when search information related to patents or patent applications of a company is leaked out, such a leakage can be very damaging to a company.

A private information retrieval (PIR) protocol allows a chooser to retrieve an item from a server (i.e. sender) containing a database without revealing the identity or the content of that item. The trivial solution is to let a sender send the entire string to a chooser, requiring n bits communication costs, where n is the number of bits in the database. In other words, the database being the sender sends the entire database to a chooser at every query so as to result in the database not knowing what is the item retrieved by the chooser.

In a way, the history and the challenge of the PIR research has always been about obtaining the lightweight scheme in communication. Figure 1 shows the history of the PIR research and the position of our note.

---

[1] This work was supported by JSPS KAKENHI 19860094.

R. Sion et al. (Eds.): FC 2010 Workshops, LNCS 6054, pp. 47–56, 2010.
© IFCA/Springer-Verlag Berlin Heidelberg 2010

In 1995, Chor et al.[4], who first formulated the PIR problem, proved that in any single server Informational (i.e. information theoretically private) PIR, we can not do better than the trivial solution (i.e. the communication is at least n bits). This result has lead PIR research results to following two approaches:

- Replicate the same database into k servers.
- Computational PIR (CPIR) based on assumptions related to cryptographic hardness.

In the former research results [1][2], each replicated server learns nothing about the chooser's item, and such assumption is slightly unrealistic. The first single-database computational PIR scheme to achieve a communication complexity less than n was developed in 1997 by E. Kushilevitz et al. [10] and achieved communication complexity of $O(n^{\frac{1}{2}})$.

In 2004, Helger Lipmaa [11](Length Flexible CPIR, in short, LFCPIR) achieved log-squared communication complexity. The security of LFCPIR is based on the semantic security of the Damgård-Jurik cryptosystem, which is a length-flexible additively homomorphic cryptosystem.

In 2006, Kwon et al proposed a new scheme (optimized LFCPIR, or OLFCPIR), which aimed at reducing the communication cost of Lipmaa's $O(\log^2 n)$ LFCPIR to $O(\log n)$[9].

In LFCPIR, a chooser has to expand his query, which consists of encryptions of 0 and 1, and this depends on the dimensions of the database; on the other hand, in OLFCPIR, the chooser does not have to expand the query (cipher text). Instead, the database expands the ciphertext with their original mapping while offline.

However, we point out a fatal error in OLFCPIR of overflow contained at their original mapping in this paper. We then correct OLFCPIR and compare the results of the corrected OLFCPIR with LFCPIR to show that the communication cost of corrected OLFCPIR is asymptotically the same as LFCPIR.

This paper is organized into the following sections; in section 2,we describe the details of LFCPIRLip05. In section 3, we describe the details of OLFCPIR [9] and point out its drawback. In section 4, we show our corrected OLFCPIR and compare the communication complexity with LFCPIR. Finally, we present the conclusions in section 5.

2   LFCPIR

2.1   DJ Cryptosystem and Hyper Rectangle Database

In order to describe Lipmaa's CPIR protocol LFCPIR, we review Damgård-Jurik public key encryption with some fixed parameters (for simplicity) [7]. Let a k-bit integer $m = pq$ be a public key for odd primes p and q. For a positive integer s, the encryption is defined as follows:

$$E_m^s : \mathbb{Z}_{m^s} \times \mathbb{Z}_{m^{s+1}}^* \longrightarrow \mathbb{Z}_{m^{s+1}}^*$$
$$(M, r) \longmapsto (1 + m)^M r^{m^s}$$

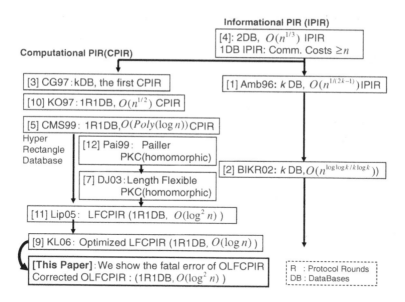

Fig. 1. The history of Private Information Retrieval

where M is a plaintext and r is a random element. Thus the encryption algorithm probabilistically maps sk-bit plaintexts to $(s+1)k$-bit ciphertexts, where $k = \log m$. For simplicity, we sometimes omit the random parameter r and write $E_m^s(M, r) = E_m^s(M)$. Now the Damgård-Jurik encryption has the following properties:

$$1. E_m^s(M_1)E_m^s(M_2) = E_m^s(M_1 + M_2)$$

$$2. E_m^s(M_1)^{E_m^s(M_2)} = E_m^{s+1}(M_1 E_m^s(M_2))$$

Another way to build LFCPIR is by using a different arrangement of the database. For a fixed $\alpha \in [\alpha]$, the database $DB = (u[1], \cdots, u[n])$ is arranged as a α- dimensional $\lambda_1 \times \cdots \times \lambda_\alpha$ hyperrectangle, where $\lambda_j, j = 1, \cdots, \alpha$ are positive integers such that $n = \Pi_{j=1}^{\alpha} \lambda_j$. We index every element $u[i]$ in the database by its coordinates $(i_1, \cdots, i_\alpha) \in \Pi_{j=1}^{\alpha} \mathbb{Z}_{\lambda_j}$ in this hypperrectangle. Thus we denote

$$u(i_1, \cdots, i_\alpha) := u[i_1 \Pi_{j=2}^{\alpha} \lambda_j + i_2 \Pi_{j=3}^{\alpha} \lambda_j + \cdots + i_{\alpha-1} \lambda_\alpha + i_\alpha +; 1]$$

for $(i_1, \cdots, i_\alpha) \in \Pi_{j=1}^{\alpha} \mathbb{Z}_{\lambda_j}$.

2.2 LFCPIR Protocol

Now we give a general description of LFCPIR for $s = \lceil l/k \rceil$, where k is a security parameter.

Algorithm 1. LFCPIR Protocol

【Step0: Parameters' Setup】
· Public Parameters
Database size n, dimension α
Chooser's public key $m = pq$
· Private Input Parameters
Chooser: secret key $\Lambda = LCM(p - 1, q - 1)$
a requested data coordinate $u = (u_1, \cdots, u_\alpha)$
Sender: Database data X
· Private Output Parameters
Chooser's retrieved data $x(u_1, \cdots, u_\alpha) \in X$
· Functions
DJ Encrypt Function : $FE(x)$
DJ Decrypt Function : $FD(x)$

begin

【Step1: Chooser Query $Q(u)$】
For j=1 to α do,
    For $t = 1$ to λ_j do:
        Generate a random r_{jt}
        If $u_j = t$ then set $b_{jt} \leftarrow 1$ else set $b_{jt} \leftarrow 0$
        Set $\beta_{jt} \leftarrow E_m^{s+j-1}(b_{jt}, r_{jt})$
Send $Q(u) = (\beta_{jt})_{j\in[\alpha], t\in\mathbb{Z}_{\lambda_j}}$

【Step2: Sender Answer $A(x_u)$】
For j=1 to α do
    For $i_{j+1} \leftarrow 0$ to $\lambda_{j+1} - 1$,
    $i_{j+2} \leftarrow 0$ to $\lambda_{j+2} - 1, \cdots, i_\alpha \leftarrow 0$ to $\lambda_\alpha - 1$ do:
        Set $x_j(i_{j+1}, \cdots, i_\alpha) \leftarrow \Pi_{t\in\mathbb{Z}_{\lambda_j}} \beta_{jt}^{x_{j-1}(t-1,i_{j+1},\cdots,i_\alpha)}$
Send $A(x_u) = x_\alpha$

【Step3: Chooser Retrieval $(x(u_1, \cdots, u_\alpha))$】
For $j \leftarrow \alpha$ downto 1 do:
    Set $x'_{j-1} \leftarrow D_{(p,q)}^{s+j-1}(x'_j)$
Output $x(u_1, \cdots, u_\alpha) = x'_0$

end

We illustrate the generic idea of the protocol by an example using $\alpha = 2, \lambda_1 = \lambda_2 = 4$. Here, the database is a 4×4 rectangle and it denotes the (i, j)-th element of sk-bits by $x(i, j)$. Assume that a chooser wants to know $u = x(2, 3)$ privately. Then the protocol proceeds as follows:

【Step1】
Chooser computes
$\beta_{11} = E_m^s(0), \beta_{12} = E_m^s(0),$
$\beta_{13} = E_m^s(1), \beta_{14} = E_m^s(0),$

$\beta_{21} = E_m^{s+1}(0), \beta_{22} = E_m^{s+1}(1),$
$\beta_{23} = E_m^{s+1}(0), \beta_{24} = E_m^{s+1}(0),$
and sends them to Sender.

【Step2】

Sender computes

$x_1(j_2) = \Pi_{i=1}^4 \beta_{1i}^{x(j,i)} = E_m^s(x(j,3))$

for each $j = 1, \ldots, 4$, and

$x_2 = \Pi_{j=1}^4 \beta_{2j}^{x_1(j_i)} = E_m^{s+1}(E_m^s(x(2,3)))$

and then, sends x_2 to Chooser.

【Step3】

Chooser recovers $x(2,3)$ by decrypting x_2 twice.

3　OLFCPIR

3.1　ι Map

In the LFCPIR protocol, β_{jt} is given by $E_m^{s+j-1}(b_{jt}, r_{jt})$, where the ciphertext is $(s + j - 1)k$-bits in size and b_{jt} is either 0 or 1. Kwon et al. introduced the following map to replace the encryptions of various sizes by those of a constant smaller size;

$$\iota_s^{s+t} : \mathbb{Z}_{m^{s+1}}^* \longrightarrow \mathbb{Z}_{m^{s+t+1}}^*$$

$$x \bmod m^{s+1} \longmapsto x^{m^t} \bmod m^{s+t+1}$$

The map $\iota_s^{s+t} : \mathbb{Z}_{m^{s+1}}^* \longrightarrow \mathbb{Z}_{m^{s+t+1}}^*$ map is well-defined and

$$\iota_s^{s+t}(E_m^s(0,r)) = E_m^{s+t-1}(0,r')$$

$$\iota_s^{s+t}(E_m^s(1,r)) = E_m^{s+t-1}(m^t,r')$$

for any $r' \in \mathbb{Z}_{m^{s+t+1}}^*$ such that $r = r' \bmod m^{s+1}$.

3.2　OLFCPIR Protocol

In LFCPIR, the chooser has to expand the query and send it. OLFCPIR presented below uses on the database side, sender, the ι Map to expand. In OLFCPIR, the expansion takes place at the database (i.e sender) while in LFCPIR the expansion takes place at the chooser. Therefore in OLFCPIR, the chooser sends and receives a relatively small ciphertext which reduces the communication cost of the scheme. The general OLFCPIR is described as follows:

Algorithm 2. OLFCPIR Protocol

【Step0: Parameters' Setup】

· Public Parameters

Database size n, dimension α

Chooser's public key $m = pq$

· Private Input Parameters

Chooser: secret key $\Lambda = LCM(p-1, q-1)$

a requested data coordinate $u = (u_1, \cdots, u_\alpha)$

Sender: Database data X

· Private Output Parameters

Chooser's retrieved data $x(u_1, \cdots, u_\alpha) \in X$

· Functions

DJ Encrypt Function: $FE(x)$

DJ Decrypt Function: $FD(x)$

begin

【Step1: Chooser Query $Q(u)$】

For j=1 to α do:

   For $t = 1$ to λ_j do:

      Generate a random r_{jt}

      If $u_j = t$ then set $b_{jt} \leftarrow 1$ else set $b_{jt} \leftarrow 0$

      Set $\beta_{jt} \leftarrow E_m^s(b_{jt}, r_{jt})$

Send $Q(u) = (\beta_{jt})_{j \in [\alpha], t \in \mathbb{Z}_{\lambda_j}}$

【Step2: Sender Answer $A(x_u)$】

For $j = 1$ to α do

   For $i_{j+1} \leftarrow 0$ to $\lambda_{j+1} - 1$,

   $i_{j+2} \leftarrow 0$ to $\lambda_{j+2} - 1, \cdots, i_\alpha \leftarrow 0$ to $\lambda_\alpha - 1$ do:

      Set $x_j(i_{j+1}, \cdots, i_\alpha) \leftarrow$

      $\Pi_{t \in \mathbb{Z}_{\lambda_j}}((\iota_s^{s+j-1}(\beta_{jt}))^{x_{j-1}(t-1, i_{j+1}, \cdots, i_\alpha)} \mod m^{s+j})$

Send $A(x_u) = x_\alpha$

【Step3: Chooser Retrieval $(x(u_1, \cdots, u_\alpha))$】

Set $x'_{\alpha-1} \leftarrow D_{p,q}^{s+\alpha-1}(x'_\alpha)$

For $j \leftarrow \alpha - 1$ down to 1 do:

   Set $x'_{j-1} \leftarrow D_{(p,q)}^{s+j-1}(x'_j / m^j)$

Output $x(u_1, \cdots, u_\alpha) = x'_0$

end

3.3   The Error

When we multiply out the Answer $A(x_u) = x_\alpha$, which is generated after multiple ι mappings at Step2,

$$x_\alpha = E_m^{s+\alpha-1}(m^{\alpha-1} * E_m^{s+\alpha-2}(\cdots$$
$$m^2 * E_m^{s+1}(m * E_m^s(x(u_1, \cdots, u_\alpha)))))$$

This implies that it comprises multiple encryptions $E_m^{s+j-1}(m^{j-1} * E_m^{s+j-2}(C))$.

Note that the domain of the E_m^{s+j-1} map and the codomain of $E_m^{s+j-2}(C)$ map are both $\mod m^{s+j-1}$.

We then describe $E_m^{s+j-2}(C)$ into base m number as $a_{s+j-2}a_{s+j-3} \cdots a_1 a_0$,

$$E_m^{s+j-2}(C) \equiv a_{s+j-2} * m^{s+j-2} + a_{s+j-3} * m^{s+j-3} +$$
$$\cdots a_1 * m + a_0 (\mod m^{s+j-1})$$

if we multiply m^{j-1}, which is derived from the ι map, with both sides,

$$m^{j-1} * E_m^{s+j-2}(C)$$
$$\equiv a_{s+j-2} * m^{s+2j-3} +$$
$$\cdots + a_{s-1} * m^{s+j-2} + \cdots + a_1 * m^j + a_0 * m^{j-1}$$
$$\equiv a_{s-1} * m^{s+j-2} + a_{s-2} * m^{s+j-3} +$$
$$\cdots + a_1 * m^j + a_0 * m^{j-1} (\mod m^{s+j-1})$$

Again, if we describe it into the base m number,

$$a_{s-1} \cdots a_1 a_0 0 \cdots 0$$

Thus, as the result of the overflow, the lower $j - 1$ digits of E_m^{s+j-1} become 0, and the coefficients with upper $s + j - 1$ to s digits of $E_m^{s+j-2}(C)$ disappear.

As a result, the chooser cannot retrieve $x(u_1, \cdots, u_\alpha)$ correctly even if he decrypts the answer $A(x_u) = x_\alpha$.

Therefore, the OLFCPIR protocol does not function as PIR.

4   Corrected OLFCPIR

In our corrected OLFCPIR depicted in Algorithm 3, we first describe the parameter setup (step 0) and the chooser quesry (step 1). Both steps are the same as in OLFCPIR. The correction of the overflow error takes place in step 2 and 3. We can avoid the aforementioned overflow error as follows:

Algorithm 3. Corrected OLFCPIR Protocol

【Step0: Parameters' Setup】
· Public Parameters
Database size n, dimension α
Chooser's public key $m = pq$
· Private Input Parameters
Chooser: secret key $\Lambda = LCM(p - 1, q - 1)$
a requested data coordinate $u = (u_1, \cdots, u_\alpha)$
Sender: Database data X
· Private Output Parameters
Chooser's retrieved data $x(u_1, \cdots, u_\alpha) \in X$
· Functions
DJ Encrypt Function: $FE(x)$
DJ Decrypt Function: $FD(x)$
begin
【Step1: Chooser Query $Q(u)$】
For j=1 to α do:
    For $t = 1$ to λ_j do:
        Generate a random r_{jt}
        If $u_j = t$ then set $b_{jt} \leftarrow 1$ else set $b_{jt} \leftarrow 0$
        Set $\beta_{jt} \leftarrow E_m^s(b_{jt}, r_{jt})$
Send $Q(u) = (\beta_{jt})_{j \in [\alpha], t \in \mathbb{Z}_{\lambda_j}}$

【Step2: Sender Answer $A(x_u)$】
For $j = 1$ to α do
  For $i_{j+1} \leftarrow 0$ to $\lambda_{j+1} - 1$,
    $i_{j+2} \leftarrow 0$ to $\lambda_{j+2} - 1, \cdots, i_\alpha \leftarrow 0$ to $\lambda_\alpha - 1$ do:
    Set $x_j(i_{j+1}, \cdots, i_\alpha)$
      $\leftarrow \Pi_{t \in \mathbb{Z}_{\lambda_j}}((\iota_s^{s+j-1}(\beta_{j,t}))^{x_{j-1}(t-1, i_{j+1}, \cdots, i_\alpha)} \mod m^{s+j(j-1)/2})$
Send $A(x_u) = x_\alpha$

【Step3: Chooser Retrieval $(x(u_1, \cdots, u_\alpha))$】
Set $x'_{\alpha-1} \leftarrow D_{p,q}^{s+\alpha-1}(x'_\alpha)$
For $j \leftarrow \alpha - 1$ down to 1 do:
  Set $x'_{j-1} \leftarrow D_{(p,q)}^{s+j-1}(x'_j/m^j)$
Output $x(u_1, \cdots, u_\alpha) = x'_0$

end

Here, we illustrate our corrected protocol with an example of the same setting as in section 2 (i.e. $\alpha = 2, \lambda_1 = \lambda_2 = 4$, 4×4 rectangle database and the chooser wants to know $u = x(2,3)$). Then our protocol proceeds as follows:

【Step1】
Chooser computes
$\beta_{11} = E_m^s(0), \beta_{12} = E_m^s(0),$
$\beta_{13} = E_m^s(1), \beta_{14} = E_m^s(0),$
$\beta_{21} = E_m^s(0), \beta_{22} = E_m^s(1),$
$\beta_{23} = E_m^s(0), \beta_{24} = E_m^s(0),$
and sends them to Sender.

【Step2】
Sender computes
$x_1(j_2) = \Pi_{i=1}^4 \beta_{1i}^{x(j,i)} = E_m^s(x(j,3))$
for each $j = 1, \ldots, 4$, and
$x_2 = \Pi_{j=1}^4 (\iota_j^{j+1}(\beta_{2j})^{x_1(j_i)} \mod m^{s+3})$
$= E_m^{s+2}(m * E_m^s(x(2,3)))$
and then, sends x_2 to Chooser.

【Step3】
Chooser decrypts x_2 to obtain $m * E_m^s(x(2,3)) \mod m^{s+2}$ and decrypts $m * E_m^s(x(2,3))/m \mod m^{s+2}$ to recover $x(2,3)$.

4.1 Comparison

LFCPIR
Let $\alpha \in [\log n]$ and $\lambda_j = n^{1/\alpha}$ for every $j = 1, \ldots, \alpha$. Then it is shown that the associated protocol LFCPIR has a chooser-side communication cost

$$\Sigma_{j=1}^\alpha \Sigma_{t=1}^{\lambda_j-1}(s+j)k$$

$$= \Sigma_{j=1}^\alpha (s+j)(n^{1/\alpha} - 1)k = \alpha(s + \frac{1}{2}(\alpha+1))(n^{1/\alpha} - 1)k$$

Table 1. Our Results (Communication costs of each protocols)

	LFCPIR	OLFCPIR (Error)	Corrected OLFCPIR
Chooser	$O(k \log^2 n + k \log n)$	$O(k \log n)$	$O(k \log n)$
Sender	$O(k \log n + k)$	$O(k \log n)$	$O(k \log^2 n + k \log n)$
Total	$O(k \log^2 n + k \log n + k)$	$O(k \log n)$	$O(k \log^2 n + k \log n)$

and a sender-side communication cost $(\alpha + s)k$.

Especially, these costs are optimized when $\alpha = \log n$.

With optimization, the chooser-side communication cost becomes: $\frac{1}{2} \log^2 n + (s + \frac{1}{2} \log n)k = O(k \log^2 n + k \log n)$.

With optimization, the sender-side communication cost becomes: $(\log n + s)k = O(k \log n + k)$.

Corrected OLFCPIR

For each $\alpha \in [\log n]$ and $\lambda_j = n^{1/\alpha}$ for every $j = 1, \ldots, \alpha$,

the associated protocol Corrected OLFCPIR has a chooser-side communication cost of

$$\alpha(s + 1)(n^{1/\alpha} - 1)k$$

and a sender-side communication cost of

$$(\frac{1}{2}\alpha(\alpha + 1) + s)k.$$

If these costs are optimized when $\alpha = \log n$, the chooser-side communication cost becomes $(s + 1) \log n \cdot k = O(k \log n)$.

while the sender-side communication cost becomes: $(\frac{1}{2} \log n(\log n + 1) + s)k = O(k \log^2 n + k \log n)$.

To summarize the comparison, the corrected OLFCPIR provides a reduced sending cost and an increased receiving cost. However the overall communication cost is asymptotically the same as in the previous LFCPIR.

5   Conclusion and Our Results

In this paper, we pointed out that the most efficient PIR (OLFCPIR) by Kwon et al. does not work due to overflow error. The overflow error provided the wrong coordinated for the item to be retrieved from the database. Basically, the expansion of the exponent needed to be bigger in order to avoid the overflow error. We therefore proposed a correction of the OLFCPIR resulting in a new protocol that we called corrected OLFCPIR. We furthermore compared out new protocol with LFCPIR, and finally showed that the communication cost of our corrected OLFCPIR is asymptotically the same as LFCPIR.

References

1. Ambainis, A.: Upper Bound on the Communication Complexity of Private Information Retrieval Automata, Languages and Programming. In: Degano, P., Gorrieri, R., Marchetti-Spaccamela, A. (eds.) ICALP 1997. LNCS, vol. 1256, pp. 401–407. Springer, Heidelberg (1997)

2. Beimel, A., Ishai, Y., Kushilevitz, E., Rayomnd, J.: Breaking on the $o(n^{(}1/(2k-1)))$ barrier for information theoretic private information retrieval. In: 41th IEEE Symposium on Foundation of Computation Science (2002)

3. Chor, B., Gilboa, M.: Computationally Private Information Retrieval. In: ACM Symposium on Theory of Computing, pp. 303–313 (1997)

4. Chor, B., Goldreich, O., Kushilevitz, E., Sudan, M.: Private Information Retrieva. In: IEEE Symposium on Foundations of Computer Science, pp. 41–50 (1995)

5. Cachin, C., Micali, S., Stadler, M.: Computationally private information retrieval with polylogarithmic communication. In: Stern, J. (ed.) EUROCRYPT 1999. LNCS, vol. 1592, pp. 402–414. Springer, Heidelberg (1999)

6. Damgard, I., Jurik, M.: A Generalisation, a Simplification and Some Applications of Paillier's Probabilistic Public-Key System. In: Kim, K.-c. (ed.) PKC 2001. LNCS, vol. 1992, pp. 119–136. Springer, Heidelberg (2001)

7. Damgård, I., Jurik, M.: A Length-Flexible Threshold Cryptosystem with Applications. In: Safavi-Naini, R., Seberry, J. (eds.) ACISP 2003. LNCS, vol. 2727, pp. 350–364. Springer, Heidelberg (2003)

8. Beimel, A., Ishai, Y., Kushilevitz, E.: General constructions for information theoretic private information retreival (2003) (Unpublished manuscripte),
http://www.cs.bgu.ac.il/beimel/pub.html

9. Kwon, D., Lee, J.: An efficient Computationally PIR protocol with Log Communication. In: The 1st Joint Workshop on Information Security (JWIS), Seoul Korea, September 20-21, pp. 491–499 (2006)

10. Kushilevitz, E., Ostrovsky, R.: Replication is not neeeded: Single database, computationally-private information retrieval. In: 38th IEEE Symposium on Foundimental of Computer Science, pp. 364–373 (1997)

11. Lipmaa, H.: An Oblivious Transfer Protocol with Log-Squared Communication. In: Zhou, J., López, J., Deng, R.H., Bao, F. (eds.) ISC 2005. LNCS, vol. 3650, pp. 314–328. Springer, Heidelberg (2005)

12. Paillier, P.: Public-Key Cryptosystems Based on Composite Degree Residuosity Classes. In: Stern, J. (ed.) EUROCRYPT 1999. LNCS, vol. 1592, pp. 223–238. Springer, Heidelberg (1999)

Reliable Food Traceability Using RFID Tagging

Guillermo Azuara, José L. Salazar, José L. Tornos, and Joan J. Piles

Universidad de Zaragoza
{gazuara,jsalazar,jltornos,jpiles}@unizar.es

Abstract. Radio Frequency IDentification (RFID) technology has numerous potential applications in various industries. One important use is for complete traceability of a specific product with the added advantage of being able to verify that quality controls have been passed, with all the necessary steps complied with and for the time required. The aim of this work is to present a food traceability system using RFID tags with contents guaranteed secure by the use of public-key cryptography and at an affordable cost without the need for substantial investment in infrastructure. Aggregate signatures are used so that all the steps can be signed in a reduced memory space. This type of signature is a cryptographic primitive that "consolidates" several signatures into one in such a way that if n users sign n messages, all the signatures can be grouped into one single signature.

Keywords: Traceability, RFID (Radio Frequency Identification), Aggregate signatures, PKC (Public Key Cryptography).

1 Introduction

Radio Frequency Identification (RFID) had its origins in the Second World War before Harry Stockman introduced the concept of passive RFID [1].

Since then the possibility of singly identifying objects even when there is no direct vision between reader and tag, together with the possibility of storing information in the tag itself and the modest cost, has resulted in the system becoming increasingly popular, gradually replacing other older identification systems such as bar codes.

For a specific definition of what we call traceability, we can refer to the definition given by the ISO in 1994 in which it is defined as "the ability to track any food, feed, food-producing animal or substance that will be used for consumption through all stages of production, processing and distribution" [2]. This is of vital importance for food safety [3] bearing in mind that, according to [4], about seven million people every year suffer food-related illnesses or poisoning. Consequently, there are various European, national, regional and local regulations requiring traceability systems for products for human consumption. Several European, national, regional and local regulations (such as some Protected Designation of Origin regulations) require traceability of products for human consumption. Although numerous implementations have been carried out in recent years, mainly with the use of bar codes, an increasing number of companies are complementing this system of identification with radiofrequency identification. RFID has several advantages summarized as follows [5]:

R. Sion et al. (Eds.): FC 2010 Workshops, LNCS 6054, pp. 57–67, 2010.
© IFCA/Springer-Verlag Berlin Heidelberg 2010

•Reduced labour costs.
•Faster production chain.
•Reduced losses (fraud, theft and administrative errors).
•More efficient product control.
•Increased knowledge of client behavior.

In the food sector in particular, there are three very important advantages:

•Better management of perishable products.
•Improvements in monitoring, locating and solving product quality problems.
•Improvement in management of withdrawal product in cases of risk.

The RFID identification is mandatory in the EU in the case of goats, sheep [6] or cows [7].

In light of the above, although some traceability systems based on RFID have already been implemented, the possibility is not usually contemplated of a client, or a verification authority such as the regulatory committee of a Protected Designation of Origin, being able to check that all the requirements have in fact been complied with in order that the product can be sold under a specific quality mark. This article describes a proposal for providing security for a traceability process based on RFID. It guarantees that products undergo a specific process and achieve quality levels that are verified, in some cases by people and in others by automated systems. In the proposed scheme, an external entity verifies the compliance of the processes by checking the validity of the digital signatures certifying the various controls, contributing an additional tool for guaranteeing quality.

It was decided to implement security by using a public-key infrastructure (PKI), and to minimize the memory space in the tags with an aggregate signature procedure, enabling a check at the end of the process that all stages have been completed with only one cryptographic operation.

The remainder of the article is organized as follows. First, we introduce the two essential elements of our proposal, an RFID system and the concept of aggregate signatures. Then, we describe a scenario, such an example, in which the system described has been developed, followed by an explanation of the proposed solution. Finally, we present our conclusions.

2 RFID Systems

RFID technology enables objects or persons to be identified with a single identifier, the information being transmitted to a receiving device (reader) using radio-frequency waves [1]. One of the most promising applications for industry is in the field of logistics, being able to track a specific object. The most widely-used system for identifying objects are bar codes that were mainly defined by two standards, the European Number Article (EAN) in Europe and another with a similar aim in the United States, the Universal Product Code (UPC). These two standards are today combined into a single standard known as GS1 [8]. A basic RFID system consists of an identification device (tag) attached to the object or person to be identified, a reader / recorder capable of reading and / or writing the tags and a protocol defining both the information format and the reading / writing procedure.

This basic system is usually expanded by a connection with a computer support system, as is shown in Fig. 1.

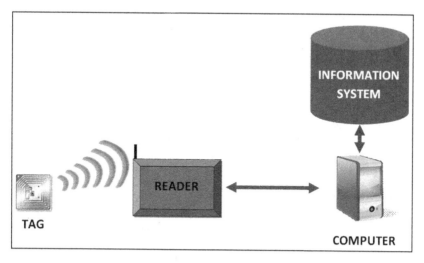

Fig. 1. Expanded RFID system

The tags, according to the EPCGlobal standard cited in [9] are classified in five classes:

- •Class 0: passive tags (obtaining their energy from the signal sent by the reader), read only and with information written on the tag by the tag manufacturer. Anti-theft or EAS (Electronic Article Surveillance) tags are included in this category.
- •Class 1: passive tags which can be written on once only. They normally contain a single identifier code such as the EPC (Electronic Product Code).
- •Class 2: passive or semi-passive tags (they include a small battery but only transmit at the request of the reader), very similar to class 1 tags but they allow multiple writing.
- •Class 3: semi-passive tags, similar to class 2 but including sensors.
- •Class 4: active tags, integrating batteries and transmitters so that they can communicate directly with other tags as well as the reader.

Note that EPC Class 5 devices correspond to readers.

The typical frequency bands at which these systems operate are LF (125-134.2 KHz), HF (13.56 MHz), UHF (865.5-867.6 MHz in Europe, 915 MHz I the United States and 950-956 MHz in Japan) and ISM (2.4 GHz). The first two bands are usually used for animal identification and "keyless" entry systems. The third one is very extensively used for intelligent tags and identification of objects for logistic purposes, and the fourth one is also used for object identification. Remember that the higher the frequency, the greater the data transmission rate, but there can be more problems transmitting in areas of high humidity, damp surfaces or a large quantity of metal surfaces.

The content of the tag is basically a unique identification number. It can also have a memory in which data can be recorded, and in secure tags there is also an area of encrypted memory for which a secret code is required.

From what we have seen above, it can easily be deduced that the architecture of one of these tags consists of the memory where the identifier and the additional data is kept, a transmitter and receiver system with its corresponding antenna and the logic necessary for managing the tasks of reading / writing and encryption (if it has this feature).

To conclude this brief description of RFID technology, it should be pointed out that it can sometimes happen that when a reader carries out a reading, multiple tags respond because of being within the operational range, in which case the use of anti-collision procedures is necessary.

3 Aggregate Signatures

The cryptographic concept of the multi-signature is based on the fact that the same message is signed by N agents in such a way that it can be checked that all the signers have in fact signed the message [10]. Improvements on this basic idea resulted in the development of a signature much smaller than that resulting from the linking together of all the signatures, with a corresponding reduction in computational time invested in the verification process [11].

Aggregate signatures represent a step beyond multi-signatures, as they allow for an untrusted third party who is not one of the users to compress all the signatures of different agents on different messages into the same aggregated signature. This signature can be verified knowing only the public keys of the signatories and the messages. In other words, given a set of U users, each one with a public and private key (K_{u+} y K_{u-}), and a subset $V \subseteq U$, if each user $u \in V$ produces a signature σ_u of a message M_u these signatures can be compacted into an aggregate signature σ by an untrusted third party different from the users of V. There are various applications of this idea, such as allowing a process to be carried out without the need for certificates [12], allowing verification of both the validity of a signature and the signing order [13], or where verification is independent of the order of signing [14].

The memory available for signing is a very limited resource in our working scenario, so that one essential property is for the aggregated signature to be of a constant size, not very large and independent of the number of compacted signatures. Having regard to these considerations, we have selected the proposal of Boneh [14] based on the use of bilinear applications as this meets our requirements. Bilinear applications emerged as cryptanalysis methods for cryptographic systems based on elliptic curves, reducing the problem of calculating the elliptic logarithm in supersingular curves to the discrete logarithm, more easily computable [15]. Later the attack was extended to include other more general types of curve [16], [17]. There is a substantial bibliography relating to algorithms enabling the application of bilinear applications based on the pairings of Weil and Tate, based also on the work of Miller [18].

4 Physical Scenario

By way of example, we can mention that we have implemented this method in a system to automate the information´s collection that the CRDO (Consejo Regulador de la Denominación de Origen / governing board of the protected designation of origin) "Jamón de Teruel" requires to guarantee the quality of the ham (pork leg) identified by this denomination. The animals, whose meat will be sold under this quality brand, must fulfill a number of specifications from the moment they are born till their entrance into the slaughterhouse. Further requirements are checked at different positions in the abattoir and at the same time extra information about the piece of meat is collected. Once the pork leg is taken apart in the slaughterhouse, it must suffer a drying process under specific conditions of temperature, humidity and salt content [19].We can distinguish three clearly defined parts in the system to be developed to tackle this task:

- A study of RFID transmission systems: the choice of components and transmission bands most appropriate for the environmental and financial conditions of the process. The financial conditions are especially important in this case owing to the large number of items to identify and the effect of the cost of the system on the final price of the product.
- The information system, including the design of how data will be compiled and processed, together with its availability for reference.
- System security, described in this work, designed to guarantee that the tags are written by the authorised entities, that the messages are electronically signed and the verification given.

The objective is to be able to provide evidence that the product has passed through a series of obligatory steps, or that it has undergone a series of pre-established checks. A separate message is created at each step, reflecting quantitatively the parameter being verified, and then signed. By using aggregate signatures, after each step the signatures are compacted into one single "aggregate".

As we are dealing with cured items, the steps that we should control, quantitatively and qualitatively, are as follows (view Fig. 2 in next page):

- Farm: to check that the pig comes from the required origin. Person responsible: farmer.
- Feedyard: this should be an authorized feedyard. The weight of the pigs and their feed types should be recorded. Person responsible: feedyard owner or farmer.
- Slaughterhouse: on reception the origin of the pigs should checked again (person responsible: controller); at the weighing point it should be checked that all the pre-established quality requirements have been complied with (person responsible: controller); in the quartering area the quality criteria should be checked again (person responsible: quartering room manager).
- Drying shed: the washing, drying and curing processes should be carried out satisfactorily in terms of processing and duration. Responsible: slaughterhouse owner.

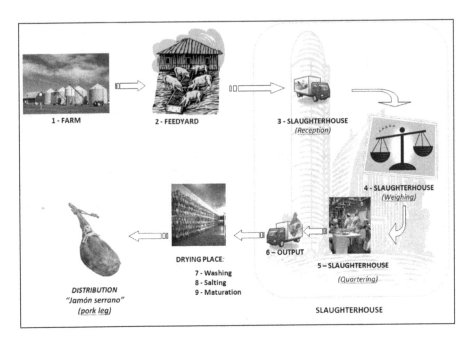

Fig. 2. Traceability in ham production

It can be appreciated that during the process it is necessary to have an entity that directly controls a part of the process, and that supervises the automated part (assigning secret keys to the different teams or equipment that record data and keeping the certificates and secret keys).

We will suppose that the RFID readers / recorders involved in the process do not need a person to carry out the verification. These devices may not be manipulated without authorization and they therefore incorporate the necessary measures to guarantee against this extreme case. Each one is assigned a private signature key, and there are periodic checks of the seals to see that the system has not been tampered with.

Once the product has completed the whole cycle, the fact that the process has been correctly complied with can be checked by verifying the aggregate signature.

As well as recording the information in a centralized information system, the data can also be written on the RFID tag which is attached to the product throughout the process, in such a way that the product history can be obtained and verified by reading the tag without the need for connection to a centralized information system.

5   Proposed Solution

As stated above, our proposed solution is to guarantee that all steps in the described process have been completed and all requirements complied with by using public key cryptography.

Specifically, we propose using tags with a memory space of 1024 bits which should be compatible with the conditions of the process and suitable for use with food products (in our implementation NPX icodeSLI). These are able to store data collected during the process, both on each tag and in the database. All this information is guaranteed by an aggregate signature verifying that all entries have been made by authorized agents.

At each check point there is a reader /recorder connected to a computer equipped with security measures to prevent unauthorized manipulation and the corresponding authorized agent signs the generated message with the private key, thus validating the quality of the product in this check point.

As regards the working parameters of the system, mainly the presence of a high humidity concentration, recommends the use of the HF band, 13.56 MHz, for the RFID elements (ISO 15693). The tag cannot affect the quality of the meat. For all these conditionings, adhesive HF tags have been chosen. The adhesive material must be suitable for being used with meat products. The information collected by the watcher will be stored on the tag and the specific number, marked with ink, can be also printed on the tag surface. The printer used is an AD Monarch 9855 HF.

Fig. 3 shows a scheme of the complete system, and it can be seen that the structure at all the control points is the same as shown in Fig. 1: a RFID reader / recorder connected to a computer, which in turn has access to the information system, to the public key infrastructure by means of a communication network.

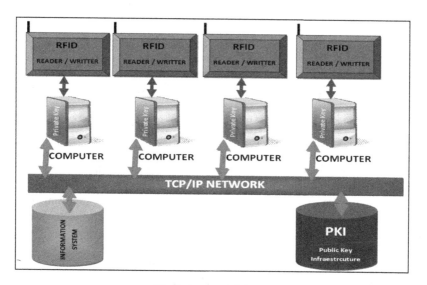

Fig. 3. Proposed Scheme

Given that the memory space of RFID tags is very limited, we had to reach a compromise between the required level of security and the size of the signature. The solution chosen was the scheme proposed by Boneh [14].

At each check point, after the signature has been verified, the corresponding control message is aggregated and the new signature aggregated.

Before signing and aggregating the new data, the whole process up to that point is verified. If the check produces a negative result, the product is immediately withdrawn from the production chain saving the producer time, money and space.

We have carried out tests [20] with keys of different sizes, evaluating also the processing time of each one and obtaining the results shown in Fig. 4 and Fig. 5.

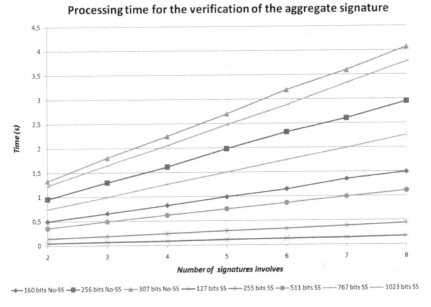

Fig. 4. Comparation of processing time for the verification of the aggregate signature

In Fig. 4 we can see the processing time for the verification of the aggregate signature depending on the number of signatures involved. It can be appreciated that they are practically linear given that the verification involves the execution of a bilinear pairing for each signatory. The curves used belong to two families, supersingular (SS) and non-supersingular (no-SS). With these different results we choose the curve typology according to the available power variables of the process and the level of security we wish to provide, as determined by the equipment available.

Turning to Fig. 5, we can also compare the processing times for the two curve typologies (supersingular and non-supersingular). It can be seen that the increase in processing time for the supersingular curves is much greater and that although in quantitative terms it might appear that the times are less for the supersingular curves, this is not the case. The level of security offered by each of the curves is determined by the length of its keys multiplied by the MOV factor of the curve, which is 2 for supersingular curves and 6 for non-supersingular curves. Therefore, we have opted for the latter because they offer a shorter processing time and a shorter length of encrypted message with the same level of security.

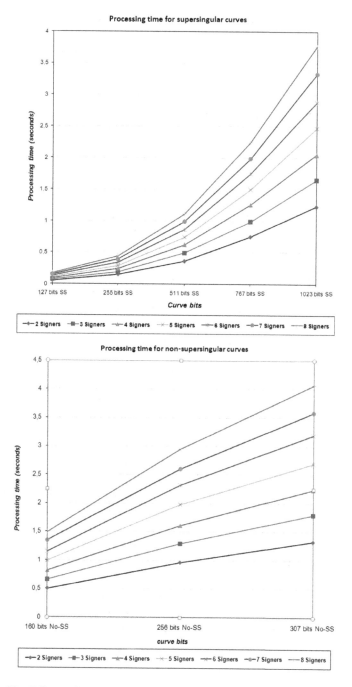

Fig. 5. Processing time for Supersingular and non-Supersingular curves

It should also be added that the choice of a degree of MOV equal to 6 is determined by the fact that this is the maximum level in which this type of curve is operational. At higher values the operations involved in the calculation of bilinear pairings become excessively complex. Therefore a signature size of 160 bits has been chosen based on non-supersingular curves.

Once the product is on the market, any user with the public keys of the signers and the messages stored in the tag itself can check whether the product has complied with the appropriate procedures. The public keys can be found in the public register of the certifying authority. By using RFID, this check can be done quickly and easily, even automatically, so that the wholesaler can act as soon as the goods are received.

6 Conclusions

The use of RFID tags in the proposed system provides evidence that all the controls in a production process have been complied with. This enables the client to verify rapidly that all the products have correctly passed through the production cycle with the guarantee of trust provided under the responsibility of the signer.

As the calculation of the signatures is done by computer, the tag is freed from this task, and this constitutes a significant saving both in cost and in processing time. The use of Light Cryptography is an interesting alternative to our method. However, the requirement of minimal logical in the tag would increase too much the cost of the system.

The fact that the production process information is stored in the tag itself makes direct inspection of the products much easier (without the need for any outside connection).

The key size can be adjusted to achieve a compromise between the level of security and a processing time compatible with the production process. For example, with a signature size of 160 bits using non-supersingular curves, verification times of aggregate signatures of less than two seconds have been achieved, in an eight signature process. This result is perfectly compatible with the system described production chain.

The memory space on the tags used for the signatures is 50 times less than what would be needed for messages signed using the RSA method and compacting the signatures (assuming eight intermediary signatures, and for example the 1024 bits provided by RSA at a basic level of security).

Acknowledgments

This work was supported in part by the Instituto Nacional de Investigación y Tecnología Agraria y Agroalimentaria (INIA) funds under Grant PET2007-08-C11-06. Also, it was partially supported by Cátedra Telefónica-Universidad de Zaragoza.

References

1. Landt, J.: The history of RFID. IEEE Potentials 24(4), 8–11 (2005)
2. ISO Standard 8402: 1994 International Organization for Standarization (ISO) (1994), http://www.iso.org

3. Regattieri, A., Gamberi, M., Manzini, R.: Traceability of food products: General framework and experimental evidence. Journal of Food Engineering 81, 347–356 (2007)
4. Sarig, Y.: Traceability of food products. CIGR Journal of Scientific Research and Developments 5(12), 54–65 (2003)
5. Sahin, E., Dallery, Y., Gershwin, S.: Performance evaluation of a traceability system. In: Proceedings of IEEE International Conference on Systems, Man and Cybernetics, vol. 3, pp. 210–218 (2002), ISSN: 1062-922X
6. Council Regulation (EC) No. 21/2004 of 17 December 2003 establishing a system for the identification and registration of ovine and caprine animals and amending Regulation (EC) No 1782/2003 and Directives 92/102/EEC and 64/432/EEC (2003)
7. Regulation (EC) No 1760/2000 of the European Parliament and of the Council of 17 July 2000, establishing a system for the identification and registration of bovine animals and regarding the labelling of beef and beef products and repealing Council Regulation (EC) No 820/97 (2000)
8. GS1, http://www.gs1.org/
9. Garfinkely, S., Holtzman, H.: Understanding RFID Technology. In: Garfinkely, S., Rosenberg, B. (eds.) RFID: Applications, Security, and Privacy, Westford, cap. 2. Pearson Education, London (2006)
10. Okamoto, T.: A digital multisignature scheme using bijective public-key cryptosystems. ACM Trans. Comput. Syst. 6(4), 432–441 (1988)
11. Boldyreva, A.: Threshold signatures, multisignatures and blind signatures based on the gap-diffie-hellman-group signature scheme. In: Kim, K.-c. (ed.) PKC 2001. LNCS, vol. 1992, pp. 31–46. Springer, Heidelberg (2001)
12. Herranz: Deterministic identity-based signatures for partial aggregation. The Computer Journal 49(3), 322–330 (2006)
13. Lysyanskaya, A., Micali, S., Reyzin, L., Shacham, H.: Sequential aggregate signatures from trapdoor permutations. In: Cachin, C., Camenisch, J.L. (eds.) EUROCRYPT 2004. LNCS, vol. 3027, pp. 74–90. Springer, Heidelberg (2004)
14. Boneh, D., Gentry, C., Lynn, B., Shacham, H.: Aggregate and verifiably encrypted signatures from bilinear maps. In: Biham, E. (ed.) EUROCRYPT 2003. LNCS, vol. 2656. Springer, Heidelberg (2003); Cryptology ePrint Archive, Report 2002/175
15. Menezes, A., Vanstone, S., Okamoto, T.: Reducing elliptic curve logarithms to logarithms in a finite field. IEEE Transactions on Information Theory 39, 1639–1646 (1993)
16. Frey, G., Müller, H.: The tate pairing and the discrete logarithm applied to elliptic curve cryptosystems. IEEE Transactions on Information Theory 45, 1717–1719 (1999)
17. Garefalakis, T.: The generalized weil pairing and the discrete logarithm problem on elliptic curves. In: Rajsbaum, S. (ed.) LATIN 2002. LNCS, vol. 2286, pp. 118–130. Springer, Heidelberg (2002)
18. Miller, V.: Short program for functions on curves (1986), http://crypto.stanford.edu/miller/miller.pdf
19. López, A.M., Pascual, E., Salinas, A.M., Ramos, P., Azuara, G.: Design of a RFID based traceability system in a slaughterhouse. In: Workshops Proceedings of the 5th International Conference on Intelligent Environments. Ambient Intelligence and Smart Environments, vol. 4 (October 2009)
20. Azuara, G., Piles, J.J., Salazar, J.L.: Securización de un sistema de trazabilidad RFID mediante firmas agregadas. VII Jornadas de Ingeniería Telemática, Libro de Actas, 57–63 (2008)

Lightweight Cryptography and DPA Countermeasures: A Survey

Amir Moradi[1] and Axel Poschmann[2]

[1] Horst Görtz Institute for IT Security, Ruhr University Bochum, Germany
[2] Division of Mathematical Sciences, School of Physical and Mathematical Sciences,
Nanyang Technological University, Singapore
moradi@crypto.rub.de, aposchmann@ntu.edu.sg

Abstract. The dawning Ubiquitous Computing age demands a new attacker model for the myriads of pervasive computing devices used: since a potentially malicious user is in full control over the pervasive device, additionally to the cryptographic attacks the whole field of physical attacks has to be considered. Most notably are here so-called *side channel attacks*, such as *Differential Power Analysis* (DPA) attacks. At the same time, the deployment of pervasive devices is strongly cost-driven, which prohibits expensive countermeasures. In this article we survey a broad range of countermeasures and discuss their suitability for ultra-constrained devices, such as passive RFID-tags. We conclude that adiabatic logic countermeasures, such as 2N-2N2P and SAL, seem to be promising candidates, because they increase the resistance against DPA attacks while at the same time lowering the power consumption of the pervasive device.

1 Introduction

Mark Weiser's famous vision of *ubiquitous computing* (ubicomp) [47], which is widely believed to be the next paradigm in information technology, seems to become reality in the near future, since increasingly everyday items are enhanced to pervasive devices by embedding computing power. The mass deployment of pervasive devices promises on the one hand many benefits (e.g. optimized supply-chains), but on the other hand, many foreseen applications are security sensitive (military, financial or automotive applications), not to mention possible privacy issues. With the widespread presence of embedded computers in such scenarios security is a striving issue, because the potential damage of malicious attacks also increases. Even worse, pervasive devices are deployed in a hostile environment, *i.e.* an adversary has physical access to or control over the devices, which enables the whole field of physical attacks. Not only the adversary model is different for ubicomp, but also its optimisation goals are significantly different from that of traditional application scenarios: high throughput is usually not an issue but power, energy and area are sparse resources. Due to the harsh cost constraints for ubicomp applications only the least required amount of computing power will be realized. If computing power is fixed and cost are variable, Moore's Law leads to the paradox of an increasing demand for lightweight solutions.

R. Sion et al. (Eds.): FC 2010 Workshops, LNCS 6054, pp. 68–79, 2010.
© IFCA/Springer-Verlag Berlin Heidelberg 2010

In this article we are going to address the issue of lightweight side-channel countermeasures. Our main contribution is a survey of countermeasures on different architectural levels (cell, gate, algorithmic) and an evaluation of their suitability for constrained devices. Our main metrics are the area and timing overhead, but we also take practical evaluations into account to identify a set of countermeasures that seem to be promising for constrained devices.

The remainder of this article is organized as follow: In Section 2 we are going to briefly highlight the hardware properties of basic building blocks, such as Boolean operations and flipflops. Subsequently in Section 3 we introduce to Side channel attacks and several previously proposed countermeasures. Then in Section 4 we will evaluate a selection of countermeasures with regard to their suitability for constrained devices. Finally this paper is concluded in Section 5.

2 Hardware Properties of Cryptographic Building Blocks

Block ciphers take a block of data and a key as input and transform it to a ciphertext, often using a roundfunction that is iterated several times. The intermediate state is called *data state* and *key state*, respectively. While software implementations have to process single operations in a serial manner, hardware implementations offer more flexibility for parallelization and serialization. Generally speaking there exist three major architecture strategies for the implementation of block ciphers: *serialized, round-based,* and *parallelized.* In a *serialized* architecture only a fraction of a single round is processed in one clock cycle. These lightweight implementations allow to reduce area and power consumption at the cost of a rather long processing time. If a complete round is performed in one clock cycle, we have a *round-based* architecture. This implementation strategy usually offers the best time-area product and throughput per area ratio. A *parallelized* architecture processes more than one round per clock cycle, leading to a rather long critical path. A longer critical path leads to a lower maximum frequency but also requires the gates to drive a higher load (fanout), which results in larger gates with a higher power consumption. By inserting intermediate registers (a technique called *pipelining*), it is possible to split the critical path into fractions, thus increasing the maximum frequency. Once the pipeline is filled, a complete encryption can be performed in one clock cycle with such an architecture. Consequently, this implementation strategy yields the highest throughput at the cost of high area demands. Furthermore, since the pipeline has to be filled, each pipelining stage introduces a delay of one clock cycle.

In the context of lightweight cryptography, clearly serialized implementations are the most important architecture, since they allow to significantly reduce the area and power demands. In order to compare the area requirements independently of the technology used, it is common to state the area as *gate equivalents* [GE]. One GE is equivalent to the area which is required by the two-input NAND gate with the lowest driving strength of the appropriate technology. The area in GE is derived by dividing the area in μm^2 by the area of a two-input NAND gate. However, it is not easy to compare the power consumption of different technologies.

In order to reuse the same hardware resources in a serialized or round-based implementation, data and key state have to be stored. Since external memory is often not available for cryptographic applications or draws too much current (e.g. on passive RFID-tags), the state has to be maintained in registers using flipflops. Unfortunately flipflops have a rather large area and power demand, for example, when using the *Virtual Silicon (VST)* standard cell library based on the *UMC L180* 0.18μ *1P6M Logic process* (UMCL18G212T3, [46]), flipflops require between 5.33 GE and 12.33 GE to store a single bit (see Table 1). The gate count differs so significantly for different cells because the first cell (HDDFFPB1) consists only of a simple D flipflop itself, while the latter one (HDSDERSPB1) comprises of a multiplexer to select one of two possible inputs for storage and a D flipflop with active-low enable, asynchronous clear and set. There exists a wide variety of flipflops of different complexity between these two extremes. A good trade-off between efficiency and useful supporting logic provide the two flipflop cells HDSDEPQ1 and HDSDFPQ1. Both are scan flipflops, which means that beside the flipflop they also provide a multiplexer. The latter one is also capable of being gate clocked, which is an important feature to lower power consumption. Storage of the internal state typically accounts for at least 50 % of the total area and power consumption. E.g. the area requirements of storage logic accounts for 55 % in the case of a round-based PRESENT [3] and for 86% in the case of a serialized PRESENT [34], while for a serialized AES it accounts for 60 % of the area and half of the current consumption (*i.e.* 52 %) [7]. Therefore implementations of cryptographic algorithms for low-cost tag applications should aim to minimize the storage required.

Table 1. Area requirements and corresponding gate count of selected standard cells of the UMCL18G212T3 library [46]

Standard cell	Cell name	Area in μm^2	GE
NOT	HDINVBD1	6.451	0.67
NAND	HDNAN2D1	9.677	1
NOR	HDNOR2D1	9.677	1
AND	HDAND2D1	12.902	1.33
OR	HDOR2D1	12.902	1.33
MUX	HDMUX2D1	22.579	2.33
XOR (2-input)	HDEXOR2D1	25.805	2.67
XOR (3-input)	HDEXOR3D1	45.158	4.67
D Flip flop	HDDFFPB1	51.61	5.33
Scan D flipflop /w enable	HDSDFPQ1	58.061	6
Scan flipflop	HDSDEPQ1	83.866	8.67
complex Scan flipflop	HDSDERSPB1	119.347	12.33

The term *combinatorial elements* includes all the basic Boolean operations such as NOT, NAND, NOR, AND, OR, and XOR. It also includes some basic logic functions such as multiplexers (MUX). It is widely assumed that the gate count for these basic operations is typically independent of the library used. However, in [34] it has been shown that ASIC implementation results of a serialized PRESENT in different technologies range from $1,000$ GE to $1,169$ GE. This indicates that also the gate count for basic logic gates differs depending on the used standard-cell library. For the *Virtual Silicon (VST)* standard cell library based on the *UMC L180* 0.18μ *1P6M Logic process* (UMCL18G212T3, [46]) the figures for selected two-input gates with the lowest driving strength is given in Table 1. Note that in hardware XOR and MUX are rather expensive when compared to the other basic Boolean operations.

In the next section we will introduce background information of *Differential Power Analysis* attacks and their countermeasures.

3   Introduction to DPA and Countermeasures

Although nowadays side-channel attacks, after the first publication of power analysis attacks in [16], are known as a serious threat for devices performing cryptographic operations, in fact this kind of attacks has been accidentally discovered in 1943 [26]. These attacks exploit the fact that the execution of a cryptographic algorithm on a physical device leaks information about the processed data and/or executed operations through side channels, e.g., power consumption [16], execution time [15] and electromagnetic radiation [8]. As presented in a number of publications, side-channel attacks particularly power analysis attacks are considered as an extremely powerful and practical tool for breaking cryptographic devices.

By measuring and evaluating the power consumption of a cryptographic device, information-dependent leakage is exploited and combined with the knowledge about the plaintext or ciphertext (in contrary to mathematical cryptanalyses which require pairs of plain- and ciphertexts) in order to extract, e.g., a secret key. Since intermediate results of the computations can be derived from the leakage, e.g., from the Hamming weight of the data processed in a software implementation, a divide-and-conquer strategy becomes possible, i.e., the secret key could be recovered byte by byte.

A *Simple Power Analysis (SPA)* attack, as introduced in [16], relies on visual inspection of power traces, e.g., measured from an embedded microcontroller of a smartcard. The aim of an SPA is to reveal details about the execution of the program flow of a software implementation, like the detection of conditional branches depending on secret information. Contrary to SPA, *Differential Power Analysis (DPA)* utilizes statistical methods and evaluates several power traces with often uniformly distributed known plaintexts or known ciphertexts. A DPA requires no knowledge about the concrete implementation of the cipher and can hence be applied to any unprotected black box implementation. According to intermediate values depending on key hypotheses the traces are divided into sets or correlated to estimated power values, and then statistical tools, e.g., difference of estimated means [16], correlation coefficient [4], and estimated mutual information [10], indicate the most probable hypothesis amongst all partially guessed key hypotheses.

Several schemes have been proposed to protect cryptographic implementations against DPA attacks. A DPA countermeasure aims at preventing a dependency between the power consumption of a cryptographic device and intermediate values of the executed algorithm [17]. *Hiding* and *Masking* are amongst the most common countermeasures on either the hardware or the software level. The goal of *Hiding* methods is to increase the noise factor [48] or to equalize the power consumption values independently of the processed data while *Masking* rely on randomizing key-dependent intermediate values processed during the execution of the cipher. The most common proposed countermeasures can be classified as follows:

- **Cell Level** (DPA-resistant logic styles): Counteracting DPA attacks at the cell level means that the logic cells of a circuit are implemented in such a way that their power consumption is independent of the processed data and the performed operations [17]. During the last years, several proposals as DPA-resistant logic style have been made and a selection is listed below:
  - **Sense Amplifier Based Logic (SABL)** [42], which is a dual-rail precharge logic, is designed to have a constant internal power consumption independent of the processed logic values. In order to achieve this aim, a full-custom design tool must be used to balance all the internal capacitances of the final layout.
  - **Wave Dynamic Differential Logic (WDDL)** [43] and **Masked Dual-rail Precharge Logic (MDPL)** [32] have been designed to avoid the usage of a full-custom design tool. However, their implementations show strong data-dependent leakage [39,31,36] which makes them vulnerable to straightforward DPA attacks.
  - **Random Switching Logic (RSL)** [38,40] employs several random bits for a non-linear combinational circuit and needs a special design flow to reach the desired level of protection. For instance a practical implementation showed vulnerability to a single-bit DPA attack [35].
  - **Dual-rail Transition Logic (DTL)** [24], which aims at randomly changing the logic values and presenting the desired data at the same time, has not been practically evaluated yet and its effectiveness is still uncertain.
  - **Charge Recovery Logics** have been proposed for low-power applications, and some of them, so-called *adiabatic logic* styles, have been investigated from DPA-resistance point of view in [22] and [14]. Adiabatic logic uses a time-varying voltage source and its slopes of transition are slowed down. This reduces the energy dissipation of each transition. In short the idea of adiabatic logic is to use a trapezoidal power-clock voltage rather than fixed supply voltage. As a consequence the power consumption of a circuit is reduced while at the same time its resistance against side-channel attacks is greatly enhanced.

- **Masking:** Randomizing the values which are processed by the cryptographic device can be performed at different levels of abstraction:

  • **Gate Level:** Masking at the gate level is performed by considering a number of mask bits for each logic value of the circuit. There are a number of proposals on how to use mask bits at the gate level, e.g., [12], [44] and [45]. However, practical realization of such schemes faces with glitches which inherently happen on logic circuit and cause vulnerability to DPA attacks [18].

  • **Algorithm Level:** According to the masking scheme, e.g., additive or multiplicative, non-linear functions of the given cipher must be redesigned to fulfill the desired level of security. There are a set of publications on contributing a masking scheme on the AES substitution function, e.g., [29] and [2]. Nevertheless, their practical investigations show vulnerability to those DPA attacks which consider glitches of the combinational circuit as the hypothetical power model [19]. Moreover, there are some proposals which are provably secure, e.g., [49] and [5]. Though they have not been practically investigated, the same vulnerability to glitches is expected.

    A threshold implementation of Sboxes has been proposed in [27,28] to avoid the effect of glitches, but it has not been practically verified yet.

- **Hiding:** Randomizing the amounts of power consumption in order to hide the sensitive operation is often performed on software implementations by shuffling the execution of operations and/or by insertion of dummy operations [17]. Although this class of countermeasures can not perfectly protect against DPA attacks, its combination with algorithmic masking, which has been introduced in [11], provides a reasonable level of protection [41].

  Randomly permuting intermediate values using permutation tables [13] also can be considered as a hiding scheme, but its efficiency has been investigated as a vulnerability has bee reported in [33]. Moreover, dynamic reconfiguration, which has been proposed in [20], can be considered as a realization of shuffling in hardware.

4   Comparison of Countermeasures

In this section we will evaluate the countermeasures introduced in the previous section with regard to the following criteria:

Area Overhead: The area overhead of every countermeasure is clearly one of the most important metrics, when low-cost devices are considered, since the cost of an ASIC are proportional to its area. These figures are either obtained from the corresponding publications or estimated. Therefore they should primarily not be seen as precise figures, but rather as an indicator in what range a countermeasures is to be expected to increase the area.

Timing Overhead: Typically timing is not critical in many low-cost applications as only rather small amounts of data are going to be processed. However, the energy consumption is directly proportional to the amount of clock cycles required. Therefore the timing overhead is an important measure for active (i.e. battery powered) constrained devices, rather than for passive (i.e. without an own power supply) constrained devices. Similar to the area overhead these figures are either obtained from the corresponding publications or are estimated and should be viewed as rough guidelines rather than precise figures.

Practical Evaluation: It has turned out that countermeasures that have been shown to be provably secure by using simulated power consumption can be attacked when real ASIC implementations are used, e.g., [29] vs. [19]. On the other hand, theoretical attacks on simulated power consumptions have been shown to be impractical on real world ASIC implementations, e.g., [32] vs. [31]. Therefore practical evaluation of a countermeasure is crucial for a more precise evaluation of the security level that can be achieved with this countermeasure. Furthermore, this column is a good indicator for future work as it shows where prototyping of an ASIC has been done already.

Known Leakages: This column lists publications that have found theoretical or practical leakages of the countermeasure.

In the following some notes on Table 2, which summarizes a comparison between the most promising countermeasures, are given. MDPL [32] has only around halve the speed, because MDPL gates consist of two P-N networks due to the usage of majority gates, i.e., a basic majority cell followed by an inverter. Area overhead ranges from 2 for a buffer, over 3.5 for a D-type flipflop and up to 6 for an XNOR gate. A prototyped ASIC implementation of the AES resulted in an area overhead factor of around 5, a power overhead factor of 11 and a timing overhead factor of 2.6 [30]. Several leakages have been found for MDPL [37,9,23,21,36] and a chip has been prototyped and evaluated by the authors of MDPL in [31]. Finally, the authors have proposed an improved MDPL, called iMDPL [31]. However, iMDPL requires 3 times more area than MDPL, thus increasing the total area overhead factor to around 15, *i.e.* an implementation in iMDPL is around 15 *times* larger than a plain CMOS implementation. Furthermore, the leakages reported in [36,9,21] also hold for iMDPL.

RSL [40,38] doubles the area requirements while halving the speed for the maximum frequency, since timing is not critical, there can no delay be expected in low frequency typical for low-cost devices. However, after prototyping an ASIC a leakage has been reported in [35].

Charge recovery logics, e.g., 2N-2N2P [22] and SAL [14], increase the area by a factor between 2 and 4. However, the power consumption is *less* than for standard CMOS circuits. Since their DPA-resistance increases with lower frequencies, it makes them particular valuable for low-power low throughput applications, such as passive RFID-tags. No charge recovery logic has been yet practically evaluated and no leakages have been fund so far. It seems to be one of the most promising candidates for future evaluation. However, since it is a full-custom design no standard-cell design flow can be used.

All gate-level masking schemes [12,44,45] have been shown to be susceptible in the presence of glitches [18] and thus are not considered any further by us.

Moreover, both algorithmic masking approaches [2] and [29] are susceptible to toggle count attacks as shown in [19].

Canright algorithmic masking [5] yields a very compact S-box of the AES that is 2.7 times as large as an unprotected S-box for the first round and 2.2 times larger for every subsequent round. A masked AES implementation would require to also store the mask bits which would double the area requirements for storage. All together the area overhead factor is estimated to be 2.5. Since it has not yet practically evaluated it seems to be an interesting candidate for further investigations, especially its resistance to glitching attacks. Zakeri algorithmic masking [49] also increases the area by a factor of around 4, which is rather large. However, there has been no practical evaluation so far and no leakage has been found.

Nikova algorithmic masking based on secret sharing [27,28] has not been practically evaluated so far. It requires to store at least two additional mask bits for every masked bit. Given the fact that especially in lightweight implementations storage accounts for the majority of the gate count, it is fair to estimate the hardware overhead with a factor of 3. However, this countermeasures has not

Table 2. Area and Timing overhead of several side channel countermeasures[1] (estimated values are denoted by *)

Countermeasure			Overhead factor		Pract.	Leakage
Level	Type/Name	Ref.	Area	Time	eval.	found in
Cell	MDPL	[32]	5	2.6	yes	[9,23,25,30,31,36,37]
	iMDPL	[31]	*15	*6	no	[9,21,36]
	RSL	[40,38]	2	2	yes	[35]
	DTL	[24]	*11	*4	no	none
	2N-2N2P	[22]	*2	(2)	no	none
	SAL	[14]	*4	(2)	no	none
Gate	Private Circuits	[12]	(3)	(3)	no	[18]
	Masking	[44,45]	*10	*5	no	[18]
Alg.	Masking	[2]	*8	*5	no	[19]
	Masking	[29]	*6	*4	no	[19]
	Masking	[5]	2.5	3	no	none
	Masking	[49]	4	3	no	none
	Secret Sharing	[27,28]	*3	*1.3	no	none
	Shuffling + Masking	[11]	7	10	yes	[41]
	Rand. Perm. Tab.	[13]	2.5	12	yes	[33]
	Dyn. Reconf.	[20]	4.75	3.36	yes	none

[1]Note that the overheads vary by different algorithms and architectures. The values presented in this table are mostly based on implementations of the AES encryption algorithm, and we did our best to consider the same architecture for all countermeasures.

[2]suitable for low-throughput applications.

[3]depends on the level of protection, e.g., area overhead would be an order of $O(nt^2)$ where n is the size of the original circuit and t is related to the desired protection level.

been practically evaluated and seems to be an interesting candidate for future investigations.

Dynamic reconfiguration [20] increases the area requirements by a factor of 4.75 and reduces the maximum clock frequency by a factor of 3.36. However, since lightweight applications typically do not need high throughput the timing overhead is not important, but the area overhead is already rather high.

5   Conclusions

The structural problem of most of todays SCA countermeasures is that they significantly increase the area, timing and power consumption of the implemented algorithm compared to an unprotected implementation. Furthermore, many countermeasures require random numbers, hence also a TRNG or a PRNG[1] has to be available. Since this will also increase the cost of an implementation of the algorithm, it will delay the break-even point and hence the mass deployment of some applications. For ultra-constrained applications, such as passive RFID tags, some countermeasures pose an impregnable barrier, because the power consumption of the protected implementation is much higher than what is available.

Power optimization techniques are an important tool for lightweight implementations of specific pervasive applications and might ease the aforementioned problem. On the one hand they also strengthen implementations against side channel attacks, because they lower the power consumption (the signal), which decreases the signal to noise ratio (SNR). However, on the other hand power saving techniques also *weaken* the resistance against side channel attacks. One consequence of the power minimization goal is that in the optimal case only those parts of the data path are active that process the relevant information. Furthermore, the width of the data path, *i.e.* the amount of bits that are processed at one point in time, is reduced by serialization. This however implies that the algorithmic noise is reduced to a minimum, which reduces the amount of required power traces for a successful side channel attack. Even worse, the serialized architecture allows the adversary a divide-and-conquer approach which further reduces the complexity of a side channel attack. Summarizing, it can be concluded that lightweight implementations greatly enhance the success probability of a side channel attack. The practical side channel attack [6] on *KeeLoq* applications [1] impressively underline this conclusions.

Adiabatic logics, like other DPA countermeasures, have an area overhead, but decrease the (instantaneous) power consumption by decreasing the frequency. As a consequence the resistance of the corresponding circuit against side-channel attacks is extremely increased. Especially for pervasive devices adiabatic logic styles seem to be a promising SCA countermeasure and practical evaluations of these logic styles will be worth reading. Furthermore, also the approach taken by Nikova *et al.* [27,28] is a promising candidate, because it has a moderate area overhead and was theoretically proven to be secure against DPA attacks.

---

[1] True Random Number Generator, Pseudo Random Number Generator.

Acknowledgment

The research was supported in part by the Singapore National Research Foundation under Research Grant NRF-CRP2-2007-03.

References

1. Keeloq Algorithm (November 2006), http://en.wikipedia.org/wiki/KeeLoq
2. Akkar, M., Giraud, C.: An Implementation of DES and AES Secure against Some Attacks. In: Koç, Ç.K., Naccache, D., Paar, C. (eds.) CHES 2001. LNCS, vol. 2162, pp. 309–318. Springer, Heidelberg (2001)
3. Bogdanov, A., Leander, G., Knudsen, L., Paar, C., Poschmann, A., Robshaw, M., Seurin, Y., Vikkelsoe, C.: PRESENT - An Ultra-Lightweight Block Cipher. In: Paillier, P., Verbauwhede, I. (eds.) CHES 2007. LNCS, vol. 4727, pp. 450–466. Springer, Heidelberg (2007)
4. Brier, E., Clavier, C., Olivier, F.: Correlation Power Analysis with a Leakage Model. In: Joye, M., Quisquater, J.-J. (eds.) CHES 2004. LNCS, vol. 3156, pp. 16–29. Springer, Heidelberg (2004)
5. Canright, D., Batina, L.: A Very Compact "Perfectly Masked" S-Box for AES. In: Bellovin, S.M., Gennaro, R., Keromytis, A.D., Yung, M. (eds.) ACNS 2008. LNCS, vol. 5037, pp. 446–459. Springer, Heidelberg (2008)
6. Eisenbarth, T., Kasper, T., Moradi, A., Paar, C., Salmasizadeh, M., Shalmani, M.T.M.: On the Power of Power Analysis in the Real World: A Complete Break of the KeeLoqCode Hopping Scheme. In: Wagner, D. (ed.) CRYPTO 2008. LNCS, vol. 5157, pp. 203–220. Springer, Heidelberg (2008)
7. Feldhofer, M., Wolkerstorfer, J., Rijmen, V.: AES Implementation on a Grain of Sand. IEE Proceedings on Information Security 152(1), 13–20 (2005)
8. Gandolfi, K., Mourtel, C., Olivier, F.: Electromagnetic Analysis: Concrete Results. In: Koç, Ç.K., Naccache, D., Paar, C. (eds.) CHES 2001. LNCS, vol. 2162, pp. 251–261. Springer, Heidelberg (2001)
9. Gierlichs, B.: DPA-Resistance Without Routing Constraints? – A Cautionary Note About MDPL Security. In: Paillier, P., Verbauwhede, I. (eds.) CHES 2007. LNCS, vol. 4727, pp. 107–120. Springer, Heidelberg (2007)
10. Gierlichs, B., Batina, L., Tuyls, P., Preneel, B.: Mutual Information Analysis. In: Oswald, E., Rohatgi, P. (eds.) CHES 2008. LNCS, vol. 5154, pp. 426–442. Springer, Heidelberg (2008)
11. Herbst, C., Oswald, E., Mangard, S.: An AES Smart Card Implementation Resistant to Power Analysis Attacks. In: Zhou, J., Yung, M., Bao, F. (eds.) ACNS 2006. LNCS, vol. 3989, pp. 239–252. Springer, Heidelberg (2006)
12. Ishai, Y., Sahai, A., Wagner, D.: Private Circuits: Securing Hardware against Probing Attacks. In: Boneh, D. (ed.) CRYPTO 2003. LNCS, vol. 2729, pp. 463–481. Springer, Heidelberg (2003)
13. Coron, J.-S.: A New DPA Countermeasure Based on Permutation Tables. In: Ostrovsky, R., De Prisco, R., Visconti, I. (eds.) SCN 2008. LNCS, vol. 5229, pp. 278–292. Springer, Heidelberg (2008)
14. Khatir, M., Moradi, A., Ejlali, A., Shalmani, M.T.M., Salmasizadeh, M.: A Secure and Low-Energy Logic Style using Charge Recovery Approach. In: SLPED 2008, pp. 259–264. ACM, New York (2008)
15. Kocher, P.C.: Timing Attacks on Implementations of Diffie-Hellman, RSA, DSS, and Other Systems. In: Koblitz, N. (ed.) CRYPTO 1996. LNCS, vol. 1109, pp. 104–113. Springer, Heidelberg (1996)

16. Kocher, P.C., Jaffe, J., Jun, B.: Differential Power Analysis. In: Wiener, M. (ed.) CRYPTO 1999. LNCS, vol. 1666, pp. 388–397. Springer, Heidelberg (1999)
17. Mangard, S., Oswald, E., Popp, T.: Power Analysis Attacks: Revealing the Secrets of Smart Cards. Springer, Heidelberg (2007)
18. Mangard, S., Popp, T., Gammel, B.M.: Side-Channel Leakage of Masked CMOS Gates. In: Menezes, A. (ed.) CT-RSA 2005. LNCS, vol. 3376, pp. 351–365. Springer, Heidelberg (2005)
19. Mangard, S., Pramstaller, N., Oswald, E.: Successfully Attacking Masked AES Hardware Implementations. In: Rao, J.R., Sunar, B. (eds.) CHES 2005. LNCS, vol. 3659, pp. 157–171. Springer, Heidelberg (2005)
20. Mentens, N., Gierlichs, B., Verbauwhede, I.: Power and Fault Analysis Resistance in Hardware through Dynamic Reconfiguration. In: Oswald, E., Rohatgi, P. (eds.) CHES 2008. LNCS, vol. 5154, pp. 346–362. Springer, Heidelberg (2008)
21. Moradi, A., Eisenbarth, T., Poschmann, A., Rolfes, C., Paar, C., Shalmani, M.T.M., Salmasizadeh, M.: Information Leakage of Flip-Flops in DPA-Resistant Logic Styles. Cryptology ePrint Archive, Report 2008/188 (2008), http://eprint.iacr.org/
22. Moradi, A., Khatir, M., Salmasizadeh, M., Shalmani, M.M.: Charge Recovery Logic as a Side Channel Attack Countermeasure. In: ISQED 2009, pp. 686–691 (2009)
23. Moradi, A., Salmasizadeh, M., Shalmani, M.T.M.: Power Analysis Attacks on MDPL and DRSL Implementations. In: Nam, K.-H., Rhee, G. (eds.) ICISC 2007. LNCS, vol. 4817, pp. 259–272. Springer, Heidelberg (2007)
24. Moradi, A., Shalmani, M.T.M., Salmasizadeh, M.: Dual-Rail Transition Logic: A Logic Style for Counteracting Power Analysis Attacks. Computers and Electrical Engineering 35(2), 359–369 (2009)
25. Mulder, E.D., Gierlichs, B., Preneel, B., Verbauwhede, I.: Practical DPA Attacks on MDPL. Cryptology ePrint Archive, Report 2009/231 (2009), http://eprint.iacr.org/
26. National Security Agency: TEMPEST: A Signal Problem. Cryptologic Spectrum 2(3) (1972) (declassified 2007)
27. Nikova, S., Rechberger, C., Rijmen, V.: Threshold Implementations Against Side-Channel Attacks and Glitches. In: Ning, P., Qing, S., Li, N. (eds.) ICICS 2006. LNCS, vol. 4307, pp. 529–545. Springer, Heidelberg (2006)
28. Nikova, S., Rijmen, V., Schläffer, M.: Secure Hardware Implementations of Non-Linear Functions in the Presence of Glitches. In: Lee, P.J., Cheon, J.H. (eds.) ICISC 2008. LNCS, vol. 5461, pp. 218–234. Springer, Heidelberg (2009)
29. Oswald, E., Mangard, S., Pramstaller, N., Rijmen, V.: A Side-Channel Analysis Resistant Description of the AES S-box. In: Gilbert, H., Handschuh, H. (eds.) FSE 2005. LNCS, vol. 3557, pp. 413–423. Springer, Heidelberg (2005)
30. Popp, T., Kirschbaum, M., Mangard, S.: Practical Attacks on Masked Hardware. In: Fischlin, M. (ed.) RSA Conference 2009. LNCS, vol. 5473, pp. 211–225. Springer, Heidelberg (2009)
31. Popp, T., Kirschbaum, M., Zefferer, T., Mangard, S.: Evaluation of the Masked Logic Style MDPL on a Prototype Chip. In: Paillier, P., Verbauwhede, I. (eds.) CHES 2007. LNCS, vol. 4727, pp. 81–94. Springer, Heidelberg (2007)
32. Popp, T., Mangard, S.: Masked Dual-Rail Pre-charge Logic: DPA-Resistance without Routing Constraints. In: Rao, J.R., Sunar, B. (eds.) CHES 2005. LNCS, vol. 3659, pp. 172–186. Springer, Heidelberg (2005)
33. Prouff, E., McEvoy, R.: First-Order Side-Channel Attacks on the Permutation Tables Countermeasure. In: Clavier, C., Gaj, K. (eds.) CHES 2009. LNCS, vol. 5747, pp. 81–96. Springer, Heidelberg (2009)

34. Rolfes, C., Poschmann, A., Leander, G., Paar, C.: Ultra-Lightweight Implementations for Smart Devices - Security for 1000 Gate Equivalents. In: Grimaud, G., Standaert, F.-X. (eds.) CARDIS 2008. LNCS, vol. 5189, pp. 89–103. Springer, Heidelberg (2008)

35. Saeki, M., Suzuki, D., Shimizu, K., Satoh, A.: A Design Methodology for a DPA-Resistant Cryptographic LSI with RSL Techniques. In: Clavier, C., Gaj, K. (eds.) CHES 2009. LNCS, vol. 5747, pp. 189–204. Springer, Heidelberg (2009)

36. Schaumont, P., Tiri, K.: Masking and Dual-Rail Logic Don't Add Up. In: Paillier, P., Verbauwhede, I. (eds.) CHES 2007. LNCS, vol. 4727, pp. 95–106. Springer, Heidelberg (2007)

37. Suzuki, D., Saeki, M.: Security Evaluation of DPA Countermeasures Using Dual-Rail Pre-charge Logic Style. In: Goubin, L., Matsui, M. (eds.) CHES 2006. LNCS, vol. 4249, pp. 255–269. Springer, Heidelberg (2006)

38. Suzuki, D., Saeki, M., Ichikawa, T.: Random Switching Logic: A Countermeasure against DPA based on Transition Probability. Cryptology ePrint Archive, Report 2004/346 (2004), http://eprint.iacr.org/

39. Suzuki, D., Saeki, M., Ichikawa, T.: DPA Leakage Models for CMOS Logic Circuits. In: Rao, J.R., Sunar, B. (eds.) CHES 2005. LNCS, vol. 3659, pp. 366–382. Springer, Heidelberg (2005)

40. Suzuki, D., Saeki, M., Ichikawa, T.: Random Switching Logic: A New Countermeasure against DPA and Second-Order DPA at the Logic Level. IEICE Transactions on Fundamentals of Electronics, Communications and Computer Sciences E90-A(1), 160–168 (2007)

41. Tillich, S., Herbst, C.: Attacking State-of-the-Art Software Countermeasures - A Case Study for AES. In: Oswald, E., Rohatgi, P. (eds.) CHES 2008. LNCS, vol. 5154, pp. 228–243. Springer, Heidelberg (2008)

42. Tiri, K., Akmal, M., Verbauwhede, I.: A Dynamic and Differential CMOS Logic with Signal Independent Power Consumption to Withstand Differential Power Analysis on Smart Cards. In: ESSCIRC 2002, pp. 403–406 (2002)

43. Tiri, K., Verbauwhede, I.: A Logic Level Design Methodology for a Secure DPA Resistant ASIC or FPGA Implementation. In: DATE 2004, pp. 246–251 (2004)

44. Trichina, E.: Combinational Logic Design for AES Subbyte Transformation on Masked Data,
http://eprint.iacr.org/2003/236

45. Trichina, E., Korkishko, T., Lee, K.H.: Small Size, Low Power, Side Channel-Immune AES Coprocessor: Design and Synthesis Results. In: Dobbertin, H., Rijmen, V., Sowa, A. (eds.) AES 2005. LNCS, vol. 3373, pp. 113–127. Springer, Heidelberg (2005)

46. Virtual Silicon Inc. 0.18 μm VIP Standard Cell Library Tape Out Ready, Part Number: UMCL18G212T3, Process: UMC Logic 0.18 μm Generic II Technology: 0.18μm (July 2004)

47. Weiser, M.: The Computer for the 21st Century. ACM SIGMOBILE Mobile Computing and Communications Review 3(3), 3–11 (1999)

48. Yang, S., Wolf, W., Vijaykrishnan, N., Serpanos, D.N., Xie, Y.: Power Attack Resistant Cryptosystem Design: A Dynamic Voltage and Frequency Switching Approach. In: DATE 2005, pp. 64-69. IEEE Computer Society, Los Alamitos (2005)

49. Zakeri, B., Salmasizadeh, M., Moradi, A., Tabandeh, M., Shalmani, M.: Compact and Secure Design of Masked AES S-Box. In: Qing, S., Imai, H., Wang, G. (eds.) ICICS 2007. LNCS, vol. 4861, pp. 216–229. Springer, Heidelberg (2007)

Securing the Use of RFID-Enabled Banknotes*

Santi Martínez, Concepció Roig, and Magda Valls

Escola Politècnica Superior, Universitat de Lleida, Spain
{santi,roig}@diei.udl.es, magda@matematica.udl.es

Abstract. The use of RFID tags (radio-frequency identification tags) in banknotes presents a main challenge that may discourage their usage: how to avoid a possible attacker to count the amount of tags. Such a drawback is faced in this paper by designing an appropriate Medium Access Control (MAC) for this scenario. A MAC is the set of mechanisms and protocols that allows devices to share the communication channel. In a RFID system, a MAC protocol makes it possible for several tags to communicate within a common environment with the RFID reader. In this paper, we present a new MAC protocol that is suitable for ensuring security in the use of RFID-enabled banknotes. It also guarantees privacy and fits scalability requirements when the number of tags is increasing.

1 Introduction

Nowadays, the use of RFID tags has been extended to several environments such as proximity cards, automated toll payment or ignition keys of automobiles, among others. In this context, the European Central Bank has been considering the possibility of including RFID tags in Euro banknotes [1, 2, 3]. This would make illegal activities such as counterfeiting and money-laundering difficult and would even prevent kidnappers from demanding unmarked bills. A possible scenario would be detecting holders of a huge amount of banknotes in an airport, since it would prevent evasion.

However, the use of RFID tags in some environments, may present some problems, given by the fact that all the tags share the same medium to communicate with the reader. On the one hand, the time needed by the reader to identify all tags may become too high when the number of tags becomes large, affecting negatively the whole system performance. On the other hand, a privacy problem arises, if an eavesdropper is able to count the number of responses sent to the reader. This, for example, will permit thieves to select their victims according to the number of banknote tags that they are carrying. Thus, it is necessary to study Medium Access Control (MAC) protocols, that take into account these kind of problems.

In this paper, we propose a new MAC protocol for RFID to provide scalability and privacy in the communication layer. In this protocol, tags respond to the

---

* This work was supported by the Generalitat de Catalunya with a Grant FIC, and the projects of the Spanish MCyT TIN2006-15662-C02-02 and MTM2007-66842-C02-02.

R. Sion et al. (Eds.): FC 2010 Workshops, LNCS 6054, pp. 80–93, 2010.
© IFCA/Springer-Verlag Berlin Heidelberg 2010

reader queries, until being identified, using random probabilities, which will be modified during the execution of the protocol. This permits to adapt the frequency of responses to the number of tags that are present in the environment, allowing a fast identification of all of them, while making the identification process scalable when the number of tags increases. To provide privacy, the number of responses is masked by means of a noisy tag, so that, under adversaries view, the amount of responding tags will not give information about the number of tags that are present.

The rest of the paper is structured as follows. Section 2 outlines some related work. In Section 3, the proposed protocol is described, and some implementation issues are also discussed. Section 4, treats the security aspects. In Section 5, an experimentation process, based on simulation, is carried out, to check feasibility and scalability of the protocol. Finally, Section 6 outlines the main conclusions.

2   Related Work

The communication system based on RFID has three layers: the physical layer, the application layer and the communication layer. The physical layer defines the physical air interface, the application layer treats user's information and the communication layer controls communications between reader and tags.

The global scalability and security of a communication system based on RFID technology relies on how these properties are solved in each individual layer [4]. In the case of the physical layer, they may be guaranteed by using a common standard and ensuring a common manufacturing process for all tags. This may be achieved if a unique manufacturer produces all tags.

For the application layer, some proposals focus only on providing different levels of security, such as the *Anonymous ID* [5], the *External Encryption* [1] or the *Random Hash Lock* [6].

Other kind of protocols are those that provide security by means of noisy tags [7], that share a common secret with the reader. When responding to reader's queries, there will be a collision between these noisy tags and a normal tag. The reader will substract all noisy tag responses and will obtain the sequence of the genuine tag.

The idea of using extra tags as a method of providing security is also used in the blocker tag protocol [8]. However, the goal is completely different: preventing identification of a tag from any reader. This makes sense in situations where tags have finished their use in the RFID environment. For instance, after buying a product. This blocker tag will confuse the reader by sending false identifiers.

There are other proposals which can fit more demanding security requirements. For instance, in [9] a scheme is proposed in which tags change their identifier using a hash function each time they are read, but it presents a high computational complexity for the database. This problem is partially solved in [10] using a time-memory trade-off; the main problem of this approach is its scalability when the number of tags increases so much. This problem is overcome in [11], where it is proposed a scheme using elliptic curve cryptography and zero knowledge reader authentication, that achieves the security requirements, maintaining scalability.

Concerning the communication layer of a RFID system, the main concern taken into account is usually its performance: to identify the largest amount of tags in the minimum time. This is the case of several existing MAC protocols for RFID, such as framed ALOHA [12] and its variations [12, 13], and Colorwave [14], among others. In general, these protocols tend to degrade the response time when the number of tags is large, so, providing scalability is an important issue. Additionally, when these protocols are applied to systems that are considered secure, the problem of an attacker counting the number of tags is not taken into account, probably because in some environments this is not considered a threat.

Nevertheless, in possible future scenarios such as having RFID tags attached to banknotes [1, 2], preventing an attacker to count the number of tags will be as important as avoiding the revelation of their denomination. A protocol to provide location privacy of a banknote holder in RFID-based bank systems has been proposed in [3], but it does not address the counting problem.

In this paper, we propose a new MAC protocol for RFID that addresses both: (a) the scalability in the system performance, by adapting the frequency of tag responses to the number of tags, and (b) the privacy problem of counting tags, by using a noisy tag to mask the number of responses. In this way, an attacker cannot tell when a real response or collision of non-noisy tags has occurred. We consider scalability and security at the application layer solved, using some of the existing proposals, as those presented in [9, 10, 11]. We also consider a common manufacturing process, in order to minimize radio fingerprint differences [4].

3   The Proposed MAC Protocol

We consider a typical RFID scenario with tags, a reader and a database containing the information of the tags. There will also be one noisy tag that is physically present in the environment and recognized by the reader.

We assume that the application layer of the RFID system is secure, i.e. the information is securely sent and only authorized readers are able to understand it [9, 10, 11]. In the example of banknotes, we assume that the banknote tag identifier (probably containing the banknote serial number and its denomination) and any additional information are securely sent to the RFID reader. Thus, an eavesdropper capable of reading this information is unable to understand it. We also assume a secure physical layer [4]. Based on these assumptions, the protocol works, in the communication layer, with the following objectives:

(a) To allow authorized RFID readers to identify the highest amount of tags in a minimum time, and to detect those that are false.

(b) To prevent unauthorized RFID readers from guessing the number of tags by just listening in on the communication channel.

The protocol proceeds by following successive time slots (referred to as *intervals* during the rest of the paper). At each of these intervals a tag may send a message to the reader or wait silently until the next interval. Each tag responds at random under a certain probability. This probability will be modified during the execution of the protocol, so that it is ensured the same distribution of responses per interval independent of the number of tags in the system. This makes the protocol scalable when the number of tags is large.

Clearly, if a system has few tags, each tag has to respond more frequently, in order to accelerate the identification of all the tags; and if a system has a large amount of tags, the frequency of tag responses should be lower, so that collisions are minimized. To do this, the reader has to collaborate with the tags informing them about the number of responses it receives.

The noisy tag will send a message to the reader at each interval, using noise pseudo-randomly generated from a secret shared with the reader, so that only the reader can substract it. This is done in order to trick an eavesdropper into thinking that all intervals have a collision. This secret is shared on the setup of the system.

At the beginning of each interval the reader sends an interval signal, informing about the amount of responses that were received during the previous interval. This must be done in a secure manner, using the application layer protocol, so that an attacker cannot obtain this information. We have considered three situations: zero responses, one response, and multiple responses (i.e. collision). The tags will modify their probabilities taking into account this information.

After informing of an one response interval the application layer protocol is executed in order to authenticate the tag that responded, while the rest of the tags wait. Similarly, after informing of a collision or a zero responses interval, the noisy tag will perform a false authentication, since otherwise, attackers could tell the difference between one response intervals and the other two kinds, if one response intervals were the only ones to include this authentication part.

The reader and tags proceed according to the algorithms exposed in next subsections. Afterwards, we will discuss about the appropriate values for the parameters that take part in these algorithms.

3.1 Reader's Algorithm

In this subsection, we expose the reader's algorithm, which is shown in Algorithm 1.

The protocol starts with the reader sending the first interval signal. After that, the main loop begins with the reader waiting for responses during the rest of the interval. Then, the pseudo-random noise from the noisy tag is subtracted, and the reader securely sends a new interval signal, with information about the situation of the amount of tags that responded during the previous interval (i.e. with the value 0, 1 or 2 corresponding to zero, one or multiple responses).

If there was one response, the tag identifier is obtained and checked for validity using the application layer protocol. If the identifier is valid, it is added to the identifiers set, *Id_Set*. If there was a collision or a zero responses interval, a spurious noisy tag identifier is obtained and automatically discarded.

The number of intervals to be executed is determined by *MAX_ITER*, whose appropriate value will be discussed in Section 3.3.

Algorithm 1. Reader's reading operation

```
     Input: MAX_ITER: Positive integer
     Output: Id_Set: Set of identifiers
 1  Send_First_Interval_Signal;
 2  for Iter ∈ {1 .. MAX_ITER} loop
 3  │   Wait_for_Responses;
 4  │   Substract_Noise;
 5  │   if there were no responses then
 6  │   │   Send_Interval_Signal (0);
 7  │   │   Obtain_Tag_Id  (* of the noisy tag *);
 8  │   else if there was one response then
 9  │   │   Send_Interval_Signal (1);
10  │   │   Id := Obtain_Tag_Id;
11  │   │   Check_Validity (Id);
12  │   │   if Id is valid then
13  │   │   │   Add (Id_Set, Id);
14  │   │   else  -- it's not valid
15  │   │   │   Notify about incorrect Id;
16  │   │   end if
17  │   else  -- there was a collision
18  │   │   Send_Interval_Signal (2);
19  │   │   Obtain_Tag_Id  (* of the noisy tag *);
20  │   end if
21  end loop
```

3.2   Tag's Algorithm

The pseudo-code corresponding to tag's algorithm is shown in Algorithm 2.

A tag will respond to the reader's interval signal under a certain probability, *Curr_Prob*. So, the key factor of the protocol is the change of this probability, that will be modified dynamically during the execution of the protocol. This modification is carried out according to the following parameters:

- An estimation, done by the tag, of the number of tags in the system, *Est_Tags*.
- The number of processed intervals, *Iter*. The modification of the current probability to respond with respect to the previous one, becomes smoother as the number of intervals increases, in order to assure that the tag will stabilize its probability to respond.
- The number of consecutive intervals with zero (*Consec_Zero*) or with multiple (*Consec_Cols*) responses. A large number of them is an indication of an unsuitable probability, so the modification should be more drastic.

The algorithm begins when the reader sends the first interval signal. Initially, the tag uses an estimation of the number of tags of 64 (this initial estimation may be adjusted depending on the expected number of tags of the environment, see Section 3.3), and the initial probability of a tag responding during the interval

Algorithm 2. Tag's reading operation

```
 1  Wait_for_First_Interval_Signal;
 2  Iter := 1; Consec_Zero := 0; Consec_Cols := 0;
 3  Est_Tags := 64; Curr_Prob := 1/Est_Tags;
 4  repeat
 5  |    Send_Response (Curr_Prob);
 6  |    Responses := Wait_for_Interval_Signal;
 7  |    Iter := Iter+1;
 8  |    switch Responses do
 9  |    |    case 0  −− No responses
10  |    |    |    Consec_Zero := Consec_Zero+1; Consec_Cols := 0;
11  |    |    |    Est_Tags := Est_Tags / Mod_Factor (Iter, Consec_Zero);
12  |    |    |    if Curr_Prob < 1/Est_Tags then
13  |    |    |    |    Curr_Prob := (Curr_Prob+1/Est_Tags)/2;
14  |    |    |    else
15  |    |    |    |    Curr_Prob := Increment (Curr_Prob, 1/Est_Tags);
16  |    |    |    end if
17  |    |    |    Wait while noisy tag authenticates;
18  |    |    case 1  −− One response
19  |    |    |    if this tag answered last interval then
20  |    |    |    |    Authenticate itself to the reader;
21  |    |    |    else
22  |    |    |    |    Consec_Zero := 0; Consec_Cols := 0;
23  |    |    |    |    Est_Tags := Est_Tags - 1;
24  |    |    |    |    Curr_Prob := Increment (Curr_Prob, 1/Est_Tags$^2$);
25  |    |    |    |    Wait while other tag authenticates;
26  |    |    |    end if
27  |    |    case 2  −− Collision
28  |    |    |    Consec_Zero := 0; Consec_Cols := Consec_Cols+1;
29  |    |    |    Est_Tags := Est_Tags * Mod_Factor (Iter, Consec_Cols);
30  |    |    |    if Curr_Prob > 1/Est_Tags then
31  |    |    |    |    Curr_Prob := (Curr_Prob+1/Est_Tags)/2;
32  |    |    |    else
33  |    |    |    |    Curr_Prob := Decrement (Curr_Prob, 1/Est_Tags);
34  |    |    |    end if
35  |    |    |    Wait while noisy tag authenticates;
36  |    |    end
37  |    end
38  until this tag has been identified ;
```

is its inverse (1/64). Based on this initial probability the tag chooses whether to respond or not during the first interval. Then, it enters the main loop.

Each iteration begins with the tag waiting for the interval signal which carries information about the three possible situations of tags responding during the previous interval (0, 1 or 2). Depending on the situation, the tag will modify the estimated number of tags and the probability in one of the three following ways:

(**case 0**) *Responses* = 0. There were no responses in the previous interval, so the tag increases the consecutive zeroes counter and resets to 0 the consecutive collisions counter. This situation means that the current probability of the tags is too low, so the estimated number of tags is too high. So, the tag decreases the estimated number of tags by dividing it by a modifier factor depending on the number of started intervals and the number of consecutive zeroes. The current probability is increased by establishing it to the arithmetic mean of the inverse of the new estimation and the previous current probability, except in the case that this inverse was lower (or equal) than the old probability, since in that situation doing the mean would decrease the probability (or leave it unaltered). Instead of this, the probability should be increased using a function for increasing it, depending on the inverse of the estimation. We will talk later about the selection of *Mod_Factor* and *Increment* functions.

(**case 1**) *Responses* = 1. There was only one response. If this tag was the one that responded, it authenticates to the reader using the application layer protocol and sets its current probability to 0. Otherwise, both the consecutive zeroes and collisions counter are reset to 0, and the estimated number of tags is decreased by one (since the tag that responded will stop the protocol). Then, the tag increases its probability in function of the inverse of the estimation squared, so that the overall probability of the reader getting one response is not modified. Finally, it waits while other tag authenticates.

(**case 2**) *Responses* = 2. There was a collision, so the tag increases the consecutive collisions counter and resets to 0 the consecutive zeroes counter. This situation means that the current probability of the tags is too high, so the estimated number of tags is too low. Thus, the estimated number of tags is increased by multiplying it by a modifier factor depending on the number of started intervals and the number of consecutive collisions. The current probability is decreased by establishing it to the arithmetic mean of the inverse of the new estimation and the old current probability, except in the case that this inverse was greater (or equal) than the old probability, since in that situation doing the mean would increase the probability (or leave it unaltered). Instead of this, the probability should be decreased using a function for decreasing it, depending on the inverse of the estimation. We will talk later about the selection of the *Decrement* function.

Note that, in case *Responses* is 0 or 2, the tag will wait during the false authentication of the noisy tag. Finally, based on the current probability, it either responds or not during this interval, and, if the tag has not been identified, a new iteration begins. Otherwise, it is deactivated for the rest of the session.

The algorithm includes an improvement that was not exposed in the pseudo-code for the sake of simplicity. This will permit an even faster achievement of the appropriate probability when the number of tags is too large or too small.

It consists on modifying the probability in a different manner when the protocol is in its initial phases. A tag considers that the protocol is in its initial phases until there has been an interval of each of the three kinds (with zero, one and multiple responses). In these initial phases, the probability has been set to the inverse of *Est_Tags*, except for the tag that responded in an one response interval, that has its probability set to 0.

It is worth to remark that the described protocol could be easily implemented in tag circuitry, because the operations involved in the algorithm are very simple.

3.3   Selection of Parameters

Some things need to be tuned for a proper performance of the system: the initial estimation of the number of tags, the *Mod_Factor*, *Increment* and *Decrement* functions, and the number of iterations to execute the protocol, *MAX_ITER*.

Initial estimation of the number of tags
For the initial estimation of *Est_Tags*, we suggest a value of 64, since it works reasonably well for environments with a number of tags between 2 and 2000, that are the example scenarios that we have considered. For other scenarios this estimation could be adapted to the appropriate value, depending on the range of possible amounts of tags.

Modification of the estimated number of tags
The goal of the function *Mod_Factor* is to dynamically adjust the number *Est_Tags*, in order to tend to the number of tags in the system. The factor returned by the function will be used to decrease the value *Est_Tags* when the estimation is too large (in case *Responses* = 0) by dividing by it, or to increase it when the estimation is too small (in case *Responses* = 2) by multiplying by it. Therefore, the function has to return a value greater than 1.

Mod_Factor receives two arguments: I is the number of started intervals, and R is the consecutive zeroes (*Consec_Zero*) or collisions (*Consec_Cols*) counter, depending on the situation. According to this, we propose the expression:

$$Mod\_Factor(I, R) = 1 + \frac{R}{I - R} + \frac{R - 1}{R} \tag{1}$$

Table 1 shows the value of $Mod\_Factor(I, R)$ for the first values of I and R. The values shown in the table correspond to those that fulfil the condition $I > R$,

Table 1. Some values of $Mod\_Factor(I, R)$

I \ R	1	2	3	4	5	6	7	8	9	10
2	2.00									
3	1.50	3.50								
4	1.33	2.50	4.67							
5	1.25	2.17	3.17	5.75						
6	1.20	2.00	2.67	3.75	6.80					
7	1.17	1.90	2.42	3.08	4.30	7.83				
8	1.14	1.83	2.27	2.75	3.47	4.83	8.86			
9	1.13	1.79	2.17	2.55	3.05	3.83	5.36	9.88		
10	1.11	1.75	2.10	2.42	2.80	3.33	4.19	5.88	10.9	
11	1.10	1.72	2.04	2.32	2.63	3.03	3.61	4.54	6.39	11.9

since the number of consecutive zeroes or collisions is allways lower than the number of started intervals. As can be observed, for the same value of I, the value of the function increases as the parameter R is also increasing (i.e. the more consecutive zeroes/collisions have happened, the higher will be the factor to divide/multiply Est_Tags by). On the other hand, for the same value of R, the value of the function decreases as the parameter I is increasing (so, Est_Tags will change smoothly). This will accomplish the goal of decreasing the value of Est_Tags in the case of no responses and increasing it in the case of a collision.

The value of $Mod\_Factor(I+1, R+1)$ is larger than $Mod\_Factor(I, R)$, since, for example, after i intervals, with the last r ones being collisions, a new collision would cause both arguments to increase by one, and we want larger factors in those cases. When the values of I and R are nearly the same, the function gives larger values, since the estimation is far from the real number of tags and needs to be modified more drastically. It can also be observed that $Mod\_Factor(I, R)$ tends to 1 when I is becoming larger and R is becoming smaller (since in that case the estimation is good).

Modification of the probability to respond
The functions $Increment$ and $Decrement$ are designed to modify the probability of responding, $Curr\_Prob$. Since the output will be stored as a new probability, the result must be in $[0, 1]$.

Both functions receive two parameters A and B, whose values are in $[0, 1]$, and they correspond to the current probability and the amount of modification. The expressions that are proposed to compute both functions are the following:

$$Increment(A, B) = A + B \cdot (1 - A) \tag{2}$$

$$Decrement(A, B) = A - B \cdot A \tag{3}$$

Table 2 shows the value of $Increment(A, B)$ and $Decrement(A, B)$ for some values of A and B. It can be observed that $Increment$ behaves like a saturated addition $A + B$; it returns a value greater or equal than A, and the increase depends on B. Similarly, $Decrement$ corresponds to a saturated substraction $A - B$; it returns a value less or equal than A, and the decrease depends on B.

Number of iterations to execute
For the number of iterations to execute the protocol, MAX_ITER, the recommended criterion is to execute always a fixed number of iterations, in order

Table 2. Some values of $Increment(A, B)$ and $Decrement(A, B)$

	Increment					Decrement			
A \ B	0.00	0.33	0.67	1.00	A \ B	0.00	0.33	0.67	1.00
0.00	0.00	0.33	0.67	1.00	0.00	0.00	0.00	0.00	0.00
0.33	0.33	0.56	0.78	1.00	0.33	0.33	0.22	0.11	0.00
0.67	0.67	0.78	0.89	1.00	0.67	0.67	0.44	0.22	0.00
1.00	1.00	1.00	1.00	1.00	1.00	1.00	0.67	0.33	0.00

not to give any hint of the number of tags present. So, deciding the number of iterations must be done beforehand.

As will be seen in Section 5.1, the number of intervals with one response tends to be one third of the total number of intervals. Because of this, *MAX_ITER* should be slightly greater than triple the maximum expected number of tags. This will permit to identify all tags.

4   Security

The protocol described in this paper is a MAC one. Thus, the only thing that needs to be guaranteed by the present protocol is precisely the difficulty of deducing the number of tags from the number of responses. We can consider three kinds of adversaries.

(a) Passive attacker eavesdropping on the communication channel. His goal is to learn the number of tags.

In order to prevent that an eavesdropper could distinguish the three kinds of responses (0, 1 or 2), a noisy tag will respond with noise at each interval, so that, from the point of view of the eavesdropper, all intervals are collision intervals. Moreover, after collision and zero responses intervals, the noisy tag will perform a false authentication, thus, attackers cannot tell the difference between one response intervals and the other two kinds. Obviously, the interval message containing the value 0, 1 or 2 should also be ciphered by the application layer protocol. In short, the attacker will only see a fixed number of iterations, and a collision and an authentication at each interval, so he will not be able to deduce the number of tags from this information.

(b.1) Active attacker controlling all tags of the environment during a period of time. His goal is to predict future noisy tag responses.

The pseudo-random noise should be generated in a manner that cannot be predicted by an attacker. If an attacker controls all the tags of the environment (except the noisy tag), he could know the responses of all the tags, so, he can substract them in order to learn the noisy tag responses. If he could predict the noise sequence of the noisy tag from these responses, he could substract the noisy tag responses when new tags (of a potential victim) enter in the environment.

A possible secure method for generating the pseudo-random sequence could be to compute an initial sequence from a seed, and then to apply a cryptographically secure hash function to each value of the sequence. So, if the noisy tag has the seed s_i, it will output $h(s_i)$ (where $h(\cdot)$ is the hash function), then it will generate the next seed value $s_{i+1} = f(s_i)$ using some proper function f. Other methods would also be possible.

(b.2) Active attacker controlling additional noisy tags. His goal is to perform a denial of service attack.

The presence of additional noisy tags would generate a denial of service type of attack. But, this is not a problem that can be controlled, since, all protocols are affected by this type of attack in the presence of uncontrolled electromagnetic noise sources in their radio frequency.

It should be noted that a single noisy tag is capable of providing the desired level of security. For instance, in the case of detecting holders of a huge amount of banknotes in an airport, the readers would be placed on specific places, so that each one has its corresponding noisy tag nearby.

5   Performance Analysis

A simulation of the proposed protocol has been performed in order to evaluate its performance and scalability, and to prove that all tags will be identified with a proper value of MAX_ITER. Concerning the time needed to identify all tags, it would be determined by the MAX_ITER value multiplied by the time needed to identify one tag, since the rest of the protocol does not represent a big overhead. So, the key factor to the total cost is the time needed by the application layer protocol.

The protocol was simulated using a multitask program, with several tasks acting as the tags and another one acting as the reader. This environment was programmed using the language Ada.

5.1   Identifying All Tags

In order to experimentally evaluate the performance of the proposed MAC protocol, several simulations have been done in order to verify that the suggested number of iterations is appropriate to identify all tags.

Table 3 collects data for simulations corresponding to amounts of tags of the form 2^n, for $3 \leq n \leq 11$. For each amount of tags, 100 simulations were done. We obtained the following data:

- *Iter.*: Mean number of iterations needed to detect all tags.
- *Zero resp.*: Mean number and percentage of zero-responses intervals.
- *One resp.*: Mean number and percentage of one-response intervals.
- *Collision*: Mean number and percentage of collision intervals.

The proportions of intervals with zero, one or multiple responses converge all of them to one third of the total number of intervals. But this does not mean that

Table 3. Simulation statistics

Tags	Iter.	Zero responses		One response		Collision	
8	24.6	8.5	34.6%	8.0	32.5%	8.1	32.9%
16	47.7	16.2	34.0%	16.0	33.5%	15.5	32.5%
32	93.6	32.7	34.9%	32.0	34.2%	28.9	30.9%
64	189.9	65.4	34.4%	64.0	33.7%	60.5	31.9%
128	365.0	123.4	33.8%	128.0	35.1%	113.6	31.1%
256	751.4	251.0	33.4%	256.0	34.1%	244.4	32.5%
512	1524.1	505.5	33.2%	512.0	33.6%	506.6	33.2%
1024	3033.5	1002.3	33.0%	1024.0	33.8%	1007.2	33.2%
2048	6067.0	2004.5	33.0%	2048.0	33.8%	2014.5	33.2%

the protocol is to be executed a variable number of intervals, since that would give a valuable information to an eavesdropper (who could deduce the number of tags from the number of intervals). This is only intended to demonstrate that the protocol scales when the number of tags is increasing.

These results may be taken into account for the problem of the appropriate number of iterations that the reader should execute in order to identify all tags (assuming that one knows the maximum expected quantity). As said in Section 3.3, this number should be slightly greater than triple the maximum expected number of tags.

5.2 Efficiency of the Protocol

In order to test the efficiency of the proposed protocol, we have experimentally tested the amount of tags that can be identified within a fixed number of iterations, incrementing the number of tags until surpassing $MAX\_ITER/3$. For doing this, several simulations have been done for amounts of tags of the form 2^n, for $4 \leq n \leq 11$, with MAX_ITER fixed to 500. As before, 100 simulations were done for each amount of tags. Table 4 collects mean data for these simulations. The number of tags identified is equal to the number of one response intervals.

It can be seen, that for amounts of tags below one third the number of intervals (from 16 to 128 tags), all tags are identified. Since each authenticated tag stops the protocol, the number of zero responses intervals is larger in these cases. On the other hand, for a large amount of tags (from 256 to 2048), the number of tags identified is near one third the number of intervals (i.e. approximately 166). This remains true for any amount of tags above that level. Note that this is not usually true for other MAC protocols, that tend to degrade throughput when the number of participant increases.

Table 4. Simulation of 500 iterations

Tags	Zero responses		One response		Collision	
16	468.4	93.7%	16.0	3.2%	15.6	3.1%
32	439.4	87.9%	32.0	6.4%	28.6	5.7%
64	375.4	75.1%	64.0	12.8%	60.6	12.1%
128	258.2	51.6%	128.0	25.6%	113.8	22.8%
256	169.4	33.9%	165.6	33.1%	165.0	33.0%
512	164.4	32.9%	168.4	33.7%	167.2	33.4%
1024	163.4	32.7%	164.8	33.0%	171.8	34.3%
2048	162.8	32.5%	164.3	32.9%	172.9	34.6%

6   Conclusions

In this paper, a scalable MAC protocol has been proposed that prevents the revelation of the number of RFID tags present in the environment to an adversary. This protocol may be specially appropriate in systems where the prevention of the revelation of that number is a big issue. This would be the case if RFID tags are attached in banknotes as the European Central Bank is planning to.

The protocol follows several intervals in which each tag may send a message or wait until the next interval, under a certain probability. This probability is modified at each interval, so that tags will tend to probabilities that ensure an even distribution of responses, independently of the number of tags. A simulation has been done to show that the system accomplishes this scalability requirement.

Security in the system will be guaranteed through fixing the number of intervals to the appropriate value according to the maximum expected number of tags, and having a noisy tag present in the environment, so that an eavesdropper cannot obtain any information from listening in on the communication channel.

References

[1] Juels, A., Pappu, R.: Squealing Euros: Privacy Protection in RFID-Enabled Banknotes. In: Wright, R.N. (ed.) FC 2003. LNCS, vol. 2742, pp. 103–121. Springer, Heidelberg (2003)

[2] Rieback, M.R., Crispo, B., Tanenbaum, A.S.: The Evolution of RFID Security. IEEE Pervasive Computing 5(1), 62–69 (2006)

[3] Choi, E.Y., Lee, S.M., Lee, D.H.: Self-updating: Strong Privacy Protection Protocol for RFID-Tagged Banknotes. In: Indulska, J., Ma, J., Yang, L.T., Ungerer, T., Cao, J. (eds.) UIC 2007. LNCS, vol. 4611, pp. 1171–1180. Springer, Heidelberg (2007)

[4] Avoine, G., Oechslin, P.: RFID Traceability: A Multilayer Problem. In: S. Patrick, A., Yung, M. (eds.) FC 2005. LNCS, vol. 3570, pp. 125–140. Springer, Heidelberg (2005)

[5] Kinoshita, S., Hoshino, F., Komuro, T., Fujimura, A., Ohkubo, M.: Nonidentifiable Anonymous-ID Scheme for RFID Privacy Protection. Joho Shori Gakkai Shinpojiumu Ronbunshu CSS (15), 497–502 (2003) (in Japanese)

[6] Weis, S.A., Sarma, S.E., Rivest, R.L., Engels, D.W.: Security and Privacy Aspects of Low-Cost Radio Frequency Identification Systems. In: Hutter, D., Müller, G., Stephan, W., Ullmann, M. (eds.) Security in Pervasive Computing. LNCS, vol. 2802, pp. 454–469. Springer, Heidelberg (2004)

[7] Castelluccia, C., Avoine, G.: Noisy Tags: A Pretty Good Key Exchange Protocol for RFID Tags. In: Domingo-Ferrer, J., Posegga, J., Schreckling, D. (eds.) CARDIS 2006. LNCS, vol. 3928, pp. 289–299. Springer, Heidelberg (2006)

[8] Juels, A., Rivest, R., Szydlo, M.: The Blocker Tag: Selective Blocking of RFID Tags for Consumer Privacy. In: Atluri, V. (ed.) Conference on Computer and Communications Security – ACM CCS, Washington, DC, USA, October 2003, pp. 103–111. ACM Press, New York (2003)

[9] Ohkubo, M., Suzuki, K., Kinoshita, S.: Cryptographic Approach to "Privacy-Friendly" Tags. In: RFID Privacy Workshop (2003)

[10] Avoine, G., Oechslin, P.: A Scalable and Provably Secure Hash-Based RFID Protocol. In: International Workshop on Pervasive Computing and Communication Security – PerSec, pp. 110–114. IEEE Computer Society Press, Los Alamitos (2005)

[11] Martínez, S., Valls, M., Roig, C., Miret, J.M., Giné, F.: A Secure Elliptic Curve-Based RFID Protocol. Journal of Computer Science and Technology 24(2), 309–318 (2009)

[12] Floerkemeier, C., Wille, M.: Comparison of Transmission Schemes for Framed ALOHA based RFID Protocols. In: International Symposium on Applications and the Internet Workshops – SAINTW, pp. 92–97. IEEE Computer Society Press, Los Alamitos (2006)

[13] Khandelwal, G., Yener, A., Lee, K., Serbetli, S.: ASAP: A MAC Protocol for Dense and Time-Constrained RFID Systems. In: IEEE International Conference on Communications – ICC, vol. 9, pp. 4028–4033 (2007)

[14] Waldrop, J., Engels, D.W., Sarma, S.E.: Colorwave: A MAC for RFID Reader Networks. Wireless Communications and Networking 3, 1701–1704 (2003)

Increasing Privacy Threats in the Cyberspace: The Case of Italian E-Passports

Vincenzo Auletta[1], Carlo Blundo[1], Angelo De Caro[1], Emiliano De Cristofaro[2], Giuseppe Persiano[1], and Ivan Visconti[1]

[1] Dipartimento di Informatica ed Applicazioni
Università degli Studi di Salerno
I-84084 Fisciano (SA) - Italy
{auletta,carblu,decaro,giuper,visconti}@dia.unisa.it
[2] University of California, Irvine
Irvine, CA, 92617 - USA
edecrist@uci.edu

Abstract. The recent introduction of electronic passports (e-Passports) motivates the need of a thorough investigation on potential security and privacy issues. In this paper, we focus on the e-Passport implementation adopted in Italy. Leveraging previous attacks to e-Passports adopted in other countries, we analyze (in)security of Italian e-Passports and we investigate additional critical issues.

Our work makes several contributions.

1. We show that in some concrete scenarios, Italian e-Passports are prone to eavesdropping attacks, where one can unnoticeably obtain private data stored in the e-Passport using RF communication, while the passport is stored in a bag/pocket. Moreover, we show how to trace e-Passports by successfully linking two or more communication transcripts related to the same e-Passport.
2. We propose a set of open-source tools that build successful attacks to the security of Italian e-Passports. Among them, we provide a simulator that produces attacks without requiring physical passports and RFID equipment.
3. We show that the random number generator included in the RFID chips produces bits that are noticeably far from the uniform distribution, thus potentially exposing Italian e-Passports to several other attacks.

1 Introduction

Electronic Passports (e-Passport) are similar to traditional passports and were first introduced in Malaysia, in 1998. They contain a small contactless integrated circuit (IC), embedded in the back cover. This RFID micro-chip stores holder's data, information about country entrances, the digital signature of the issuer Authority, a digital picture (it enables biometric comparison at international borders, through the use of facial recognition technology) and, potentially, other biometric data. The paper part of the e-Passport contains a page with holder's data (first name, family name, birth-date, expiration date), a picture, and a

R. Sion et al. (Eds.): FC 2010 Workshops, LNCS 6054, pp. 94–104, 2010.
© IFCA/Springer-Verlag Berlin Heidelberg 2010

character sequence, namely MRZ (Machine Readable Zone), necessary to access the document content. The e-Passport standard was defined by the International Civil Aviation Organization (ICAO)[1]. The ICAO defines the RFID micro-chips ISO 14443 stored inside the passports as "integrated contactless circuits". The ICAO standard requires that RFID passports must be identifiable by a standard logo on the cover. More applications have been envisaged for the future, such as storing visa information on the chip [26].

Personal data stored on the RF-chip is highly sensitive, thus it is necessary to guarantee its confidentiality, integrity, and authenticity. However, the e-Passport initiative and the proposed schemes have been subject of diverse political and technical debates and criticisms. Advocates of e-Passports claim that they enhance security, protect against forgery and manipulation of travel documents, identity theft, and speed up identification of individuals allowing governments to build uniform data bases in standardized format [3]. On the other hand, they generated several concerns regarding security and privacy offered by current specifications and particularly by the current implementation. Prior notable works investigating such issues include [19,24,25,26].

Protocols for e-Passports and Known Attacks. The main cryptographic protection mechanisms of e-Passport are: Passive Authentication (PA), Basic Access Control (BAC), and Active Authentication (AA). However, at time of publication, a transition to the more advanced Extended Access Control (EAC) is being carried out [1].

PA provides authenticity by means of digital signatures to authenticate all relevant data stored on the chip. Such signatures are generated by a trusted Document Signer in the personalization phase of the MRTD chip [21].

BAC aims to provide confidentiality and integrity of communications between the reader — part of the inspection system — and the e-Passport. Current realizations of BAC use symmetric cryptography and generate corresponding encryption and authentication keys from passport information, e.g. from the Machine Readable Zone (MRZ).

Unfortunately, weak implementations of such mechanisms have been the targets of successful eavesdropping attacks. We refer the reader to such attacks of several countries' e-Passports, such as the Netherlands [6,33], Germany [15] and Belgium [10]. Moreover, special machines, e.g. the Cost-Optimized Parallel Code Breaker (COPACABANA) [27] have been used to break BAC [29].

Among the most interesting studies, the work in [11], provides an extensive investigation of the Belgian e-Passport based on the ICAO specifications. Authors show that entropy of the MRZ is as low as 38 bits, and such value can be further reduced to 23 for targeted attacks where date of birth is known. Since MRZ is the source of randomness to generate encryption and authentication keys, such low entropies result into successful attacks to BAC by exhaustive search.

Recent Advances. Recently, the EU parliament has decided that the e-Passport issued by Member States will include biometric information [8]. Parliament

---

[1] Document 9303, Part 1, Volumes 1 and 2 (6th edition, 2006).

members foresee that the use of fingerprints will help preventing identity theft. The EU parliament also introduced the principle of "one person, one passport", so that children will have their own travel documents. Until the age of 12, no detection of fingerprints will be enforced, as they are still evolving.

Starting August 2009, two Italian counties, those of Grosseto and Potenza, are testing the new e-Passport carrying additional biometric data. The use of this new e-Passport is planned to be gradually extended to all Italian counties. Biometric data are protected by a more advanced mechanism referred to as Extended Access Control (EAC). Although using stronger underlying cryptographic primitives, however, EAC is not immune from attacks either, as pointed out in [13,31,34]. In particular, an adversary might play as a man-in-the-middle, in order to transfer the proofs given by the e-Passport to another reader to be accepted as the victim. Moreover, an adversary might show to someone else evidence of an interaction with an e-Passport, thus violating user privacy irreversibly.

Our Contribution. This paper presents a security analysis of Italian e-Passports. Starting from the successful attempts that have been carried out in other European countries, we propose similar attacks but adapted to Italian e-Passports. We have evaluated out attacks by developing a suite of ad-hoc open-source tools. Among them, we provide a simulator that produces attacks without requiring physical e-Passports and RFID equipment. Finally, we report our negative evaluation about the quality of the random number generator contained in the Italian e-Passports.

Paper Organization. Section 2 presents an overview of the protocols involved in e-Passports implementations. In Section 3, we show how Italian e-Passports can be successfully attacked, as previously done for other countries. Next, in Section 3.2, we present our python-based software, the Basic Access Control Knocker (BACK), which aims at extracting private data from Italian e-Passports. This software first attempts to reduce the quantity of unknown information in the MRZ. Then, it performs a brute force attack to guess values of the MRZ that can not be predicted. Finally, in Section 3.3 we analyze the *quality* of the randomness used by Italian e-Passport during RFID communication, showing that the random number generator included in the RFID chips is extremely weak.

2   E-Passports

We now discuss in more details the current protocols that are used by e-Passports as enforced by ICAO.

Passive Authentication (PA). PA provides authenticity by means of digital signatures to authenticate all relevant data stored on the chip. Such signatures are generated by a trusted Document Signer in the personalization phase of the MRTD chip [21]. The PA protocol checks that the digital signature calculated by the reader (and based on the passport content) matches the digital signature stored inside the passport. Passive authentication does not prevent skimming (unauthorized reading), eavesdropping (communication wire-tapping), and cloning (reproduction of an identical tag). However, it guarantees that e-Passport content was not altered.

Basic Access Control (BAC). The Basic Access Control (BAC) is the first protocol to be run between the reader and the e-Passport. It is designed to prevent skimming and eavesdropping. As previously discussed, the e-Passport is provided with the MRZ, i.e., a character sequence which can be read both by the holder and by the RFID reader, only if the document is opened. The BAC protocol consists of three messages, as depicted in Figure 1. Both the reader and the e-Passport deterministically obtain a couple of keys (K_{ENC} and K_{MAC}) from the MRZ. Then the passport generates a couple of random strings (r_{PICC}, k_{PICC}) and sends r_{PICC} to the reader, which in turn generates a couple of random strings (r_{PCD}, k_{PCD}) and will create a ciphertext containing ($r_{PCD}, r_{PICC}, k_{PCD}$) (in this order). The MAC is calculated on this ciphertext and the couple (ciphertext, MAC) is sent to the passport. The passport decrypts the message and tests that: (i) it contains the random string, r_{PICC}, generated at the beginning of the protocol, and, (ii) the MAC is successful verified. In case such tests fail, the protocol is interrupted. Otherwise, the passport encrypts the message composed of $r_{PICC}, r'_{PCD}, k_{PICC}$. Again, the MAC is computed and the passport sends to the reader the couple (ciphertext, MAC). Then the reader decrypts the ciphertext and performs the same two tests executed by the passport before (the string to match is no longer r_{PICC}, but r_{PCD}). On a successful protocol execution, the reader and the passport will share the keys k_{PICC}, k_{PCD}, which will be used for encryption and authentication of the following protocol messages.

Active Authentication (Å). Å is designed to prevent cloning by introducing a key pair unique to each chip: While the public key is authenticated through the PA, the corresponding private key is stored in secure memory and cannot

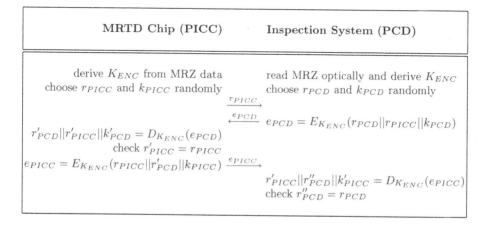

Fig. 1. The BAC protocol

be read out. The chip then proves knowledge of this private key by means of a challenge-response protocol: the MRTD chip signs a challenge randomly chosen by the reader which recognizes the MRTD chip as genuine. Although Å protects against cloning, it introduces a privacy threat known as *Challenge Semantic* [1]. In Å, the reader challenges the chip to sign a value which the reader chooses randomly according to the specification.[2] A manipulated reader, however, may tailor the challenge such that one can recognize it later obtaining a proof that the e-Passport holder/owner has passed a certain border. ICAO requires that e-Passports contain a metallic membrane to make unauthorized reading (skimming) more difficult while the passport is closed. However, it is currently easy to overcome the metallic protection and read the content of the e-Passport. Since in most countries, including Italy, only PA and BAC are actively enforced, we will concentrate our analysis on BAC. Other results about e-Passport security and privacy threats can be found in [12,13,14].

Extended Access Control (EAC) [1]. The proposed specification for Advanced Security Mechanisms for MRTD [1] considers two different access control mechanisms, depending on the degree of data sensitivity. On the one hand, less-sensitive data (e.g., the MRZ, the facial image, and other data that is relatively easy to acquire from other sources) is protected by Basic Access Control (BAC). On the other hand highly sensitive data (e.g., fingerprints, iris scan, and other data that cannot be obtained easily from other sources at a large scale) must only be available to authorized inspection systems. Highly sensitive data is protected by the Extended Access Control (EAC) which additionally verifies that the inspection system is entitled to read this data. European Union pushes ICAO to replace BAC by EAC in the future so that less-sensitive data can be protected by stronger cryptography.

The main protocols in EAC are *Chip Authentication* and *Terminal Authentication*. Chip authentication provides a key agreement to be used for secure communication.[3] The procedure is as follows: At the border an e-Passport holder presents her e-Passport to the border control who scans the MRZ on the e-Passport and then places the e-Passport near an inspection terminal to fetch data from the chip. The e-Passport and the terminal establish an encrypted communication channel by executing the Basic Access Control (BAC) protocol. Then the terminal and the e-Passport perform a mandatory Chip Authentication followed by a Passive Authentication. Finally, a Terminal Authentication is performed by the chip challenging the reader who signs the challenge together with the hash of the ephemeral Diffie-Hellman public key to authenticate the key agreement. The protocol does not protect against the challenge semantics, and one could get a proof that a given terminal has communicated with the chip. However, the work in [1] argues that reader privacy is not a concern since readers do not correspond to citizens and do not change location.

---

[2] The signature is used to prove signature capabilities with respect to the public key which in turn is authenticated from the Logical Data Structure.

[3] Chip authentication in EAC could thus replace both, BAC and Å, to improve security.

Notice that even though additional security guarantees will be provided by next generation e-Passport, currently available e-Passports with their weaknesses and limitations will be circulating for the next 10 years.

2.1   Related Work

Belgium was the first country worldwide to issue ICAO-compliant electronic passports, using the RFID technology. Nowadays, more than 50 countries issue e-Passports. The Italian Government adopted this standard since October 26th, 2006. RFID tags have specific computational and memory constraints, but have the capability to communicate with an RFID reader in order to identify the passport's owner. In this scenario, user privacy is heavily threaten. In fact, several weak versions of these passport (like the ones released in Belgium in 2004) can be read by any RFID reader [17] that is compliant with the public standard. Other solutions, like the Basic Access Protocol (BAC) [24], introduce the need of providing to the reader some information, which can be get by only opening the passport and reading inside it. Juels et al. [24], besides presenting some privacy threats as for US passports, discussed the BAC low entropy of the US passport. Kc and Karger [26] also discussed additional issues related to slice attacks (encountered in hotels and banks) and fake fingers. Hoepman et al. [22] analyzed BAC within the context of Dutch passport, and the related threats of e-Passport based new applications, such as traceability. Monnerat, Vaudenay, and Vuagnoux [16] reviewed the e-Passport privacy issues, and focused on the Active Authentication side effects. They proposed a GQ-based authentication protocol as a possible countermeasure. Lehtonen et al. [30] proposed combining RFID with optical memory devices in order to improve the security of machine readable documents. Witteman [35] established a practical attack against the BAC of the Dutch passport. Grunwald executed a similar attack on the German e-Passport [18]. Laurie also successfully cloned a UK e-Passport while it was hidden in an envelope [28]. All of them, however, assume some known information about the passport's owner. Recently, Halvac and Rosa [20] investigated the feasibility of performing a relay attack on Czech e-Passport, and Ortiz-Yepes [32] supplied a short overview of security mechanisms recommended by ICAO. Finally, Avoine et al. [9] showed that those schemes can be attacked, because of a lack of entropy of data to be inserted into the reader. In fact, this information is usually related with personal data, such as name, age, etc.

3   (In)Security of Italian e-Passports

In this Section, we discuss our analysis of Italian e-Passports. We show that the generation of an MRZ with high entropy has been fallacious. As a result, Italian e-Passport are insecure as well. We also discuss the suite of open source tools that we have developed in order to evaluate our analysis. Finally we discuss the quality of the random number generator used in Italian e-Passports.

3.1 The MRZ Is Predictable

As we have already stressed, BAC uses the MRZ data to deterministically derive the keys employed for encrypting and authenticating messages. Our analysis
focuses on showing that MRZ data have low entropy. Indeed, we try to reconstruct all bits of the MRZ, and we find out that many of them are predictable,
as they correspond to information about the e-Passport's owner (e.g., her name)
or about the document itself (e.g., expiration date). In Italian e-Passports, information contained in the MRZ is: passport number, issuing country, owner's
birth date, owner's gender and passport expiration date.

  We now evaluate the entropy of all fields. The issuing country and the owner's
gender are considered as known and do not contribute to the relative entropy.
The passport number consists of two characters concatenated to 7 numerical
digits. Assuming this sequence to be fully random, its entropy would be around
of 32 bits. The owner's birth date format is YY / MM / DD. Assuming that
owner's age is in the range from 1 to 100 years then we have an entropy of around
15 bits. As for the document expiration date, since Italian e-Passports have a
long validity period, we can assume that this date is in the interval from the
current date to next 10 years, giving an entropy of 12 bits. Therefore, we have
a total potential entropy of amounting to about 59 bits. However, in practice it
is possible to use heuristics to significantly reduce the entropy of the MRZ. For
instance, the physical features of e-Passport's owner can be used to approximate
the date of birth to a smaller interval. The expiration date can also be guessed
by considering that all the current Italian e-Passports are less than 3 years old
—they were first released in October 2006. Thus, the most unpredictable element
of the MRZ appears to be the passport number. However, a statistical analysis
shows that passport numbers appear to increase as the expiration date increases,
not excluding the possibility that the number assignment was implemented essentially as a counter. Therefore, the entropy can be sensibly decreased, resulting
in a drastic reduction of BAC security.

3.2 The Simulator

In this Section, we propose our tool, namely BACK (Basic Access Control
Knocker), designed to access e-Passports. BACK can be downloaded for free
(we refer the reader to [2] for more details). BACK is written in Python and it
uses free-ware libraries [28] to manage the interaction with the RFID reader. It
can work with a wide set of RFID readers (for a comprehensive list of the compatible RFID readers can be found at http://www.rfidiot.org/#Hardware).
In order to access the e-Passport, BACK requires the user to type at command
line the range of values in which to guess MRZ data (i.e., min and max passport number, min and max date of birth, gender, min and max expiration date).
Then, BACK tries to reconstruct the MRZ by brute force and to access the
e-Passport through the BAC protocol.

Off-line Attack. BACK is a very flexible tool, which can be configured in
several modalities (described in details in [2]). In particular, it is possible to

configure BACK in simulation mode and have it to work without an RFID reader. In this case, all the requests are sent to a Python module (Server) that emulates the reader, and that is connected to a XML file representing the e-Passport.

Additionally, there is another way to conduct an off-line attack which requires a ciphertext. This attack is possible when an adversary is able to eavesdrop a communication between a passport and a reader. Now a brute-force attach can be performed until one of the messages in the eavesdropped communication, is correctly interpreted.

Efficiency. All tests have been carried out by using a Compaq nx6125 notebook with AMD Turion 64 Mobile ML-32 processor and 879MB of RAM. When BACK works on real e-Passport and RFID reader, its efficiency obviously also depends on the speed of the reader, as well as on the speed of the e-Passport to perform all the operations (e.g., random strings generation, encryption, authentication). The number of checks per minute is an appropriate parameter to measure the tool efficiency. On Omnikey Cardman 5321 RFID reader, BACK performs (on average) 760 checks per minute. Concretely, when partial information about the e-Passport are successfully guessed, our tool allows one to retrieve all the information in a few hours. On the other hand, we observed a remarkable speed up when BACK works in simulation mode. This is due to the absence of communication latency between the RFID reader and the e-Passport and to the greater computation speed of the simulator compared to the RFID tag microprocessor. In this setting, BACK performs on average 33,000 checks per minute. Such results provide evidence that when more efficient (and with lower latency) RFID readers will be available, our tool can be effectively used to break the BAC protocol—and thus achieve unauthorized access to e-Passports—within a small amount of time.

Forward Security. In the following, we consider another critical issue: forward security. We believe that brute-force attacks are extremely slow when executed using real RFID devices exchanging proper messages in radio-frequency identification. Hence, we consider a different form of attack where RFID chips can be bypassed. To this aim, we first collect real transcripts from conversations between e-Passports and readers. Then, we mount an off-line brute force attack trying to link the conversations and trace the e-Passports. The performance of these attacks are comparable to the use of our simulator.

3.3 Analysis of the Random Number Generator

The use of random and pseudo-random numbers is common in most cryptographic applications. In fact, security of cryptographic schemes often depends on the quality of the pseudo-random generator. As we have seen in Section 2, the passport is requested to choose some values at random. One of this value, r_{PICC}, is the challenge which is sent to the reader in clear. We now focus on this aspect to analyze the quality of randomness used by Italian e-Passport during RFID communication.

Since 1997, the RNG-TWG (Random Number Generation Technical Working Group) [7] has been working on developing a "battery" of statistical tests suitable in the evaluation of random number generators and pseudo-random number generators used in cryptographic applications. The result of their work has been the NIST Statistical Test Suite (STS) [4]. STS is a statistical package consisting of 15 tests developed to test the randomness of (arbitrarily long) binary sequences produced by either hardware or software based cryptographic random or pseudo-random number generators. More details on this package can be found in [5].

Using as challenge values ten bitstreams of one million bits each (collected through the use of BACK), we execute the STS statistical tests. All collected data has been stored in a file in a suitable format to be processed by STS. The analysis report generated by the STS package is quite surprising: it turns out that only one of the 15 statistical tests has been passed by the random generator implemented in the Italian e-Passports used for the tests.

We conclude that the random number generator included in the RFID chips does not produce an output close enough to the uniform distribution, thus exposing Italian e-Passports to several other threats. It is very likely that this issue about bad randomness does not apply only to the BAC but also affects the other protocols executed by Italian e-Passports.

4   Conclusion

In this paper, we have studied the security of Italian e-Passports, considering the remarkable weaknesses of the BAC protocol stressed in the literature [9,18,22,23,35]. In particular, we showed that the BAC protocol suffers from low entropy of MRZ data. To this aim, we developed an efficient tool to guess the MRZ and attack the BAC protocol. Our experimental results show that it is possible to execute unauthorized readings of user data in realistic scenarios. Concrete attacks require a few hours to succeed. Other improvements have been achieved assuming that the attack is mounted off-line, having as input the transcript of a successful BAC execution, thus attacking forward security. Finally, we showed that the random number generator currently implemented in Italian e-Passports is extremely weak, thus exposing protocols to further attacks.

Unfortunately, the very recent introduction (August 2009) of additional biometric information in Italian e-Passports and the weaknesses discussed in this work show once more that cryptographic and security tools can not be used as black boxes but instead need to be carefully understood, adapted and integrated in larger frameworks. In critical and massive applications as e-Passports, this task should be carried out by proper experts.

We hope that our security analysis will persuade governments of the relevant dangers for user privacy and security of deploying critical infrastructure without appropriate expertise.

Future Work. At time of publication, we are investigating the use of machine learning techniques to predict some additional values (i.e., mainly the passport number) by using a bunch of passports, along with their numbers, expiration dates and place of delivery. We believe that Lagrange polynomial interpolation could help in this direction. However, we acknowledge the need of further analysis (as well as the availability of many e-Passports), in order to refine and test effectiveness of our intuition.

Acknowledgments. We thank Marco Comentale, Giancarlo De Maio, Vito Poeta and Maurizio Quaranta for their Python programming and software testing, making BACK reality. Moreover, we thank Aniello Del Sorbo, and Ahmad-Reza Sadeghi for several useful discussions about e-Passport security in theory and practice. Finally we thank Aniello Castiglione for suggesting the use of NIST Statistical Test Suite for the randomness evaluation of e-Passports.

The work of the authors has been supported in part by the European Commission through the EU ICT program under Contract ICT-2007-216646 ECRYPT II, and in part through the FP7 Information Communication Technologies programme, under Contract FET-215270 FRONTS.

References

1. Advanced security mechanisms for Machine Readable Travel Documents - Extended Access Control,
   http://www.bsi.bund.de/fachthem/epass/EACTR03110_v110.pdf
2. BACK User Guide, http://rfid.dia.unisa.it/epass/UserGuide.pdf
3. Benefits of MRTD, http://mrtd.icao.int/content/view/28/203/
4. NIST Statistical Test Suite,
   http://csrc.nist.gov/groups/ST/toolkit/rng/documents/sts-2.0b.zip
5. NIST Statistical Test Suite Documentation,
   http://csrc.nist.gov/publications/nistpubs/800-22-rev1/
   SP800-22rev1.pdf
6. Privacy issues with new digital passport,
   http://www.riscure.com/news/passport.html
7. Random Number Generation Technical Working Group,
   http://csrc.nist.gov/groups/ST/toolkit/rng/index.html
8. Security features and biometrics in passports,
   http://www.europarl.europa.eu/sides/getDoc.do?language=EN&type=
   IM-PRESS&reference=20090114IPR46171
9. Avoine, G., Kalach, K., Quisquater, J.: E-Passport: Securing international contacts with contactless chips. In: Tsudik, G. (ed.) FC 2008. LNCS, vol. 5143, pp. 141–155. Springer, Heidelberg (2008)
10. Avoine, G., Kalach, K., Quisquater, J.-J.: Belgian biometric passport does not get a pass... your personal data are in danger!,
    http://www.dice.ucl.ac.be/crypto/passport/index.html
11. Avoine, G., Kalach, K., Quisquater, J.-J.: epassport: Securing international contacts with contactless chips. In: Tsudik, G. (ed.) FC 2008. LNCS, vol. 5143, pp. 141–155. Springer, Heidelberg (2008)
12. Blundo, C., Persiano, G., Sadeghi, A., Visconti, I.: Identification protocols revisited -episode i: E-passports. In: Secure Component and System Identification, SECSI 2008 (2008)

13. Blundo, C., Persiano, G., Sadeghi, A., Visconti, I.: Improved security notions and protocols for non-transferable identification. In: Jajodia, S., Lopez, J. (eds.) ES-ORICS 2008. LNCS, vol. 5283, pp. 364–378. Springer, Heidelberg (2008)
14. Blundo, C., Persiano, G., Sadeghi, A., Visconti, I.: Resettable and non-transferable chip authentication for e-passports. In: Workshop on RFID Security (RFIDSec 2008) (2008)
15. Carluccio, D., Lemke-Rust, K., Paar, C., Sadeghi, A.-R.: E-passport: The global traceability or how to feel like an ups package. In: Lee, J.K., Yi, O., Yung, M. (eds.) WISA 2006. LNCS, vol. 4298, pp. 391–404. Springer, Heidelberg (2007)
16. Courses, E., Surveys, T.: E-Passport Threats. IEEE Security & Privacy Magazine 5(6), 61–64 (2007)
17. Avoine, G., Kalach, K., Quisquater, J.-J.: Belgian Biometric Passport does not get a pass... (2007),
    http://www.dice.ucl.ac.be/crypto/passport/index.html
18. Grunwald, L.: New attacks against RFID-Systems (2006),
    http://www.blackhat.com/presentations/bh-usa-06/BH-US-06-Grunwald.pdf
19. Kc, G.S., Karger, P.A.: Security and Privacy Issues in Machine Readable Travel Documents (MRTDs). RC 23575, IBM T. J. Watson Research Labs (April 2005)
20. Halvac, M., Rosa, T.: A Note on the Relay Attacks on e-passports: The Case of Czech e-Passports. Cryptology ePrint Archive, Report 2007/244 (2007)
21. ICAO. Machine Readable Travel Documents, PKI for Machine Readable Travel Documents offering ICC Read-Only Access (2004), http://www.icao.int/mrtd
22. H. J.H., H. E., J. B., and O.M. S.R. W
23. Juels, A., Molnar, D., Wagner, D.: Security and Privacy Issues in E-passports. Technical report
24. Juels, A., Molnar, D., Wagner, D.: Security and Privacy issues in e-Passports. In: SecureComm (2005)
25. Juels, A., Molnar, D., Wagner, D.: Security and privacy issues in e-passports. In: SecureComm 2005, First International Conference on Security and Privacy for Emerging Areas in Communication Networks, Athens, Greece (September 2005)
26. Kc, G., Karger, P.: Security and Privacy Issues in Machine Readable Travel Documents, MRTDs (2006)
27. Kumar, S., Paar, C., Pelzl, J., Pfeiffer, G., Rupp, A., Schimmler, M.: How to Break DES for 8,980. In: SHARCS 2006 – Special-purpose Hardware for Attacking Cryptographic Systems, pp. 17–35 (2006),
    http://www.hyperelliptic.org/tanja/SHARCS/talks06/copa_sharcs.pdf
28. Laurie, A.: RFIDIOt, http://www.rfidiot.org
29. Liu, Y., Kasper, T., Lemke-Rust, K., Paar, C.: E-passport: Cracking basic access control keys with copacobana. In: SHARCS 2007 (2007)
30. Lehtonen, M., Michahelles, F., Staake, T., Fleisch, E.: Strengthening the security of machine readable documents by combining rfid and optical memory devices. In: Proceedings of Int. Conf. on Ambient Intelligence Development (2006)
31. Monnerat, J., Vaudenay, S., Vuagnoux, M.: About machine-readable travel documents – privacy enhancement using (weakly) non-transferable data authentication. In: International Conference on RFID Security (2007)
32. Ortiz-Yepes, D.: ePassports: Authentication and Access Control Mechanisms (2007)
33. Robroch, H.: ePassport Privacy Attack, Presentation at Cards Asia Singapore (April 26, 2006), http://www.riscure.com
34. Vaudenay, S.: E-passport threats, vol. 5, pp. 61–64. IEEE Computer Society, Los Alamitos (2007)
35. Witteman, M.: Attacks on digital passports. What the Hack

RLCPS Preface

The workshop "Real-Life Cryptographic Protocols and Standardization" is intended to gather the experiences of the designers and implementers of cryptographic protocols that are deployed in real-life systems. Designing and implementing real-life systems puts forth many challenges – not only technical issues regarding the use of hardware and software, but also usability, manageability, interoperability and timing to deploy the system. Designing to fulfill all these restrictions while not degrading security frequently requires tremendous efforts. The resulting cryptographic protocols may not always be interesting at the theoretical cryptography level, but the documentation of the challenges they face and the ways such challenges were met is important to be shared with the community. Standardization also promotes the use of cryptographic protocols where the best practices from these experiences are condensed in a reusable way.

We were happy to organize the first workshop in conjunction with the Financial Cryptography and Data Security Conference 2010 in Tenerife, Spain. The selected papers focus on real-life issues and discuss all the design criteria and relevant implementation challenges. We hope the proceedings from the series of this workshop serve as a place where researchers and engineers find the documentation of the necessary know-how for designing and implementing secure systems that have a tangible impact in real life; eventually, we hope that this contributes to a future generation of usable real-life systems where security would be one of their intrinsic qualities.

March 2010

Aggelos Kiayias
Kazue Sako

SPAKE: A Single-Party Public-Key Authenticated Key Exchange Protocol for Contact-Less Applications

Jean-Sébastien Coron[1], Aline Gouget[2,3], Pascal Paillier[2,3], and Karine Villegas[3]

[1] University of Luxembourg
[2] CryptoExperts
[3] Gemalto Security Labs

Abstract. SPAKE is a cryptographic protocol that provides lightweight transactions in contact-less applications. In this protocol a verifier (a reader or terminal) authenticates a prover (a contact-less card) relative to a certification authority. Additionally, the prover and the verifier must establish a session key for secure messaging. Contrarily to previous solutions such as MIFARE, the protocol is *asymmetric* in order to allow SAM[1]-less, low cost readers. Because contact-less transactions are subject to very strong time limitations, the protocol also achieves *high-speed computations* while providing a customizable security level.

1 Introduction

In typical contact-less transactions, authentication between a card and a reader is based on proprietary symmetric cryptography, such as MIFARE Classic [11], CALYPSO [4] or FELICA [18]. Usually, a dedicated hardware circuit is embedded in both contact-less cards and readers, and a common secret key is shared between the two parties. This architecture may suffer from dramatic security weaknesses when relying on adhoc cryptographic mechanisms, as exemplified by the recent attacks on MIFARE [12,13,14,15]. Until now, it seems that little or no industrial effort has been undertaken to design cryptographic replacements that would provide both efficiency and provable security.

We describe SPAKE (Single-party Public-key Authenticated Key Exchange), a protocol that allows fast authentication for contact-less applications. In SPAKE, a verifier called Proximity Coupling Device (PCD) authenticates a prover called Proximity Integrated Circuit Card (PICC) relative to some certification authority. Additionally, the PCD and PICC establish a session key for secure messaging and user-dependent data are then securely transmitted by the PICC to the PCD.

The originality of SPAKE is that it achieves public key authentication, thereby allowing SAM-less, low cost readers. The protocol is also fast because the card's data must be sent within very strong time limitations, namely about 150 milliseconds. The main targeted applications for this protocol are access control

---

[1] SAM: Secure Application Module.

R. Sion et al. (Eds.): FC 2010 Workshops, LNCS 6054, pp. 107–122, 2010.
© IFCA/Springer-Verlag Berlin Heidelberg 2010

and transport. Our SPAKE protocol is based on a public-key encryption scheme called *RSA for paranoids*, a variant of RSA designed by Adi Shamir [17] that enjoys very fast decryption. This is especially useful in our context since decryption must be performed inside the smart-card, where a cryptographic coprocessor is commonly available. The security requirements for SPAKE are the following: (i) Chip unforgeability (it should be impossible to authenticate as a PICC without knowing that PICC's private key sk); (ii) Channel secrecy (it should be infeasible to recover the session key K of a recorded transaction).

In this paper, we describe a formal security model for these two security properties. We first provide a security analysis of the SPAKE protocol generically in term of the underlying public-key encryption primitive. We show that SPAKE is secure (in the ideal cipher model) if the underlying public-key scheme is one-way under chosen-ciphertext attack *i.e.* OW-CCA-secure [3]. We then describe a variant of RSA for paranoids that achieves the OW-CCA property. This enables to make SPAKE secure against active attacks. Additionally, we show that RSA moduli with a fixed common part can be used, without degrading the overall system security. This allows to reduce transmissions, since in this case only a fraction of the modulus needs to be transmitted from the PICC to the PCD. Next, we provide a full specification of SPAKE for various levels of security, based on either DES or AES. Finally, we report benchmarks of SPAKE performances.

2   High-Level Objectives for SPAKE

2.1   Functional Requirements

A Single-Party Public-key Authenticated Key Exchange (SPAKE) protocol is a two-party cryptographic protocol played between a prover PICC and a verifier PCD. The goals of the protocol are:

1. The PCD authenticates the PICC relative to a certification authority CA;
2. The PCD and PICC establish a session key later used for secure messaging.

We note that there is no authentication of the PCD by the PICC. This implies that any attacker can fake a PCD and establish a session key with the PICC. Formally, a SPAKE protocol is a 4-uple of probabilistic algorithms:

- Keygen: given a security parameter κ, the algorithm generates a key pair (pk, sk). The public key pk gets certified by a CA and the corresponding certificate is denoted σ. Then (pk, sk, σ) is securely transmitted to the PICC.
- Challenge: the PICC sends its certified public key (pk, σ) to the PCD who checks the certificate. Optionally the PICC can send additional data denoted *data* (for example, a commitment). Then the PCD generates a challenge

$$chal \leftarrow \mathsf{Challenge}(pk, \sigma, data)$$

and sends *chal* to the PICC.

– Response: the PICC uses sk to generate a pair of strings

$$(res, K) \leftarrow \text{Response}(sk, chal) .$$

The response res is sent to the PCD while K is kept private by the PICC, to be used as the session key.

– Verif: the PCD computes $K' \leftarrow \text{Verif}(pk, \sigma, data, chal, res)$. If $K' = \bot$, then the PCD aborts the protocol. Otherwise, it uses K' as the session key.

We require that if the PICC has computed (res, K) and the PCD has obtained K', then $K' = K$. For simplicity, we assume that the public keys are certified and that the PCD always checks the certificate sent by the PICC.

The implementations of SPAKE that we consider are somewhat dictated by the quest for optimized performances. When the hardware architectures of the reader and the contact-less card both embed a coprocessor for a blockcipher such as DES or AES, it makes sense to make SPAKE rely on that primitive. In typical contact-less applications, cards are in general equipped with a cryptographic coprocessor and SPAKE may therefore take advantage of this. A cryptoprocessor is however hardly ever available on the reader side, and a desired feature of the protocol is that a simple CPU must be powerful enough to carry out all cryptographic computations on the reader.

2.2 Security Requirements

Real-life access control applications require two security properties:

1. Unforgeability: no attacker can impersonate a PICC without knowing that PICC's private key sk.
2. Channel secrecy: no attacker can recover the session key K of an eavesdropped transaction.

During an *active* attack, the adversary $\mathcal{A}$ can additionally interact with a PICC; otherwise the attack is only passive. For unforgeability under an active attack, $\mathcal{A}$ can therefore interact with a PICC before trying to pass an authentication towards the PCD. However, since there is no authentication of the PCD, an active adversary can easily fake a PCD and establish a session key with a PICC. Therefore security against active attacks cannot be achieved for the secrecy property; in this paper we only consider passive attacks for the secrecy property. Formally, we consider the following scenario between an attacker $\mathcal{A}$ and a challenger $\mathcal{C}$:

1. $\mathcal{C}$ generates a key pair (pk, sk) and sends pk to $\mathcal{A}$, along with its public-key certificate σ.
2. Using sk, $\mathcal{C}$ simulates n protocol executions between a chip and a terminal, and sends the protocol transcripts $(T_1, \ldots, T_n)$ to $\mathcal{A}$.
3. $\mathcal{A}$ can request any of the session keys used in the transcripts $(T_1, \ldots, T_n)$.
4. (Active attack). $\mathcal{A}$ can engage in up to n protocol executions with $\mathcal{C}$, who plays the role of the PICC. $\mathcal{C}$ answers using sk. A the end of each protocol execution, $\mathcal{A}$ obtains the corresponding session key.

5. (Secrecy). $\mathcal{A}$ outputs one of the session keys matching the protocol transcripts $(T_1, \ldots, T_n)$, not previously revealed in step 3.
6. (Unforgeability). $\mathcal{C}$ plays the role of the PCD and $\mathcal{A}$ plays the role of the PICC. $\mathcal{A}$ must output res such that $\mathsf{Verif}(pk, \sigma, data, chal, res) \neq \perp$.

Definition 1. *A SPAKE protocol is said to be (t, ε)-secure if no adversary running in at most t elementary steps can impersonate a PICC or recover the session key of an observed transaction with probability greater than ε.*

The security is proven using the well-known Ideal Cipher Model (ICM). Although it is better to obtain a protocol that does not rely on this assumption, the ICM is recognized as a powerful tool for obtaining both secure and efficient constructions. We note that the ICM has recently been shown to be equivalent to the Random Oracle Model (ROM) [6].

The adversary's goal differs from the adversary's goal in [2]. Namely in [2] the adversary is only asked to distinguish between a real session key and a random one; here the adversary is required to output the full session key. It is easy to see that a scheme proven secure in the ICM can be turned into a scheme secure in the ROM in the sense of [2] and vice-versa.

We want to provably achieve unforgeability and secrecy. We consider the following scenario between an attacker and a challenger. The adversary can interact at most n times with the chip. Eventually the adversary must be able to authenticate (unforgeability) or to output a session key (secrecy).

3   The SPAKE Protocol: Generic Construction

The SPAKE protocol relies on a blockcipher E as well as on a public-key encryption scheme $\mathcal{E}$. Viewing E as an ideal cipher, we further prove that our construction is secure under appropriate security assumptions on $\mathcal{E}$.

3.1   High-Level Description of SPAKE

SPAKE makes use of a blockcipher $E : \{0,1\}^\alpha \times \{0,1\}^\beta \rightarrow \{0,1\}^\beta$ where $\{0,1\}^\alpha$ is the key-space and $\{0,1\}^\beta$ is the message and ciphertext space. We require that $\alpha \leq \beta$, which applies to both DES ($\alpha = 56$, $\beta = 64$) and AES ($\alpha = \beta = 128$). We denote by $\mathcal{M}_{pk}$ the message space of $\mathcal{E}_{pk}$ and we assume that $\{0,1\}^\alpha \subset \mathcal{M}_{pk}$. We denote by $\mathcal{D}_{sk}$ the corresponding decryption algorithm. The SPAKE protocol is as follows:

- KeyGen: generate a key pair (pk, sk) for the public-key primitive. The CA issues a certificate σ on the public key pk.
- Challenge: the PICC randomly selects $k \leftarrow \{0,1\}^\alpha$ and computes $y = E_k(0)$. It then sends (pk, σ, y) to the PCD. The PCD picks a random number $r \in \{0,1\}^\alpha$ and sends $c = \mathcal{E}_{pk}(r)$ to the PICC.

- Response: the PICC recovers $r = \mathcal{D}_{sk}(c)$. If $r = \perp$ then the PICC aborts the protocol. The PICC computes $res = E_r(k)$ and $K = r \oplus k$; it then sends res to the PCD.
- Verification: the PCD verifies the certificate σ, decrypts $k = E_r^{-1}(res)$ and checks that $E_k(0) = y$. In this case it sets $K = r \oplus k$, otherwise a failure is reported.

After authentication, the PICC and PCD both use K as the session key to initiate secure messaging.

3.2 Generic Security of SPAKE

In this section we formulate the security of SPAKE in generic terms towards the underlying public-key encryption scheme $\mathcal{E}$. We start by describing the security assumptions we will make on $\mathcal{E}$ to yield a secure protocol.

Definition 2 (OW-CPA [3]). *A public-key encryption scheme $\mathcal{E}$ is said to be (t, ε)-OW-CPA if no adversary running in time t, given a random public key pk and $c = E_{pk}(m)$ where m is generated at random in the message space, can output m with probability better than ε.*

Definition 3 (OW-CCA [3]). *A public-key encryption scheme $\mathcal{E}$ is said to be (t, ε)-OW-CCA if no adversary running in time at most t, given a random public key pk and $c = E_{pk}(m)$ where m is generated at random in the message space, can output m with probability better than ε, with oracle access to a decryption oracle for any $c' \neq c$.*

The following two theorems show that SPAKE achieves the requirements of active unforgeability and passive secrecy.

Theorem 1 (Active Unforgeability). *The SPAKE protocol is (t, ε)-secure against unforgeability under active attacks, in the ideal cipher model, assuming that $\mathcal{E}$ is (t', ε')-OW-CCA, where $t = t' - \text{poly}(\kappa, q, n)$ and $\varepsilon = \varepsilon' + 2^{-\beta}$, where q is the number of queries to the ideal cipher, and n is the number of protocol transcripts.*

Theorem 2 (Passive Secrecy). *The SPAKE protocol is (t, ε)-passively secure against secrecy, in the ideal cipher model, assuming that $\mathcal{E}$ is (t', ε')-OW-CPA, where $t = t' - \text{poly}(\kappa, q, n)$ and $\varepsilon = n \cdot \varepsilon' + n \cdot 2^{-\alpha}$, where q is the number of queries to the ideal cipher, and n is the number of protocol transcripts.*

The proofs of Theorems 1 and 2 are provided in Appendices A and B.

4 Revisiting RSA for Paranoids

4.1 Description

The RSA for paranoids scheme (RSAP) is an asymmetric encryption scheme defined by Adi Shamir in [17]. It consists in using an unbalanced modulus $N = pq$ and in decrypting ciphertexts only modulo the smallest prime factor p. The scheme is described as follows:

- KeyGen: given the security parameter κ and a public exponent e, generate a prime p with $|p| = \kappa$ such that $\gcd(e, p-1) = 1$. Then generate a prime q such that $p \ll q$ and compute $N = p \cdot q$. Compute $d = e^{-1} \mod (p-1)$. The public key is (N, e) and the private key is (p, d). Let γ be a parameter such that $\gamma \leq \kappa - 1$.

- Encryption: given $m \in \{0, 1\}^{\gamma}$, compute $c = m^e \mod N$.

- Decryption: given c, compute $m = c^d \mod p$.

This completes the description of Shamir's scheme. It is easy to see that the decryption procedure recovers the full plaintext m because we always have $0 \leq m < 2^{\gamma} < p$. In Shamir's scheme, decryption is very fast because it is performed only modulo p, and the size of p can be made smaller than in textbook RSA encryption where the two prime factors are balanced.

4.2 Chosen-Ciphertext Attacks against RSAP

There exists a straightforward chosen-ciphertext attack against RSAP: one generates a random $c \in \mathbb{Z}_N$ and requests its decryption to the private key holder. Given $m = c^d \mod p$, it is easy to compute $c' = m^e \mod N$ and $\gcd(c - c', N)$ then discloses p with overwhelming probability.

For our purposes, we want to design a variant of RSAP that achieves the OW-CCA property. One option is to apply the OAEP construction [1] to encrypt m as $c = (\text{OAEP}(m, r))^e \mod N$ where r is a random string of appropriate size. However, the OAEP construction is proven secure only when the underlying encryption scheme is a one-way trapdoor *permutation*, as in the case of textbook RSA. Here the RSAP is *not* a permutation since the message space $\{0, 1\}^{\gamma}$ is much smaller than the ciphertext space $\mathbb{Z}_N$.

In the following we describe a different encoding that provably achieves the OW-CCA property. Note that since we are only interested in realizing the OW-CCA property and not the (stronger) IND-CCA property, our encoding (and the corresponding security proof) is substantially simpler than OAEP. In particular it is deterministic whereas OAEP is probabilistic.

4.3 Enhancing the Security of RSA for Paranoids

Our OW-CCA-secure variant of RSAP is defined as follows:

- KeyGen: given the security parameter κ and a public exponent e, generate a prime p with $|p| = \kappa$ such that $\gcd(e, p-1) = 1$. Then generate a prime q such that $p \ll q$ and compute $N = p \cdot q$. Compute $d = e^{-1} \mod (p-1)$. The public key is (N, e) and the private key is (p, d).

  The message space is $\{0, 1\}^{\alpha}$. Let $H : \{0, 1\}^{\alpha} \rightarrow \{0, 1\}^{\ell}$ be a hash function, where the output size ℓ is such that $\alpha + \ell \leq \kappa - 1$.

- Encryption: given $m \in \{0, 1\}^{\alpha}$, compute $c = (m \| H(m))^e \mod N$.

– Decryption: given c, compute $x = c^d \bmod p$ and parse x as $m\|h$ where $m \in \{0,1\}^\alpha$ and $h \in \{0,1\}^\ell$. If the parsing fails or if $h \neq H(m)$, return $\bot$. Otherwise return m.

We will refer to this scheme as the RSAP-H variant. The following theorem shows that RSAP-H is OW-CCA secure assuming that RSAP is partially one-way.

Definition 4 (P-OW-CPA [5]). *A public-key encryption scheme $\mathcal{E}$ is said to be (t,ε)-partially-OW-CPA (P-OW-CPA secure) if given a random public key pk and $c = \mathcal{E}_{pk}(m)$ where $m = m_1\|m_2$ is generated at random in the message space and $m_1 \in \{0,1\}^{k_1}$, no adversary running in time t can output m_1 with probability better than ε.*

Theorem 3. *RSAP-H is (t,ε)-OW-CCA secure in the random oracle model, assuming that RSAP is (t',ε')-P-OW-CPA secure with $k_1 = \alpha$ and posing $\varepsilon = q_h \cdot \varepsilon' + q_c \cdot 2^{-\ell}$ where q_h is the number of hash queries and q_c is the number of ciphertext queries.*

We refer to Appendix C for the proof of Theorem 3.

4.4   Instantiating SPAKE with RSAP-H

We define $H(m) = E_m(0) \bmod 2^\ell$ where ℓ is a parameter such that $\ell \leq \beta$. The blockcipher E must be independent from the blockcipher used in SPAKE. This can be done by pre-pending a dedicated bit in the key input. The full SPAKE protocol based on the blockcipher $E : \{0,1\}^\alpha \times \{0,1\}^\beta \to \{0,1\}^\beta$ where again $\alpha \leq \beta$ is described as follows:

– KeyGen: given the security parameter $\kappa > \alpha + \beta$ and a public exponent e, generate a prime p with $|p| = \kappa$ such that $\gcd(e, p-1) = 1$. Then generate a prime q such that $p \ll q$ and compute $N = p \cdot q$. Compute $d = e^{-1} \bmod (p-1)$. The public key is (N, e) and the private key is (p, d). The CA issues a certificate σ on the public key pk.
– Challenge: the PICC randomly selects $k \leftarrow \{0,1\}^{\alpha-1}$ and computes $y = E_{0\|k}(0)$. The tuple (pk, σ, y) is then sent to the PCD. The PCD picks a random number $r \in \{0,1\}^{\alpha-1}$, and lets h be the ℓ least significant bits of $E_{1\|r}(0)$; it then sends c to the PICC, where $c = (r\|h)^e \bmod N$.
– Response: the PICC computes $x = c^d \bmod p$ and parses x as $r\|h$ where $r \in \{0,1\}^{\alpha-1}$ and $h \in \{0,1\}^\ell$. If the parsing fails or if h is not equal to the ℓ least significant bits of $E_{1\|r}(0)$, the PICC aborts the protocol. The PICC computes $res = E_{0\|r}(k)$ and $K = r \oplus k$. Then res is sent to the PCD.
– Verification: the PCD verifies the certificate σ, decrypts $k = E_{0\|r}^{-1}(res)$ and checks that $E_{0\|k}(0) = y$. If the verification succeeds, the PCD sets $K = r \oplus k$. Otherwise PCD aborts the protocol.

After the protocol is executed, the PICC and PCD both use $K \in \{0,1\}^{\alpha-1}$ as the session key. The passive secrecy and active unforgeability properties follow from Theorems 1, 2 and 3.

5   RSA Moduli with Predetermined Bits

In this section, we show that SPAKE supports the use of RSA moduli with a fixed common part without degrading the security properties. This enables to reduce the size of transmissions, since in this case only a fraction of the modulus needs to be transmitted between the PICC and the PCD. Thus the global process execution time could be reduced.

5.1   The Key Generation Algorithm

In [17], the following RSA generation algorithm with predetermined part is proposed (here we use slightly different notations):

Generation of an RSA modulus with a predetermined part

Input: κ, n and t, and predetermined string $s = 1\|s'$ with $s' \in \{0,1\}^{n-\kappa-t-1}$

Output: a modulus N such that $s \cdot 2^{\kappa+t} \leq N < (s+1) \cdot 2^{\kappa+t}$

1. Generate a prime p in the interval $[2^{\kappa-1}, 2^{\kappa}[$.
2. Let $a \leftarrow \lfloor s \cdot 2^{\kappa+t}/p \rfloor$
3. Let $b \leftarrow \lfloor (s+1) \cdot 2^{\kappa+t}/p \rfloor$
4. Generate a random prime q in the interval $[a, b[$.
5. Return $N = p \cdot q$

The parameter t must be large enough so that there are enough primes in the interval $[a, b[$. One can take for example $t = 50$. It is argued in [17] that an RSA modulus with a predetermined part offers the same level of security than a standard RSA modulus. Namely, one can show that the distribution of q in the previous algorithm is close to the distribution of q in a standard RSA modulus, when the predetermined part s is generated at random. Therefore, any factoring algorithm against a modulus N with predetermined part would work equally well against a standard RSA modulus.

5.2   Using a Common Predetermined Part in SPAKE

In the following we show that all users can actually share the same predetermined part s, where s is initially generated at random by the Certificate Authority. The CA will only certify moduli N with this predetermined part. Formally, we consider the following adaptation of the SPAKE protocol.

Setup: Given parameters n, κ and t, the Certificate Authority generates $s = 1\|s'$ where $s' \leftarrow \{0,1\}^{n-\kappa-t-1}$ is chosen at random. The CA publishes s.

SPAKE: The rest of the SPAKE protocol is identical to the description given in Section 3.1, except that every user will generate an RSA modulus with the same predetermined part s.

The following theorem shows that if SPAKE is secure with a single user, then it remains secure if all users share the same predetermined part in their RSA modulus.

Theorem 4. *If RSAP-H-SPAKE is secure when the modulus of one user has a predetermined part $s = 1\|s'$ where $s' \leftarrow \{0,1\}^{n-\kappa-t-1}$, then RSAP-H-SPAKE remains secure when all the moduli of users share the same predetermined part.*

Proof. We consider an attacker $\mathcal{A}$ which can adaptively corrupt all users except one. Let n be the number of users. We are given as input a public key corresponding to a single user $\mathcal{U}$, with predetermined part s. We select a random index j in $[1, n]$. Then for user j we use the public key of $\mathcal{U}$; for the other users we generate a RSA modulus with the same predetermined part s. The attacker $\mathcal{A}$ cannot distinguish between user j and the other users, because all RSA moduli follow the same distribution. With probability at least $1/n$, his attack applies against user j; in this case, this gives an attack against the original user $\mathcal{U}$. □

6   Real-Life Implementations of SPAKE

Since it is common for embedded hardware platforms to feature a coprocessor for DES or AES, we consider implementations of SPAKE using one or the other blockcipher. We consider four possible levels of security: 55 bits, 64 bits, 80 bits and 100 bits. For each of these levels of security, we specify which blockcipher to use, the required bit-size of N, the bit-size of p, the value of e and the number of predetermined bits of N.

6.1   Basing SPAKE on DES

As described in previous sections, we can use DES to instantiate the blockcipher in the SPAKE protocol, thus posing $\alpha = 56$ and $\beta = 64$. In this case, the security level is at most $\alpha - 1 = 55$ bits. To obtain a higher security level, one could think of using 3-DES instead of DES; we stress that this is not possible in the context of SPAKE. Namely the security proofs of Theorems 1 and 2 rely on the Ideal Cipher Model, and it is easy to see that 3-DES does *not* behave as an ideal cipher. To justify this claim, consider the 3-DES blockcipher

$$3\mathsf{DES}(k_1\|k_2\|k_3, m) = \mathsf{DES}(k_3, \mathsf{DES}^{-1}(k_2, \mathsf{DES}(k_1, m)))\ .$$

Assume that k_1 and k_2 are unknown to the attacker, but k_3 is known. Then given $c = 3\mathsf{DES}(k_1\|k_2\|k_3, m)$, the attacker can easily compute $c' = 3\mathsf{DES}(k_1\|k_2\|k_3', m)$ for any k_3' since $c' = \mathsf{DES}(k_3', \mathsf{DES}^{-1}(k_3, c))$. It is easily seen that this is impossible to do with an ideal cipher. Therefore 3-DES cannot be viewed as an ideal cipher, even when DES is viewed as an ideal cipher. This implies that we cannot hope to increase the security of SPAKE by using 3-DES instead of DES.

6.2   Basing SPAKE on AES

We can also use AES-128 to instantiate the blockcipher of SPAKE, in which case $\alpha = \beta = 128$. The security level is then at most $\alpha - 1 = 127$ bits.

6.3   Tuning the Size of N and p

The RSA for paranoid scheme RSAP uses an unbalanced RSA modulus $N = pq$ with $p \ll q$, and in our search for best performance the sizes of N and p would tend to be as small as possible. The security strength [7] of generated moduli therefore depends on their resistance to integer factoring algorithms. There are two categories of factoring techniques:

1. Factoring algorithms whose running time depends on the size of N; the fastest such algorithm is the General Number Field Sieve (GNFS) [9].
2. Factoring algorithms whose running time depends on the size of p: the fastest such algorithm is the Elliptic Curve Method (ECM) [8].

For GNFS, we use the same complexity estimates as in [7], where the following expression for the security strength of an n-bit RSA modulus N is given as $s_{\mathsf{GNFS}}(n) = \left(\frac{64}{9}\right)^{1/3} \cdot \log_2(e) \cdot (n \ln 2)^{1/3} \cdot (\ln(n \ln 2))^{2/3} - 14$. For ECM, we use the following formula (see Appendix D), which gives the security strength of a κ-bit prime p: $s_{\mathsf{ECM}}(\kappa) = (\ln 2)^{-1/2} \cdot (2 \cdot \kappa \ln(\kappa \ln 2))^{1/2} + 5$. We summarize the required key size for the 55-bit, 64-bit, 80-bit and 100-bit security levels in Section 6.6.

6.4   Coppersmith's Attack and Shamir's Bound

In this section we describe an attack based on Coppersmith's theorem for finding small roots of polynomial equations. The attack applies when a small public exponent e is used.

Theorem 5 (Coppersmith). *Let $N = pq$ be a RSA modulus of unknown factorization and $f(x)$ by a polynomial of degree δ. There exists a polynomial-time algorithm that finds all roots x_0 of $f(x) = 0 \mod N$ such that $0 \le x_0 < N^{1/\delta}$.*

If $m^e < N$, then the message can be recovered by taking an e-th root in $\mathbb{Z}$. Coppersmith's algorithm allows to go beyond this bound using exhaustive search. More specifically, we consider the RSA for paranoids encryption scheme $c = m^e \mod N$ where $m \in \{0,1\}^\gamma$. We write $m = m_0 \cdot \lfloor N^{1/e} \rfloor + x_0$ where $x_0 < N^{1/e}$. This gives $c = (m_0 \cdot \lfloor N^{1/e} \rfloor + x_0)^e \mod N$. If we are given m_0, this gives a polynomial equation of degree e in x which has a small root $|x_0| < N^{1/e}$. We can then apply Coppersmith's theorem and recover the full value of m. Since m_0 is unknown, we must perform an exhaustive search on m_0 and apply Coppersmith's theorem for each possible value of m_0. Since the size of m is γ bits, the size of m_0 in bits is $|m_0| = \gamma - |N|/e$. For a targeted security level of k bits, we must have $|m_0| > k$, which gives the condition $\gamma \ge (\log_2 N)/e + k$, thus leading to the condition $e \ge \frac{\log_2 N}{\gamma - k}$ where k is the security parameter.

In our OW-CCA-secure variant of RSA for paranoids implemented with the blockcipher $E : \{0,1\}^\alpha \times \{0,1\}^\beta \to \{0,1\}^\beta$, we have $\gamma = \alpha + \ell - 1$. This gives the condition $e \ge \frac{\log_2 N}{\alpha + \ell - 1 - k}$. We also consider Shamir's bound in [17]. It consists in taking e such that the size of m^e before modular reduction is at least twice the size of m, as in Rabin encryption. This gives the bound $e \geq \frac{2 \log_2 N}{\alpha + \ell - 1}$. In this paper, we use the strictest of those two bounds. We note that if $\alpha + \ell \geq 2k$, Coppersmith's bound is automatically satisfied when Shamir's bound is satisfied. This is the case for the parameters considered in this paper.

6.5 Predetermined Bits

We refer to the algorithm of Section 5. Given an n-bit modulus with $|p| = \kappa$ and $p \ll q$, the size of the predetermined part is set to $n - \kappa - t - 1$ bits, where t is a parameter that must be large enough so that the prime generation algorithm succeeds with overwhelming probability. One can take for example $t = 50$. Then the size of the predetermined part is $n - \kappa - 51$ bits. The size of the remaining bits which are different for each user is therefore $\lambda = \kappa + 51$ bits.

6.6 Summarizing

In light of the previous sections, we summarize in Table 1 the parameters corresponding to the various security levels. We recommend to consider a security level of at least 80 bits, since 55 bits or 64 bits of security might not be enough in practice for secure applications.

Table 1. Security level, size of N, size of p, number λ of non-predetermined bits in N, minimal value for e, blockcipher, and key-size α and block-size β of the block cipher, and output size ℓ of the redundancy used in SPAKE with RSAP-H

SPAKE Security	$|N|$	$|p|$	λ	e	blockcipher	α	β	ℓ
55 bits	640	192	243	11	DES	56	64	64
64 bits	832	240	291	11	AES-128	128	128	104
80 bits	1248	352	403	11	AES-128	128	128	128
100 bits	2048	560	611	17	AES-128	128	128	128

7 Proof of Concept/Prototype

We have realized a proof of concept based on NXP's SmartMX P5CT072 platform, which features the FameXE cryptoprocessor and a hardware DES processor. In contactless applications the CPU clock can be set to 31 MHz, the hardware DES can be clocked at 36 MHz and the FameXE at 48 MHz. We have used a specific Mini OS for test and benchmarking purposes. The PCD was simulated on a PC via a transparent contact-less reader.

The code size of our SPAKE library is 1.6 KB. The library supports all cryptographic operations, thus excluding APDU treatment executed by the OS. Tables 2 and 3 provide the benchmarks of the various stages of a typical transport transaction in two different settings. The initialisation stage (Init) initiates the anti-collision protocol, selects the application and performs a PPS negotiation of the transmission baudrate. The *Get Challenge* APDU command consists in running the Challenge algorithm of SPAKE, where the PICC sends the commitment y and the certificate σ. We assume that, since a significant fraction of the bits of the public key N are fixed, the signature scheme of the certificate is a Rabin-Williams signature with message recovery. Therefore only the certificate needs to be sent, and the PCD recovers N when verifying it. The *Get Response* command consists of the decryption stage using our variant of RSA for paranoids. Execution times on the PICC side are separated from the time required by contact-less transmissions, which we provide at 106 and 424 Kbits per second respectively. Also note that the code is executed from EEPROM, which is more time consuming than when the code is executed from ROM — so performances can be improved in an actual product. Finally when the *Get Data* command is played, the card sends three typical files (user data and profile w.r.t the transport application) over the secure channel to the reader.

Table 2 reports performances for $\kappa = |p| = 224$, $|N| = 512$ and $|\sigma| = 1280$. The RAM consumption in this case is about 800 bytes and 216 bytes of non-volatile memory (EEPROM) are required to store (σ, p, d). The total transaction time in this case is close to 96 milliseconds.

Table 2. Benchmarks (in microseconds) of a contact-less transaction for $\kappa = 224$

$p = 224$	Proc PICC	Com@106	Com@424
Init	1521	5400	3986
Get Challenge	7446	15873	4022
Get Response	24367	7693	1961
Get Data	7045	12120	3143
Deselect	146	727	219
Total	40525	41813	13331

Table 3 provides performances for $\kappa = 352$, $|N| = 1248$, where $|\sigma|$ is still 1280. In this case, about 900 bytes of RAM and 248 bytes of EEPROM are required. A full transaction is then completed in about 156 ms.

Table 3. Benchmarks (in microseconds) of a contact-less transaction for $\kappa = 352$

$p = 352$	Proc PICC	Com@106	Com@424
Get Response	73101	17015	4291
Total	89259	51135	15661

Countermeasures against Radio-Frequency Analysis have been undertaken. Classical protections against the RF versions of SPA/DPA and related attacks can be carried out by randomizing the private exponent d and the prime factor p. We assume that the hardware blockcipher is inherently immune against side-channel attacks.

Finally, we stress that this prototype is intended for test purposes only and that the chosen parameters provide a low security level of 49 bits in the case of Table 2. These parameters should be adjusted as indicated in Table 1 to reach an appropriate security level in actual products.

8   Conclusion

In this paper, we have provided a new protocol for authenticated key exchange. We have shown that our protocol is secure against active attacks if the underlying public-key scheme is One-Way Chosen-Ciphertext (OW-CCA) secure. For this we have designed a variant of RSA for paranoids that achieves that OW-CCA property. Additionally, we have shown that RSA moduli with a fixed common part can be used, without degrading the overall system security. This enables to reduce the communication bandwidth, since in this case only a fraction of the modulus needs to be transmitted between the PICC and the PCD, when the certificate does not support message recovery. Then, we have provided a full specification of SPAKE for various levels of security. Finally, the details of a prototype have been reported along with performance benchmarks.

References

1. Bellare, M., Rogaway, P.: Optimal Asymmetric Encryption. In: De Santis, A. (ed.) EUROCRYPT 1994. LNCS, vol. 950, pp. 92–111. Springer, Heidelberg (1995)
2. Bellare, M., Pointcheval, D., Rogaway, P.: Authenticated key exchange secure against dictionary attacks. In: Preneel, B. (ed.) EUROCRYPT 2000. LNCS, vol. 1807, p. 139. Springer, Heidelberg (2000)
3. Bellare, M., Desai, A., Pointcheval, D., Rogaway, P.: Relations Among Notions of Security for Public-Key Encryption Schemes. In: Krawczyk, H. (ed.) CRYPTO 1998. LNCS, vol. 1462, p. 26. Springer, Heidelberg (1998)
4. Technical documents available, http://www.calypsotechnology.net/
5. Fujisaki, E., Okamoto, T., Pointcheval, D., Stern, J.: RSA-OAEP is Secure under the RSA Assumption. In: Kilian, J. (ed.) CRYPTO 2001. LNCS, vol. 2139, p. 260. Springer, Heidelberg (2001)
6. Coron, J.S., Patarin, J., Seurin, Y.: The Random Oracle Model and the Ideal Cipher Model are Equivalent. In: Wagner, D. (ed.) CRYPTO 2008. LNCS, vol. 5157, pp. 1–20. Springer, Heidelberg (2008)
7. European Network of Excellence ECRYPT, Yearly Report on Algorithms and Keysizes (2007-2008), www.ecrypt.eu.org/ecrypt1/documents/D.SPA.28-1.1.pdf
8. Lenstra Jr., H.W.: Factoring Integers with Elliptic Curves. Ann. Math. 126, 649–673 (1987)
9. Lenstra, A.K., Lenstra Jr., H.W.: The development of the number field sieve. Lecture Notes in Math, vol. 1554. Springer, Heidelberg (1993)
10. Girault, M., Poupard, G., Stern, J.: On the Fly Authentication and Signature Schemes Based on Groups of Unknown Order. Journal of Cryptology 19(4), 463–487 (2006)
11. NXP Semiconductors. MF1ICS70 functional specification (January 2008), http://mifare.net

12. Nohl, K., Plötz, H.: Little Security, Despite Obscurity. In: Chaos Communication Congress
13. Nohl, K.: Mifare security. In: Chaos Communication Congress
14. Courtois, N., Nohl, K., O'Neil, S.: Algebraic Attacks on the Crypto-1 Stream Cipher in MiFare Classic and Oyster Cards. Cryptology ePrint Archive, http://eprint.iacr.org/2008/166
15. Courtois, N.: Conditional Multiple Differential Attack on MiFare Classic. In: Rump session of Eurocrypt 2009 (2009)
16. SAGE mathematics library, http://www.sagemath.org
17. Shamir, A.: RSA for paranoids. CryptoBytes 1, 1–4 (1995)
18. Sony Global - FeliCa Web Site, Technical documents available, http://www.sony.net/Products/felica/
19. Zimmermann, P.: The ECMNET Project, http://www.loria.fr/~zimmerma/records/ecmnet.html
20. Zimmermann, P., Dodson, B.: 20 Years of ECM. In: Hess, F., Pauli, S., Pohst, M. (eds.) ANTS 2006. LNCS, vol. 4076, pp. 525–542. Springer, Heidelberg (2006)

A   Proof of Theorem 1

We receive a public key pk and a challenge $c^* = \mathcal{E}_{pk}(m^*)$, and we must recover m^*, using an adversary that breaks the active unforgeability property with probability ε. We also have access to a decryption oracle that can decrypt any ciphertext except c^*.

The ideal cipher E is simulated in the standard way. We start our interaction with the PICC by generating the n protocol transcripts; we can do this without knowing the private key sk. Eventually the adversary tries to impersonate the PICC. In the active attack phase, we use the decryption oracle from the OW-CCA challenge in order to decrypt the ciphertext sent by the adversary; for the rest we proceed as in the passive attack phase.

Eventually the adversary tries to impersonate the PICC. The adversary first sends the commitment y^*; we send the challenge ciphertext c^* to the adversary. The adversary sends res.

To solve the OW-CCA challenge we look at the history of E; for all triples of the form (r, k, res), we compute $c = \mathcal{E}_{pk}(r)$. If $c = c^*$ we return r as the decryption of c^*.

We now provide an analysis of the success probability of our reduction. Our simulation of E is perfect; moreover, our ciphertext c^* has the same distribution has in the original attack scenario. Therefore, when interacting with our simulation the attacker succeeds with the same probability as in the original attack scenario, that is with probability at least ε; in this case by definition we must have $y = E_k(0)$ where $k = E_{m^*}^{-1}(res)$.

If there is no triple of the form $(m^*, \cdot, res)$ in the history of E, then the distribution of $k = E_{m^*}^{-1}(res)$ is independent from the adversary's view; then the probability that $y = E_k(0)$ is at most $2^{-\beta}$. Therefore, with probability at least $\varepsilon - 2^{-\beta}$, the triple (m^*, k, res) belongs to history of E. Since by assumption the PK encryption scheme is deterministic, our reduction can check that c^* is indeed the encryption of m^* and therefore output m^*. Therefore, with probability at least $\varepsilon - 2^{-\beta}$, our reduction outputs the correct solution m^* to the OW-CCA challenge.

B   Proof of Theorem 2

We receive a public key pk and a challenge $c^* = \mathcal{E}_{pk}(m^*)$, and we must output m^*. The ideal cipher E is simulated in the standard way. We also generate the protocol transcripts as in the proof of Theorem 1, except that for a randomly chosen index j in $[1, n]$, we use the challenge ciphertext c^* instead of $c = \mathcal{E}_{pk}(r)$. More precisely, for the j-th protocol transcript, we generate a random $k \in \{0, 1\}^\alpha$ and let $y = E_k(0)$; we also generate a random $res \in \{0, 1\}^\beta$; the corresponding j-th transcript is then (y, c^*, res); this implicitly defines $E_{m^*}(k) = res$. If the adversary requests the session key for this j-th transcript, we abort. Eventually, the attacker outputs the session key corresponding to one of the previous n transcripts, not previously revealed.

To solve the OW-CPA challenge, our reduction determines the list of triples of the form $(r, \cdot, res)$ in the history of E, where res is the response in the j-th transcript, and for each of these triples it determines whether $c = \mathcal{E}_{pk}(r)$; in this case, it outputs r as a solution to the OW-CPA challenge.

Now we analyze the success probability of our reduction. We denote by S the event that in the original attack scenario, the adversary eventually outputs the session key for the j-th transcript, for an index j chosen uniformly at random in $[1, n]$; we have: $\Pr[\mathsf{S}] \geq \frac{\varepsilon}{n}$. We denote by Bad the event that the adversary makes a query for $E_{m^*}^{-1}(res)$. We have that conditioned on $\neg$Bad, our simulation of E is perfect and the adversary's view has the same distribution as in the original scenario; therefore, the event Bad has the same probability in the original scenario and in our reduction.

Moreover, if event Bad does not occur in the original scenario, then the adversary's view is independent from the value of k in the j-th transcript; therefore, the probability that the adversary outputs $K = r \oplus k$ is at most $2^{-\alpha}$, which gives: $\Pr[\mathsf{S}|\neg\mathsf{Bad}] \leq 2^{-\alpha}$. We have $\Pr[\mathsf{S}] = \Pr[\mathsf{S}|\mathsf{Bad}] \cdot \Pr[\mathsf{Bad}] + \Pr[\mathsf{S}|\neg\mathsf{Bad}] \cdot \Pr[\neg\mathsf{Bad}] \leq \Pr[\mathsf{Bad}] + \Pr[\mathsf{S}|\neg\mathsf{Bad}]$. Therefore, we obtain that $\Pr[\mathsf{Bad}] \geq \Pr[\mathsf{S}] - \Pr[\mathsf{S}|\neg\mathsf{Bad}] \geq \frac{\varepsilon}{n} - 2^{-\alpha}$. Finally, we have that our reduction succeeds if event Bad occurs. Namely since by assumption the underlying PK encryption scheme, we can check that c^* is indeed the encryption of m^* and therefore output m^*. This gives that $\Pr[\mathsf{Succ}] \geq \frac{\varepsilon}{n} - 2^{-\alpha}$.

C   Proof of Theorem 3

We receive a P-OW-CPA challenge (N, e, y^*) where $y^* = (x_1 \| x_2)^e \mod N$, where $x_1 \in \{0, 1\}^\alpha$ and $x_1 \| x_2$ is randomly generated in $\{0, 1\}^\gamma$, where $\gamma = \alpha + \ell$; our goal is to recover x_1. The adversary is run with public key (N, e) and target ciphertext y^*; this implicitly defines $H(x_1) = x_2$. We answer H-queries and ciphertext queries as follows:

H-queries: given a fresh hash query for $H(m)$, we generate a random $h \in \{0, 1\}^\ell$ and store (m, h) in a H-table; then we return h.

Ciphertext queries: given a ciphertext query c, we proceed as follows. For all (m, h) in H-table: compute $c' = (m\|h)^e \mod N$; if $c = c' \mod N$, return m; if $\gcd(c - c', N) = p$, return m. If $\gcd(c, y^*) = p$, recover d and x_1, and return x_1. Else return $\perp$.

Adversary "type 1": the adversary does not make a hash query to x_1. The simulation of H is perfect. Consider a ciphertext query for c, and let $x = c^d \mod p$. We denote by $\mathcal{D}$ the regular decryption oracle and $\mathcal{S}_D$ our simulated oracle. Then, if x cannot be parsed as $m\|u$, then both $\mathcal{D}$ and $\mathcal{S}_D$ return $\perp$. Else, x can be parsed as $m\|u$ and there are two cases. If (m, u) is in H-table, then both $\mathcal{D}$ and $\mathcal{S}_D$ return m. Else, (m, u) is not in H-table, and:

1. If $m = x_1$, then if $u = x_2$ both $\mathcal{D}$ and $\mathcal{S}_D$ return x_1, otherwise both return $\perp$.
2. If $m \neq x_1$, then $\mathcal{D}$ returns m if $u = H(m)$ and $\perp$ otherwise, whereas $\mathcal{S}_D$ always returns $\perp$.

Therefore, $\mathcal{D}$ and $\mathcal{S}_D$ only differ for case 2, which happens with probability at most $2^{-\ell}$. Since there are at most q_c ciphertext queries, our simulation of $\mathcal{D}$ is perfect except with probability at most $q_c \cdot 2^{-\ell}$. Therefore the adversary eventually outputs x_1 with probability at least $\varepsilon' \geq \varepsilon - q_c \cdot 2^{-\ell}$.

Adversary "type 2": the adversary makes a hash query for x_1. In this case, our simulation selects a random query among the list of H queries; therefore our simulation outputs x_1 with probability at least $\varepsilon' \geq \frac{\varepsilon - q_c \cdot 2^{-\ell}}{q_h}$, where q_h is the number of hash queries.

D   Security against the ECM Algorithm

The largest prime factor found using the ECM is a 222-bit integer (a table of the largest factors found by the ECM is maintained in [19]). It is estimated in [20] that the factorization of a 216 bits prime factor takes 24 years on a single 2.4 GHz PC, which corresponds to 2^{61} operations. Moreover the complexity of the ECM is $C(p) = \exp\left((\sqrt{2} + o(1))\sqrt{\log p \log \log p}\right)$. Ignoring the $o(1)$ term and using $C'(p) = C_0 \cdot \exp\left((\sqrt{2} + o(1))\sqrt{\log p \log \log p}\right)$ instead (where C_0 is a constant), the security level in bits can be estimated as $\log_2 C'(p) = \log_2 C_0 + \frac{\sqrt{2 \cdot \log p \log \log p}}{\log 2}$ where C_0 is taken such that $\log_2 C'(2^{216}) = 61$. We obtain the following formula, which gives the security level of a κ-bit prime p: $s_{\mathsf{ECM}}(\kappa) = (\ln 2)^{-1/2} \cdot (2 \cdot \kappa \ln(\kappa \ln 2))^{1/2} + 5$.

A Secure and Privacy-Preserving Targeted Ad-System

Elli Androulaki and Steven M. Bellovin

Columbia University
{elli,smb}@cs.columbia.edu

Abstract. Thanks to its low product-promotion cost and its efficiency, targeted online advertising has become very popular. Unfortunately, being profile-based, online advertising methods violate consumers' privacy, which has engendered resistance to the ads. However, protecting privacy through anonymity seems to encourage click-fraud. In this paper, we define consumer's privacy and present a privacy-preserving, targeted ad system (PPOAd) which is resistant towards click fraud. Our scheme is structured to provide financial incentives to all entities involved.

1 Introduction

Thanks to its ability to target audiences combined with its low cost, online advertising has become very popular throughout the past decade. However, current profile-based advertising techniques raise privacy risks and may contravene users' expectations, while privacy-preserving techniques, e.g., anonymous browsing, create many opportunities for fraud. In this way, security and privacy seem to contradict each other. In this paper we show that the aforementioned concepts are not mutually exclusive. In particular, we analyze the privacy concerns raised by online advertising as well as the subsequent security issues, and propose a privacy preserving set of protocols that provide targeted ads with guaranteed fraud detection.

Privacy Concern: Targeted Ads. To increase their banner-ads' effectiveness, *publishers* — usually service oriented websites paid to show advertising spots of other companies' products — choose their ads based on users' browsing activity. More specifically, third party cookies enable special ad networks to track users' browsing activity across multiple websites, construct very accurate user-profiles [KW06], and target ads accordingly. These advertising models track users even on sensitive sites, such as medical information websites, which could result in embarrassing advertisements appearing on other sites and in other contexts. A recent study [TKH+09] show broad rejection of the concept:

> Contrary to what many marketers claim, most adult Americans (66%) do not want marketers to tailor advertisements to their interests. Moreover, when Americans are informed of three common ways that marketers gather data about people in order to tailor ads, even higher percentages –between 73% and 86%—say they would not want such advertising.

R. Sion et al. (Eds.): FC 2010 Workshops, LNCS 6054, pp. 123–135, 2010.
© IFCA/Springer-Verlag Berlin Heidelberg 2010

The study found that over half of Americans felt that the punishment for illegal use of personal information should be jail time for the executives or that the company "be put out of business". The privacy issues become more serious when a conversion takes place, i.e., an online credit-card-based purchase or any activity which requires a login, thus linking a profile to a particular identity.

Security Concerns: Fraudulent Clicks. In the mechanism described before, publishers and ad-networks get paid by the advertisers in proportion to the number of clicks an advertisment receives from users. To dishonestly increase their revenue, publishers often fake clicks on ads. The existing privacy-preserving techniques, such as anonymizing networks, make detection of fraudulent clicks more difficult as all user identification elements are concealed.

Our Contribution. In this paper we present an online target advertising technique combining both privacy and security, PPOAd. More specifically,

1. we provide a concrete defintion of consumers' privacy
2. we present a privacy-preserving mechanism for the current ad-system infrastructure guaranteeing similar or better revenues for all the entities involved
3. we present a privacy-preserving mechanism for click-fraud detection and show how this mechanism is applied in our system, and
4. we based our protocols on ecash and unlinkable credential systems

Organization. In the following section we present current ad-systems' architecture. In sections 3 and 4 we demonstrate our system's requirements, threat model and protocols, while in sections 5 and 6, we elaborate on our system's security, privacy and innovation w.r.t. the exising work.

2   Targeted-Ads System Architecture

Except for **users** — the online consumers — in a typical advertising mechanism, the principle parties are **advertisers, ad networks** and the **publishers**. **Advertisers** are the companies selling and promoting a particular product or group of products. **Publishers** are usually service-oriented websites paid to *publish* advertisements of advertisers' products. **Ad networks** are paid by advertisers to choose the list of advertisements which will appear on publishers and filter the clicks the ads receive. Typical examples of ad-networks are Doubleclick (owned by Google), Atlas Solutions (owned by Microsoft), Brightcove, and more. It is often the case that an ad network offers various services and also acts as a publisher.

When a user visits a website (publisher), the browser sends to the publisher some pieces of information called cookies, which link multiple visits of the same user. In fact, a special type of cookies, the *third party cookies*, are sent during the publishers' visit to the corresponding ad networks, who can now trace user activity across multiple websites. In this way, especially as ad networks collaborate with many publishers, they construct very accurate user profiles and target ads accordingly. There are many policies regarding how ad-networks and publishers are paid. The most popular one is the "cost per click" (CPC), where both parties are paid by the advertisers in proportion to the number of clicks the latters' ads receive.

As clearly shown before, targeted ads violate privacy, while CPC payment method motivates many attacks: publishers may fake clicks on ads they publish to increase their income, while advertisers may generate clicks on their competitors' advertisements to deplete the latter's daily advertising budget. Detection of click-fraud is currently the responsibility of ad networks. Unfortunately, it is apparent that any conventional mechanism concealing users' browsing activity may strengthen click fraud.

3   Requirements-Threat Model

In this section we will define *privacy*, *security* and *deployability* in the context of our system w.r.t. our system's requirements and threat model.

Requirements. Application layer *privacy* and *security* are the core requirements in our system. Privacy refers to the user-protection, while security refers to the protection of the other entities of the system. More specifically, we define privacy, as the union of:

- *User Activity Unlinkability.* No system entity should be able to profile a particular honest user, i.e., link two or more browsing activities as having originated by the same party, and
- *User Anonymity.* No system entity should be able to link a particular browsing activity to an identity.

In addition, we define security as the combination of the following properties:

- *Correctness.* We require that if all parties are honest, advertisers will pay publishers and ad networks in accordance to the number of clicks their ads have received, while privacy is maintained.
- *Fairness.* We require that parties in our system will be paid if and only if they do their duty properly.
- *Accountability.* Our system should also be accountable, i.e., misbehaving parties should be detected and identified.
- *Unframability.* We require that no user can frame an honest user for being responsible for a misbehavior, i.e., for click-fraud. It is conceivable that strong accountability implies unframability.
- *Mis-Authentication.* Unless authorized, no user should be able to make use of our system.

We can easily see how the click fraud detection requirement is covered through the fairness and accountability requirements: fairness requires that publishers should not receive payments for fake clicks on a particular advertisement, while accountability requires that the attacker is traced.

In addition, we require that our system provide *similar ad-efficiency*, which would result in similar profitability to the parties involved. At least as important, it must be deployable. Similar ad-efficiency and, thus, *similar profitability* for publishers and ad networks aims to eliminate any monetary constraints against the adoption of a new system. *Deployability* is important for the same reasons. We examine deployability from two aspects: *(a)* w.r.t. our system's architecture: not substantial changes in current ad-system architecture should be required for our protocols to be applied; *(b)* w.r.t. our threat model, where we make real world assumptions.

It is essential to note that both privacy and security provisions are required in the application layer. Also, we extend the current ad-system architecture with a single entity — which may or may not be distributed — the User Ad Proxy (UAP), which acts as a mediator between the user and each visiting website.

Threat Model. Ad-systems' strong monetary nature, imposes "following the money" the safest way to define our adversaries' motives and powers. In what follows, we examine our adversary w.r.t. users' privacy and ad-system's security.

Publishers may be "curious" w.r.t. users' privacy, i.e., they may collaborate with ad networks, advertisers or other users in order to reveal the identity of a particular user or to link browsing activities of the same user. In addition, we assume that publishers are "honest and dishonest" w.r.t. the ad networks and advertisers. In particular, we assume that they do provide correct user-profile related information to the ad networks, but may attempt to fake clicks to the advertisements they publish in order to increase their revenues.

Ad networks' revenues depend on the efficiency of the way they list ads in the various publishers, as well as on their credibility. Ads' efficiency depends on the accuracy of users-profiling, while credibility depends of the ad network's click frauds' detectability. It is, consequently, reasonable to assume that ad networks are "honest but curious", w.r.t. users, while they are "honest" w.r.t. advertisers.

Advertisers are considered to be "curious" w.r.t. the users. In particular, since advertisers have no direct interaction with them, we believe that they may collaborate with publishers or ad-networks to make user-profiling more accurate.

UAP is considered to be "honest but curious" w.r.t. the users. More specifically, we assume that UAP is trusted to perform its functional operations honestly towards the users, but may collaborate with publishers or any other entity to link separate browsing activities of the same user. We also adopt a economic model so that UAP does not have a motive to cheat the advertisers.

4   A Privacy preserving Targeted-Ad System

As mentioned in the previous section, we extend the current ad-system architecture with the User Ad Proxy (UAP). UAP may be considered either as a single entity or as a group of collaborating entities and acts as a communication mediator between a user U visiting a publisher-website Pub and Pub. It is important to note that to hide any lower layer information emitted, U interacts with the rest of the system entities through an anonymizing network, while to automatically erase any cookies acquired and to be able to communicate with UAP or an UAP-member (if distributed), user-side installs a piece of software, which basically establishes an anonymous — communication layer — registration of user with the UAP.

The three core operations of our system: *(a)* the registration procedure of a user U at PPOAd, during which U obtains credentials to use the services of UAP, *(b)* the visit to a publisher, where a PPOAd-user requests a webpage, and *(c)* the ad-clicking procedure, where the user clicks on one of the publisher's ads (fig. 1). For convenience, we will assume that a user U is interacting with a publisher Pub. In addition, we will assume a single UAP, while in section 5, we will refer to the distributed UAP case.

Our scheme is based on the use of two types of tokens, issued by the user-UAP collaboration during the registration procedure: a registration credential regtick, which authorizes U as member of PPOAd multiple times anonymously and unlinkably, and a wallet with adticks, W_{adtick}, which will enable U to click on ads. regticks are blind towards the UAP, their possession can be demonstrated by their owner anonymously and unlinkably many times, each time resulting in a session-oriented ticket tick. Issued by the valid collaboration between U and the UAP, adticks are blind towards the UAP and can only be used for a limited number of times (MaxClicks) strictly by the person who issued them. For security purposes, U's identity is revealed in the following two cases: *(a)* when U attempts to make use of the same adtick more than once, or *(b)* if more than MaxClicks adticks of U are used for the same ad. We make use of regticks to achieve privacy w.r.t. UAP and adticks to achieve privacy and security w.r.t. to all the entities. Both tokens have an expiration date, so that users need to update their subscription on a monthly basis. In this way, we avoid unessessary computations, as misbehaving parties can be detected and removed from the system.

When requesting for a webpage, U sends to UAP his ad-preferences, demonstrates knowledge of his regtick and proves that his regtick is not among the blacklisted ones. UAP contacts the website and provides it with the U-specified ad-preferences. Ads are then shown to U accordingly.

When U clicks on an ad (see fig.1), he uses one of the adticks he has obtained at the registration procedure. The adtick is then linked to the following combination:

Fig. 1. Clicking on Ads

$$\{publisher \ || \ ad \ network \ || \ product\text{-}serial\},$$

where product-serial is the product identification number within the ad network. It is apparent that the triplet mentioned before identifies the particular ad. If U clicks intentionally on the same ad more than a pre-defined number of times using his adtick s, he will risk his privacy, as his identity will be revealed. However, U can choose instead to open an account for clicking on that particular ad, which will enable the ad network to decide whether series of U's clicks on that ad are legal or fraudulent. If classified as malicious, U's membership credential will be blacklisted.

As we will see later on, we use the blacklistable version of unlinkable credential system of [TAKS07] for the registration credentials regticks and the accountable ecash [SHJCL06] scheme for adticks.

In what follows, we will elaborate on the building blocks we used to construct our protocols and based on them we will proceed with the detailed description of our scheme.

4.1 Building Blocks

In this section, we present our primitives: group signature schemes, blacklistable anonymous credential systems as well as digital cash systems.

Ecash. An E-Cash [CHL05][SHJCL06] system consinsts of three types of players: the *bank, users* and *merchants*. Through this protocol, users withdraw coins from the bank, which may spend anonymously and unlinkably to merchants. Merchants deposit the coins to the bank which checks coins' validity. Users having spent the same coins twice or more than a particular number of coins to the same merchant have their identities revealed. The input and output specifications of the basic operations are as follows. For convenience, we will assume that the operations take place between a merchant M, a user U and the Bank B.

- $(pk_B, sk_B) \leftarrow$ EC.BKeyGen$(1^k, params)$ and $(pk_U, sk_U) \leftarrow$ EC.UKeyGen$(1^k, params)$, which are the key generation algorithm for the bank and the users respectively.
- $\langle W, \top \rangle \leftarrow$ EC.Withdraw(pk_B, pk_U, n) [U(sk_U), B(sk_B)]. In this interactive procedure, U withdraws a wallet W of n coins from B.
- $\langle W', (S, \pi) \rangle \leftarrow$ EC.Spend(pk_M, pk_B, n) [U(W), M(sk_M)]. In this interactive procedure, U spends a digital coin with serial S from his wallet W to M. When the procedure is over, W is reduced to W', M obtains as output a coin (S, π), where π is a proof of a valid coin with a serial number S.
- $\langle \top/\bot, L' \rangle \leftarrow$ EC.Deposit(pk_M, pk_B) [M(sk_M, S, π), B(sk_B, L)]. In this interactive procedure, M deposits a coin (S, π) into its account in the bank. If this procedure is successful, M's output will be $\top$ and the bank's list L of the spent coins will be updated to L'.
- $(pk_U, \Pi_G) \leftarrow$ EC.Identify$(params, S, \pi_1, \pi_2)$. When the bank receives the two coins with the same serial number S and validity proofs π_1 and π_2, it executes this procedure, to reveal the public key of the violator accompanied with a violation proof Π_G.
- $\top/\bot \leftarrow$ EC.VerifyGuilt$(params, S, pk_U, \Pi_G)$. This algorithm, given Π_G publicly verifies the violation of pk_U.
- $\{(S_i, \Pi_i)\}_i \leftarrow$ EC.Trace$(params, S, pk_U, \Pi_G, D, n)$. This algorithm provides the list of serials S_i of the ecoins a violator pk_U has issued, with the corresponding ownership proofs Π_i.
- $\top/\bot \leftarrow$ EC.VerifyOwnership$(params, S, \Pi, pk_U, n)$. This algorithm allows to publicly verify the proof Π that a coin with serial number S belongs to a user with public key pk_U.

[SHJCL06] is a money-laundering prevention version of [CHL05], where anonymity is revoked when the spender spends more coins to the same merchant than a spending limit. In this case ecoins are upgraded to $C = (S, V, \pi)$, where V is a merchant-related locator, while EC.Identify and EC.VerifyGuilt procedures are upgraded to the DetectViolator and VerifyViolation to support the extended violation definition.

Security Properties: (a) Correctness. (b) Balance. No collection of users and merchants can ever spend more coins than they withdrew. *(c) Identification of Violators.* Given a violation and the corresponding proofs of guilt, the violator's public pk_U key is revealed such that EC.VerifyViolation accepts. *(d) Anonymity of users.* The bank, even when cooperating with any collection of malicious users and merchants, cannot learn anything about a user's spendings other than what is available from side information from the environment. *(e) Exculpability.* An honest user U cannot be accused for conducting a violation such that EC.VerifyViolation accepts. *(f) Violators' Traceability.* Given a violator U with a proof of violation Π_G, this property guarantees that EC.Trace will output the serial numbers of all coins that belong to U along with the corresponding proofs of ownership, such that for each one of them EC.VerifyOwnership accepts.

Blacklistable Anonymous Credentials (BLAC). The entities in the blacklistable credential system BLAC of [TAKS07] are the Group Manager GM, a set of service providers SPs and users. Through this system users can register to receive a particular service multiple times without users' access activity being able to be traced. However, misbehaving users are blacklisted. The procedures supported are the following:

- $\langle \text{gpk}, \text{gsk} \rangle \leftarrow$ BLAC.Setup[GM(1^k)]. This algorithm generates a group public key gpk and the GM's secret group information gsk .
- $\langle \text{cred}_U, \text{JLog}_U \rangle \leftarrow$ BLAC.Register(gpk)[U, GM(gsk)]. When this interactive registration ends, U has obtained his membership credential cred_U.
- $\langle \top/\bot \rangle \leftarrow$ BLAC.Authenticate(gpk) [U(cred_U), SP(BL)]. In this interactive procedure, U proves to SP that he is a valid (non-blacklisted) member of the group.
- $\langle BL' \rangle \leftarrow$ BLAC.BLAdd[SP(BL)], where a service provider ads a credential (ticket) to the blacklist BL.
- $\langle tick \rangle \leftarrow$ BLAC.BLExtract[SP(BL)], where SP extracts an element from the blacklist.
- $\langle BL' \rangle \leftarrow$ BLAC.BLRemove[SP(BL)], where SP removes a credential from the blacklist.

Security Properties: (a) Correctness. (b) Mis-authentication Resistance. No unregistered user or collection of unregistered users should be able to authenticate themselves. *(c) Blacklistability.* SPs may blacklist any misbehaving user of the system and restrict him from any ability of authenticating himself. *(d) Anonymity.* SPs may only learn whether a user is blacklisted or not; no identification information may be leaked. *(e) Non-framability.* An honest user should never be blocked from access.

Group Signature Schemes (GSS). In a typical GSS, there is a group manager (GM), the group-members, who act as signers (let each be S) and produce signatures on behalf of the group, without being able to be accurately identified. The procedures supported are the following:

- (gpk, gsk) $\leftarrow$ GS.Setup(1^k). This algorithm generates a group public key gpk and the GM's secret group information gsk .
- $\langle \text{bgusk}_S, \text{JLog}_S \rangle \leftarrow$ GS.Join(gpk)[S, GM(gsk)]. When this interactive join procedure ends, an S obtains a secret signing key bgusk_S, and the GM (group manager) logs the join transcript JLog_S in the the group manager's database D.
- $\sigma \leftarrow$ GS.Sign(gpk, bgusk_S, m). This algorithm generates a group signature on a message m.
- $\langle \top/\bot \rangle \leftarrow$ GS.Verify(gpk, m, σ). This is a verification algorithm.
- Ms $\leftarrow$ GS.Open(gsk, σ, D). With this algorithm the GM determines the identity of the group member who generated the signature σ.

Security Properties: (a) Anonymity. Given a signature, the adversary can identify its originator among the group members no better than randomly. *(b) Unforgeability.* The adversary cannot produce a valid group signature without owning group membership information. *(c) Non-framability.* The adversary cannot create a valid group signature that opens to another group member.

4.2   The PPOAd **Protocol in Detail**

UAP runs EC.BKeyGen twice to establish the two accountable ecash schemes, which will be used for adticks (see, section **??**). In addition to its keys' generation, UAP runs the BLAC.Setup procedure of the blacklistable anonymous credential (BLAC) scheme for user-registration purposes, while it maintains two blacklists: the TempBL, where it stores the credentials in question, and, the PermBL, which is the official blacklist of the system.

Each ad network AdNet runs GS.Setup to generate the administration information for the group of publishers G^{AdNet} it provides ads with: $\{gpk^{AdNet}, gsk^{AdNet}\}$. In response, each publisher collaborating with AdNet, runs GS.Join with AdNet to obtain membership in G^{AdNet}.

Registration (PPOAd.Register) This is the case where a user U registers to UAP such that the former makes use of PPOAd's privacy services:

1. U provides the UAP with a piece of identification information. This can be a credit card, which will be used to pay U's subscription. U runs EC.UKeyGen to issue his system identity, the signature key pair (pk_U, sk_U).
2. U and UAP collaborate in a BLAC.Register procedure, where U's credential $regtick_U$ is issued. $regtick_U$ is blind towards UAP.
3. U and UAP collaborate in a BLAC.Authenticate procedure, so that UAP obtains a transcript of the $regtick_U$ authentication phase, mem_U. Note that the mem_U which was obtained by UAP in this way, serves blacklistability purposes and cannot be linked to later authentications of U through $regtick_U$.
4. U and UAP collaborate in two EC.Withdraw procedure, for the former to obtain two wallets $W_{ads}^{f,l}$ of accountable ecash each corresponding to the two different settings of accountable ecash established in the setup phase.
5. UAP stores in its membership database the new user's entry: $\{U, pk_U, mem_U\}$, and provides U with a signed proof of payment: $PaymRec = Sig_{UAP}(timestamp, U)$.

In what follows, we will assume that a user U visits a website Pub, which is in contract with a number of ad networks $Adv_1, \ldots, Adv_m$, who provide the website with ads.

Ad-targeting (PPOAd.Target) This procedure involves the targeting of ads taking place when U visits Pub.

1. *User Authorization*: U interacts with UAP in a BLAC.Authenticate procedure to authenticate himself as a non-blacklisted member of the PPOAd system. In this procedure U demonstrates knowledge — in a zero knowledge fashion — of his membership credential $regtick_U$. Let AuthT be the corresponding transcript of U-UAP interactions.
2. tick *issue phase*: UAP issues a signed, dated permission tick, which will enable U to access the website requested. tick may have the form of

$$tick = Sig_{UAP}(timestamp, AuthT).$$

3. *Preferences setup*. In this phase, U sets up his ad-preferences and sends them to the UAP. UAP then sends the webpage http request with U's preferences. As we will see later, the preferences-related info provided to UAP does not enable U activity-tracking neither by the UAP, nor by the requested website.
4. *Targeting*. Ad networks, who receive U's preferences as coming from UAP itself, process the ad-preferences and provide Pub with the corresponding list of ads.
5. Pub *Visit*. U provides tick to Pub and the Pub-webpage is presented to U.

Ad-clicking (PPOAd.Adclick) This operation refers to the case, where U has already visited Pub and clicks on one of the ads an ad network AdNet$_i$ provided to Pub. The series of interactions involve the following:

1. *Clicked Ad's website request*. Pub sends the ad-click information to the clicked ad's website, which is essentially one of the advertisers in contract with AdNet$_i$. Let Adv$_j$ be the one. The ad-click information includes AdNet$_i$, Pub, AuthT and a timestamp. Note that this step is currently performed in ad-systems and serves billing and user-profiling purposes. Note that AuthT can be considered as a session identifier for the U.
2. AdID *construction*. In this phase the ad network, advertiser and clicked-product's identifier is popularized to U. The complete ad's identity would then be the following:

$$AdID = \{Pub||AdNet_i||product\ ID\},$$

where we assume that the same products of different advertisers have different identification numbers. As we will discuss in section 5, in addition to the AdID, an AdID-related key-pair is constructed (pk_{AdID}, sk_{AdID}).
3. adtick-*based Authorization*. Let MaxClicks be the number of times an honest user usually clicks on an ad.[1] Based on how many times U has — over all his browsing activity — clicked on that particular AdID, we have three adclick protocols of U-AdNet$_i$ interaction:
   (a) If U has clicked on the same AdID fewer than MaxClicks times, he and AdNet$_i$ collaborate in EC.Spend procedure, so that U spends one of his W^i_{ads} digital coins to the AdID related key-pair.
   (b) If U has clicked exactly MaxClicks times to the same AdID, he and AdNet$_i$ commit in an EC.Spend procedure for one of the coins of U's W^i_{ads} wallet. In addition, U and AdNet$_i$ collaborate in EC.UKeyGen for U to create an account $(pk_U^{AdID}, sk_U^{AdID})$ within AdNet$_i$ for that particular AdID. AdNet$_i$ stores $\{pk_U AdID, AuthT, AdID\}$ to its database.
   (c) If U has clicked on the same AdID more than MaxClicks times, he has already been issued an AdID-account. Thus, he demonstrates knowledge of sk_U^{AdID}. In this way, his behavior towards this AdID will be traceable.
   We can see that a user trying to attack an advertiser using PPOAd will eventually have his click-activity for that particular ad traced. In this way, AdNet$_i$ may have all the information necessary to characterize the sequence of clicks on that AdID as malicious or benign. Different CPC rates may apply in this case.
4. If everything is fine, the the Adv$_j$ website is presented to U.

---

[1] This number varies from two to four, depending on how interesting that product is, and should be defined after suitable research.

If at any point of the procedure, U declines to cooperate, $AdNet_i$ or Pub report AuthT to UAP, who can then run BLACK.BLAdd on TempBL to put a temporary hold on $regtick_U$ which corresponds to AuthT. Note that thanks to the properties of BLAC system adopted, UAP does not need to know the user U or his $regtick_U$. On the other hand, if U tries to click on the same AdID more MaxClicks times using his adticks, he will need to spend more than MaxClicks coins of his W_{ads}^i wallet or more than one coin of his W_{ads}^i to the same AdID. Because of the accountable ecash properties, this will result in revocation of pk_U, while $regtick_U$ will be immediately blacklisted (through mem_U).

Update Membership (PPOAd.UpdateMembership) To enforce payment of its registered members' regular contribution, at the end of each prefixed period, UAP changes its credentials' parameters. To continue making use of PPOAd's services, users contact UAP by providing identification and payment (most recent PaymRec) information. Each user and UAP commit in a BLAC. Authenticate protocol, for the former to prove that his old credential is not among the blacklisted ones. If a user's $Uregtick_U$ is not blacklisted, U pays his monthly contribution, issues a new $regtick_U$ and receives new PaymRec. On the other hand, if $regtick_U$ is blacklisted or U does not pay, his old credential will be invalid and thus will not be possible for him to use PPOAd's services.

5 System Considerations

In this section, we will elaborate on the *security* and *privacy* properties of our system, as well as on other practical issues.

Implementation Issues. *System Software Components.* We have already mentioned that for our system purposes, we extended the current ad system infrastructure with the UAP entity, while users of the system install a PPOAd-specific software, which involves the following: *(a)* the User-ad-preferences software, where the users specify their public and topic-related ad-preferences which will occasionally be sent to UAP, *(b)* the cookie-clean-up section, which removes all the cookies of users' browsing activity, *(c)* the UAP/ad-network-communication part, which consists of the withdrawer side of the accountable ecash system, the user side of the anonymous credential system presented in 4.1. In addition, user side makes use of an anonymizing network to contact UAP. UAP installs the bank and server side of the ecash and BLAC systems respectively to authorize PPOAd-users to browse online. Ad networks and publishers just need to assign their products identity numbers and install the spender part of the ecash protocol.

User-ad-preferences play an important role for our system's *ad-efficiency*. As mentioned in previous section, after his registration to the PPOAd (PPOAd. Register) the user obtains and installs software to handle the PPOAd's interactions. Depending on how targeted wishes his ads to be, the user creates many partial profiles by choosing various types of products he is interested in and the particular products in each category individually that may be of his interest. When the user visits a website and after the

PPOAd.Authenticate phase — the user-software obtains the classification of the requested website and forwards to UAP the corresponding partial profile. Assuming that the lower layer information, i.e., consumer's machine's IP is hidden towards the UAP, because of the BLAC system unlinkability property, the latter cannot link the partial profiles of the same user. In addition, being partial (related to the website), while prone to change at any time, the same partial profile may commonly be met across different users and will not be enough to link browsing activities of the same consumer across different websites.

AdID *key-pair construction.* To preserve security and privacy, it is essential that each AdID-combination: {Pub, AdNet, productID}, where Pub is the visited website, AdNet is the ad network providing the ad and productID the serial of the product, is assigned a different key-pair. To achieve this, AdNet constructs AdID's key-pair by contributing to the key-generation algorithm a pre-specified hash of the following quantity: $gpk_{Pub}||pk_{AdNet}||productID$, where gpk_{Pub} is the Pub's public information in the G^{AdNet}, and pk_{AdNet} the public key of AdNet. In this way, the same key will be generated for the same AdID, without the need of precalculating it, while the probability that the same key is generated for two AdIDs is negligible.

Distributed UAP is critical if PPOAd is intended for large-scale use. This can be achieved through the use of blind group and group signatures, where UAP-related blind and plain signatures were used. In addition, depending on our privacy and computation efficiency requirements, we may group UAPs serving users of the same geographical area together. In this way, operations such as validity checks will be accelerated.

Privacy. Assuming that the partial profiles reveal nothing w.r.t. the consumer, and that user-cookies are successfully erased through the PPOAd-software installed, privacy in our system is guaranteed through the ecash and BLAC systems' security properties (see, section 4.1). In particular, consumers' anonymity and activity unlinkability is provided directly via the anonymity and unlinkability properties of the blacklistable anonymous credentials used in PPOAd.Register and PPOAd.Target procedures and anonymity and unlinkability properties of the ecash schemes used in PPOAd.Adclick procedure. Note that even when a consumer clicks on the same AdID more than MaxClicks times, the former's behavior towards that particular AdID is only traceable (when and how often the consumer clicks on it) and not his overall browsing activity.

Security. Each part of PPOAd's security is satisfied. Correctness is guaranteed through the correctness of the schemes adopted. Mis-authentication resistance is achieved through the corresponding property of the blacklistable anonymous credential system used at the authorization phase of our protocols. Unframability is guaranteed through the combination of the mis-authentication resistance property and the ecash nature of the adticks: being unforgeable and ecash-based, only an authenticated PPOAd-user who issued the adticks can use them successfully. Fairness and accountability are achieved also through the accountable ecash security properties (see, section 4.1): a user trying to click at the same ad many times will either have his public key revealed or his click-activity w.r.t. that ad traced. If the latter is the case, and the user is classified as malicious, he will be automatically be blacklisted and his ad-clicks ignored.

A Market Model. Incentivising users to use our system is critical for the latter's adoption since, if popular, both ad networks and ad agencies would be motivated to feed our system with advertisements. Users' motive is the combination of receiving ads related to their interests while maintaining their privacy.

On the other hand, it is necessary that all the participating entities behave properly for users to continue using the system. Threats towards security continue to exist. In our threat model, we assumed that UAP restricts users to a single registration to PPOAd. However, it is conceivable that in the real world, corrupted UAP entities — since they are paid by the users — may be tempted to issue multiple accounts to the same party, which would enable the latter to forge clicks without limit. It is thus critical that we offer monetary incentive for the system entities to behave according to our threat model. In addition, since targeted advertising is already very profitable, we need to create incentives to direct it as we propose. In this section we elaborate on a market model towards for both cases.

In response to our threat model issue, we require that UAP entities are paid by both, the user — through his PPOAd-subscription — and by the ad networks who also benefit from click-fraud. Wanting to maintain their clientele, UAP will be forced to be "honest" in their functional operations towards both entities: users and ad networks.

As far as the PPOAd application is concerned, ad networks already have incentives to participate in our system: through the PPOAd click-fraud detection mechanism, ad networks' fraud detection ability — thus their credibility — will be enhanced. In addition, despite our privacy provisions, ad networks may still target ads even more effectively: the targeting procedure is now based on partial profiles provided by the user himself, while it is likely that their audience is extended with users who — strictly for privacy reasons — had so far removed ads from their browsers. Being offered better click-fraud detection rates, advertisers would also benefit from PPOAd.

6   Related Work

Fraudulent Click detection has been attempted in the past. In particular, Jakobsson, MacKenzie and Stern in [JMS99] introduce an ad system where advertisers (in their system are called merchants) utilize e-coupons to detect malicious actions. However, in their scheme they do not deal with privacy the same way we defined it.

Combining targeted ads and privacy has been attempted in the past. Juels in [J01] has suggested a target ad technique with the use of third parties, the nogotiants, which would update a bulletin board with users' ad-preferences. Although perfectly secure in terms of privacy, they do not deal with our second security concern. Claessens and Diaz in [CDFP03] in fact suggested a more lightweight privacy preserving target ad system, where users would be grouped in terms of profiles for them to be presented with ads. V. Toubiana et al. in [TNB+09] have transferred the targeting mechanism to a browser extension, in a private way towards ad networks and publishers. However, though there are some suggestions, they do not consider click fraud. To privately target ads, iPrivacy [SS01] ecommerce system, had their clients obtain anonymous email accounts — held by the company itself or the banks — bound to specific advertising profiles; in this way users only receive ads of their interests.

7   Conclusion

In this paper we have addressed privacy and security in the area of online targeted advertising. In particular, we provided a set of protocols providing targeted ads with similar ad-effectiveness as current systems and in a privacy preserving way. At the same time, the privacy provided in our system is conditional, guaranteed only for honest users.

Acknowledgments

We'd like to thank Chris Jay Hoofnagle and Christopher Soghoian for their comments on this paper.

References

[CDFP03]   Claessens, J., Diaz, C., Faustinelli, R., Preneel, B.: Secure and privacy-preserving web banner system for targeted advertising. COSIC internal report (2003),
           http://citeseerx.ist.psu.edu/viewdoc/summary?doi=10.1.1.15.4382

[CHL05]   Camenisch, S.H.J., Hohenberger, S., Lysyanskaya, A.: Compact e-cash. In: Cramer, R. (ed.) EUROCRYPT 2005. LNCS, vol. 3494, pp. 302–321. Springer, Heidelberg (2005)

[J01]   Juels, A.: Targeted advertising... and privacy too. In: Naccache, D. (ed.) CT-RSA 2001. LNCS, vol. 2020, pp. 408–424. Springer, Heidelberg (2001)

[JMS99]   Jakobsson, M., MacKenzie, P.D., Stern, J.P.: Secure and lightweight advertising on the Web. Computer Networks (Amsterdam, Netherlands) 31(11-16), 1101–1109 (1999)

[KW06]   Krishnamurthy, B., Wills, C.E.: Generating a privacy footprint on the internet. In: IMC 2006: Proceedings of the 6th ACM SIGCOMM conference on Internet measurement, pp. 65–70. ACM, New York (2006)

[SHJCL06] Jan Camenisch, S.H., Hohenberger, S., Lysyanskaya, A.: Balancing accountability and privacy using E-cash (Extended abstract). In: De Prisco, R., Yung, M. (eds.) SCN 2006. LNCS, vol. 4116, pp. 141–155. Springer, Heidelberg (2006)

[SS01]   Stolfo, S.J., Smith, J.M.: Method and system for user defined filtering of communications to anonymous users in a computer network. U.S. patent WO/2001/065442 (2001)

[TAKS07]   Tsang, P.P., Au, M.H., Kapadia, A., Smith, S.W.: Blacklistable anonymous credentials: blocking misbehaving users without ttps. In: CCS 2007: Proceedings of the 14th ACM conference on Computer and communications security, pp. 72–81. ACM, New York (2007)

[TKH+09]   Turow, J., King, J., Hoofnagle, C.J., Bleakley, A., Hennessy, M.: Americans reject tailored advertising and three activities that enable it (September 2009),
           http://ssrn.com/abstract=1478214

[TNB+09]   Toubiana, V., Narayanan, A., Boneh, D., Nissenbaum, H., Solon, B.: Priveads: Privacy preserving targeted advertising (2009),
           http://crypto.stanforf.edu/privads/

Cryptographic Cloud Storage

Seny Kamara and Kristin Lauter

Microsoft Research
{senyk,klauter}@microsoft.com

Abstract. We consider the problem of building a secure cloud storage service on top of a public cloud infrastructure where the service provider is not completely trusted by the customer. We describe, at a high level, several architectures that combine recent and non-standard cryptographic primitives in order to achieve our goal. We survey the benefits such an architecture would provide to both customers and service providers and give an overview of recent advances in cryptography motivated specifically by cloud storage.

1   Introduction

Advances in networking technology and an increase in the need for computing resources have prompted many organizations to outsource their storage and computing needs. This new economic and computing model is commonly referred to as cloud computing and includes various types of services such as: infrastructure as a service (IaaS), where a customer makes use of a service provider's computing, storage or networking infrastructure; platform as a service (PaaS), where a customer leverages the provider's resources to run custom applications; and finally software as a service (SaaS), where customers use software that is run on the providers infrastructure.

Cloud infrastructures can be roughly categorized as either private or public. In a private cloud, the infrastructure is managed and owned by the customer and located on-premise (i.e., in the customers region of control). In particular, this means that access to customer data is under its control and is only granted to parties it trusts. In a public cloud the infrastructure is owned and managed by a cloud service provider and is located off-premise (i.e., in the service provider's region of control). This means that customer data is outside its control and could potentially be granted to untrusted parties.

Storage services based on public clouds such as Microsoft's Azure storage service and Amazon's S3 provide customers with scalable and dynamic storage. By moving their data to the cloud customers can avoid the costs of building and maintaining a private storage infrastructure, opting instead to pay a service provider as a function of its needs. For most customers, this provides several benefits including availability (i.e., being able to access data from anywhere) and reliability (i.e., not having to worry about backups) at a relatively low cost.

While the benefits of using a public cloud infrastructure are clear, it introduces significant security and privacy risks. In fact, it seems that the biggest hurdle

R. Sion et al. (Eds.): FC 2010 Workshops, LNCS 6054, pp. 136–149, 2010.
© IFCA/Springer-Verlag Berlin Heidelberg 2010

to the adoption of cloud storage (and cloud computing in general) is concern over the confidentiality and integrity of data. While, so far, consumers have been willing to trade privacy for the convenience of software services (e.g., for web-based email, calendars, pictures etc), this is not the case for enterprises and government organizations. This reluctance can be attributed to several factors that range from a desire to protect mission-critical data to regulatory obligations to preserve the confidentiality and integrity of data. The latter can occur when the customer is responsible for keeping personally identifiable information (PII), or medical and financial records. So while cloud storage has enormous promise, unless the issues of confidentiality and integrity are addressed many potential customers will be reluctant to make the move.

To address the concerns outlined above and increase the adoption of cloud storage, we argue for designing a *virtual private storage service* based on recently developed cryptographic techniques. Such a service should aim to achieve the best of both worlds by providing the security of a private cloud and the functionality and cost savings of a public cloud. More precisely, such a service should provide (at least):

– confidentiality: the cloud storage provider does not learn any information about customer data
– integrity: any unauthorized modification of customer data by the cloud storage provider can be detected by the customer

while retaining the main benefits of a public storage service:

– availability: customer data is accessible from any machine and at all times
– reliability: customer data is reliably backed up
– efficient retrieval: data retrieval times are comparable to a public cloud storage service
– data sharing: customers can share their data with trusted parties.

An important aspect of a cryptographic storage service is that the security properties described above are achieved based on strong cryptographic guarantees as opposed to legal, physical and access control mechanisms. We believe this has several important benefits which we discuss further in Section 3.

This article is organized as follows. In Section 2 we describe, at a high level, a possible architecture for a cryptographic storage service. We consider both consumer and enterprise scenarios. We stress that this design is not intended to be a formal specification (indeed many important business and engineering questions would need to be addressed) but is only meant to serve as an *illustration* of how some of the new and non-standard cryptographic techniques that have been developed recently could be combined to achieve our goals. In Section 3 we give an overview of the benefits of a cryptographic storage service, e.g., reducing the legal exposure of both customers and cloud providers, and achieving regulatory compliance. In Section 4 we describe in more detail the relevant cryptographic techniques, including searchable encryption, proofs of storage and attribute-based encryption. Finally, in Section 5, we mention some cloud services that could be built on top of a cryptographic storage service such as secure back-ups, archival, health record systems, secure data exchange and e-discovery.

2   Architecture of a Cryptographic Storage Service

We now describe, at a high level, a possible architecture for a cryptographic storage service. At its core, the architecture consists of three components: a *data processor* (DP), that processes data before it is sent to the cloud; a *data verifier* (DV), that checks whether the data in the cloud has been tampered with; and a *token generator* (TG), that generates tokens that enable the cloud storage provider to retrieve segments of customer data; and a *credential generator* that implements an access control policy by issuing credentials to the various parties in the system (these credentials will enable the parties to decrypt encrypted files according to the policy). We describe designs for both consumer and enterprise scenarios.

2.1   A Consumer Architecture

Consider three parties: a user Alice that stores her data in the cloud; a user Bob with whom Alice wants to share data; and a cloud storage provider that stores Alice's data. To use the service, Alice and Bob begin by downloading a client application that consists of a data processor, a data verifier and a token generator. Upon its first execution, Alice's application generates a cryptographic key. We will refer to this key as a master key and assume it is stored locally on Alice's system and that it is kept secret from the cloud storage provider.

Whenever Alice wishes to upload data to the cloud, the data processor is invoked. It attaches some metadata (e.g., current time, size, keywords etc) and encrypts and encodes the data and metadata with a variety of cryptographic primitives (which we describe in more detail in Section 4). Whenever Alice wants to verify the integrity of her data, the data verifier is invoked. The latter uses Alice's master key to interact with the cloud storage provider and ascertain the integrity of the data. When Alice wants to retrieve data (e.g., all files tagged with keyword "urgent") the token generator is invoked to create a token. The token is sent to the cloud storage provider who uses it to retrieve the appropriate (encrypted) files which it returns to Alice. Alice then uses the decryption key to decrypt the files. Data sharing between Alice and Bob proceeds in a similar fashion. Whenever she wishes to share data with Bob, the application invokes the token generator to create an appropriate token, and the credential generator to generate a credential for Bob. Both the token and credential are sent to Bob who, in turn, sends the token to the provider. The latter uses the token to retrieve and return the appropriate encrypted documents which Bob decrypts using his credential.

This process is illustrated in Figure 1. We note that in order to achieve the security properties we seek, it is important that the client-side application and, in particular, the core components be either open-source or implemented or verified by someone other than the cloud service provider.

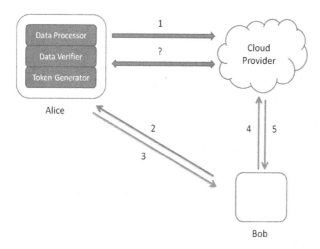

Fig. 1. (1) Alice's data processor prepares the data before sending it to the cloud; (2) Bob asks Alice for permission to search for a keyword; (3) Alice's token and credential generators send a token for the keyword and a credential back to Bob; (4) Bob sends the token to the cloud; (5) the cloud uses the token to find the appropriate encrypted documents and returns them to Bob. (?) At any point in time, Alice's data verifier can verify the integrity of the data.

2.2   An Enterprise Architecture

In the enterprise scenario we consider an enterprise MegaCorp that stores its data in the cloud; a business partner PartnerCorp with whom MegaCorp wants to share data; and a cloud storage provider that stores MegaCorp's data.

To use the service, MegaCorp deploys dedicated machines within its network. Depending on the particular scenario, these dedicated machines will run various core components. Since these components make use of a master secret key, it is important that they be adequately protected and, in particular, that the master key be kept secret from the cloud storage provider and PartnerCorp. If this is too costly in terms of resources or expertise, management of the dedicated machines (or specific components) can alternatively be outsourced to a trusted entity.

In the case of a medium-sized enterprise with enough resources and expertise, the dedicated machines include a data processor, a data verifier, a token generator and a credential generator. To begin, each MegaCorp and PartnerCorp employee receives a credential from the credential generator. These credentials will reflect some relevant information about the employees such as their organization or team or role. Whenever a MegaCorp employee generates data that needs to be stored in the cloud, it sends the data together with an associated decryption policy to the dedicated machine for processing. The decryption policy specifies the type of credentials necessary to decrypt the data (e.g., only members of a particular team). To retrieve data from the cloud (e.g., all files generated by a particular employee), an employee requests an appropriate token

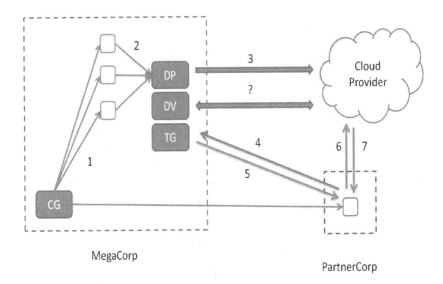

Fig. 2. (1) Each MegaCorp and PartnerCorp employee receives a credential; (2) Mega-Corp employees send their data to the dedicated machine; (3) the latter processes the data using the data processor before sending it to the cloud; (4) the PartnerCorp employee sends a keyword to MegaCorp's dedicated machine ; (5) the dedicated machine returns a token; (6) the PartnerCorp employee sends the token to the cloud; (7) the cloud uses the token to find the appropriate encrypted documents and returns them to the employee. (?) At any point in time, MegaCorp's data verifier can verify the integrity of MegaCorp's data.

from the dedicated machine. The employee then sends the token to the cloud provider who uses it to find and return the appropriate encrypted files which the employee decrypts using his credentials. Whenever MegaCorp wants to verify the integrity of the data, the dedicated machine's data verifier is invoked. The latter uses the master secret key to interact with the storage provider and ascertain the integrity of the data.

Now consider the case where a PartnerCorp employee needs access to Mega-Corp's data. The employee authenticates itself to MegaCorp's dedicated machine and sends it a keyword. The latter verifies that the particular search is allowed for this PartnerCorp employee. If so, the dedicated machine returns an appropriate token which the employee uses to recover the appropriate (encrypted) files from the service provider. It then uses its credentials to decrypt the file. This process is illustrated in Figure 2. Similarly to the consumer architecture, it is imperative that all components be either open-source or implemented by someone other than the cloud service provider.

In the case that MegaCorp is a very large organization and that the prospect of running and maintaining enough dedicated machines to process all employee data is infeasible, consider the following slight variation of the architecture described

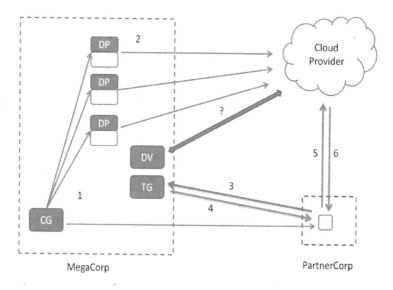

Fig. 3. (1) Each MegaCorp and PartnerCorp employee receives a credential; (2) Mega-Corp employees process their data using their own data processors and send them to the cloud; (3) the PartnerCorp employee sends a keyword to MegaCorp's dedicated machine; (4) the latter returns a token; (5) the employee sends the token to the cloud; (6) the cloud uses the token to find the appropriate encrypted documents and returns them to the employee. (?) At any point in time, MegaCorp's data verifier can check the integrity of MegaCorp's data.

above. More precisely, in this case the dedicated machines only run data verifiers, token generators and credential generators while the data processing is distributed to each employee. This is illustrated in Figure 3. Note that in this scenario the data processors do not include the master secret key so the confidentiality of the data is not affected. The data processors, however, do include some keying material which, if revealed to the service provider, could enable it to compromise the confidentiality of the tokens it receives (i.e,. it could learn which keywords are being searched for).

3   Benefits of a Cryptographic Storage Service

The core properties of a cryptographic storage service are that (1) control of the data is maintained by the customer and (2) the security properties are derived from cryptography, as opposed to legal mechanisms, physical security or access control. Therefore, such a service provides several compelling advantages over other storage services based on public cloud infrastructures. In this section, we recall some of the main concerns with cloud computing as outlined in the Cloud Security Alliances recent report [7] and highlight how these concerns can be mitigated by such an architecture.

Regulatory compliance. Most countries have laws in place that make organizations responsible for the protection of the data that is entrusted to them. This is particularly so for the case of personally identifiable information, medical records and financial records. And since organizations are often held responsible for the actions of their contractors, the use of a public cloud storage service can involve significant legal risks. In a cryptographic storage service, the data is encrypted on-premise by the data processor(s). This way, customers can be assured that the confidentiality of their data is preserved irrespective of the actions of the cloud storage provider. This greatly reduces any legal exposure for both the customer and the provider.

Geographic restrictions. Data that is stored in certain legal jurisdictions may be subject to regulations even if it was not collected there. Because it can be difficult to ascertain exactly where one's data is being stored once it is sent to the cloud (i.e., many service providers have data centers deployed throughout the world) some customers may be reluctant to use a public cloud for fear of increasing their legal exposure. In a cryptographic storage service data is only stored in encrypted form so any law that pertains to the stored data has little to no effect on the customer. This reduces legal exposure for the customer and allows the cloud storage provider to make optimal use of its storage infrastructure, thereby reducing costs.

Subpoenas. If an organization becomes the subject of an investigation, law enforcement agencies may request access to its data. If the data is stored in a public cloud, the request may be made to the cloud provider and the latter could even be prevented from notifying the customer. This can have severe consequences for customers. First, it preempts the customer from challenging the request. Second, it can lead to law enforcement having access to data from clients that are not under investigation (see, e.g., [34]). Such a scenario can occur due to the fact that service providers often store multiple customer's data on the same disks. In a cryptographic storage service, since data is stored in encrypted form and since the customer retains possession of all the keys, any request for the (unencrypted) data must be made directly to the customer.

Security breaches. Even if a cloud storage provider implements strong security practices there is always the possibility of a security breach. If this occurs the customer may be legally responsible. In a cryptographic storage service data is encrypted and data integrity can be verified at any time. Therefore, a security breach poses little to no risk for the customer.

Electronic discovery. Digital information plays an important role in legal proceedings and often organizations are required to preserve and produce records for litigation. Organizations with high levels of litigation may need to keep a copy of large amounts of data on-premise in order to assure its integrity. This can obviously negate the benefits of using a cloud storage service. Since, with a cryptographic storage service, a customer can verify the integrity of its data at any point in time (e.g., every hour) a provider has every incentive to preserve the data's integrity.

Data retention and destruction. In many cases a customer may be responsible for the retention and destruction of the data it has collected. If this data is stored in the cloud, however, it can be difficult for a customer to ascertain the integrity of the data or to verify whether it was properly discarded. A cryptographic storage service alleviates these concerns since data integrity can be verified and since the information necessary to decrypt data (i.e., the master key) is kept on-premise. Secure data erasure can be effectively achieved by just erasing the master key.

4   Implementing the Core Components

The core components of a cryptographic storage service can be implemented using a variety of techniques, some of which were developed specifically for cloud storage. When preparing data for storage in the cloud, the data processor begins by indexing it and encrypting it with a symmetric encryption scheme (e.g., AES) under a unique key. It then encrypts the index using a *searchable encryption* scheme and encrypts the unique key with an *attribute-based encryption* scheme under an appropriate policy. Finally, it encodes the encrypted data and index in such a way that the data verifier can later verify their integrity using a *proof of storage*.

In the following we provide high level descriptions of these new cryptographic primitives. While traditional techniques like encryption and digital signatures could be used to implement the core components, they would do so at considerable cost in communication and computation. To see why, consider the example of an organization that encrypts and signs its data before storing it in the cloud. While this clearly preserves confidentiality and integrity it has the following limitations. To enable searching over the data, the customer has to either store an index locally, or download all the (encrypted) data, decrypt it and search locally. The first approach obviously negates the benefits of cloud storage (since indexes can grow large) while the second has high communication complexity. Also, to verify the integrity of the data, the organization would have to retrieve all the data first in order to verify the signatures. If the data is large, this verification procedure is obviously undesirable. Various solutions based on (keyed) hash functions could also be used, but all such approaches only allow a fixed number of verifications.

4.1   Searchable Encryption

At a high level, a searchable encryption scheme provides a way to "encrypt" a search index so that its contents are hidden except to a party that is given appropriate tokens. More precisely, consider a search index generated over a collection of files (this could be a full-text index or just a keyword index). Using a searchable encryption scheme, the index is encrypted in such a way that (1) given a token for a keyword one can retrieve pointers to the encrypted files that contain the keyword; and (2) without a token the contents of the index are hidden. In addition, the tokens can only be generated with knowledge of a secret key and the retrieval procedure reveals nothing about the files or the keywords except that the files contain a keyword in common.

This last point is worth discussing further as it is crucial to understanding the security guarantee provided by searchable encryption. Notice that over time (i.e., after many searches) knowing that a certain subset of documents contain a word in common *may* leak some useful information. This is because the server could make some assumptions about the client's search pattern and use this information to make a guess about the keywords being searched for. It is important to understand, however, that while searching does leak *some* information to the provider, what is being leaked is exactly what the provider would learn from the act of returning the appropriate files to the customer (i.e., that these files contain some keyword in common). In other words, the information leaked to the cloud provider is not leaked by the cryptographic primitives, but by the manner in which the service is being used (i.e., to fetch files based on exact keyword matches). This leakage seems almost inherent to any efficient and reliable cloud storage service and is, at worst, less information than what is leaked by using a public cloud storage service. The only known alternative, which involves making the service provider return false positives and having the client perform some local filtering, is inefficient in terms of communication and computational complexity.

There are many types of searchable encryption schemes, each one appropriate to particular application scenarios. For example, the data processors in our consumer and small enterprise architectures could be implemented using symmetric searchable encryption (SSE), while the data processors in the large enterprise architecture could be based on asymmetric searchable encryption (ASE). In the following we describe each type of scheme in more detail.

Symmetric searchable encryption. SSE is appropriate in any setting where the party that searches over the data is also the one who generates it. Borrowing from storage systems terminology, we refer to such scenarios as single writer/single reader (SWSR). SSE schemes were introduced in [32] and improved constructions and security definitions were given in [23,16,19].

The main advantages of SSE are efficiency and security while the main disadvantage is functionality. SSE schemes are efficient both for the party doing the encryption and (in some cases) for the party performing the search. Encryption is efficient because most SSE schemes are based on symmetric primitives like block ciphers and pseudo-random functions. As shown in [19], search can be efficient because the typical usage scenarios for SSE (i.e., SWSR) allow the data to be pre-processed and stored in efficient data structures.

The security guarantees provided by SSE are, roughly speaking, the following:

1. without any tokens the server learns nothing about the data except its length
2. given a token for a keyword w, the server learns which (encrypted) documents contain w without learning w.

While these security guarantees are stronger than the ones provided by both asymmetric and efficiently searchable encryption (described below), we stress that they do have their limitations. In addition to the issues outlined above, all currently known constructions have deterministic tokens which essentially means that the service provider can tell if a query is repeated (though it won't know what the query is).

The main disadvantage of SSE is that the known solutions tradeoff efficiency and functionality. This is easiest to see by looking at two of the main constructions proposed in the literature. In the scheme proposed by Curtmola et al. [19], search time for the server is optimal (i.e., linear in the number of documents that contain the keyword) but updates to the index are inefficient. On the other hand, in the scheme proposed by Goh [23], updates to the index can be done efficiently but search time for the server is slow (i.e., linear in the total number of documents). We also remark that neither scheme handles searches that are composed of conjunctions or disjunction of terms. The only SSE scheme we are aware of that handles conjunctions [24] is based on pairings on elliptic curves and is as inefficient as the asymmetric searchable encryption schemes discussed below. Another limitation of some searchable encryption constructions is that they are only secure in a setting where the queries are generated non-adaptively (i.e., without seeing the answers to previous queries). Schemes secure in an adaptive setting (i.e., where queries can depend on the answers of previous queries) are considered in [19].

Asymmetric searchable encryption (ASE). ASE schemes are appropriate in any setting where the party searching over the data is different from the party that generates it. We refer to such scenarios as many writer/single reader (MWSR). ASE schemes were introduced in [11] while improved definitions were given in [1]. Several works have shown how to achieve more complex search queries in the public-key setting, including conjunctive searches [28,13] and range queries [13,31]. Other issues related to the application of ASE in practical systems have been studied [5,6,22], as well as very strong notions of ASE that can guarantee the complete privacy of queries (at the cost of efficiency) [12].

The main advantage of ASE is functionality while the main disadvantages are inefficiency and weaker security guarantees. Since the writer and reader can be different, ASE schemes are usable in a larger number of settings than SSE schemes. The inefficiency comes from the fact that all known ASE schemes require the evaluation of pairings on elliptic curves which is a relatively slow operation compared to evaluations of (cryptographic) hash functions or block ciphers. In addition, in the typical usage scenarios for ASE (i.e., MWSR) the data cannot be stored in efficient data structures.

The security guarantees provided by ASE are, roughly speaking, the following:

1. without any tokens the server learns nothing about the data except its length,
2. given a token for a keyword w, the server learns which (encrypted) documents contain w.

Notice that 2 here is weaker than in the SSE setting. In fact, as pointed out by Byun et al. [15], when using an ASE scheme, the server can mount a dictionary attack against the token and figure out which keyword the client is searching for. It can then use the token (for which it now knows the underlying keyword) and do a search to figure out which documents contain the (known) keyword.

Efficient ASE (ESE). ESE schemes are appropriate in any setting where the party that searches over the data is different from the party that generates it and where the keywords are hard to guess. This falls into the MWSR scenario as well. ESE schemes were introduced in [8]. The main advantage of efficient ASE is that search is more efficient than (plain) ASE. The main disadvantage, however, is that ESE schemes are also vulnerable to dictionary attacks. In particular, the dictionary attacks against ESE can be performed directly against the encrypted index (as opposed to against the token like in ASE).

Multi-user SSE (mSSE). mSSE schemes are appropriate in any setting where many parties wish to search over data that is generated by a single party. We refer to such scenarios as single writer/many reader (SWMR). Multi-user SSE schemes were introduced in [19].

In a mSSE scheme, in addition to being able to encrypt indexes and generate tokens, the owner of the data can also add and revoke users' search privileges over his data.

4.2   Attribute-Based Encryption

Another set of cryptographic techniques that has emerged recently allows the specification of a decryption policy to be associated with a ciphertext. More precisely, in a (ciphertext-policy) attribute-based encryption scheme each user in the system is provided with a decryption key that has a set of attributes associated with it (this is how the "credentials" in Section 2 would be implemented). A user can then encrypt a message under a public key and a policy. Decryption will only work if the attributes associated with the decryption key match the policy used to encrypt the message. Attributes are qualities of a party that can be established through relevant credentials such as being a PartnerCorp employee or living in Washington State.

Attribute-based encryption was introduced in [29]. Improved constructions are given in [25,27,10]. The setting where attributes can be distributed by multiple parties is considered in [17,18].

4.3   Proofs of Storage

A proof of storage is a protocol executed between a client and a server with which the server can prove to the client that it did not tamper with its data. The client begins by encoding the data before storing it in the cloud. From that point on, whenever it wants to verify the integrity of the data it runs a proof of storage protocol with the server. The main benefits of a proof of storage are that (1) they can be executed an arbitrary number of times; and (2) the amount of information exchanged between the client and the server is extremely small and independent of the size of the data.

Proofs of storage can be either privately or publicly verifiable. Privately verifiable proofs of storage only allow the client (i.e., the party that encoded the file) to verify the integrity of the data. With a publicly verifiable proof of storage, on the other hand, anyone that possesses the client's public key can verify the data's integrity.

Proofs of storage were introduced in [2] and [26]. Improved definitions and constructions were given in [30,14,20,3] and dynamic proofs of storage (where the data can be updated) are considered in [4,21,33].

5   Cloud Services

Secure extranet. In addition to simple storage, many enterprise customers will have a need for some associated services. These services can include any number of business processes including sharing of data among trusted partners, litigation support, monitoring and compliance, back-up, archive and audit logs. We refer to a cryptographic storage service together with an appropriate set of enterprise services as a secure extranet and believe this could provide a valuable service to enterprise customers.

Electronic health records. In February 2009, 19 billion dollars were provisioned by the U.S. government to digitize health records. This move towards electronic health records promises to reduce medical errors, save lives and decrease the cost of healthcare. Given the importance and sensitivity of health-related data, it is clear that any storage platform for health records will need to provide strong confidentiality and integrity guarantees to patients and care givers (see [9] for more regarding these issues).

Interactive scientific publishing. As scientists continue to produce large data sets which have broad value for the scientific community, demand will increase for a storage infrastructure to make such data accessible and sharable. To incent scientists to share their data, scientific societies such as the Optical Society of America are considering establishing a publication forum for data sets in partnership with industry. Such an interactive publication forum will need to provide strong guarantees to authors on how their data sets may be accessed and used by others, and could be built on a cryptographic cloud storage system like the one proposed here.

References

1. Abdalla, M., Bellare, M., Catalano, D., Kiltz, E., Kohno, T., Lange, T., Lee, J.M., Neven, G., Paillier, P., Shi, H.: Searchable encryption revisited: Consistency properties, relation to anonymous IBE, and extensions. In: Shoup, V. (ed.) CRYPTO 2005. LNCS, vol. 3621, pp. 205–222. Springer, Heidelberg (2005)

2. Ateniese, G., Burns, R., Curtmola, R., Herring, J., Kissner, L., Peterson, Z., Song, D.: Provable data possession at untrusted stores. In: Ning, P., De Capitani di Vimercati, S., Syverson, P. (eds.) ACM Conference on Computer and Communication Security (CCS 2007), ACM Press, New York (2007)
3. Ateniese, G., Kamara, S., Katz, J.: Proofs of storage from homomorphic identification protocols. In: Matsui, M. (ed.) ASIACRYPT 2009. LNCS, vol. 5912, pp. 319–333. Springer, Heidelberg (2009)
4. Ateniese, G., Di Pietro, R., Mancini, L.V., Tsudik, G.: Scalable and efficient provable data possession. In: Proceedings of the 4th international conference on Security and privacy in communication netowrks (SecureComm 2008), pp. 1–10. ACM, New York (2008)
5. Baek, J., Safavi-Naini, R., Susilo, W.: On the integration of public key data encryption and public key encryption with keyword search. In: Katsikas, S.K., López, J., Backes, M., Gritzalis, S., Preneel, B. (eds.) ISC 2006. LNCS, vol. 4176, pp. 217–232. Springer, Heidelberg (2006)
6. Baek, J., Safavi-Naini, R., Susilo, W.: Public key encryption with keyword search revisited. In: Gervasi, O., Murgante, B., Laganà, A., Taniar, D., Mun, Y., Gavrilova, M.L. (eds.) ICCSA 2008, Part I. LNCS, vol. 5072, pp. 1249–1259. Springer, Heidelberg (2008)
7. Bardin, J., Callas, J., Chaput, S., Fusco, P., Gilbert, F., Hoff, C., Hurst, D., Kumaraswamy, S., Lynch, L., Matsumoto, S., O'Higgins, B., Pawluk, J., Reese, G., Reich, J., Ritter, J., Spivey, J., Viega, J.: Security guidance for critical areas of focus in cloud computing. Technical report, Cloud Security Alliance (April 2009)
8. Bellare, M., Boldyreva, A., O'Neill, A.: Deterministic and efficiently searchable encryption. In: Menezes, A. (ed.) CRYPTO 2007. LNCS, vol. 4622, pp. 535–552. Springer, Heidelberg (2007)
9. Benaloh, J., Chase, M., Horvitz, E., Lauter, K.: Patient controlled encryption: ensuring privacy of electronic medical records. In: ACM workshop on Cloud computing security (CCSW 2009), pp. 103–114. ACM, New York (2009)
10. Bethencourt, J., Sahai, A., Waters, B.: Ciphertext-policy attribute-based encryption. In: IEEE Symposium on Security and Privacy, pp. 321–334. IEEE Computer Society, Los Alamitos (2007)
11. Boneh, D., di Crescenzo, G., Ostrovsky, R., Persiano, G.: Public key encryption with keyword search. In: Cachin, C., Camenisch, J.L. (eds.) EUROCRYPT 2004. LNCS, vol. 3027, pp. 506–522. Springer, Heidelberg (2004)
12. Boneh, D., Kushilevitz, E., Ostrovsky, R., Skeith, W.: Public-key encryption that allows PIR queries. In: Menezes, A. (ed.) CRYPTO 2007. LNCS, vol. 4622, pp. 50–67. Springer, Heidelberg (2007)
13. Boneh, D., Waters, B.: Conjunctive, subset, and range queries on encrypted data. In: Vadhan, S.P. (ed.) TCC 2007. LNCS, vol. 4392, pp. 535–554. Springer, Heidelberg (2007)
14. Bowers, K., Juels, A., Oprea, A.: Proofs of retrievability: Theory and implementation. Technical Report 2008/175, Cryptology ePrint Archive (2008)
15. Byun, J.W., Rhee, H.S., Park, H.-A., Lee, D.H.: Off-line keyword guessing attacks on recent keyword search schemes over encrypted data. In: Jonker, W., Petković, M. (eds.) SDM 2006. LNCS, vol. 4165, pp. 75–83. Springer, Heidelberg (2006)
16. Chang, Y., Mitzenmacher, M.: Privacy preserving keyword searches on remote encrypted data. In: Ioannidis, J., Keromytis, A., Yung, M. (eds.) ACNS 2005. LNCS, vol. 3531, pp. 442–455. Springer, Heidelberg (2005)
17. Chase, M.: Multi-authority attribute based encryption. In: Vadhan, S.P. (ed.) TCC 2007. LNCS, vol. 4392, pp. 515–534. Springer, Heidelberg (2007)

18. Chase, M., Chow, S.M.: Improving privacy and security in multi-authority attribute-based encryption. In: ACM conference on Computer and communications security (CCS 2009), pp. 121–130. ACM, New York (2009)

19. Curtmola, R., Garay, J., Kamara, S., Ostrovsky, R.: Searchable symmetric encryption: Improved definitions and efficient constructions. In: Juels, A., Wright, R., De Capitani di Vimercati, S. (eds.) ACM Conference on Computer and Communications Security (CCS 2006), pp. 79–88. ACM, New York (2006)

20. Dodis, Y., Vadhan, S., Wichs, D.: Proofs of retrievability via hardness amplification. In: Reingold, O. (ed.) TCC 2009. LNCS, vol. 5444, pp. 109–127. Springer, Heidelberg (2009)

21. Erway, C., Kupcu, A., Papamanthou, C., Tamassia, R.: Dynamic provable data possession. In: ACM conference on Computer and communications security (CCS 2009), pp. 213–222. ACM, New York (2009)

22. Fuhr, T., Paillier, P.: Decryptable searchable encryption. In: Susilo, W., Liu, J.K., Mu, Y. (eds.) ProvSec 2007. LNCS, vol. 4784, pp. 228–236. Springer, Heidelberg (2007)

23. Goh, E.-J.: Secure indexes. Technical Report 2003/216, IACR ePrint Cryptography Archive (2003), http://eprint.iacr.org/2003/216

24. Golle, P., Staddon, J., Waters, B.: Secure conjunctive keyword search over encrypted data. In: Jakobsson, M., Yung, M., Zhou, J. (eds.) ACNS 2004. LNCS, vol. 3089, pp. 31–45. Springer, Heidelberg (2004)

25. Goyal, V., Pandey, O., Sahai, A., Waters, B.: Attribute-based encryption for fine-grained access control of encrypted data. In: ACM conference on Computer and communications security (CCS 2006), pp. 89–98. ACM, New York (2006)

26. Juels, A., Kaliski, B.: PORs: Proofs of retrievability for large files. In: Ning, P., De Capitani di Vimercati, S., Syverson, P. (eds.) ACM Conference on Computer and Communication Security (CCS 2007). ACM, New York (2007)

27. Ostrovsky, R., Sahai, A., Waters, B.: Attribute-based encryption with non-monotonic access structures. In: ACM conference on Computer and communications security (CCS 2007), pp. 195–203. ACM, New York (2007)

28. Park, D., Kim, K., Lee, P.: Public key encryption with conjunctive field keyword search. In: Lim, C.H., Yung, M. (eds.) WISA 2004. LNCS, vol. 3325, pp. 73–86. Springer, Heidelberg (2005)

29. Sahai, A., Waters, B.: Fuzzy identity-based encryption. In: Cramer, R. (ed.) EUROCRYPT 2005. LNCS, vol. 3494, pp. 457–473. Springer, Heidelberg (2005)

30. Shacham, H., Waters, B.: Compact proofs of retrievability. In: Pieprzyk, J. (ed.) ASIACRYPT 2008. LNCS, vol. 5350, pp. 90–107. Springer, Heidelberg (2008)

31. Shi, E., Bethencourt, J., Chan, T., Song, D., Perrig, A.: Multi-dimensional range query over encrypted data. In: IEEE Symposium on Security and Privacy, Washington, DC, USA, pp. 350–364. IEEE Computer Society, Los Alamitos (2007)

32. Song, D., Wagner, D., Perrig, A.: Practical techniques for searching on encrypted data. In: IEEE Symposium on Research in Security and Privacy, pp. 44–55. IEEE Computer Society, Los Alamitos (2000)

33. Wang, Q., Wang, C., Li, J., Ren, K., Lou, W.: Enabling public verifiability and data dynamics for storage security in cloud computing. In: Backes, M., Ning, P. (eds.) ESORICS 2009. LNCS, vol. 5789, pp. 355–370. Springer, Heidelberg (2009)

34. Zetter, K.: Compay caught in texas data center raid loses suit against FBI. Wired Magazine (April 2009)

Extending IPsec for Efficient Remote Attestation

Ahmad-Reza Sadeghi and Steffen Schulz

System Security Group, Ruhr-University Bochum
{ahmad.sadeghi,steffen.schulz}@trust.rub.de   .

Abstract. When establishing a VPN to connect different sites of a network, the integrity of the involved VPN endpoints is often a major security concern. Based on the Trusted Platform Module (TPM), available in many computing platforms today, remote attestation mechanisms can be used to evaluate the internal state of remote endpoints automatically. However, existing protocols and extensions are either unsuited for use with IPsec or impose considerable additional implementation complexity and protocol overhead.

In this work, we propose an extension to the IPsec key exchange protocol IKEv2. Our extension (i) allows for continuous exchange of attestation data while the IPsec connection is running, (ii) supports highly efficient exchange of attestation data and (iii) requires minimal changes to the IKEv2 protocol logic. The extension is fully backwards compatible and mostly independent of the employed low-level attestation protocol. Our solution has much less overhead than the TCG TNC design, however, we also discuss integration with TNC deployments.

1   Introduction

Secure communication between computer systems is typically established using secure channel technologies such as TLS [1] or IPsec [2]. While these protocols ensure secure transmission of data and the authenticity of the communication endpoints, they do not provide any guarantee on the integrity of the involved endpoints. In many cases however, it is highly desirable to ensure the *trustworthiness* of the involved remote endpoints, i.e., to have assurance that the remote system conform to a defined policy.

The secure remote assessment of a remote system's state is called *remote attestation*. It involves a mutually trusted attestor to assure that the possibly compromised system cannot lie about its current state. The attestor vouches for the correctness of the *attestation data* transmitted in one or more *attestation reports*. The Trusted Computing Group (TCG), a large consortium of hard- and software vendors, recently approached this problem by publishing several vendor-independent specifications to introduce Trusted Computing into the mainstream computer industry [3]. The core component of the TCG Trusted Computing Infrastructure [4] is the Trusted Platform Module (TPM) [5], a security module specifically designed to securely store and report a record of system events. Many computer vendors already ship the TPM in Laptops and PCs today. The TPM

R. Sion et al. (Eds.): FC 2010 Workshops, LNCS 6054, pp. 150–165, 2010.
© IFCA/Springer-Verlag Berlin Heidelberg 2010

is already used by some commercial applications such as Microsoft BitLocker [6] which is a full disk encryption software delivered with some versions of Windows Vista and "Sirrix.TrustedVPN" that is VPN infrastructure utilizing a broader set of TPM functionalities [7].

In the TCG approach to attestation, also called *binary attestation*, relevant system events are reported to the TPM in form of measurements. More specifically, SHA-1 hash values of binary code that is about to be executed are *extended* (stored) into Platform Control Registers (PCRs) of the TPM such that the order and value of all measurements can be verified. By requiring each software component to measure any other component before executing it, a chain of measurements is created from the initial bootstrapping phase to the start of individual user applications. For each running application, this chain of measurements can be followed back to the first component started in the system, which is typically part of the platform firmware (BIOS). For remote attestation of the current system state, the local TPM simply signs the current set of recorded measurements (*TPMQuote(PCRlist)*) such that a remote peer can verify an authenticated list of measurements. There have been several enhancements to this architecture: Examples are the Integrity Measurement Architecture (IMA) [8] that implements a TCG-style measurement architecture in the Linux kernel or the concept of a Dynamic Root of Trust for Measurement, where a CPU extension is used to initialize a trusted system state that can serve as a new root of the chain of measurements [9], or property-based attestation [10,11]. Another enhancement is the concept of *Runtime Attestation*. While normal attestation typically only records the state of a program at startup, by measuring its program code and configuration, runtime attestation attempts to track or enforce the state transitions of running applications. Known approaches for such protocols either attest to a certain behavior that is enforced at runtime [12,13,14] or attempt to inspect the state of a running program to detect compromise [15,16,17]. Unfortunately, existing runtime attestation mechanisms are often tuned to specific use cases and only detect specific attacks. Several attack classes, for example using Return-Oriented Programming [18], are not yet reliably detected.

A major issue with the TCG approach to the concept of attestation is the large number of possible states that modern computer system can assume. Due to the complexity of todays operating systems and applications, it is very hard to create and maintain a list all valid states of a system. As a result, a lot of effort is invested into minimizing the Trusted Computing Base (TCB) of a system, i.e., the number and the size of components that must be trusted. Projects like NGSCB [19], EMSCB [20], OpenTC [21] and sHype [22] attempt to reduce complexity and enhance reliability and security of critical subsystems through modularization and isolation of the system components. In particular, an IPsec-based VPN service was recently presented in [23] that is optimized for security and low internal complexity. By using a microkernel-based operating system and by delegating all uncritical functionality like network card drivers and IP stack into isolated software modules, the so-called Secure VPN (sVPN) allows to create IPsec gateways with a small TCB. The obvious next step to enhance the security of such deployments is to combine sVPN with remote attestation. *Trusted Channels*, secure (i.e., authentic, integral, confidential) channels with remote attestation, have been considered in [24,25,26,27,28,29]. However, no proposal exists that specifically targets IPsec VPNs, much less one that focuses on simplicity and allows efficient exchange of remote attestation reports at runtime, i.e., while the associated secure channel remains operational.

Contribution. We propose an extension to the IPsec key exchange protocol, the Internet Key Exchange version 2 (IKEv2) [30], to allow for continuous exchange of attestation data while the IPsec connection is running. As will be elaborated in Section 3, the IKEv2 protocol regularly establishes its own secure channel as a control channel for the actual IPsec communication channels. We propose an extension to IKEv2 to use this control channel for the exchange of remote attestation reports. This design allows for efficient exchange of attestation data during connection setup and during the whole lifetime of any associated communication channel. Thus, our solution can modularly and flexibly handle the underlying attestation protocol supporting various attestation protocols and architectures, an mentioned above (e.g., binary, property-based, IMA, etc.), and is highly suited for future developments in remote attestation. Our extension is fully backwards compatible to IKEv2 and need only minor changes to the IKEv2 protocol logic. Last but not least our solution can be implemented with significantly less components and protocol overhead than the TCG Trusted Network Connect (TNC) framework, nevertheless, we also discuss how our extension can be incorporated into TNC deployments.

Outline. We identify the requirements for our trusted channel in Section 2. Following a short introduction to the IKEv2 protocol flow and message format in Section 3, we then describe the details of our extension in Section 4. We demonstrate the security of our proposal in Section 5 and discuss the relation of our work to the TCG TNC framework in Section 6.

2   Requirements for Remote Attestation with IKEv2

The security requirements for remote attestation protocols are not difficult to identify and many solutions are known [24,25,26,27,28,29,31]. However, as mentioned in Section 1, the practicability and scalability of available approaches is questionable. We feel that minimal complexity and modularization is the best available approach to achieve scalable trustworthy systems. By isolating critical functionality from the remaining software, the TCB of a system is expected to become less complex and thus more reliable and also more stable over time.

Our goal is thus to integrate existing and future solutions for binary, property-based or even runtime attestation protocols with system designs that feature TCBs with high modularity and low complexity, like the Secure VPN (sVPN) design presented in [23]. For successful integration, we thus identify the following technical requirements for our protocol extension:

R1 *Security.* The attestation reports must be cryptographically linked to the endpoints of the associated secure channel to prevent a compromised endpoint from relaying attestation reports of other parties (cf. [24]).

R2 *Privacy.* Confidentiality of transferred attestation messages can be a requirement depending on the usage scenario, e.g., to comply with a company's security policy.

R3 *Simplicity and Modularity.* As costs to validate and maintain software rise with its internal complexity, low software complexity is one of the main design goals of the sVPN architecture. To support this goal, the complexity added by our protocol extension should be minimal.

R4 *Efficiency.* For general usability and to limit server load, our extension must support the exchange of attestation data with minimal additional protocol overhead, message roundtrips and computational load.

R5 *Interoperability and Flexibility.* The protocol extension must be backwards compatible to IKEv2 and should support centralized management similar to TNC. As remote attestation is still a subject of research (cf. Section 1), the protocol must be extensible to support future developments in this field.

3   The Internet Key Exchange Protocol (IKEv2)

In this section, we briefly introduce the IKEv2 protocol specified in [30]. We focus on the general protocol flow and some details on the message format in order to give the reader a better understanding on the impact of the protocol extension presented in Section 4.

Overview. The Internet Key Exchange (IKE) protocol was designed as a general protocol for negotiation of Security Associations (SAs), i.e., of keys, algorithms and other attributes needed to establish a secure channel. Its most prominent application is the negotiation of *Child SAs* for IPsec, the Security Extension of the Internet Protocol. It is important for the reader to recognize that IKEv2 will always first negotiate the SA pair[1] for a secure control channel (*IKE SAs*). Within this control channel, SAs for the actual communication channels are be negotiated (*Child SAs*), refreshed or revoked without the need for further authentication. It is this control channel that we will use to transport the attestation reports.

Protocol Flow. Figure 1 depicts the basic message flow of IKEv2 and the required payloads in each exchange phase. The protocol works with pairs of messages, so-called exchanges. The first message of each exchange is sent by the *Initiator* and answered (possibly with an empty message) by the *Responder*. The standard IKEv2 protocol flow iterates through multiple phases, each of which consists of at least one message exchange with certain allowed payloads. The first phase, INIT, is used to exchange Diffie-Hellman public keys (K_i, K_r) and to negotiate attributes of the IKE SA pair ($SA1$). The resulting (unauthenticated)

---

[1] Since SAs are unidirectional, they are typically created and managed in pairs.

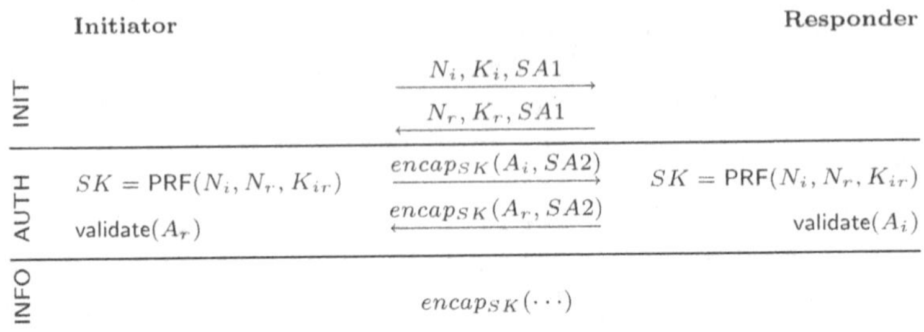

Fig. 1. Standard IKEv2 protocol flow with the IKEv2 Payloads for Diffie-Hellman key exchange (K), SA proposals for IKE SA ($SA1$) and first Child SA ($SA2$), nonces (N) and authentication of Initiator (A_i) and Responder (A_r)

shared secret K_{ir} is used to generate a session key SK that protects subsequent exchanges under the IKE SA ($encap_{SK}()$). The AUTH exchange is started in the second phase to mutually authenticate the endpoints of the IKE SAs and to negotiate a first set of Child SAs ($SA2$) that can be used for actual data transfer. After the authentication phase succeeded, the peers may use the established IKE channel secured by the IKE SAs to transmit additional notifications or to negotiate additional Child SAs for secure communication channels (INFO phase).

Message Format. An IKEv2 message consists of the IKEv2 header followed by a list of payloads, each of which may contain several substructures. Each of the IKEv2 payloads start with a *Generic Payload Header* that specifies the type and offset of the next payload in the message. This allows Initiator and Responder to add optional or non-standard payloads to any message without interfering with the main handshake. If not supported or unexpected by the implementation of the receiver, payloads are simply ignored by jumping to the next available payload. However, the sender may also enforce processing of non-standard payloads by setting a flag in that payload's Generic Payload Header. In that case, the receiver must produce a corresponding error message if the payload could not be processed.

The *Security Association Payload* (SA Payload) used to negotiate attributes of an SA is the most complex payload in IKEv2. Each SA Payload contains a list of *SA Proposal Substructures* that represent alternative choices for the SA to be negotiated. Each SA Proposal in turn contains a list of *Transform Substructures* that correspond to the available algorithms that can be negotiated as part of the SA. The Transform Substructures are categorized according to the available types of algorithms, e.g., algorithms for encryption, employed pseudo-random functions or authentication. Finally, each Transform Substructure can contain a list of *Transform Attributes* to signal the allowed parameters for the respective algorithm. To illustrate the recursive encoding of SA Proposals, Figure 2 (a) depicts an example SA Payload where the first SA Proposal structure proposes the use of Encapsulated Security Payload (ESP) with AES-CBC encryption and HMAC-SHA1-96 authentication. Note that the AES-CBC algorithm is supplied with a Transform Attribute specifying possible key lengths, while the key length of HMAC-SHA1-96 is implicit in the algorithm (96 bit [32]). Order and numbering of structures is used to efficiently encode preferences and available combinations algorithms. Also note that the type of an SA Proposal restricts its allowed Transform Substructures: While an SA Proposal for the Authenticated Header (AH) protocol only contains the authentication Transform, an SA of type IKE SA contains at least four different types of Transform Substructures, negotiating attributes for encryption, authentication, Diffie-Hellman group and Pseudo-Random Function (PRF). For a general introduction to IPsec we refer to [33,34].

4   An IKEv2 Extension for Remote Attestation

Our extension is implemented in three steps. First, we define an additional SA Transformation type *Remote Attestation* as an optional component of the IKE SA. This allows a peer to propose and select remote attestation as part of the negotiated set of algorithms. Secondly, we define a new IKE payload *Attestation Data* to tunnel the actual remote attestation data. Finally, we show how the actual attestation is securely linked to the IKE SA.

4.1   Remote Attestation in the IKE SA

As explained in Section 3, the IKEv2 protocol negotiates algorithms, key lengths and other attributes of an SA by formulating them in an ordered list of SA Proposal Substructures. For each SA negotiation, such a list is sent in an SA Payload by the Initiator. The Responder parses the SA Payload, selects a set of SA parameters and returns them in a corresponding response SA Payload. Figure 2 (b) and (c) depict the format of the Transform and Transform Attribute Substructures that are encapsulated in the SA Proposals.

Since the message format of IKEv2 is extensible by design and contains large ranges of identifiers that are "reserved for private use", we can simply define a new Transform Substructure of type Remote Attestation and use its Transform ID field to identify up to 2^{16} specific remote attestation protocols. This makes the class of remote attestation algorithms available to the IKEv2 ciphersuite negotiation and, in case it is selected by both peers, allows us to define the additional semantics in Sections 4.2 and 4.3.

Unfortunately, since such protocols can be quite complex and are still subject to research, they may exist in multiple variations. While the exact version can be negotiated within the attestation protocol, merging it with the SA negotiation step is more efficient and consistent. In particular it prevents the case where two parties agree on an attestation algorithm only to notice, multiple roundtrips later, that they do not support the same version of it.

We therefore also define a new Transform Attribute to encode protocol version numbers. Specifically, we use a simple Transform Attribute ($F = 1$ in

```
(a) SA-Payload              (b) Transform Substructure

+------------------------+           0 1 2 3 4 5 6 7 8 9 0 1 2 3 4 5 6 7 8 9 0 1 2 3 4 5 6 7 8 9 0 1
|SA-Payload              |           ---------  +---------------------------------------------------------------+
| +--------------------+ |  Transform | 0 (last) or 3 |  RESERVED     |        Transform Length       |
| |SA-Proposal #1 [ESP]| |  Structure +---------------------------------------------------------------+
| | +----------------+ | |  Header    |Transform Type |  RESERVED     |        Transform ID           |
| | |Transform #1 [enc]| |           ---------  +---------------------------------------------------------------+
| | |       [AES-CBC]| | |  List of   |                                                               |
| | | +------------+ | | |  Transform ~                    <Transform Attributes>                   ~
| | | |Transf.Attr. #1 | |  Attrs.    |                                                               |
| | | |  [key len=128]| | |           ---------  +---------------------------------------------------------------+
| | | +------------+ | | |
| | |Transform #2 [auth]| |  (c) Transform Attribute Substructure
| | |   [HMAC-SHA1-96]| | |
|_|_+----------------+ | |           0 1 2 3 4 5 6 7 8 9 0 1 2 3 4 5 6 7 8 9 0 1 2 3 4 5 6 7 8 9 0 1
| +--------------------+ |           ---------  +---------------------------------------------------------------+
| |SA-Proposal #2 [...]| |  Header    |F|     Attribute Type        | F=1: Attr. Value; F=0: Length |
| | ...                | |           ---------  +---------------------------------------------------------------+
| +--------------------+ |  If F=0,   ~               F=0: Attribute Value                          ~
| ...                  |  Payload   |               F=1: Not Transmitted                            |
+------------------------+           ---------  +---------------------------------------------------------------+
```

Fig. 2. Illustration of the recursive structure of an SA Payload (a). Details of the IKEv2 Transform (b) and Transform Attribute (c) structures as depicted in [30].

Figure 2 (c)) and split the resulting 16 bit attribute value field into two 8 bit version numbers. The two numbers V_{min} and V_{max} are interpreted as an inclusive range of acceptable versions or, if V_{min} is higher than V_{max}, as a negated version range. Similar to the Key Length Attribute, multiple Version Attributes can be included in a single Transform to encode intersections of version ranges. As an example, a Remote Attestation Transform with a Transform ID set to 1 might identify the property-based attestation protocol presented in [10] and an attached Version Attribute with $V_{min} = V_{max} = 2$ might identify the revised version of that protocol from [11].

This design allows an Initiator to propose an IKE SA with a remote attestation protocol in the same way it proposes different encryption or authentication algorithms. It can suggest multiple alternative protocols at once or make remote attestation optional by also including SA Proposals without a Remote Attestation Transform. The Responder has to select one complete set of parameters and express this set in its reply, or report an error that none of the proposals is acceptable. Selecting an appropriate Remote Attestation Transform thus imposes minimal overhead for the peers and is fully backwards compatible.

4.2   The Attestation Data Payload

Once a remote attestation protocol is negotiated, the messages of this protocol must be transmitted through IKEv2. To send these messages within the IKEv2 exchange, we have to define the layout and semantics of a payload structure that transports these messages. As creation and verification of attestation messages is a separate task that can be useful to many different applications besides IPsec, we assume that actual attestation messages are handled by some external *Attestation Service*, however, such a component could also be included into the IKEv2 server directly.

```
Attestation Data Payload (ADP)

Generic        0 1 2 3 4 5 6 7 8 9 0 1 2 3 4 5 6 7 8 9 0 1 2 3 4 5 6 7 8 9 0 1
Payload
Header        +--------------------------------------------------------------+
              | Next Payload  |C|  RESERVED  |          Payload Length        |
              +--------------------------------------------------------------+
Header        |                          Data Length                         |
              +--------------------------------------------------------------+
Attestation   |                                                              |
Protocol      ~                    <Attestation Data>                        ~
Data          |                                                              |
              +--------------------------------------------------------------+
```

Fig. 3. New payload to transport attestation messages through IKEv2

As shown in Figure 3, the Attestation Data Payload (ADP) consists of the Generic Payload Header, a Data Length field and an opaque Attestation Data field. To rule out possible problems with duplicated or maliciously manipulated attestation requests as well as privacy concerns, ADPs must only be transmitted protected by the IKE SA, after the last IKE_AUTH exchange succeeded. The opaque content of the payload may consist of multiple subsequent messages or logical channels, as for example supported by the TNC Client Server (TNCCS) protocol specified in [35]. The ADP defined here thus does not itself implement aggregation of multiple messages into a single payload but delegates this functionality to the Attestation Service (AS). However, to also support simple attestation protocols in an efficient manner the IKEv2 server may include multiple ADPs within a single IKEv2 message and thus transmit multiple queued attestation messages at once. In this case, the IKEv2 server is responsible for maintaining the order of Attestation Data messages. This order is already well-defined through the order of IKEv2 messages and the order of payloads within a message.

More sophisticated attestation mechanisms like property-based attestation may require the exchange of larger attestation messages than the maximum message size of a UDP datagram, $2^{16} - 1$ bytes or 64 KB, allows [10]. Following the example of [29], we thus include the separate Data Length field to allow an overall attestation message of up to $2^{32} - 1$ bytes or 4 GB to be fragmented over multiple ADPs. Since the order of IKEv2 messages and payloads within a message is well-defined and the secure channel provided by the IKE SA addresses packet loss and Denial of Service (DoS) attacks, reassembling such fragments is straightforward. Since IKEv2 messages are always exchanged in pairs, fragments are acknowledged with an empty IKEv2 message as defined in [30]. Defragmentation errors can be handled as IKEv2 payload parsing errors.

4.3 The Shared Attestation Key

As specified in [30], the peers involved in the IKEv2 exchange initialize an internal PRF for each of the two negotiated IKE SAs. Based on the exchanged nonces and the shared Diffie-Hellman key K_{ir}, the PRF is used to extract shared

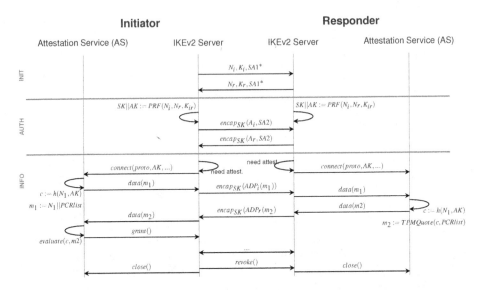

Fig. 4. Modified IKEv2 protocol flow from Figure 1 using new Transformation Structures in the $SA1^*$ payloads (cf. Section 4.1) and additional ADP payloads that carry attestation messages m_1, m_2 in the third protocol phase (cf. Section 4.2). The involved IKEv2 servers are ignorant of the attestation protocol details. They relay the messages of their responsible ASs and act upon any received policy decisions (cf. Section 4.4). A simple unilateral attestation protocol is used in phase three to clarify the distinct roles of AS and IKEv2 server.

fresh symmetric keys for each algorithm of the two IKE SAs. The length of the keys depend on the respective negotiated algorithms and their attributes and is computed accordingly.

We extend this definition to create a shared Attestation Key AK if a remote attestation algorithm is selected as part of the IKE SA negotiation. As shown in Figure 4, we define the extraction process as $SK||AK := \mathsf{PRF}(N_i, N_r, K_{ir})$. This is a simplified version of the extraction process defined in [30] which includes additional data into the PRF input and defines how to generate several keys for encryption, authentication etc. that we represent with SK here. Note that all the keys extracted in this manner are statistically independent from each other as long as the PRF is secure. Therefore, the order in which they are extracted is not relevant for their security. More importantly, this allows us to use the Attestation Keys (AKs) as input for attestation protocols that potentially disclose these values, e.g., when used as nonces in the TCG `TPMQuote()` operation.

4.4 Attestation Service (AS) Interface

As flexibility is one of our main goals, we do not intend to restrict our protocol extension to one or more remote attestation protocols. Instead, we delegate interpretation, verification and creation of attestation data to an external generic

Attestation Service (AS). In the following, we present the semantics of the Inter-Process Communication (IPC) interface between the IKEv2 server and its (implicitly trusted) AS. A sample communication flow for a unilateral attestation of the Responder is illustrated in Figure 4.

Connect(): After the last AUTH exchange succeeds, the IKEv2 server uses the *connect()* call to inform the AS that an attestation of the local platform or evaluation of a remote platform's attestation report is needed. The call to the AS contains (1) the negotiated remote attestation protocol and attributes (*proto*), (2) the symmetric key AK of respective IKE SA, (3) the public key certificates, if used to authenticate the IKE SA and (4) an identifier of the corresponding network channel. Note that in case of mutual attestation, the IKEv2 server will receive attestation requests and responses under the same IKE SA, and will thus also provide them to the AS under the same channel identifier.

Data(): This call implements the exchange of attestation data between the local AS and IKEv2 server. It contains the channel identifier and the opaque attestation message m that was received or is to be sent by the IKEv2 server.

Grant()/deny(): The *deny()* call can be used by the Attestation Service (AS) at any time to revoke all Child and IKE SAs associated with the connection. The *grant()* call informs the IKEv2 server that the attestation succeeded and the associated Child SAs can be disclosed to the respective subsystems. The signaling of error messages or alternative attestation exchanges is the responsibility of the involved ASs.

Close(): This call can be issued by both, AS and IKEv2 server to signal that the respective IPC connection and its associated IKE SA shall be closed. Any associated Child SAs are revoked (*revoke()*).

5   Security Considerations

In this section, we discuss the security of the trusted channel that can be established using the extension proposed above. Since our proposal is not restricted to a particular remote attestation protocol, we will use the unilateral challenge-response attestation shown in the third protocol phase of Figure 4 to show by example that our design achieves the following security goals.

G1 Based on the security of the IKEv2 secure channel and careful choice of the attestation protocol, the IKEv2 extension allows to establish a trusted channel that meets our security requirements **R1** and **R2** of Section 2.

G2 A compromise of the attested platform can be recognized in subsequent attestation exchanges if it is detected by the employed attestation protocol.

Assumptions. To show that **G1** and **G2** can be met with the protocol shown in Figure 4, we need the following additional assumptions.

A1 *IKEv2 Security.* As specified in [30], the IKEv2 protocol establishes a secure channel based on the fresh shared keys stream that can be extracted from the PRF in the second phase. After the second phase succeeded, this channel provides an ordered exchange of authenticated and encrypted messages secure against packet loss, replay and downgrade or version rollback attacks.

A2 *TCG PKI.* A Public Key Infrastructure (PKI) exists that allows the Initiator to validate the result of the attestation report of the Responder (e.g., result of `TPMQuote()` operation plus measurement log) to gain assurance that the report is authentic and executed by a mutually trusted attestor component.

A3 *Attestation.* The attestation mechanism (e.g., the `TPMQuote()` operation) on the Responder is secure in the sense that a *compromise* of the platform's system state is reflected in subsequent attestation reports. In this context, *compromise* denotes any change to a platform's state that violates the security policy of the Initiator.[2]

A4 *IPsec Security* The security of the IKEv2 channel (**A1**) extends to the associated Child SAs and how they are used within IPsec. More precisely, the communication channels that are associated with a secure IKEv2 channel provide a secure channel with the properties negotiated in the Child SA negotiation, according to the security policies of Initiator and Responder (e.g., authentication, confidentiality, partial sequence integrity as specified in [36].

Adversary. The adversary considered here is provided with two major attack vectors. Firstly, we assume that the network channel used by Initiator and Responder to communicate is fully under control of the attacker (**V1**). Secondly, we assume that the attacker can take control the platform of the Responder at any time, even while the trusted channel is already established (**V2**), with the exception that the mutually trusted attestor component of the platform remains integral.

V1 The control of the network channel allows the attacker to launch downgrade, version rollback, replay, injection and many more attacks on IKEv2 and associated communication channels. Due to assumptions **A1** and **A4** however, these attacks are all prevented by the employed secure channel protocols. The adversary is still capable of launching a DoS attack, however, this is always possible with the given level of control on the network and thus trivial. In a more selected DoS attack, the adversary may attempt to either prevent the exchange of attestation messages after the secure channel is already

---

[2] Our goal is to show that the proposed system design is sound *if* a sufficiently secure attestation protocol is used, i.e., the attestation protocol is out of scope. We thus use this definition to obviate any discussion of the attestation scheme, including the problem of runtime attestation.

established. However, as specified in Section 4.1, the use of attestation is negotiated in IKEv2 phase one and thus known and confirmed at both peers as soon as authentication succeeded. As specified in Section 4.4, the IKEv2 servers will thus wait for the decision of the Attestation Service to grant or deny the use of the actual associated communication channels. In face of selective DoS in later IKEv2 exchanges, the involved ASs can simply deny all further communication due to attestation timeout. As the attestation messages are only exchanged once the IKEv2 authentication phase succeeded, requirement **R2** of goal **G1** is met in case of **V1**.

V2 When taking over control of a platform (in our example, that of the Responder) the adversary is free to modify or inspect its state, including, e.g., long term authentication keys and session keys for the secure channel established via IKEv2. However, by assumption **A3** any such action is detected by the employed attestation protocol and reflected in subsequent attestation reports if it is relevant to the Initiator[3]. Based on the example attestation protocol illustrated in Figure 4, one can easily see how the Initiator can assure in this case that any subsequent attestation reports either report the compromise or fail the authentication:

P1 When requesting an attestation report (m_1 with requested property list PCRlist), the freshness of the response is assured by including a fresh nonce (N_1) in the request that must be used in combination with a one-way function when computing the response.

P2 The attestation protocol must be designed such that attestation reports cannot be spoofed. In our example, this is achieved by combining the TCG TPMQuote operation with assumption **A2**.

P3 The remaining option for the adversary is to reflect the request of the Initiator to an uncompromised third party to receive a fresh and valid attestation report to answer the original request. This is prevented in our example by including the shared Attestation Key (AK) into the attestation report using a one-way function $h()$. More precisely, the Responder hashes the nonce together with the shared Attestation Key of the associated connection and uses the result $c = h(N_1, AK)$ as additional input to the digital signature computed in the TPMQuote() command. With growing bit length of AK, the adversary has exponentially decreasing probability that the AK' used by the third party is the same as the AK used in the connection between Initiator and Responder, so that the attestation report is linked to the respective channel endpoint as required by **R1**. Alternatively, we also provide the certificate data used to authenticate the peers of the IKEv2 channel, thus providing additional ways to meet **R1**.

Finally, the adversary may choose not to send a response at all. However, the Initiator may simply signal the IKEv2 server to close the associated connections after some timeout to address this issue. Unfortunately, the violation

---

[3] In practical systems, the platform configuration may be divided into isolated compartments that prevent the instant compromise of the whole system, thus allowing the relevant components to detect the compromise.

of **R2** is always possible (and thus trivial) if the peer that validates an attestation report is compromised and the attestation protocol discloses the state it attests to. This can be solved using privacy-preserving remote attestation protocols like [10,11,37].

With appropriate choice of the employed attestation protocol, our design thus achieves the security goals **G1** and **G2**. The argument is easily extended to multilateral attestation and repeated attestation exchanges at runtime. In fact, any attestation protocol that follows the requirements in **P1** to **P3** meets our security goals under aforementioned assumptions **A1** to **A4** if only communicating using our extension.

6   Related Work - TCG Trusted Network Connect

The TCG work group for Trusted Network Connect (TNC) published several specifications on the integration of remote attestation into existing secure channel protocols. Their proposed TNC architecture [38] is a general framework for request, transmission and validation of attestation reports: Attestation data is exchanged between multiple *Agents* on the involved network endpoints. The messages are collected from the Agents [39,40], and encapsulated in the TNC Client Server (TNCCS) signaling protocol [35]. Two alternative protocols are specified to transport these TNCCS messages to the peer, one using the Extensible Authentication Protocol (EAP) framework [41] and one using a separate dedicated Transport Layer Security (TLS) [42] channel.

Several modern secure channel protocols support EAP, a protocol framework that supports many different authentication mechanisms as sub-protocols (*EAP methods*). The TCG thus defined the *IF-T Binding to EAP* [29] to describe a way to tunnel TNCCS messages within EAP methods (inner EAP method). Alternatively, if EAP is not available, the *IF-T Binding to TLS* [42] specifies how the TNCCS messages can be transmitted through a separate dedicated TLS [1] connection.

While the TNC framework is highly flexible and integrates well with EAP-based centralized network access control management, it fails to meet our requirements for simplicity and efficiency: The use of EAP imposes a significant protocol overhead in terms of roundtrips and relies on the secure configuration and implementation of multiple additional protocol layers. The additional layers introduced by the TNC framework aggravate this problem. Further, the design requires to repeat the EAP handshake and possibly reset the channel when additional attestation exchanges are desired after the channel is established (e.g., to report changes to the local policy of a peer at runtime). The IF-T Binding to TLS on the other hand requires a dedicated TLS channel for the exchange of attestation messages. This allows to exchange additional attestation reports at runtime, however, the cost of implementing and negotiating TLS as well as the associated certificate management is considerable. The approach is complicated by the requirement to cryptographically link the remote attestation reports to the secure channel. As we have shown, an extension of the IKEv2 protocol is the less cumbersome and more flexible solution.

6.1   TNC Compatibility

As explained in Section 2, the primary goal of our proposal is the efficient and flexible transport attestation messages over the IKEv2 protocol. From perspective of the TNC architecture, our proposal can thus be seen as a new *IF-T Binding to IKEv2* which leverages the existing secure channel.

In fact, our extension meets the requirements of the TNCCS protocol. Specifically, the requirements for *Chunking*, *Transport* and *Security* are met through transparent in-order transfer of messages of up to $2^{32} - 1$ bytes and the secure channel provided by the IKE SA[4]. Our protocol extension can thus be used to transport TNCCS messages transparently, however, with one major caveat: As our design leverages the secure channel provided by IKEv2, exchanged attestation messages are only protected during transmission between the two involved IKEv2 servers. Our protocol does not explicitly support the case where (part of) the Attestation Service is on a remote system. However, where such a design is desired, the existing IPsec implementation can be used to configure additional secure tunnels towards the AS.

7   Conclusion

In this work we proposed an extension to the IKEv2 key exchange protocol used in IPsec VPNs. We leverage the high flexibility of IKEv2 to implement the transport of remote attestation messages within the IKEv2 channel, resulting in a highly efficient and simple design. The result is particularly interesting for use with resource constrained devices or if formal verification is desired. As IKEv2 is designed as a generic key exchange server, our solution is also more versatile than previous TLS-based trusted channels. We are currently working to integrate our extension into the Turaya Secure VPN service [23], together with a simple attestation protocol to continuously report changes to the low-level IPC access control. The result can be used to build highly reliable VPN appliances based on the Turaya Secure OS, featuring a minimal TCB with a small set of security services on top of a microkernel [43,44].

References

1. Dierks, T., Rescorla, E.: The Transport Layer Security (TLS) Protocol Version 1.2. RFC 5246 (2008)
2. Kent, S., Seo, K.: Security Architecture for the Internet Protocol. RFC 4301 (2005)
3. Trusted Computing Group (TCG): Tcg homepage (2009), https://www.trustedcomputing.org
4. Trusted Computing Group: TCG Architecture Overview, v1.4 (2007)
5. Trusted Computing Group: TPM Main Specification, v1.2 (2005)
6. Microsoft TechNet: Bitlocker drive encryption technical overview (2008), http://technet.microsoft.com/en-us/library/cc732774.aspx

---

[4] If an insecure IKE SA is negotiated, by design the lack of security also extends to its Child SAs and thus to all communication channels.

7. Sirrix AG security technologies: Homepage (2009), http://www.sirrix.com
8. Sailer, R., Zhang, X., Jaeger, T., van Doorn, L.: Design and implementation of a TCG-based integrity measurement architecture. Research Report RC23064, IBM Research (2004)
9. McCune, J.M., Parno, B., Perrig, A., Reiter, M.K., Seshadri, A.: Minimal TCB code execution. In: Proceedings of the IEEE Symposium on Research in Security and Privacy, Oakland, CA. Technical Committee on Security and Privacy, IEEE Computer Society, Los Alamitos (2007)
10. Chen, L., Landfermann, R., Loehr, H., Rohe, M., Sadeghi, A.R., Stüble, C.: A protocol for property-based attestation. In: [45]
11. Korthaus, R., Sadeghi, A.R., Stüble, C., Zhan, J.: A practical property-based bootstrap architecture. In: STC 2009: Proceedings of the 2009 ACM workshop on Scalable trusted computing, pp. 29–38. ACM, New York (2009)
12. Alam, M., Zhang, X., Nauman, M., Ali, T., Seifert, J.P.: Model-based behavioral attestation. In: SACMAT 2008: Proceedings of the 13th ACM Symposium on Access Control Models and Technologies, pp. 175–184. ACM, New York (2008)
13. Peng, G., Pan, X., Zhang, H., Fu, J.: Dynamic trustiness authentication framework based on software's behavior integrity. In: 9th International Conference for Young Computer Scientists, pp. 2283–2288. IEEE Computer Society, Los Alamitos (2008)
14. Nauman, M., Alam, M., Zhang, X., Ali, T.: Remote attestation of attribute updates and information flows in a ucon system. In: [46], pp. 63–80
15. Loscocco, P.A., Wilson, P.W., Pendergrass, J.A., McDonell, C.D.: Linux kernel integrity measurement using contextual inspection. In: [47], pp. 21–29
16. Petroni Jr., N.L., Hicks, M.: Automated detection of persistent kernel control-flow attacks. In: CCS 2007: Proceedings of the 14th ACM Conference on Computer and Communications Security, pp. 103–115. ACM, New York (2007)
17. Baiardi, F., Cilea, D., Sgandurra, D., Ceccarelli, F.: Measuring semantic integrity for remote attestation. In: [46], pp. 81–100
18. Buchanan, E., Roemer, R., Shacham, H., Savage, S.: When good instructions go bad: generalizing return-oriented programming to RISC. In: CCS 2008: Proceedings of the 15th ACM conference on Computer and communications security, pp. 27–38. ACM, New York (2008)
19. England, P., Lampson, B., Manferdelli, J., Peinado, M., Willman, B.: A trusted open platform. IEEE Computer 36, 55–63 (2003)
20. EMSCB Project Consortium: The European Multilaterally Secure Computing Base (EMSCB) project (2004), http://www.emscb.org
21. The OpenTC Project Consortium: The Open Trusted Computing (OpenTC) project (2005), http://www.opentc.net
22. Sailer, R., Valdez, E., Jaeger, T., Perez, R., van Doorn, L., Griffin, J.L., Berger, S.: sHype: Secure hypervisor approach to trusted virtualized systems. Technical Report RC23511, IBM Research Division (2005)
23. Schulz, S., Sadeghi, A.R.: Secure VPNs for trusted computing environments. In: [46], pp. 197–216
24. Goldman, K., Perez, R., Sailer, R.: Linking remote attestation to secure tunnel endpoints. In: [45], pp. 21–24
25. Asokan, N., Ekberg, J.E., Sadeghi, A.R., Stüble, C., Wolf, M.: Enabling Fairer Digital Rights Management with Trusted Computing. Research Report HGI-TR-2007-002, Horst-Görtz-Institute for IT-Security (2007)
26. Stumpf, F., Tafreschi, O., Röder, P., Eckert, C.: A robust integrity reporting protocol for remote attestation. Revised version (2006)

27. Gasmi, Y., Sadeghi, A.R., Stewin, P., Unger, M., Asokan, N.: Beyond secure channels. In: [47], pp. 30–40
28. Armknecht, F., Gasmi, Y., Sadeghi, A.R., Stewin, P., Unger, M., Ramunno, G., Vernizzi, D.: An efficient implementation of trusted channels based on OpenSSL. In: Xu, S., Nita-Rotaru, C., Seifert, J.P. (eds.) STC, pp. 41–50. ACM, New York (2008)
29. Trusted Computing Group: TNC IF-T: Protocol Bindings for Tunneled EAP Methods, v1.1 (2007)
30. Kaufman, C.: Internet Key Exchange (IKEv2) Protocol. RFC 4306 (2005)
31. Trusted Computing Group: Subject Key Attestation Evidence Extension, v1.0 (2005)
32. Krawczyk, H., Bellare, M., Canetti, R.: HMAC: Keyed-Hashing for Message Authentication. RFC 2104 (1997)
33. Paterson, K.G.: A Cryptographic Tour of the IPsec Standards (2006), http://citeseer.ist.psu.edu/737404.html
34. Doraswamy, N., Harkins, D.: IPsec: The new Security Standard for the Internet, Intranets and Virtual Private Networks, 2nd edn. Prentice-Hall, Englewood Cliffs (2003)
35. Trusted Computing Group: TNC IF-TNCCS: Trusted Network Connect Client-Server, v1.2 (2009)
36. Kent, S.: IP Encapsulating Security Payload (ESP). RFC 4303 (2005)
37. Chen, L., Löhr, H., Manulis, M., Sadeghi, A.R.: Property-based attestation without a trusted third party. In: Wu, T.-C., Lei, C.-L., Rijmen, V., Lee, D.-T. (eds.) ISC 2008. LNCS, vol. 5222, pp. 31–46. Springer, Heidelberg (2008)
38. Trusted Computing Group: TNC Architecture for Interoperability, v1.3 (2008)
39. Trusted Computing Group: TNC TNC IF-IMC Specification, v1.2 (2007)
40. Trusted Computing Group: TNC TNC IF-IMV Specification, v1.2 (2007)
41. Aboba, B., Blunk, L., Vollbrecht, J., Carlson, J., Levkowetz, H.: Extensible Authentication Protocol (EAP). RFC 3748 (2004) (Updated by RFC 5247)
42. Trusted Computing Group: TNC IF-T: Binding to TLS, v1.0 (2009)
43. Pfitzmann, B., Riordan, J., Stüble, C., Waidner, M., Weber, A.: The PERSEUS system architecture. In: Fox, D., Köhntopp, M., Pfitzmann, A. (eds.) VIS 2001, Sicherheit in komplexen IT-Infrastrukturen, pp. 1–18. DuD Fachbeiträge, Vieweg Verlag (2001)
44. Alkassar, A., Stüble, C.: Die Sicherheitsplattform Turaya, pp. 86–96. Vieweg+Teubner (2008) (German)
45. Juels, A., Tsudik, G., Xu, S., Yung, M. (eds.): Proceedings of the 1st ACM Workshop on Scalable Trusted Computing (STC 2006). ACM Press, New York (2006)
46. Chen, L., Mitchell, C.J., Martin, A. (eds.): Trust 2009. LNCS, vol. 5471. Springer, Heidelberg (2009)
47. Ning, P., Atluri, V., Xu, S., Yung, M. (eds.): Proceedings of the 1st ACM Workshop on Scalable Trusted Computing (STC 2007). ACM Press, New York (2007)

Open Mobile Alliance Secure Content Exchange: Introducing Key Management Constructs and Protocols for Compromise-Resilient Easing of DRM Restrictions

David William Kravitz

Motorola Applied Research Center
David.Kravitz@motorola.com

Abstract. This paper presents an insider's view of the rationale and the cryptographic mechanics of some principal elements of the Open Mobile Alliance (OMA) Secure Content Exchange (SCE) Technical Specifications. A primary goal is to enable implementation of a configurable methodology that quarantines the effects that unknown-compromised entities have on still-compliant entities in the system, while allowing import from upstream protection systems and multi-client reuse of Rights Objects that grant access to plaintext content. This has to be done without breaking compatibility with the underlying legacy OMA DRM v2.0/v2.1 Technical Specifications. It is also required that legacy devices can take at least partial advantage of the new import functionality, and can request the creation of SCE-compatible Rights Objects and utilize Rights Objects created upon request of SCE-conformant devices. This must be done in a way that the roles played by newly defined entities unrecognizable by legacy devices remain hidden.

Keywords: DRM, key management, cryptographic protocol, certificate, PKI, secure authenticated channel, extended key usage, domain key, rights object.

1 Introduction

We are concerned with three major areas within the scope of Open Mobile Alliance (OMA) Secure Content Exchange (SCE) [5] that enable more flexible sharing of licenses (i.e., "Rights") to purchased content than that specified under the predecessor OMA DRM v2.1: (1) "Move" of Rights between Devices; (2) extension of the Domain construct to "User Domains" that are supplied with Rights Objects each of which can be created by any one of the multiple Rights Issuers authorized to do so; (3) "Import" that converts content originally protected by Non-OMA DRM mechanisms to content that can be consumed by SCE Devices in accordance with derivative OMA DRM Rights.

While we acknowledge that to ensure system viability it is necessary that there be efficient means for mutually authenticating entities, for designating revocation status of specific entities, and for effectively disseminating and acting upon that status information, we maintain that these tools need to be augmented by well-designed attention to "oblivious containment," i.e. to limiting the extent of damage that can be perpetrated by

R. Sion et al. (Eds.): FC 2010 Workshops, LNCS 6054, pp. 166–181, 2010.
© IFCA/Springer-Verlag Berlin Heidelberg 2010

Table 1. *Glossary* briefly explaining many of the terms referred to in this paper

Agent-to-Agent (A2A)	Communications directly between two SCE DRM Agents, where a Secure Authenticated Channel (SAC) is established using certified keys, e.g. RSA keys.
Authorized Domain	A group of devices under dynamic membership, where the "Authorized Domains" framework is referred to in [6].
Constraint	A restriction on a Permission over DRM Content.
Content Encryption Key (*CEK*)	Key used to encrypt content, where a DCF (DRM Content Format) file includes the encrypted content.
Content Provider	In the model of [6], Content Provider organizations/companies directly distribute to Content Managers within an Authorized Domain.
Device	The entity (hardware/software or combination thereof) within a user equipment that implements a DRM Agent.
Device Rights Object (Device RO)	A Rights Object that is initially targeted to a specific entity. Subsequently, the Rights Object may be allowed to be targeted to other entities to be consumed, serially or in parallel, independently of membership in a Domain or User Domain.
Diversified Domain Key (*DDK*)	An entity-specific key derived from a Master Domain Key (*MDK*). This construction is used in [1], but not in (Candidate) OMA SCE [5].
Domain	A set of v2.x and/or SCE DRM Agents that can consume Domain Rights Objects.
Domain Authority (DA)	The entity to specify the Domain Policy for a User Domain. The DA can convey entity-specific policy via User Domain Authorizations.
Domain Enforcement Agent (DEA)	The entity to enforce the Domain Policy on behalf of the Domain Authority. It may reside in the network as a service or in a user's device.
Domain Policy	A collection of attributes which defines the policy determining characteristics of the membership of a User Domain, as set by a Domain Authority, which a Domain Enforcement Agent will enforce.
Domain Rights Object (Domain RO)	A Rights Object that is targeted to a specific v2.x Domain [4]. The Rights Object can be consumed independently by each v2.x or SCE DRM Agent that is a member of the Domain.
DRM Agent	The entity in the Device that manages Permissions and Constraints for media objects on the Device.
DRM Content	Media objects that are consumed according to a set of Permissions and Constraints in a Rights Object.
Dual-Managed	A type of RO for which usability requires a Device to be a User Domain member and to be targeted by an RI, LRM, or another Device.
Heimdall	Entity that acts as a proxy for RIs for domain management [7].

Table 1. (*Continued*)

Import	To convert content and associated Rights derived from Non-OMA DRM-sourced data into a form usable by OMA DRM Agents.
Local Rights Manager (LRM)	An entity that is responsible for aspect(s) of Import. LRM functionality would typically be deployed within a home or other client-side device.
Message Authentication Code (MAC)	The key used to generate a MAC value is denoted by K_{MAC}. HMAC-SHA1 http://www.w3.org/2000/09/xmldsig#hmac-sha1 is a MAC algorithm that uses hash function SHA-1.
Move	To make Rights existing initially on a source Device fully or partially available for use by a recipient Device, such that the Rights or parts thereof that become usable on the recipient Device can no longer be used on the source Device.
Permission	Actual usage or activities allowed by a Rights Issuer or Local Rights Manager over DRM Content.
Rights	The collection of Permissions and Constraints defining the circumstances under which access is granted to DRM Content as a "license" for use.
Rights Issuer (RI)	An entity that issues Rights Objects to OMA DRM conformant Devices.
Rights Object (RO)	A collection of Permissions and other attributes which are linked to DRM Content.
Rights Object Encryption Key (REK)	A key used to encrypt a *CEK* (by applying, e.g., AES-WRAP http://www.w3.org/2001/04/xmlenc#kw-aes128); *REK* is also designated as K_{REK}; *Protected* K_{REK} (*PREK*) is derived from K_{REK} and *UDK* for Move via RI of User Domain ROs.
User Domain	A set of v2.x and/or SCE DRM Agents that can consume User Domain Rights Objects.
User Domain Authorization	A digitally signed data object that provides proof of authorization related to a User Domain.
User Domain Key (UDK)	A 128 bit symmetric encryption key that is used by a member of the User Domain; the key is User Domain Generation- specific.
User Domain Rights Object (User Domain RO)	A Rights Object that is targeted to a specific User Domain. Besides requiring membership in the User Domain, consumption may require being targeted to an SCE DRM Agent.
v2.x DRM Agent	A DRM Agent that is conformant to either DRM v2.0 or DRM v2.1 Technical Specifications [4].

entities that are *not* known to have been compromised. This is particularly applicable to the Secure Content Exchange scenarios, in that they are geared towards enabling considerable legitimate multi-device usage of purchased content licenses via communications both within and across content protection system boundaries. Consequently, Devices as well as other types of entities in SCE are provided with the means to make more comprehensive checks of one another. To this end, each entity conveys its basic roles through the key purpose(s) of the extended key usage (extKeyUsage) extension in its pre-provisioned X.509 (identity) certificate that contains the public key corresponding to its secretly held private key. "User Domain Authorizations" that are akin to attribute certificates are used to layer on User Domain associations, where Domains and User Domains will be discussed below. A crucial property of User Domains is that there is outsourcing of domain management consistent with multiple Rights Issuers and/or "Local Rights Managers" generating Rights Objects for use within the same User Domain.

SCE introduces into OMA DRM a home-placed Local Rights Manager (LRM) entity, the purpose of which is to facilitate Import of content and associated content-access licenses (i.e., Rights or Rights Objects) as the conversion point between an upstream content protection system and OMA DRM. An LRM can be restricted by means of pre-configuration of its certificate's key purposes to generating only User Domain Rights Objects, where the limitation on the number of member Devices concurrently belonging to the User Domain is managed by a User Domain Authorization-issuing entity, namely, a "Domain Enforcement Agent" (DEA) that is functionally distinct from the LRM. Thus, such an LRM can be effectively barred from issuing Rights Objects (ROs) that will be fully usable by all arbitrarily chosen initially targeted or Move-recipient Devices, since full Rights-usability requires such Devices to attain DEA-managed User Domain membership. A gray area develops, however, if a licensing/Trust Authority allows an LRM to generate User Domain ROs that can be shared outside of the User Domain, where (limited-usage) consumption by the recipient Device (under, e.g., a "lend" Permission or "adhoc-share" Permission) does not require User Domain membership. Some Permissions and Constraints on usage may be set within the RO by the LRM rather than being preemptively (and perhaps too restrictively) hard-coded into Devices. To limit abuse, the viral spread of revocation status information pertaining to Devices can be extended to also include information concerning the status of other entities, such as LRMs and Rights Issuers, which can be acted upon by compliant Devices as a condition of accepting access to Rights that have been digitally signed by a particular LRM or Rights Issuer (RI).

We will demonstrate how steps can be taken to mitigate the extent to which still-compliant Devices can be conned by unknown-compromised/rogue Devices into taking action that unwittingly escalates or mushrooms the amount of damage. Such mitigation is applicable even if the users of still-compliant Devices are dishonest in that they intend to knowingly take advantage of pirated content by accessing it at a discount relative to legitimate-acquisition pricing. Since this type of piracy does not rely on cloning of compromised keys into circumvention devices distributed to customers of the pirate, mitigation cannot be based on forensic examination of illegal/black-market devices. We focus on security mechanisms that have been agreed to by the OMA DRM Working Group for incorporation into the 'Candidate' SCE enabler Technical Specifications [5]. An important design criterion for the SCE key management that had to be met was unified treatment of LRMs and RIs, and of local- and back-end/network- Domain Enforcement Agents.

1.1 Organization of the Paper

In section 2 we will set the context of SCE in terms of related work. Section 3 discusses key management for Device RO, Domain RO, and backwards-compatible and non-backwards-compatible (i.e. RI & DEA "Dual-Managed") User Domain RO, as a preamble to the protocols presentation in sections 4 and 5. We conclude in section 6.

2 Related Work

2.1 Aspects of Revocation

The Authorized Domain Manager and Content Manager in [6] are somewhat analogous at a high level to the SCE constructs of DEA and LRM, respectively, but their approach – to countering the threat of Authorized Domain Manager compromise by having each Content Manager routinely report the identity of the Authorized Domain Manager to Content Providers so that they are equipped to suppress content delivery to any Content Manager for which its associated Authorized Domain Manager is known to have been compromised – is not applicable to a system as flexible as required by SCE[1]. DEAs are under oversight control by a Domain Authority (DA), which can stop its delivery of User Domain Authorizations for DEAs that it considers suspect.

SCE introduces another home-based entity besides LRM, namely, a local DEA, as represented by a certificate with domainEnforcementAgentLocal key purpose as opposed to domainEnforcementAgentNetwork key purpose that is reserved for service-provider/back-end- based DEAs. The DA-signed User Domain Authorization that associates a DEA to a User Domain identifies only up to User Domain Base ID, since the DA delegates responsibility of upgrading to later User Domain Generations in accordance with the DA's policy to the DEA.

The OMA DRM Working Group consensus was that a recipient Device relative to a Move is not required to already be a member of the User Domain in order to complete the Move, whether conducted directly, i.e. Agent-to-Agent (A2A), or via an RI. This decision precludes solutions such as [6] and [3] that are based on domain-specific "pairing" of Devices. On the other hand, the reason that certain User Domain ROs need to be Moved to a recipient Device in order for that Device to be able to decrypt the associated content is because such ROs require a recipient Device to be

---

[1] SCE must be able to handle the contribution of ROs by full-blown (network) RIs as well as by LRMs, where Content Providers relevant to LRMs exist in one or more upstream systems separate from the one that is specified by OMA DRM, and LRMs can gain access to content through an upstream device (such as a set-top box) rather than necessarily directly from an upstream Content Provider. ROs are not, in general, restricted to just those that are for a User Domain, which are the only type that are under DEA control. Furthermore, an RI may have simultaneous relationships with multiple DEAs. Thus, suspending delivery of content to LRMs or RIs is not a workable solution in general.

cryptographically targeted, so that User Domain membership is not sufficient to enable content decryption. In this paper, we will denote ROs that require both specific User Domain membership and Device targeting by an RI or LRM or by another Device in order to be usable as "Dual-Managed," rather than using the less descriptive SCE terminology of "<userDomain>-constrained" to refer to such ROs.

The device targeting aspect of Dual-Managed ROs implies the opportunity for revocation-status checking of the intended recipient Device prior to enabling decryption. Analogously to [6], if in SCE the only User Domain ROs that are issued by all RIs and LRMs that contribute to a User Domain are Dual-Managed, then Device revocation does not automatically precipitate upgrade to a new Generation of the User Domain. Because of the cryptographic targeting requirement, knowledge of the appropriate User Domain Key (*UDK*) is insufficient for the purpose of processing a Dual-Managed RO to decrypt the associated content. That said, there is still an advantage to upgrading the User Domain if since the last upgrade, one or more *non-revoked* Devices have left the User Domain and have not re-joined the User Domain, or have been reported as inoperable, lost or stolen, since such a Device may be unknown-compromised and thus may have retained *UDK*(s), possibly despite indicating it had left the User Domain. Since a recipient Device is not required to already be in the User Domain, a solution such as [6] that adds all removed Devices (revoked or not) to a (local) revocation list is unworkable here. Checking based on a current Certificate Revocation List (CRL) is conducted as part of Mutual Authentication and Key Exchange (MAKE) processing that initiates a Secure Authenticated Channel (SAC) Context between two SCE Devices.

It is true that even when working under an existing SAC Context that stores symmetric keys to handle encryption and integrity, and where the *UDK* is also a symmetric key, public-key- based signature verification is required in order to check User Domain Authorizations and the RI/LRM signature over the "<rights>" element. The security that this provides is greater, however, than that provided by the [6] system. Even disregarding the domain management aspects, in that system the Content Manager's or Content Provider's intentions with regard to Permissions and Constraints are not securely relayed throughout the Rights lifecycle in an independently verifiable way, and in fact [6] does not consider any such restrictions.

As in the conditional access- only (vs. full-DRM) approach of [6], [7] is "only concerned with the cryptographic components of ROs." SCE, however, has Devices, RIs, LRMs, DEAs and DAs check certificate key purposes, has recipient SCE Devices, RIs and LRMs check User Domain Authorizations, and has recipient Devices verify that state information offered by source Devices over an A2A SAC is consistent with any limits in the accompanying RI- or LRM- signed <rights> element. Since Device-to-Device transfer operations are no longer limited, as they were by OMA DRM v2.x [4], to non-cryptographic out-of-band exchanges of encrypted content and Domain ROs, there can't be wholesale prevention of damage caused by rogue Devices resetting stateful ROs or propagating usable illicit copies of ROs.

2.2 Separating Domain Management from Domain RO Creation

Vasanta et al. [7] offers three modes/options within a framework for offloading OMA DRM domain management to a new broker entity, as a proxy for RIs that the authors denote as *Heimdall* "after the Norse deity charged with guarding the bridge that links the realm of the gods with the realm of humans." Neither option 1 nor option 2 satisfactorily addresses backwards-compatibility with OMA DRM v2.0/v2.1: In option 1, through "Initialization" the Join Domain responses are prepared in bulk by the RI for the set of user-proposed members of the domain and made available to Heimdall in advance of actual Join Domain requests by Devices. This precludes a Device from receiving the expected nonce value in the Join Domain response, i.e., the same nonce value that the Device included in the Join Domain request. To get around this problem, in option 2 Heimdall registers with the RI to establish an RI Context (as do Devices) and subsequently establishes a Domain Context with that RI for one of the RI's domains in order to receive the Domain Key generated by the RI for that domain. Heimdall can then trigger a Device registered with that RI to join the domain, where the URL that Heimdall places in the trigger can supersede the RI URL that the RI had put in the Registration response that it had previously sent to the Device. Heimdall can use its knowledge of the Domain Key to generate a Join Domain response that matches the nonce in the Join Domain request sent by the Device to Heimdall in response to the trigger. But the Device will not expect Heimdall's certificate chain and a Heimdall-generated digital signature in the Join Domain response: These are inconsistent with the public key that the Device had locally stored in an RI Context as a result of Registration. Although Heimdall can place information in the Extensions field of the Join Domain response that proves its relationship with the RI, a standard legacy OMA DRM v2.0/v2.1 Device would not be equipped to interpret this information.

To get around this problem, in option 3 Heimdall is a full-fledged RI that acts on behalf of the "real" RI to meet that RI's domain policy guidelines and requirements. Although Heimdall is supposed to limit its activity to "re-branding" ROs that are initially generated by the "real" RI, by suitably replacing the nonces and signatures that appear in RO responses sent by the "real" RI to Heimdall, there is no means to cryptographically enforce this restriction.

The essential elements of the three options (1, 2 & 3) are depicted in [7].

This relationship between the domain manager and the Rights Issuer is backwards from the trust model that SCE considers appropriate, whereby in their interactions with RIs, legacy Devices are unaware of the Domain Enforcement Agent (DEA) that is responsible for managing the User Domain which appears to be a standard RI-managed Domain from the v2.x DRM Agent's perspective. Furthermore, the Heimdall model has the "real" RI generate the Domain Key and so, unlike SCE, does not support the situation where multiple RIs feed ROs into the same domain. As we discussed relative to option 2 of [7], only a single RI can feed ROs into a legacy domain because of the need to match the signature on the RO to the entity with which the legacy Device registered and subsequently joined the domain. We observe, however, that this does not preclude the design of a domain system for which knowledge of a single key is sufficient for *non-legacy* Devices to access all of the Rights Objects created by all of the RIs for a given Generation of a given domain.

In that vein, unlike [7], [1] does introduce the concept of multiple RIs feeding a single "OMA DRM" domain, but fails to address backwards compatibility with legacy (i.e. OMA DRM v2.0/v2.1) Devices. In order to deny knowledge to a Rights Issuer of the plaintext content corresponding to ROs that were submitted to the

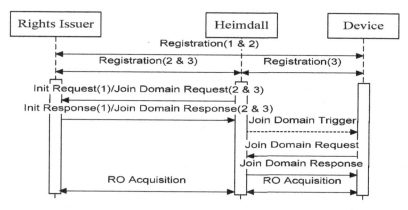

Fig. 1. Representation of basic elements of Heimdall options 1, 2, and 3

domain by another RI, [1] gives each RI an individually degraded form of the "Master" Domain Key (*MDK*). But it turns out that this key management technique adds unnecessary complexity, and, more importantly, if adopted by a system that actually does address backwards compatibility by handling legacy Devices that join a User Domain through an RI as well as SCE Devices that join a User Domain through a DEA, is less secure than it should be: It gives an RI the cryptographic capability to join v2.0/v2.1 Devices to a User Domain without the knowledge of the DEA that is responsible for managing that User Domain. This is because the RI has knowledge of the same degraded / "Diversified" Domain Key (*DDK*) that is used by v2.0/v2.1 Devices and SCE Devices to process the RO. The v2.0/v2.1 Devices acquire the Diversified Domain Key when they join the domain through the RI, and SCE Devices compute all Diversified Domain Keys from their knowledge of the Master Domain Key. Note that a v2.0/v2/1 Device can request the creation of User Domain ROs usable by it as well as by other v2.0/v2.1 Devices that joined the User Domain through that RI *and* by all SCE Devices that joined the User Domain through a DEA, and can use ROs created for these other v2.0/v2.1 Devices *or* for these other SCE Devices. As described later in this paper, the unintended situation of an RI being able to unilaterally accomplish User Domain Joins is remedied by the alternative key management architecture that the SCE Technical Specifications [5] ultimately adopted instead. The new key management architecture also does not interfere with hash chain utilization by v2.0/v2.1 Devices, while hash chaining relationships between consecutive Generations of Master Domain Keys, e.g. $MDK(j-1) = \text{hash}(MDK(j))$, are not preserved under Diversification such as the [1]-prescribed $DDK_i = 1^{st}$ 128 bits of HMAC-SHA1($PubKey_{RI\,i}$, MDK) for RI$_i$ public key $PubKey_{RI\,i}$.

Under the new backwards-compatible system an SCE Device has to register with an RI/LRM in order to establish an RI/LRM Context as a condition of requesting a User Domain RO directly from that RI/LRM, but, unlike a v2.0/v2.1 Device, not to simply consume a User Domain RO.

SCE needs to preserve the legacy architecture aspect of a requesting Device or other recipient Device not having to be in the User Domain in order to merely acquire User Domain ROs that are not Dual-Managed. This precludes the use of a Device pairing mechanism, even for SCE Devices. The DEA-signed User Domain Authorizations for RI/LRMs can be incorporated into the User Domain ROs to serve as proof of the RI/LRM's eligibility to generate User Domain ROs for the User Domain cited by User Domain Base ID and User Domain Generation. Even under imposition of the most stringent currency checking conditions required of the recipient Device relative to the RI/LRM's fitness to provide usable ROs, this can be accomplished asynchronously such that communications between the RI/LRM and SCE Device are not needed even if the RI/LRM's User Domain Authorization provided within the RO is now expired or of lapsed User Domain Generation and has possibly since been replaced with a new one. Such new User Domain Authorizations are available from the DEA by the same means by which an SCE Device acquires its own initial or updated User Domain Authorization when it first joins the User Domain or requests a subsequent refresh.

Hierarchical User Domain Authorizations (discussed next) and key purposes within the certificate profiles play a role in limiting what even unknown-compromised entities can get away with. In a multi-party interoperable deployment, it is up to a Trust Authority to contractually establish compliance and robustness criteria. In particular, certain combinations of key purposes within a single certificate may be disallowed, perhaps depending in part on specifics of the equipment into which the certificate is provisioned and the level of trust to be placed in that installed equipment environment. Additional key purposes may actually restrict the allowed functionalities, as is the case of an LRM vs. that of an RI. The separation of User Domain management from User Domain RO creation serves two primary functions: It enables a business model that supports independent RO contributions by multiple entities into a single domain, and it enables selective control of LRMs through the ability to configure key purposes in their certificates.

2.3 Domain Policy

The DA can indicate elements of domain policy via the User Domain Authorizations that it signs: The DA may perform oversight on how many compliant RI/LRMs in total can associate with the DEA by indicating that the DEA is required to gain and provide RI/LRM- and DEA- specific authorizations signed by the DA. The required or not-required status is signaled by the "RI/LRM authorization required" flag within the User Domain Authorization that the DA signs for the particular DEA relative to a specific User Domain. As a refinement of the layered approach introduced in [3], the DA may perform oversight on how many SCE Devices can associate with the DEA by having each compliant SCE Device check whether or not it is eligible to associate with the DEA, where the DA may require the particular DEA to gain and provide such Device- and DEA- specific authorization signed by the DA. The DA signals its intent by the "Device authorization required" flag. The DA can set whether or not it allows a particular DEA to handle collaborative joining (with RI/LRMs) of v2.x Devices to the User Domains it handles on behalf of the DA, by setting an "allow proxy join" flag in the authorization for the DEA that the DA signs. Each RI/LRM can self-police the number of v2.x Devices it allows to (proxy-) join a User Domain (taking into account any leave domain operations it has executed), even if the DEA would allow more joins. It may be appropriate to enable larger User Domain sizes if all ROs in a User Domain are Dual-Managed, which is important for corporate-level domains.

In order to make the SCE mechanisms introduced above and described in more detail in the following sections operate effectively, it is necessary that LRMs, DAs, DEAs, SCE Devices, and SCE-supportive RIs be able to distinguish SCE Devices from v2.0/v2.1 Devices. This is accomplished based on presence or absence of sceDrmAgent key purpose in addition to drmAgent key purpose in Device certificate.

3 Rights Object Key Management: Creation

Fig. 2 depicts the Rights Object Acquisition Protocol (ROAP) basic flow. The Device must be registered with the RI or LRM in order for ROAP to complete successfully.

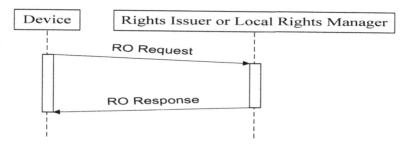

Fig. 2. RO Acquisition Protocol (ROAP) basic flow for use in requesting and delivering all of the Rights Object (RO) types discussed below

An LRM is differentiated from an RI by having at least one of localRightsManagerDevice and localRightsManagerDomain key purposes and not necessarily having rightsIssuer key purpose. An LRM with a rightsIssuer key purpose or an RI can generate Device ROs and Domain ROs for use by v2.x Devices. An LRM with a localRightsManagerDevice key purpose or an RI can create Device ROs for use by SCE Devices. An LRM with a localRightsManagerDomain key purpose or an RI can create User Domain ROs for use by SCE Devices. An LRM with a localRightsManagerDomain key purpose and a rightsIssuer key purpose or an RI can create backwards-compatible User Domain ROs. Note that an LRM without rightsIssuer key purpose is rejected by v2.x Devices.

3.1 Device RO Key Management

OMA DRM [4] employs an RSA-based key encapsulation mechanism to transport, from an RI to a Device, symmetric key material K comprised of the concatenation of Message Authentication Code key K_{MAC} and Rights Object Encryption Key K_{REK}, where K_{REK} is used to encrypt Content Encryption Key(s) (CEK(s)). Key derivation function KDF is used to derive key-encryption key KEK of octet-length $kekLen$ from integer Z chosen randomly in the interval $[0, m-1]$, where m is the Device's RSA modulus of octet-length $mLen$ and I2OSP converts a non-negative integer to an octet string of the specified length.

The target DRM Agent receiving C uses the Device's private key corresponding to its RSA public key $PubKey_{Device} = (m,$ public exponent $e)$ to recover Z from C_1, applies KDF to derive KEK, and AES-UNWRAPs to recover K from C_2, where:

$$KEK = \text{KDF(I2OSP}(Z, mLen), NULL, kekLen) ; \tag{1}$$

$$C_2 = \text{AES-WRAP}(KEK, K) = \text{AES-WRAP}(KEK, K_{MAC} \mid K_{REK}) ; \tag{2}$$

$$C_1 = \text{I2OSP(RSA.ENCRYPT}(PubKey_{Device}, Z), mLen) = Z^e \bmod m ; \tag{3}$$

$$\text{Set } C = C_1 \mid C_2. \tag{4}$$

K_{MAC} is used to handle key confirmation, where the information that is MAC'ed using K_{MAC} includes, in particular, the identity of the RI and C. Thus, an RI, even if rogue, cannot unilaterally reissue another Rights Issuer's ROs for successful use by another (or even the same) Device. A rogue RI could substitute a known K_{MAC}' value to use as a MAC key and a known Z' and corresponding KEK' and C_1' values, but cannot successfully substitute use of a known K_{REK}' value in computing C_2' for KEK', K_{MAC}' and K_{REK}'. The original K_{REK} must be used in C_2' if it is to be consistent with the existing supplied AES-WRAP of CEK(s) under K_{REK}. Certain critical elements of the RO, such as AES-WRAP of CEK(s) under K_{REK} and the permissions and constraints on usage, are signed by the RI. Even a rogue DRM Agent/Device cannot forge or alter these signatures because a Device is generally not legitimately provisioned with a private key corresponding to an RI certificate.

The construction above for an RI targeting a particular Device by using its certified RSA public key was designed with the *intent* that in order for any other Device to legitimately gain access to the plaintext content it would have to be similarly individually targeted by an RI that is licensed to create ROs for that particular content. This *intent* has not been fully met: For non-ROAP delivery of Device ROs, i.e., where the dedicated protocol with overall-message signature is not used, reliance on the RI's signature over the <rights> element is problematic because the signed data is not specific to the target Device. An unknown-compromised Device that has knowledge of K_{REK} can generate an acceptable MAC value for a forged C directed toward any Device chosen by the attacker. If a given RI generates only Device ROs, successful rerouting of these ROs can be prevented if each RO is indirectly bound to a user or Device by identifying under the RI-generated signature over the <rights> element something uniquely associated with a user or Device, such as a subscriber ID that can be confirmed via presence of an appropriate SIM card. This is not practical, however, for ROs for which such associations are not known at the time of generating the ROs. A classic case is that of Domain ROs (discussed next) where Domain membership changes over time through Domain Join or Domain Leave by Devices. We note that the RO rerouting attack is entirely thwarted for SCE Devices [5].

3.2 Domain RO Key Management

To deliver a Domain Key K_D to a Device during a v2.x Domain Join, K_{REK} is replaced by K_D in the Device RO formula above, so that transported $K = K_{MAC} \mid K_D$.

Then each Domain RO is delivered with $C = \text{AES-WRAP}(K_D, K_{MAC} | K_{REK})$ rather than with $C = C_1 | C_2$ as in the Device RO case above.

3.3 Backwards-Compatible User Domain RO Key Management

Thus there is a bandwidth-efficient means to enable RI/LRM-generation of User Domain ROs for use by v2.x and SCE Devices that denies the RI/LRM knowledge of the (Generation-specific) *UDK*, so that the DEA needs to get involved in the (Proxy-) Domain Join of v2.x Devices. The DEA also supplies the RI or LRM with an RI/LRM-specific DEA-signed User Domain Authorization that is verified by SCE Devices as a condition of accepting a User Domain RO. SCE Devices are aware that the *UDK* is usable across RI/LRMs while legacy v2.x Devices are not.

Table 2. Information supplied to RI or LRM when it is associated with a User Domain

Key	Description
K_{MAC}, K_{REK}	DEA-generated keys for RI/LRM-specific creation of User Domain ROs; AES-WRAP(UDK, $K_{MAC}|K_{REK}$), as provided by DEA, is incorporated by RI/LRM into the ROs.
$K_{MAC\text{-}Leave}$	DEA-generated MAC key used by specific RI/LRM to trigger Domain Leave of a v2.x Device; DEA-provided AES-WRAP(UDK, $K_{MAC\text{-}Leave}$) is incorporated by RI/LRM into Domain Leave trigger.

3.4 Dual-Managed RO Key Management -- For SCE Devices Only

The Device RO structure is reused, but with an extension in the ROAP RO request message that carries the Device's User Domain Authorization. Unlike in the backwards-compatible User Domain RO case, K_{REK}(s) must be unique per content, but that does not cause a bandwidth problem since these K_{REK}(s) are RI/LRM-generated.

The requirement for the Device to already be in the User Domain at the time of initial creation/delivery of a Dual-Managed RO can be advantageous in Import. An LRM can thus ensure that none of the potentially limited number of copies of ROs per Content ID is wasted by not being usable, as bounded through coordination with or proclamation by an upstream system. For security reasons, a non- User Domain member Device cannot make a successful outbound A2A Move or Move via RI.

4 Dual-Managed RO Key Management: Move

The source SCE Device in an A2A Move RO transaction or Move-via-RI protocol run may have previously received the RO as an original recipient from an RI or LRM, as an A2A recipient, or as a Move-via-RI recipient.

4.1 The A2A Move RO Transaction

Since a compliant Move-source Device uses the latest-Generation *UDK*, a recipient Device that has left the User Domain during an earlier Generation will not be able to use the RO unless it rejoins the User Domain. A Device that has left the User Domain will not be able to successfully source the RO to a compliant recipient Device that is already in a later Generation of the User Domain at the time of performing Move. The inclusion of the source Device's User Domain Authorization enables an *immediate* test by the recipient Device of the suitability of the source Device even if the recipient Device is not in the User Domain when performing Move. Fig. 3 depicts Move. Mutual Authentication and Key Exchange (MAKE) is necessary only if a Secure Authenticated Channel between the two Devices has not already been established.

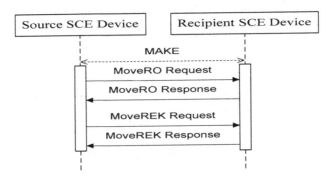

Fig. 3. Flow for conducting Agent-to-Agent (A2A) Move RO transaction, including delivery of the Rights Object Encryption Key (*REK*) if MoveRO Response message indicates 'success'

4.2 The Move via RI Protocol

Following a successful run of the Move via RI protocol with a source SCE Device, that same RI (equipped with a User Domain Authorization) generates and delivers ROs using ROAP to a recipient SCE Device. Only SCE Devices currently in the User Domain (as proven to the RI, and vice-versa) are permitted to request a Move via RI, and only SCE Devices (as evident from the Device certificate) are permitted to receive any resultant Dual-Managed ROs. Fig. 4 depicts Move via RI at a high level.

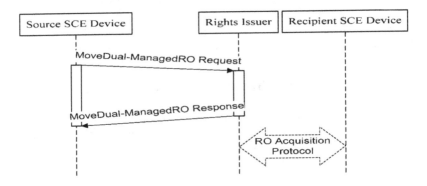

Fig. 4. Basic flow for Move via RI of Dual-Managed ROs, and ensuing RO generation and delivery if MoveDual-ManagedRO Response message indicates 'success'

Let *Hash16* denote the first 16 bytes of the SHA-1 hash of the "<moveIndication>" element (within an RO for which Move is requested by the Device) that lists the RO-originating RI/LRM, and the RIs (and RI URLs) that it authorizes to perform Move.

Let *PREK* denote *Protected K_{REK}*: $PREK$ = AES-WRAP(UDK, K_{REK} XOR *Hash16*).

$C = C_1 | C_2$ is transmitted from the source SCE Device to the RI, where:

KEK = KDF(I2OSP(Z, *mLen*), *NULL*, *kekLen*), where *kekLen* is set to 16 (128 bits), and *mLen* is the length in octets of the RI's RSA modulus m;

C_2 = AES-WRAP(KEK, K_{MAC} | $PREK_1$ | ... | $PREK_n$) (n is number of ROs Moved);

C_1 = I2OSP(RSA.ENCRYPT($PubKey_{RI}$, Z), *mLen*).

After receiving C, RI splits it into C_1 and C_2 and RSA-decrypts C_1, yielding Z = RSA.DECRYPT($PrivKey_{RI}$, c_1) = c_1^d mod m for c_1 = OS2IP(C_1) and d = RSA private exponent, where OS2IP converts an octet string to a non-negative integer.

Using Z, RI recovers KEK, and then AES-UNWRAPs C_2 to yield K_{MAC} and n $PREK_i$:

KEK = KDF(I2OSP(Z, *mLen*), *NULL*, *kekLen*);

K_{MAC} | $PREK_1$ | ... | $PREK_n$ = AES-UNWRAP(KEK, C_2).

When creating an RO for the recipient SCE Device to be delivered using ROAP with an extension that signifies it was generated following a run of the Move via RI protocol, the RI uses *PREK* in place of K_{REK} in C_2 = AES-WRAP(KEK, K_{MAC} | K_{REK}). The Device, once it is a User Domain member, uses UDK to AES-UNWRAP *PREK*, and calculates *Hash16* from RO's <moveIndication> element to recover K_{REK}.

The Move-via-RI functionality is constructed such that rather than relying on "transitive trust," an RI requested by a Device to Move a Dual-Managed RO can first consider the extent to which it trusts other RIs also authorized to Move the RO by the RI/LRM that originated the RO, as evident by the static <moveIndication> element. The construction ensures that an RI cannot successfully add or erase its ID from this element of the RO or provide a usable version of the RO to a legacy v2.x Device. The RI does not learn the RO encryption key, K_{REK}, since it does not have knowledge of UDK needed to AES-UNWRAP *PREK*.

5 Device RO Creation *Revisited*: RI as LRM Proxy

In order to enable v2.x Devices to reap some benefit from the new Import functionality, an LRM can create Device ROs with RI assistance, where the RI can control on an LRM-specific basis the range of Devices that can use these ROs, as first proposed in Method 2 of [2]. The LRM-RI Create Device RO protocol follows:

For the ith of n ROs to be created jointly by the LRM and RI, the LRM generates:

KEK_i = KDF(I2OSP(Z_i, *mLen_{Device}*), *NULL*, *kekLen*);

Ci_2 = AES-WRAP(KEK_i, K_{MAC} | $K_{REK\,i}$);

Ci_1 = I2OSP(RSA.ENCRYPT($PubKey_{Device}$, Z_i), *mLen_{Device}*);

Set $Ci = Ci_1 | Ci_2$.

For the LRM to securely transmit K_{MAC} and calculated Ci values to the RI (for n Imported ROs), the LRM sends $C = C_1 \mid C_2$, where:

$KEK = \text{KDF}(\text{I2OSP}(Z, mLen_{RI}), \textbf{NULL}, kekLen)$;

$K = K_{MAC} \mid C1 \mid ... \mid Cn$;

$C_2 = \text{AES-WRAP}(KEK, K)$;

$C_1 = \text{I2OSP}(\text{RSA.ENCRYPT}(PubKey_{RI}, Z), mLen_{RI})$.

After receiving C, the RI splits it into C_1 and C_2 and decrypts C_1 using its private key, yielding $Z = \text{RSA.DECRYPT}(PrivKey_{RI}, c_1)$ for $c_1 = \text{OS2IP}(C_1)$.

Using Z, RI recovers KEK in order to AES-UNWRAP C_2 to yield K_{MAC} and n Ci:

$KEK = \text{KDF}(\text{I2OSP}(Z, mLen_{RI}), \textbf{NULL}, kekLen)$;

$K_{MAC} \mid C1 \mid ... \mid Cn = \text{AES-UNWRAP}(KEK, C_2)$.

The recovered K_{MAC} and Ci values are used by the RI in standard ROAP delivery. The RI does not gain knowledge of any $K_{REK\ i}$.

Although an LRM can digitally sign a request to an RI, an LRM cannot successfully hijack another LRM's requests to the RI because the MAC key, K_{MAC}, that is used to authenticate request information that includes the LRM ID is sent encrypted under the RI's public key and must match the K_{MAC} delivered from the LRM to the RI under the Device's public key in order for the Device to ultimately accept the RO and use a $K_{REK\ i}$ that is concatenated with K_{MAC} to recover CEK(s). Simple replay of LRM's requests will fail because of replay cache.

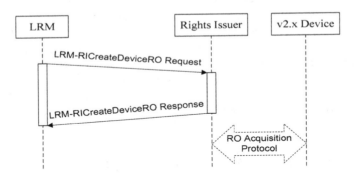

Fig. 5. Basic flow for request and response between LRM and RI, and ensuing RO creation and delivery if LRM-RICreateDeviceRO Response message indicates 'success'

6   Conclusions

We have demonstrated extension of the PKI-based rights management to include peer-level secure authenticated channels and forwarded signatures accompanied by associated certificate chains. Hierarchical User Domain Authorizations are issued in addition to long-term identity certificates. SCE Devices can by means of RO re-targeting increase the number of Devices that utilize certain ROs, while v2.x Devices cannot target or be directly targeted by other Devices. v2.x Devices and SCE Devices co-exist in the enhanced system, and certain aspects of the new Import and User Domain functionalities are, by construction, accessible to v2.x Devices.

References

1. Koster, P., Montaner, J., Koraichi, N., Iacob, S.: Introduction of the Domain Issuer in OMA DRM. In: 4th IEEE Consumer Communications and Networking Conference, pp. 940–944. IEEE Press, Los Alamitos (2007)
2. Kravitz, D.W., Messerges, T.S.: Achieving Media Portability through Local Content Translation and End-to-End Rights Management. In: 5th ACM DRM Workshop, pp. 27–36. ACM Press, New York (2005)
3. Kravitz, D.W., Messerges, T.S.: Hybrid Peer-to-Peer/Network-Based Rights Transfer in the Presence of Unknown Compromises. In: 5th IEEE Consumer Communications and Networking Conference, pp. 1065–1069. IEEE Press, Los Alamitos (2008)
4. Open Mobile Alliance Digital Rights Management (Approved Release) v2.0.2 and v2.1, http://www.openmobilealliance.org/Technical/released_enablers.aspx
5. Open Mobile Alliance Secure Content Exchange (Candidate Release) v1.0, http://www.openmobilealliance.org/Technical/released_enablers.aspx
6. Popescu, B.C., Crispo, B., Tanenbaum, A.S., Kamperman, F.L.A.J.: A DRM Security Architecture for Home Networks. In: 4th ACM DRM Workshop, pp. 1–10. ACM Press, New York (2004)
7. Vasanta, H., Safavi-Naini, R., Sheppard, N.P., Surminen, J.M.: Distributed Management of OMA DRM Domains. In: Lee, J.-K., Yi, O., Yung, M. (eds.) WISA 2006. LNCS, vol. 4298, pp. 237–251. Springer, Heidelberg (2007)

How to Evaluate the Security of Real-Life Cryptographic Protocols?
The Cases of ISO/IEC 29128 and CRYPTREC

Shin'ichiro Matsuo[1], Kunihiko Miyazaki[2], Akira Otsuka[3], and David Basin[4]

[1] NICT
[2] Hitachi Ltd.
[3] AIST
[4] ETH Zurich

Abstract. Governments and international standards bodies have established certification procedures for security-critical technologies, such as cryptographic algorithms. Such standards have not yet been established for cryptographic protocols and hence it is difficult for users of these protocols to know whether they are trustworthy. This is a serious problem as many protocols proposed in the past have failed to achieve their stated security properties. In this paper, we propose a framework for certifying cryptographic protocols. Our framework specifies procedures for both protocol designers and evaluators for certifying protocols with respect to three different assurance levels. This framework is being standardized as ISO/IEC 29128 in ISO/IEC JTC1 SC27/WG3, in which three of the authors are project co-editors. As a case study in the application of our proposal, we also present the plan for the open evaluation of entity-authentication protocols within the CRYPTREC project.

Keyword: Cryptographic protocols, formal verification, standardization.

1 Introduction

1.1 Background

Over the past 20 years, many security technologies have been developed using cryptographic protocols. For example, the widely deployed Secure Socket Layer (SSL) protocol, uses a combination of digital signatures, public key cryptography, and symmetric key cryptography. From the viewpoint of users of such security technologies, a major concern is whether they should trust their security.

For cryptographic algorithms, such as block ciphers, stream ciphers, hash functions, and public key encryption, open competitions are held by NIST, NESSIE, ECRYPT, and CRYPTREC. Thanks to such procedures, national and international organizations can select standard cryptographic algorithms and have confidence in the trustworthiness of the results. Moreover, governments can make recommendations for particular application domains, such as e-government or military systems, where algorithms are selected that meet the domain-specific

R. Sion et al. (Eds.): FC 2010 Workshops, LNCS 6054, pp. 182–194, 2010.
© IFCA/Springer-Verlag Berlin Heidelberg 2010

requirements. Again, these recommendations provide a starting point for companies and administrations building trustworthy systems.

In contrast to cryptographic *algorithms*, analogous evaluation procedures do not exist for cryptographic *protocols*. In practice, cryptographic protocols are often designed in industry by inexperienced engineers, who lack a deep knowledge of cryptography. Even for protocols that make their way to international standards, few cryptographers participate in the review process. The resulting protocols are often flawed, e.g., the vulnerabilities in the international standard ISO/IEC 11770-2 key-establishment protocol.

We propose here standardization activities for cryptographic protocols, analogous to those for cryptographic algorithms. Namely, a clearly defined evaluation process should be used where the evaluation results are certified by national and international organizations. By defining a clear evaluation process based on scientifically well-founded methods, the resulting protocols can be widely trusted and used as building blocks for security-critical systems. This would result in a substantial improvement over the current situation, where protocols are proposed and standardized (e.g., within organizations like the IETF and IEEE) without such a process. Moreover, once this process is standardized as a third party certification scheme, such as the Common Criteria or ISO/IEC 15408, newly developed cryptographic protocols may be certified to be secure under this process. This opens up the playing field for developing certified, internationally-recognized security protocols that can be widely accepted and deployed.

The starting points for our proposal are the different formal methods that currently exist for (symbolic) protocol verification. Experience shows that existing verification methods and associated tools can detect many flaws in standard cryptographic protocols. In doing so, the results can be used to improve the quality of the resulting protocols and ultimately to prove their correctness. These tools have become increasingly mature in recent years and can now provide a fine-grained analysis of the security of cryptographic protocols, which is lacking in less-principled engineering methods.

We believe such tools are now ready to be used to aid the design and, in particular, the certification of cryptographic protocols. Hence we propose a process based on the use of such tools to evaluate protocols with respect to different levels of assurance. Our evaluation process is generic: protocol designers and national organization should be able to apply it uniformly to certify a wide variety of cryptographic protocols.

1.2   Contributions

To begin with, we classify the state-of-the-art in security protocol analysis methods into three categories. Our classification is based on the capability of the method used, the skill required by the designer to use the method, and the security requirement of the protocol in question. Afterwards, we propose a certification process, which certifies the result of a security analysis performed by the protocol designer. Because the process of designing cryptographic protocols is similar to designing cryptographic products, our process is analogous to the Common Criteria. Moreover, three of the authors are project editors of the ISO standard, ISO 29128 "Verification of Cryptographic Protocols," which standardizes the above certification process. Currently this standardization is in the Committee Draft (CD) process and is under discussion. We outline this standard as well as some of the issues that have arisen during the standardization process.

We also report on a plan for the evaluation of cryptographic protocols by CRYPTREC, which is the Japanese governmental organization certifying cryptographic techniques. CRYPTREC is leading a standardization effort for entity-authentication protocols, which is taking place through 2013. The call for protocol contributions has already been made and CRYPTREC will use formal methods to evaluate the incoming proposals. Hence, this will be a good example of the application of ISO 29128. We take stock of the current plans for this evaluation.

2   Evaluation of Cryptographic Protocols

2.1   Formal Methods for Cryptographic Protocol Analysis

Designing cryptographic protocols is a very challenging problem. In open networks, such as the Internet, protocols should work even under worst-case assumptions, namely messages may be eavesdropped or tampered with by an attacker (also called the intruder or adversary) or dishonest or careless principals. Surprisingly, severe attacks can be conducted even without attacking and breaking cryptography, but rather by attacking communication itself. These attacks exploit weaknesses in the protocol's design whereby protocols can be defeated by cleverly manipulating and replaying messages in ways not anticipated by the designer. This includes attacks such as: *man-in-the-middle attacks*, where an attacker is involved in two parallel executing sessions and passes messages between them; *replay attacks*, where messages recorded from previous sessions are played in subsequent ones; *reflection attacks*, where transmitted information is sent back to the originator; and *type flaw (confusion) attacks*, where messages of different types are substituted into a protocol (e.g., replacing a name with a key). Typically, these attacks are simply overlooked, as it is difficult for humans, even by a careful inspection of simple protocols, to determine all the complex ways that different protocol sessions could be interleaved together, with possible interferences coming from a malicious intruder.

What is needed are methods to speed up the development and analysis of cryptographic protocols. Moreover, if these methods are to be used to certify protocols, then they must be mathematically precise, so that exact statements are possible about the scope and significance of the analysis results. This role can be filled by formal methods.

Over the last two decades, the security community has made substantial advances in developing formal methods for analyzing cryptographic protocols and thereby preventing the kinds of attacks mentioned above. These methods and tools can be categorized by several points of view. Here we categorize them by

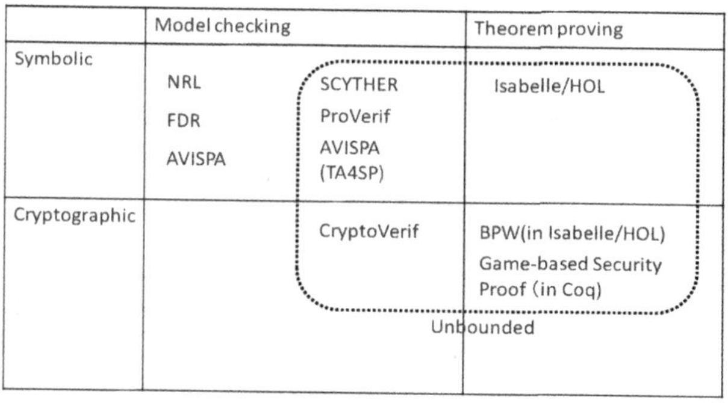

	Model checking		Theorem proving
Symbolic	NRL FDR AVISPA	SCYTHER ProVerif AVISPA (TA4SP)	Isabelle/HOL
Cryptographic		CryptoVerif	BPW(in Isabelle/HOL) Game-based Security Proof (in Coq)
		Unbounded	

Fig. 1. Categorization of Formal Methods for cryptographic protocol analysis

"Symbolic versus Cryptographic", "Bounded versus Unbounded", and "Model checking versus Theorem proving" as follows (Fig.1).

Model Checking versus Theorem Proving. Model checking establishes that a model M, typically formalized as a Kripke structure, has a property ϕ, i.e., $M \models \phi$. Model checking is a form of *algorithmic verification*, as opposed to *deductive verification*, in that $M \models \phi$ is established by executing an algorithm, rather than constructing a proof in some deductive system. Many model checking problems in security (e.g., secrecy and also authentication, see [1]) can be reduced to reachability problems, at which point the model checking algorithms amount to state enumeration. When the state space is finite, model checking constitutes a decision procedure. Initial work on model checking for cryptographic protocols began in the 1980s, starting with Kemmerer's InaTest tool [2]. Since then many successful methods and tools have been developed such as NRL [3], CSP and FDR [4,5], OFMC [6,7] and the AVISPA tool [8], ProVerif [9,10,1,11], CryptoVerif [12], and SCYTHER [13].

In theorem proving, one reduces verification to proving a theorem in first-order or higher-order logic. The model M formalizes directly the semantics of the protocol as a set of traces, i.e., the sequence of communication events that result from interleaving runs of the protocol between different principals as well as interference from the intruder. The drawback is that inductive theorem proving requires considerable expertise as well as substantial time and effort. Still, in the hands of an experienced user, this approach has been shown to be effective for verifying protocols with respect to unbounded protocol models. In theorem proving, the *inductive approach* developed by Larry Paulson [14] has been used extensively.

Bounded versus Unbounded. Protocols can often be attacked by cleverly manipulating and replaying messages in ways not anticipated by their developers. Such attacks can be quite complex and, in particular, they may require multiple parallel executing sessions. For this reason, it is necessary to model (in M)

the possibility of principals participating in an *unbounded* number of protocol sessions. However, even with simple, abstract, term-based models, the general security problem is undecidable [15].

One strategy for handling this complexity is to carry out verification by interactive theorem proving, thereby shifting the complexity to the human who guides the theorem prover. This is the case, for example, when constructing proofs using Isabelle/HOL, as in Paulson's method.

Alternatively, if we are interested in automatic verification, then essentially two options are available: to bound the model so that the problem becomes decidable, or to attempt to produce, algorithmically, a finite characterization of the infinite set of reachable states (or traces) in the unbounded model. Most of model checkers choose the first option, but some advanced model checkers, such as AVISPA with TA4SP [16] backend, ProVerif [9,10,1,11], CryptoVerif [12], and SCYTHER [13], realize the second option.

Symbolic versus Cryptographic. The standard Dolev-Yao model is employed in most formal methods for analyzing cryptographic protocols. This model provides a strong idealization of actual cryptographic operations by representing them as term constructors (function symbols) in a term algebra with cancellation rules. This idealization, which we call here the *symbolic approach*, simplifies proof construction by freeing proofs from cryptographic details such as computational restrictions, probabilistic behavior, and error probabilities.

In contrast to this is the *cryptographic approach* (also called the *computational-complexity approach* or *provable security*), where proofs are constructed by reduction, as in complexity theory [17]. Under this approach, one reduces the security of the overall system to the security of the cryptographic primitives with respect to their cryptographic definitions (for example, adaptive chosen-message security for signature schemes). The cryptographic definitions themselves are defined in terms of probability theory and complexity theory. Proving schemes secure with respect to such definitions is a complex endeavor, but one has much stronger guarantees than under the symbolic approach. In [18,19], a formalization of the BPW model is presented that is a very general model that provides cryptographic guarantees (cryptographic soundness) with respect to the cryptographic approach. This model is formalized in Isabelle/HOL and, using this model, the security (authenticity) of the (corrected) Needham-Schroeder protocol is verified. This is the first such formalization, in logic, of this model and its first application to formal, machine-checked proofs. [20] presents a refinement of the game-based approach to security proofs and its implementation using the proof assistant Coq. Another tool following the cryptographic approach is CryptoVerif [12], which is an automatic protocol prover developed by Bruno Blanchet.

3   Framework for Protocol Certification

3.1   Objectives

As we mentioned in the last section, there are many formal methods that are effective for verifying (or falsifying) the security of cryptographic protocols. The problem today is not that there is a shortage of formal methods for cryptographic protocol analysis, but rather that there are too many! There is no consensus on which methods should be used and the scope of their effectiveness. Moreover, the relationships between the different methods is not yet well understood.

This situation is problematic for practitioners who design or use cryptographic protocols because they can neither select appropriate methods to verify their protocols nor have sufficient confidence in their results. Hence we propose a framework for protocol certification whose objectives are to establish means to provide defined levels of confidence (or assurance) concerning the security of the cryptographic protocols.

3.2 ISO/IEC 29128 Verification of Cryptographic Protocols

ISO/IEC JTC 1/SC 27 has started in 2007 the project "Verification of cryptographic protocols (ISO/IEC 29128)" to provide a technical basis for the assessment of the security of cryptographic protocols. This project is on ballot to proceed at the Committee Draft (CD) stage at the time of writing this article and will become an International Standard by 2011 after several revisions and further ballots.

The current draft text of ISO/IEC 29128 does not specify precisely what proof methods or tools shall be used, but instead only specifies their properties. This encourages protocol designers to use state-of-the-art approaches for protocol verification in terms of models, methods, and tools. It also encourages tool designers to develop better tools.

The draft defines minimal requirements for specifying cryptographic protocols and different protocol assurance levels. To certify a cryptographic protocol, this standard requires a document that covers the following four aspects.

protocol specification: specification of the cryptographic protocol
adversarial model: specification of the adversarial model
security properties: specification of the objectives and security properties that the protocol should satisfy
self-assessment evidence: evidence that the specification of the cryptographic protocol in its adversarial model achieves its objectives and satisfies its security properties

The different protocol assurance levels lead to different requirements for these four aspects as shown in next subsection. The protocol designer prepares a document describing these four aspects of the protocol and provides it to the evaluator. The evaluator then checks whether these requirements are satisfied by the document in the sense defined for each protocol assurance level.

3.3 Cryptographic Protocol Assurance Levels

Table 1 presents the three levels of our assurance requirements and the associated requirements for each of the four protocol aspects. These levels provide increasingly strong guarantees about the security of cryptographic protocols.

Table 1. Cryptographic protocol assurance levels

Protocol assurance levels	Protocol Assurance Level 1 (PAL1)	Protocol Assurance Level 2 (PAL2)	Protocol Assurance Level 3 (PAL3)
Protocol Specification	Semiformal description of protocol specification	Formal description of protocol specification in a tool-specific specification language, whose semantics is mathematically defined	
Adversarial model	Informal description of adversarial model	Formal description of adversarial model	
Security property	Informal description of security property	Formal description of security property	
Self-assessment evidence	Informal argument or mathematically formal paper-and-pencil proof that the specification of the cryptographic protocol satisfies the given objectives and properties with respect to the adversarial model	Tool-aided bounded verification that the specification of the cryptographic protocol satisfies the given objectives and properties with respect to the adversarial model	Tool-aided unbounded verification that the specification of the cryptographic protocol satisfies the given objectives and properties with respect to the adversarial model

The difference between PAL1 and PAL2 is whether all aspects of the protocol description, such as the specification, security properties, and adversarial model, are formally described or not. If these are not sufficiently formal, a rigorous analysis is not possible and the designer cannot search for attacks or construct correctness proofs. At best, the designer can search for typical weaknesses and evaluate the protocol with respect to those attacks that she has thought of. Hence, PAL1 gives only minimal guarantees about the protocol's security. However, PAL1 may be sufficient for some closed network environment, such as a company intranet, lacking committed adversaries.

In contrast, in PAL2, the protocol designer provides a formal specification. Thus she can capture all traces consistent with the specification within some bound specified for the verification. Designers are typically poor at anticipating all possible (interleaved) traces and hence these traces will usually include complex ones, not considered in advance by the protocol designer. PAL2 generally gives reasonable guarantees that there does not exist any other successful adversary within some bound on the number of protocol sessions. We recommend PAL2 for open network environment such as the Internet.

The difference between PAL2 and PAL3 is whether or not the analysis (and hence the evidence presented) is for unbound verification. Verification in PAL2 is bounded and thus the designer cannot prove a protocol secure when complex attacks lie outside of the given bound. In contrast, PAL3 gives strong guarantees on that no successful (symbolic, Dolev-Yao) adversary exists, even allowing for unbounded numbers of sessions. With unbounded verification, a protocol designer can prove her protocol secure against all adversaries, even those willing to carry out complex and expensive attacks. PAL3 is effective for critical information systems, such as those providing social infrastructures or financial systems.

3.4 Discussion during the Standardization Process

Before the Committee Draft (CD) stage, ISO/IEC 29128 has been revised three times in the Working Draft (WD) stage. We have received various comments, which we have taken into account in the revisions. The following three points are the most important ones considered.

Neutrality to specific methods and tools. Since the state-of-the-art for protocol verification is progressing rapidly in terms of models, methods, and tools, this standard should not focus on specific methods or tools. Hence the draft standard provides only minimal requirements for specifying cryptographic protocols to keep them as general as possible.

Computational model. In very early stages of the standard, the highest assurance level required protocol verification in the computational model. However, because very few tools currently support this model and this approach requires both a very high degree of expertise and effort, cryptographic approaches based on the computational model (with unbounded verification) was included in PAL3 in the current draft. In the future, the use of the computational model might be defined at a higher level, such as PAL4, when verification tools are up to the task and usable by practitioners.

Paper-and-pencil proof. Both informal arguments and mathematically formal paper-and-pencil proofs are allowed under PAL1 in the current draft. Although formal proofs usually provides much more confidence than informal arguments, proofs by hand can be error-prone. Moreover, it is very difficult for protocol evaluators to confirm whether the proof is correct or not. Hence this standard requires mechanized proof for higher levels than PAL1.

3.5 Is Our Framework Effective?

Currently, when a non-expert user uses a standardized cryptographic protocol, he cannot evaluate its security by himself. Instead he trusts the standardization body, which evaluated the protocol. In other words, the security of a cryptographic protocol is reduced to trusting the standardization body. As noted previously, this trust is not always well placed. In contrast, our proposed framework will provide the practitioner with trustworthy results based on sound, scientifically verifiable evidence.

So far, not all useful and practical protocols can be evaluated in the framework. One of the reason is the immaturity of tools. Although there are many tools as mentioned in Section 2, each tool has its own limitations. For example, few of the existing tools can effectively handle all of the different algebraic properties required to formalize the different cryptographic operators used in protocols. As a result, we may not be able to prove and certify the security of some protocols in the framework, even if they are actually secure because of lacking tool support. Another problem for the framework to be practical is the lack of experts. Each tool requires some expertise, but currently only a limited number of researchers have such expertise.

These problems could be improved by progress within the research community working on formal methods for protocol verification. They can also be improved by educating developers on existing formal methods. Note that, as we mentioned in Section 3.4, the proposed framework is open with respect to future progress in methods and tools.

4   Protocol Evaluation in a National Project: The CRYPTREC Case

4.1   Overview

As explained in the previous section, ISO/IEC 29128 is a framework for certifying cryptographic protocols using formal verification methods. To improve this framework and increase its usability, we must gather experience using it in actual evaluations. Afterwards we can revise the framework based on our experience. One of the authors is involved in a Japanese national project on the selection of cryptographic protocols within CRYPTREC.[1] Within this project, formal methods are being applied to verify selected entity-authentication protocols based on the certification framework described in Section 3. We plan to use the project results and experience gained there to evaluate and improve our framework.

The CRYPTREC project aims to evaluate and monitor the security of ciphers recommended for e-Government applications, as well as to study the establishment of evaluation criteria for cryptographic modules. In 2002, CRYPTREC produced an "e-Government Recommended Ciphers List"[21]. CRYPTREC is now conducting a renewal of this list. This includes recommending a list of entity-authentication protocols. In this renewal, CRYPTREC is asking for entity-authentication protocols that use cryptographic algorithms given in the e-Government Recommended Ciphers List or that use cryptographic algorithms that have a security reduction to computationally difficult problems.

The submitted entity-authentication protocols should assure the correctness of the communication partners. In particular, the protocol designer can specify the protocol property as being mutual authentication or unilateral authentication. Examples of international standard protocols are:

– ISO/IEC 9798 series, which contain protocols based on symmetric encryption algorithms (9798-2), digital signature techniques (9798-3), cryptographic

---

[1] CRYPTREC abbreviates "CRYPTography Research and Evaluation Committees". See http://www.cryptrec.go.jp/english/index.html

check functions (9798-4), zero knowledge techniques, (9798-5) and manual data transfer (9798-6),
- Kerberos and SASL (IETF), and
- One-time passwords.

In the evaluation by CRYPTREC, protocols are evaluated assuming that, if the cryptographic algorithms used are in the e-Government Recommended Ciphers List, then they are ideally secure. If other cryptographic algorithms are used, then the protocol is evaluated without their idealization. We describe the reasons for this below.

As indicated in Sections 2 and 3, there are many mature verification tools and different ways (corresponding to different assurance levels) that these tools can be used. When considering the maturity of current tools, CRYPTREC mainly considers verification without computational soundness. CRYPTREC already has recommended symmetric and asymmetric cryptographic algorithms, a hash function, and a pseudorandom generator. Thus, in the verification, we assume that the cryptographic algorithms in the list are ideal cryptographic algorithms. Hence, we do not require complicated computationally-sound proofs in this case. If the submitted protocol uses only cryptographic algorithms in the list, the efforts required of the protocol designer and the evaluator are reduced. Of course, this does not rule out entity-authentication protocols that use cryptographic algorithms not in the list. For example, we expect that many protocols will use a variant of the Diffie-Hellman protocol or the Fiat-Shamir heuristic. In this case, their security must be proven in a computationally-sound sense.

When submitting a proposal, the protocol designer gives an informal description of the proposed protocol, the desired properties, and the adversarial model to the evaluator who conducts the verification. The protocol designer also provides the evaluator with a formal description of the proposed protocol, the adversarial model, the result of executing the verification tool, and information on the tool itself. The protocol designer can use a formal verification tool that is publicly available or a proprietary (private) one. If the protocol designer uses a publicly available tool, he must provide the name of the tool and its version number. If he uses a proprietary verification tool, he must provide access to the verification tool itself as well as its specification.

The evaluator in CRYPTREC will investigate the correctness of the protocol description and the effectiveness of the verification tool. Then the evaluator performs verification using the same tool and compares the result with those submitted by the protocol designer.

4.2 Discussion

The main issue in the certification process is how to confirm the soundness of the verification tool. To obtain reliable verification results, the tool must not contain bugs that could lead to erroneous results. In practice, however, tools often do contain bugs. In some cases, different versions of the same tool may even produce different outputs. This is a serious problem for evaluators.

Solutions discussed within the CRYPTREC project are as follows.

- The evaluator collects information about reliable tools and their stable versions. Then the evaluator provides a list of them after obtaining consensus by experts. International consensus about the reliability of different tools is therefore needed.
- Alternatively, CRYPTREC provides a single standard verification tool so that the protocol designer and the evaluator can work using this (trusted) tool.

Eliminating bugs and producing stable versions of verification tools is quite important for certification. However, the current situation is insufficient for evaluating the correctness of the tools themselves. We expect to see methods available for evaluting the correctness of tools or their results in near future. We see three possibilities here. The first option is white-box testing of the tool by several experts. To carry out the tests, the protocol designer prepares

- a documented formal model underlying the tool,
- documentation on how the formalism is implemented in the tool,
- and the tool's source code.

The evaluator checks the soundness of the formalism from the description of the formal model, then checks if this is properly implemented by referencing the implementation document and the source code itself. This type of evaluation takes substantial time and efforts.

If time and effort are limited, a second option is to perform black-box tests on the tool. For cryptographic algorithms, the "test vectors" are a widely trusted tool for verification. To verify protocol tools, a test vector would consist of three parts: a test protocol, an adversarial model, and the expected verification result.

A final option is to use model-checking tools that produce proof scripts that can be independently checked. For example, the model-checking tool could generate a proof that can be checked using a standard theorem prover, e.g., one for higher-order logic like Isabelle/HOL. Recent research results suggest that this is a promising option.

Once the verification tool (or its output) is assured to be sound, the evaluator must still verify whether the formal description of the protocol specification correctly models the actual protocol. Moreover, it must be checked that security property correctly formalizes the actual security requirements and that the adversarial model is realistic for the protocol's intended application. Hence, even with this framework, the reasonableness of the security notion is finally assured by human experts.

5   Conclusion

In this paper, we have presented two activities related to the evaluation of cryptographic protocols, the ISO/IEC 29128 project, and the CRYPTREC project, which are being conducted in parallel.

ISO/IEC 29128 is a newly proposed international standard that uses formal methods to improve the security assurance of cryptographic protocols based on mathematically rigorous, machine-checkable, security proofs. Once a cryptographic protocol is certified with ISO/IEC 29128, in particular under its highest assurance level, the protocol is absolutely secure up to the assumption under which the security proofs are made and the soundness of the underlying verification tool. Thus, with this new standard, we should enjoy substantially higher levels of security than at present time.

The CRYPTREC project is a Japanese government project that evaluates the security of cryptographic algorithms and protocols as described in this paper. CRYPTREC is now planing to conduct a security evaluation for entity-authentication protocols using formal methods. We plan to combine the findings of the CRYPTREC project with the development of ISO/IEC 29128. In this way we hope to further improve ISO/IEC 29128 and its practicality.

References

1. Blanchet, B.: From secrecy to authenticity in security protocols. In: Hermenegildo, M.V., Puebla, G. (eds.) SAS 2002. LNCS, vol. 2477, pp. 342–359. Springer, Heidelberg (2002)
2. Kemmerer, R.: Using formal methods to analyze encryption protocols. IEEE Journal of Selected Areas in Communication 7(2), 448–457 (1989)
3. Meadows, C.: The NRL protocol analyzer: An overview. Journal of Logic Programming 19 (1994)
4. Hoare, C.: Communicating sequential processes. CACM 21, 666–677 (1978)
5. Hoare, C.A.: Communicating Sequential Processes. Prentice-Hall, Englewood Cliffs (1995)
6. Basin, D.: Lazy infinite-state analysis of security protocols. In: Baumgart, R. (ed.) CQRE 1999. LNCS, vol. 1740, pp. 30–42. Springer, Heidelberg (1999)
7. Basin, D., Mödersheim, S., Viganò, L.: OFMC: A symbolic model checker for security protocols. International Journal of Information Security 4(3), 181–208 (2005)
8. Armando, A., Basin, D., Boichut, Y., Chevalier, Y., Compagna, L., Cuellar, J., Drielsma, P.H., Heám, P.C., Kouchnarenko, O., Mantovani, J., Mödersheim, S., von Oheimb, D., Rusinowitch, M., Santiago, J., Turuani, M., Viganò, L., Vigneron, L.: The AVISPA Tool for the Automated Validation of Internet Security Protocols and Applications. In: Etessami, K., Rajamani, S.K. (eds.) CAV 2005. LNCS, vol. 3576, pp. 281–285. Springer, Heidelberg (2005)
9. Abadi, M., Blanchet, B.: Analyzing Security Protocols with Secrecy Types and Logic Programs. Journal of the ACM 52(1), 102–146 (2005)
10. Blanchet, B.: An efficient cryptographic protocol verifier based on prolog rules. In: Proceedings of CSFW 2001, pp. 82–96. IEEE Computer Society Press, Los Alamitos (2001)
11. Blanchet, B.: A computationally sound mechanized prover for security protocols. In: IEEE Symposium on Security and Privacy, Oakland, California, May 2006, pp. 140–154 (2006)
12. Blanchet, B.: A computationally sound automatic prover for cryptographic protocols. In: Workshop on the link between formal and computational models, Paris, France (June 2005)

13. Cremers, C.: Scyther — Semantics and Verification of Security Protocols. PhD thesis, University of Eindhoven (2006)
14. Paulson, L.C.: The inductive approach to verifying cryptographic protocols. Journal of Computer Security 6, 85–128 (1998)
15. Durgin, N., Lincoln, P.D., Mitchell, J.C., Scedrov, A.: Undecidability of Bounded Security Protocols. In: Proceedings of the FLOC 1999 Workshop on Formal Methods and Security Protocols, FMSP 1999 (1999)
16. Boichut, Y., Heam, P.C., Kouchnarenko, O., Oehl, F.: Improvements on the Genet and Klay Technique to Automatically Verify Security Protocols. In: Automated Verification of Infinite States Systems (AVIS 2004). ENTCS (2004)
17. Goldwasser, S., Micali, S.: Probabilistic encryption. Journal of Computer and System Sciences 28, 270–299 (1984)
18. Sprenger, C., Backes, M., Basin, D., Pfitzmann, B., Waidner, M.: Cryptographically sound theorem proving. In: 19th IEEE Computer Security Foundations Workshop, Venice, Italy, July 2006, pp. 153–166. IEEE Computer Society, Los Alamitos (2006)
19. Sprenger, C., Basin, D.: Cryptographically-sound protocol-model abstractions. In: Computer Security Foundations (CSF 2008), pp. 115–129. IEEE Computer Society, Los Alamitos (2008)
20. Nowak, D.: A framework for game-based security proofs. In: Qing, S., Imai, H., Wang, G. (eds.) ICICS 2007. LNCS, vol. 4861, pp. 319–333. Springer, Heidelberg (2007)
21. CRYPTREC: e-government recommended ciphers list (2003), http://www.cryptrec.go.jp/english/images/cryptrec_01en.pdf

WECSR Preface

The First Workshop on Ethics in Computer Security Research (WECSR 2010, http://www.cs.stevens.edu/~spock/wecsr2010/), organized by the International Financial Cryptography Association (IFCA, http://www.ifca.ai/), was held on Tenerife, Canary Islands, Spain, January 28, 2010. It was part of the first multi-workshop event co-located with Financial Cryptography 2010.

The goal was to find a new path in computer security that is acceptable for institutional review boards at academic institutions, and is also compatible with ethical guidelines for professional societies or government institutions. However, no exact ethical guidelines exist for computer security research yet.

The goal was met: there were nine submissions, out of which two case studies and two position papers were selected. Each submission was reviewed by at least three Program Committee members. The Program Committee carefully reviewed the submissions during an online discussion phase in fall 2009. We would like to thank all submitters for the papers and their hard work, and hope that the comments received from the reviewers will allow them to progress with their work. The program also featured a keynote talk given by Kenneth Fleischmann via videoconference despite the time difference with the United States and repeated connectivity problems, and a panel discussion with Lorrie Cranor, Erin Kenneally, and Len Sassaman on ethical standards.

The workshop brought together about 25 participants, including computer security researchers, practitioners, policy makers, and legal experts, and fostered often fervent ethical and philosophical debates among participants, in order to shape the future of ethical standards in the field. The relaxed local atmosphere allowed for many continued discussions beyond the day itself, including on the excursion kindly organized by the conference General Chair Pino Caballero.

I would like to thank Jean Camp, Radu Sion, Rafael Hirschfeld, and the local arrangements team for their hard work and help in getting this workshop off the ground. Many thanks also to those who traveled far to this island off the coast of Morocco.

February 2010   Sven Dietrich

Preaching What We Practice: Teaching Ethical Decision-Making to Computer Security Professionals

Kenneth R. Fleischmann

College of Information Studies, University of Maryland, College Park, MD 20742-4345 USA
kfleisch@umd.edu

1 Recognizing Ethical Decisions in Technology Development

The biggest challenge facing computer security researchers and professionals is not learning how to make ethical decisions; rather it is learning how to recognize ethical decisions. All too often, technology development suffers from what Langdon Winner terms technological somnambulism – we sleepwalk through our technology design, following past precedents without a second thought, and fail to consider the perspectives of other stakeholders [1]. Computer security research and practice involves a number of opportunities for ethical decisions. For example, decisions about whether or not to automatically provide security updates involve tradeoffs related to caring versus user autonomy. Decisions about online voting include tradeoffs between convenience and security. Finally, decisions about routinely screening e-mails for spam involve tradeoffs of efficiency and privacy. It is critical that these and other decisions facing computer security researchers and professionals are confronted head on as value-laden design decisions, and that computer security researchers and professionals consider the perspectives of various stakeholders in making these decisions.

Values directly and significantly impact how we make decisions involved in developing technologies such as computer security systems. Given the important role played by values in the development, management, and use of technologies, "it is unethical to ignore the values embedded in technological artifacts" [2, p. 80]. Values are formed early in our lives, long before the choice to become a computer security researcher or professional. They are learned through a variety of experiences and contexts in childhood and throughout our lives, including family, school, religious services and instruction, athletics and other extracurricular activities, and many other activities. Thus, instead of focusing computing and information ethics courses on trying to make computer security researchers and professionals better people, it is instead more fruitful to focus on making them better researchers and professionals, by fine tuning their own self-awareness of the ethical significance of their work and their ability to consider others' needs and values when developing and testing computer security systems. This paper considers describe complementary research directions that explore both how we can both understand ethical decision-making and increase awareness of ethical decision-making among computer security researchers and professionals.

2 Understanding Ethical Decision-Making

One major focus of my independent and collaborative research projects has been to understand the role that ethical decision-making plays in technology development by

R. Sion et al. (Eds.): FC 2010 Workshops, LNCS 6054, pp. 197–202, 2010.
© IFCA/Springer-Verlag Berlin Heidelberg 2010

studying the ethical decision-making of information technology researchers and professionals. For example, research on the role of values in the design of frog dissection simulations used in biology education has demonstrated that values can be included both in the technology itself and in its packaging. Values can determine the interface with the frog body, such that animal advocacy values can be expressed through alternatives to the traditional experience of dissecting a frog, including simulations that focus on making the layers of a frog transparent or even building a frog instead of taking it apart. Values can also influence marketing and packaging, as in the use of the phrase "Frog-Friendly Software" which explicitly uses animal advocacy values to promote the use of frog dissection simulations [3].

Given the importance of technologies in our everyday lives, it is important that users are able to ensure that technologies reflect their values. Research on the role of values in the development and use of educational simulations used in biology and medicine reveals a particular approach that allows users to do achieve this goal: the *role hybridization of user-designers*, such that users become developers and are thus empowered to develop the technologies they need. In some domains and in some situations, users may find that technology developers are unable to develop technologies that meet their needs and match their values. Counter-intuitive as it may seem, it actually appears based on this research that it's easier for a biology teacher to learn to be a computer programmer than it is for a programmer to learn to become a biology teacher. Participatory design is a viable alternative, yet in practice, there are limitations to participatory design such as insufficient time or incentives for users to participate in the design process, power imbalances and communication difficulties between designers and users, and users' potential to "go native" and to adopt the designers' perspectives and as a result to lose touch with the everyday concerns of end-users. Thus, role hybridization of user-designers presents an alternative whereby users can ensure that the technologies that are developed match their needs and values [4].

To explain how values shape technology development, it is useful to develop new theories about the complex and mutually constitutive relationship between values and technology. For example, the *boundary objects with agency* concept explains that technologies not only evolve as a result of the values of different stakeholder groups, but also can play an active role in reshaping the values of those constituent groups [5]. The concept of *cyberagency* argues that the agency of technologies evolves over time, similar to the *bioagency* of humans [6]. The concept of *cyborg-cyborg interaction* explains how human-computer interaction has evolved from a field that considers how individual and distinct people interact with individual and distinct technologies to a more diverse field that also considers the increasing interactions among *groups* of people and technologies as well as the growing *convergence* between people and technologies [7]. Spanning these theoretical concepts, it is possible to build a larger theory that views humans and technologies as interacting and converging entities, each with their own interconnected and interrelated values.

All developers begin their lives as users. Similarly, scientists and engineers begin their lives as members of the reading, listening, viewing, and playing public, and as such, are influenced by a wide range of media. Thus, it is important to consider the social influences on the career choices and research trajectories of scientists and engineers. Specifically, science fiction is one form of popular media that can serve as an initial exposure and inspiration to youth to pursue careers in science and engineering [8,9].

Values play an important role in all stages of the technology development process, especially in the case of computational modeling [10]. In particular, the value of transparency plays a key role in the development and use of computational models. Transparency can enter at the beginning of the modeling process as one of the key goals. Transparency can then play a role in the selection of the modeling paradigm used, since some approaches to modeling are more easily explained to users than others. In building the model, it may be the logic rather than the technical details that need to be transparent. In assessing the model, transparency can be considered as an evaluation criterion. Finally, in the deployment stage, transparency can have an impact on how the model is used [11]. Thus, it is important that, in addition to the *covenant with reality* and *covenant with values* [12], it is also important that computational modelers follow a *covenant with transparency* that allows users to check that a technology matches their reality and values by designing for transparency [13]. Trust also plays an important role in information technology development and use [14]. Values such as trust and transparency can also be studied through automated approaches that combine human and computational expertise [15-18]. Modelers' values are also connected to their awareness of, familiarity with, and perspectives on professional codes of ethics [19].

3 Increasing Awareness of Ethical Decision-Making

Educators have a responsibility to prepare future computer security professionals for all of the major challenges that they will face during their careers, including ethical challenges such as value-laden technology design decisions. Part of this need can be fulfilled by increasing awareness of professional codes of ethics, as well as educating future computer security professionals about the implications of the concepts embedded within these codes of ethics for their work [19-23]. While much research has been done on best practices for computing and information ethics education, there is still a need for additional research on this topic [24].

It is especially important that ethics education prepares students to face the difficult challenges presented by our global information society, including sensitivity to other cultures as well as a broadening of ethical perspectives beyond the traditional Western canon. Educational cases with multiple interacting perspectives allow students to take different roles and to see how the decisions made by one individual within a case can affect the scenarios faced by other individuals. These cases can then be implemented within an educational simulation, facilitating the ease of use of the cases as well as helping to ensure the potential for broad dissemination of the cases as educational tools [25].

4 Conclusions

Teaching computer security professionals how to recognize ethical decisions in technology development is an opportunity to preach what we practice. Certainly, it is important for our teaching to be consistent with our practice, with both adhering to high ethical standards – thus, we must also of course practice what we preach. Education and practice go together well, as our experiences in research and practice can make excellent educational guides for students that can help to prepare them for many of the types of ethical challenges that they may face in the workplace. Ensuring that the next generation of computer security professionals is aware of and able to cope with the challenging ethical decisions that they will face throughout their careers is of paramount importance given the increasing reliance of government, commerce, and society as a whole on information technology.

Values such as transparency play a huge role in the development and use of information technologies [11]. Information technology professionals need to be prepared to face these challenges, and their current educational experiences as well as their familiarity with professional codes of ethics, currently leave significant room for improvement [19]. To prepare information technology professionals to face these challenges, we must first understand all of the challenges that they will face, and then develop new pedagogical tools and approaches, including new technologies, that can be effective in helping to prepare them to successfully engage in ethical decision-making, ensuring that values are embedded in technologies through conscious design rather than through sleepwalking through the design process [1]. Thus, computer security researcher should work to ensure that their research follows the highest ethical standards of research practice. Computer security professionals should ensure that the computer security systems that they develop are compatible with the needs and values of their users. Finally, Computer security educators should make sure to incorporate ethical decision-making as an integral part of course and curriculum design, not only through elective courses that focus exclusively on the ethics of information technology and which often focus on 'preaching to the choir' since only students already aware of and interested in the importance of ethical decision-making in information technology development are likely to enroll in and complete these courses, but also through significant emphasis on information ethics as a core topic in required courses, rather than merely as a tacked-on topic that receives underwhelming emphasis.

Information technology can be used to the great benefit of a large number of people, but it can also be used to increase existing inequalities and create new inequalities, to perpetuate identity theft, and to destabilize markets or even nations. Thus, preparing computer security professionals to confront ethical challenges is a nontrivial matter with broad societal implications. Computer security educators and computing and information ethics educators need to work together to ensure that computer security professionals will be able to act in both a highly skilled and highly ethical manner, and will be able to reflect on the societal importance of their work and their professional and ethical responsibilities.

Acknowledgments. This material is based in part upon work supported by the National Science Foundation under Grant Numbers SES-0217996, SES-0521117, SES-0639897, SES-0646392, IIS-07299459, and IIS-0734894. Thanks also go to John Bertot, Allison Druin, Jimmy Lin, Doug Oard, Jenny Preece, Dagobert Soergel, Al Wallace, and Bo Xie for reading and commenting on early drafts of portions of this paper.

References

1. Winner, L.: The Whale and the Reactor. University of Chicago Press, Chicago (1986)
2. Martin, C.D., Huff, C.W., Gotterbarn, D., Miller, K.: Implementing a Tenth Strand in the CS Curriculum: The Second Report from Project ImpactCS. Comm. ACM 39, 75–84 (1996)
3. Fleischmann, K.R.: Frog and Cyberfrog are Friends: Dissection Simulation and Animal Advocacy. Soc. Anim. 11, 123–143 (2003)
4. Fleischmann, K.R.: Do-It-Yourself Information Technology: Role Hybridization and the Design-Use Interface. J. Am. Soc. Info. Sci. Tech. 57, 87–95 (2006)
5. Fleischmann, K.R.: Boundary Objects with Agency: A Method for Studying the Design-Use Interface. Info. Soc. 22, 77–87 (2006)
6. Fleischmann, K.R.: The Evolution of Agency: Spectra of Bioagency and Cyberagency. Info. Soc. 23, 361–371 (2007)
7. Fleischmann, K.R.: Sociotechnical Interaction and Cyborg-Cyborg Interaction: Transforming the Scale and Convergence of HCI. Info. Soc. 25, 227–235 (2009)
8. Fleischmann, K.R., Templeton, T.C.: Past Futures and Technoscientific Innovation: The Mutual Shaping of Science Fiction and Science Fact. In: Proceedings of the 71st Annual Meeting of the American Society for Information Science and Technology, Columbus, OH (2008)
9. Fleischmann, K.R., Templeton, T.C.: Science Fiction in the Lives of Scientists and Engineers. In: Proceedings of Digital Humanities 2009, College Park, MD (2009)
10. Fleischmann, K.R., Wallace, W.A.: Ethical Implications of Values Embedded in Computational Models: An Exploratory Study. In: Proceedings of the 69th Annual Meeting of the American Society for Information Science and Technology, Austin, TX (2006)
11. Fleischmann, K.R., Wallace, W.A.: Ensuring Transparency in Computational Modeling. Comm. ACM 52, 131–134 (2009)
12. Mason, R.O.: Morality and Models. In: Wallace, W.A. (ed.) Ethics in Modeling. Elsevier, Tarrytown (1994)
13. Fleischmann, K.R., Wallace, W.A.: A Covenant with Transparency: Opening the Black Box of Models. Comm. ACM 48, 93–97 (2005)
14. Kelton, K., Fleischmann, K.R., Wallace, W.A.: Trust in Digital Information. J. Am. Soc. Info. Sci. Tech. 59, 363–374 (2009)
15. Cheng, A.-S., Fleischmann, K.R., Wang, P., Oard, D.W.: Advancing Social Science Research by Applying Computational Linguistics. In: Proceedings of the 71st Annual Meeting of the American Society for Information Science and Technology, Columbus, OH (2008)
16. Fleischmann, K.R., Oard, D.W., Cheng, A.-S., Wang, P., Ishita, E.: Automatic Classification of Human Values: Applying Computational Thinking to Information Ethics. In: Proceedings of the 72nd Annual Meeting of the American Society for Information Science and Technology, Vancouver, BC, Canada (2009)
17. Cheng, A.-S., Fleischmann, K.R., Wang, P., Ishita, E., Oard, D.W.: Values of Stakeholders in the Net Neutrality Debate: Applying Content Analysis to Telecommunications Policy. In: Proceedings of the 43rd Hawai'i International Conference on System Sciences, Kauai, HI (2010)
18. Zhou, Y., Fleischmann, K.R., Wallace, W.A.: Automatic Text Analysis of Values from the Enron Email Dataset: Clustering a Social Network Using the Value Patterns of Actors. In: Proceedings of the 43rd Hawai'i International Conference on System Sciences, Kauai, HI (2010)

19. Fleischmann, K.R., Wallace, W.A., Grimes, J.M.: The Values of Computational Modelers and Professional Codes of Ethics: Results from a Field Study. In: Proceedings of the 43rd Hawai'i International Conference on System Sciences, Kauai, HI (2010)

20. Gotterbarn, D.: Reconstructing the ACM Code of Ethics and Teaching Computer Ethics. ACM SIGCSE Bull. 30, 9–11 (1998)

21. Gotterbarn, D.: How the New Software Engineering Code of Ethics Affects You. IEEE Software 16, 58–64 (1999)

22. Martin, C.D.: What Is Computer Ethics? ACM SIGCSE Bulletin 30, 8–9 (1997)

23. Martin, C.D., Martin, D.H.: Professional Codes of Conduct and Computer Ethics Education. Soc. Sci. Comp. Rev. 8, 96–108 (1990)

24. Robbins, R.W., Fleischmann, K.R., Wallace, W.A.: Computing and Information Ethics: Challenges, Education, and Research. In: Luppicini, R., Adell, R. (eds.) Handbook of Research on Technoethics. The Idea Group, New York (2009)

25. Fleischmann, K.R., Robbins, R.W., Wallace, W.A.: Designing Educational Cases for Intercultural Information Ethics: The Importance of Diversity, Perspectives, Values, and Pluralism. J. Ed. Lib. Info. Sci. 50, 4–14 (2009)

A Case Study on Measuring Statistical Data in the Tor Anonymity Network*

Karsten Loesing[1], Steven J. Murdoch[1,2], and Roger Dingledine[1]

[1] The Tor Project
[2] Computer Laboratory, University of Cambridge, UK

Abstract. The Tor network is one of the largest deployed anonymity networks, consisting of 1500+ volunteer-run relays and probably hundreds of thousands of clients connecting every day. Its large user-base has made it attractive for researchers to analyze usage of a real deployed anonymity network. The recent growth of the network has also led to performance problems, as well as attempts by some governments to block access to the Tor network. Investigating these performance problems and learning about network blocking is best done by measuring usage data of the Tor network. However, analyzing a live anonymity system must be performed with great care, so that the users' privacy is not put at risk. In this paper we present a case study of measuring two different types of sensitive data in the Tor network: countries of connecting clients, and exiting traffic by port. Based on these examples we derive general guidelines for safely measuring potentially sensitive data, both in the Tor network and in other anonymity networks.

1 Introduction

Tor [1] is an anonymous communication system that permits its users to surf on the Net without revealing their identity or location. Tor is used by private citizens, corporations, and governments to protect their online communications, as well as by users trying to circumvent censorship. Its basic principle is to redirect traffic over virtual tunnels through three independent Tor nodes, to make it hard for an attacker to link origin to destination.

The scale of the Tor network makes it attractive for researchers who want to study real deployed anonymity networks. McCoy *et al.* published a study [8] that characterizes the usage of Tor; they tried to answer how Tor is used and mis-used, as well as discover what types of users are using Tor. We have talked to other researchers who have performed similar studies in the Tor network (or would like to), but they have not published their results because of technical or legal concerns around safe data collection. From a technical point of view, measuring data in the Tor network can easily be performed by setting up a Tor relay and logging all relayed user traffic. However, this approach raises ethical questions ranging from legal issues over hurting users' privacy to lack of community acceptance. The big threat is that an adversary could make use of this

* This research was funded, in part, by NSF grant CNS-0959138.

data to correlate Tor users with traffic exiting the Tor network. If researchers measure the live Tor network in a way that does not protect the users' privacy, and the underlying data of these studies are leaked, the protection that Tor aims to provide might be in danger. Worse, if the conservative researchers choose not to publish in case their data or process is not safe enough, then the only groups that do publish will be ones that are confident (whether rightly or wrongly) that they got every detail right.

In this paper we describe a case study of safely measuring two types of sensitive data in the Tor network: client IP addresses and exiting traffic. We consider this data to be necessary to make Tor better by making it faster, giving us a better sense of the level of anonymity Tor can provide, and making it harder for censors to block the Tor network. At the same time, both types of data could help an adversary de-anonymize Tor users if measured without caution. We identify possible problems with measuring this data and present our measurement approach which avoids putting the Tor users at risk. At the end of the paper we derive general guidelines for measuring potentially sensitive data that could be used by other researchers and in other anonymity networks.

The next section gives a brief background on Tor. Section 3 describes the goals of statistical analysis in the Tor network. Section 4 discusses the potential ethical problems when doing so. In Section 5 we present our case study of measuring client IP addresses and exiting traffic, and summarize general guidelines for similar cases in the future. Section 6 concludes the paper.

2   Background on Tor

Tor aims to prevent users from being linked with their communication partners; i.e. someone monitoring a client should be unable to find out which servers he is accessing, and a server (or someone monitoring the server) should be unable to find out the identity of clients using Tor to access it. While the original goal of Tor was to enhance privacy, recently Tor has become popular amongst users who wish to circumvent national censorship systems, such as those in countries like Iran and China. Tor's primary security property (an attacker cannot find out which websites a user is visiting) also makes it useful for circumvention because the censor is not able to selectively block access to blacklisted sites.

Tor users download and install the Tor client software, which acts as a SOCKS proxy interfacing their client software (typically a web browser) with the Tor network. This software first connects to one of the *directory authorities*, which are operated by (currently seven) individuals trusted by the Tor Project. From these authorities the software downloads a list of available Tor *nodes* which are relays run by volunteers. The Tor client then selects three of these nodes, and builds an encrypted channel to the first one (called the entry node). Over this encrypted channel, the Tor client builds an encrypted channel to the middle node, and then via this channel, connects to the third node (the exit node).

In this way, the client has a connection to the exit node, but the exit node is not aware of who the entry node or client is; similarly the entry node does not know which exit node the client has selected. The client can then request that the exit node connects to a particular destination server, such as a website accessed by the user. Messages to the server are encrypted multiple times: first to the exit node, then the middle node, and finally to the entry node. As a message is relayed by each node, one layer of encryption is removed. Thus the original message is known only to the exit node. Replies from the server are encrypted by each node along the path, and then decrypted by the client. Therefore messages coming into a node cannot be matched, based on content, to the corresponding message leaving the node.

However, Tor does not prevent an attacker from using traffic analysis to de-anonymize users. Here, the timing of packets in streams leaving the Tor network is recorded. Then, a target stream which is coming into the network is correlated with each candidate output stream. Because nodes do not significantly delay packets, it is likely that the output stream corresponding to the target incoming stream will become clear. Experiments have shown that this conclusion can be reached after only a few packets [10].

Only very capable adversaries are likely to be able to simultaneously record network traffic across the entire Internet, so this attack is unlikely to be a concern to most Tor users. However, traffic analysis can still work even given incomplete information; it just takes more data to get the same level of confidence. For example, by only recording 1 in 2000 packets, it is still possible to de-anonymize streams [9]. In general, it is impossible to accurately estimate how much distortion must be applied to a data set before it is no longer useful to an attacker. This is primarily a consequence of *auxiliary information* [2] – data which is known by the attacker but not by the individual distorting the data set.

Even excluding the problem of auxiliary information, it is not possible to estimate whether a particular conclusion that could be reached by traffic analysis is sensitive, because we cannot accurately know the privacy requirements of users. For example, the mere fact that Tor is being used can be problematic, for example if there are only a small set of candidates for a particular action. Therefore the safe option is to not collect any information about an anonymous communication network. However this extreme approach can harm users too, e.g. data which could be used to detect attacks against the network would be unavailable. Instead, in this paper we discuss approaches that can be taken to allow useful data collection, while minimizing the potentially harmful consequences.

3   Goals of Statistical Analysis

The number of Tor relays has increased from 32 in May 2004 [1] to roughly 1500 in October 2009 carrying a total of 250 MiB/s. There are estimated to be hundreds of thousands Tor users every day routing their data through the Tor network. This volume and diversity makes the Tor network an interesting object of study, both to learn more about deployed anonymity networks and to improve Tor for its users.

Performing statistical analysis in the Tor network can serve various purposes. Statistics based on the list of publicly known relays [5] can help observe trends in the structure of the Tor network: which countries are contributing relays and bandwidth, what software versions are deployed, how many relays are running on dynamic IP addresses, etc. Statistics based on performance measurements [13, 6, 4] can help detect performance bottlenecks and evaluate the effect of performance improvements. These performance measurements are conducted with self-generated requests rather than by observing other users' requests.

The next step of statistical analysis in the Tor network is evaluating network data, i.e. data that is based on real user requests. The first thing we want to learn about usage of the Tor network is *who* uses Tor. Tor is meant to provide anonymity and censorship circumvention to people worldwide. In particular, one goal is to make Tor more useful for people in various possibly censoring countries around the world. Usage statistics can help in detecting in which of these countries Tor's efforts are succeeding and which ones need more work, e.g. by performing additional trainings.

As an example, the statistics shown in Figure 1 (a) indicate that Tor usage significantly increased from Iranian IP space in June 2009 after the Iranian elections. (Note that neither of the graphs contains actual user numbers, but rather data that might be used in the future to estimate user numbers; however, the relative increase in usage is already meaningful.) After publishing these statistics, more people were motivated to set up relays and help support the Tor network and Iranian Tor users, in turn improving the security and performance of the network.

Similarly, usage statistics can help discover attempts to block users from reaching the Tor network. Such a blocking event has been observed in late September 2009 when China blocked access to most Tor relays as shown in Figure 1 (b). At the same time, bridge usage from Chinese IP addresses increased significantly by a factor of 70 as compared to the time before the blocking. Bridges are Tor relays that are not listed in the public directory, making it harder for the censor to locate and block them; we deployed the bridge design preemptively as one of the steps in the arms race, so users would have another option ready when a government decided to block connections to the public Tor relays [11]. Statistics on usage by country can help build an automatic early warning system to detect country-wide blocking events.

Another motivation for statistics on usage of the Tor network is to make Tor faster by finding out *what* Tor is used for. These statistics include the observation of what kind of applications are used over the Tor network by looking at exiting traffic. Such statistics can help reveal what share of traffic is used for low-latency applications, like web browsing or IRC, or for bulk file transfers, like file sharing. While low-latency networks like Tor have been designed to support low-latency applications, applications like file sharing increase the load on the network and increase latencies for everyone. It would be desirable to know – and to track over time – what portion of Tor traffic is used for each application class.

Another type of statistics, related to the question of what Tor is used for, is the comparison of overall traffic volume per TCP port versus the advertised bandwidth capacity per port. Each Tor relay has an *exit policy* that specifies

(a)   (b)

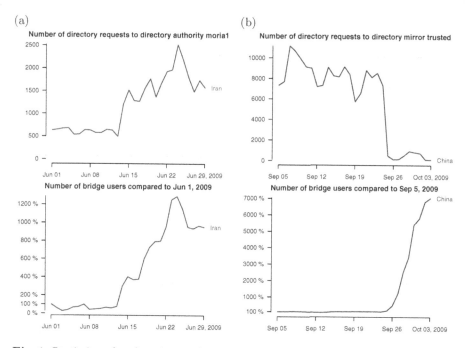

Fig. 1. Statistics related to the number of Tor users in Iran in June 2009 (a) and China in September 2009 (b)

what addresses and ports it is willing to connect to. When a client chooses its path for a given application request, it chooses a relay at random from those that permit the client's request. Selection is weighted by the relays' advertised bandwidths in order to achieve load balancing among relays. However, this approach has the drawback that relays with more permissive exit policies attract far more clients than relays that permit only a small number of addresses or ports. Statistics on exiting traffic per port can help improve load balancing by learning about the overall traffic volume per TCP port. Subsequently, clients could direct more traffic to relays with less permissive exit policies if possible.

Table 1 shows an example of the distribution of traffic to ports. Of these ports, port 80 is the one that has the largest share of read bytes (1.8 GiB) and opened streams (867896). We cannot say what fraction of this traffic can be amounted to web surfing, but the small amount of read bytes and the large number of opened streams speaks for the web surfing assumption and against file sharing. The measuring exit node permitted exiting to all ports, so is not representative for exit nodes in general. In particular, this exit node has seen a disproportional share of traffic on the non-default ports. For example, port 4662, which is typically used for file-sharing applications, sees the largest share of written bytes with a total of 6.3 GiB.

Questions like the ones described above can only be answered by performing statistical analysis on network data in the deployed Tor network. In some cases

Table 1. Statistics on traffic as seen by an exit node with unrestricted exit policy over one day distributed to TCP ports

Port	MiB written	MiB read	Streams opened in K	Default exit policy
80	666 (1.5 %)	1799 (31.7 %)	868 (16.4 %)	Yes
4661	756 (1.7 %)	10 (0.2 %)	25 (0.5 %)	No
4662	6432 (14.8 %)	75 (1.3 %)	176 (3.3 %)	No
6881	291 (0.7 %)	63 (1.1 %)	47 (0.9 %)	No
51413	387 (0.9 %)	40 (0.7 %)	46 (0.9 %)	Yes

it may be sufficient to make assumptions about user behavior to build an anonymity system. But with recent growth of the Tor network, these assumptions need to be questioned. Statistics can help make Tor more useful for censored users and improve performance for all Tor users.

4   Ethical Problems

Performing statistical analysis in an anonymity network is problematic per se, not to mention statistics on network data. The problem is that statistics must not undermine the security properties that the anonymity system is designed to provide. There are several sets of guiding principles which can be followed when collecting statistics in an anonymity network. These include: legal requirements, user privacy, ethical approval, informed consent, and community acceptance.

Legal requirements. We cannot gather any statistical data in the Tor network that is against the law. This limitation becomes even more complicated because data collection needs to take place at multiple locations in the Tor network which are subject to different laws. Therefore, in order to be safe, data collection should be performed on the lowest common denominator of the various laws of countries with measuring nodes. These laws typically fall into two categories: laws specifically prohibiting wiretapping (common worldwide), and generic personal information data protection regulations (in the EU). However in both cases, how these apply to data collection in Tor is uncertain. Wiretapping legislation differentiates between traffic data (headers) and content, but on the Internet there are so many nested protocol layers it is difficult to point to a single boundary. Data protection regulations are even more vague, merely specifying general principles such as only collecting enough information necessary for business purposes, and ensuring that is is not improperly processed. But even though we are bound by laws, only following laws is insufficient from an ethical perspective anyway – especially in our case of an anonymity network. The constraints as described below force us to be even stricter than laws would require.

User privacy. The statistics that we gather must not harm Tor's security properties. In the simplest case, the gathered and subsequently published statistical data must not be useful for an adversary to de-anonymize users. In particular, an adversary that is running one or more Tor relays herself and thereby observing one side of a circuit must not learn any useful information from our statistics about the other side of the circuit. Further, the collection of possibly sensitive data must not make the measuring relays a more attractive target for hacking attempts. The measuring relays should therefore not store sensitive information that an adversary might learn about by hacking other Tor relays, as far as possible. Finally, the code that is used for measuring statistical data should not help an adversary to extend their own logging capabilities more than necessary. A less tech-savvy adversary should not be able to misuse the measurement code to find the places in the Tor source code that could be changed to log even more sensitive network data too easily. Obviously, some of these threats cannot be solved, but only mitigated. The goal of statistical analysis in the Tor network should be to sacrifice as little user privacy as necessary while making the impact of statistics as large as possible.

Ethical approval. For research performed in academic institutions it is sometimes necessary to gain ethics approval from the Institutional Review Board (IRB). However, while such committees are well established in medical research or psychology, they are not in computer science. Faculty-level boards may not have the necessary experience to decide whether a particular experiment is ethically justifiable. There is also significant variation between countries and even institutions on what types of activities require submission to such a committee. As an example, McCoy *et al.* responded to controversy over their PETS 2008 study [8] by asking their IRB whether their experiment would have needed approval. The committee's conclusion was that the research was not classified as using human subjects and was outside their remit [7].

Informed consent. A common principle for ethical approval is that researchers obtain informed consent from subjects. This approach is particularly difficult for an anonymity network where the identity of users is in itself sensitive information. In cases where this is not possible, for example psychology experiments where it is necessary to deceive subjects, stricter ethical rules must be applied and it is more common for IRB approval to be needed. While our data collection methodology will always be public information, we cannot be sure that users will read this documentation before using the system. We must therefore only carry out actions which we believe will cause no harm.

Community acceptance. Even if statistics are perfectly legal and do not harm any security properties, it is important to have the community of users, relay operators, and researchers accept them. An anonymity network like Tor depends to some extent on the trust in the other participants. The biggest threat is probably that we might fail to communicate our plans to gather statistics in the Tor network to our community. It is important that our community understands the need for gathering statistics and exactly how measurements take place. If our community starts thinking that we might not be honest in how we gather our statistics or might not be doing what is best for the Tor network, we lose their trust and the Tor network might lose their support. One approach to openness is to publish all the data we collect; but this may conflict with ethical or legal requirements that data is not improperly processed, and it requires that we apply very strict anonymization methods at the time of collection. In the networking research field, on the other hand, collected data is often only partially anonymized (so as to maximize their usefulness), but data sets are only available on signing a legal agreement to not attempt to de-anonymize users.

5   Case Study

In the following case study we demonstrate the challenges of measuring statistical data in the live Tor network. We consider network data like countries of connecting clients and exiting traffic by port, both of which belong to the most sensitive types of data in an anonymity network. After all, the main purpose of an anonymity network is to keep the correlation between the users' IP addresses and the requests that they send to the network distinct. Measuring either client IP addresses or exiting traffic bears the risk of misuse by an adversary. Therefore, special caution must be taken when deciding how to measure these network data and how to process them in a way that they cannot aid an attacker. Subsequent to the two example cases, we derive a few general guidelines for measuring statistics in the Tor network that might be applied by other researchers studying the Tor network and in other anonymity systems as well.

5.1   Countries of Connecting Clients

The first question to answer is *who* uses the Tor network. This question can be answered by looking at IP addresses of connecting clients. In particular, we want to learn how Tor usage is distributed by countries and how this distribution changes over time. Similarly, statistics about Tor usage can be used to automatically detect blocking of the Tor network. Sudden changes in Tor usage by country would indicate country-wide blocking events.

There are various places at which clients "enter" the Tor network and where their IP addresses can be recognized. The first group is *entry nodes*, which are the first relays in the clients' circuits. Clients need to connect directly to entry nodes in order to hide their IP addresses from subsequent relays and the target they are connecting to. Hence, entry guards learn about the clients' IP addresses, but not what actions they perform over the Tor network. Relays can easily recognize whether a connecting IP address is a client or a relay from the directory of all relay IP addresses. If the connecting IP address is a known relay, they are acting as middle or exit node in a circuit. If not, the connecting IP address is a client. This classification may not be perfect, e.g. clients acting as relays at the same time, but is sufficient for statistical purposes.

The second group of places that can observe client IP addresses are *bridges*. Bridges are relays that are only known to a small set of clients that could otherwise not connect to the Tor network. Similar to entry nodes, bridges learn about client IP addresses from incoming connections. In contrast to entry nodes, bridges can be sure that every connection they see is from a client, so when making a list of clients they do not need to filter out relay IP addresses.

The third group of places at which clients connect directly to the Tor network are *directory nodes*, which are either the directory authorities or directory mirrors. Clients connect to the directory authorities during the bootstrapping process when they do not know about any relays other than the hard-coded directory authorities. Clients download the current network status (a list of relays through which they can build circuits), and then periodically connect to directory mirrors to update their view on the network. In most cases clients connect directly to the directory mirrors instead of building a circuit to fetch the information privately, because there are little or no privacy issues in downloading a network status. The requests that clients send to the directories are categorized into two versions of network status formats, one of them requested by clients up to Tor version 0.1.x and the other one by clients running Tor version 0.2.x.

It becomes immediately obvious that client IP addresses are highly sensitive information in an anonymity network. The mere fact that someone connects to the Tor network is not (and cannot be) protected by the Tor protocol. However, this information should not leak to an adversary easily. An adversary that is trying to break the anonymity properties of Tor tries to link a client's IP address to a request leaving the Tor network. If there were such a list of client IP addresses, an adversary could monitor the traffic exiting the Tor network and try to correlate clients to outgoing requests or incoming responses.

As a first step to protect client IP addresses from leaking to an adversary, they should be resolved to a country as soon as possible. Since analysis takes place on the country level, we do not need to keep the exact IP addresses of clients. This resolution can be done using a local GeoIP database that maps IP addresses to country codes. Tor versions since June 2008 include such a GeoIP database that is 2.5 MB in size. In the case of counting events per country, e.g. directory requests, this resolution can take place immediately. However, if the goal is to count unique IP addresses per country, IP addresses need to be stored in memory in some form in order to detect duplicates. In the process of writing this data to disk, IP addresses can be resolved to countries and the number of unique IP addresses per country can be summed.

The resolution of IP addresses to countries is an important first step, but it is not sufficient. The information that a client from a certain country has connected to the Tor network at a certain time might still be too sensitive to be published, especially for countries with only few Tor users. Therefore, as a second step, events are accumulated over an amount of time that makes the data less useful for an adversary. We assume that an accumulation of events over the course of one day is sufficient to prevent an adversary from learning too much. This accumulation means that statistics will not be able to discover changes in Tor usage by time of day, but this seems like a reasonable compromise.

Finally, the exact number of events from a certain country per day might still reveal sensitive information if that number is very low. In general, exact numbers

```
dirreq-stats-end 2009-08-20 17:16:35 (86400 s)
dirreq-v2-ips us=4136,de=3744,cn=3552,gb=1120,ir=1024,kr=952,it=848,
    fr=768,ru=768,??=688,ca=616,se=480,es=392,pl=392,au=368,[...]
dirreq-v3-ips us=6024,de=5176,cn=3384,fr=2208,kr=1328,it=1288,ru=1120,
    gb=1048,se=816,ca=808,pl=800,??=744,ir=728,jp=600,br=576,[...]
dirreq-v2-reqs us=7136,cn=5608,de=4728,kr=3816,gb=1568,ir=1464,ru=1136,
    it=1120,fr=1096,??=968,ca=936,tw=720,se=664,jp=576,au=552,[...]
dirreq-v3-reqs us=7800,de=5944,kr=4368,cn=4208,fr=2632,ru=1616,it=1576,
    gb=1272,ir=1096,ca=1024,??=1016,se=976,pl=944,tw=792,au=784,[...]
```

Fig. 2. Number of IP addresses and requests for network statuses as observed by a directory mirror

pose a risk when the adversary can generate such events herself and observe how many other events have occurred in the same time. As a third step, the exact number of events is concealed by introducing artificial imprecision. This is done by rounding up event numbers to the next multiple of 8.

All statistics based on client IP addresses are processed by the measuring entry node, bridge, or directory before publication as described above. Figure 2 shows an example of unique client IP addresses and number of requests for relay lists on a directory mirror. The first line indicates when the data were written and what time interval is covered. The remaining lines state how many unique IP addresses or directory requests have been observed from which country for the two possible network status versions. For example, this directory mirror has observed 7800 requests for version 3 network statuses from 6024 unique IP addresses from the United States. The country code ?? stands for IP addresses that could not be resolved to a country. The exact data format is described in the directory protocol specification document [12].

The statistics from entry nodes and bridges look similar, except that they only contain unique IP addresses and no requests of any kind. Directory mirrors and entry nodes upload their statistics to the directory authorities where they can be downloaded by anyone who is interested. Bridges upload their statistics to the bridge authority. Before publication of bridge statistics, all possibly identifying information about the bridge needs to be removed. Otherwise, bridge statistics might reveal to an adversary where bridges are located. Instead, bridges are assigned a unique bridge identifier, so that statistics of the same bridge can be observed over time.

5.2   Exiting Traffic by Port

The analogue of IP addresses of clients connecting to the Tor network is traffic exiting from the Tor network to the Internet. In contrast to the question *who* is using the Tor network that can be answered by looking at client IP addresses, exiting traffic can reveal more information about *what* the Tor network is used for. Statistics of exiting traffic include what kind of applications are used over the Tor network, or the comparison of overall traffic volume per TCP port versus the advertised bandwidth capacity per port.

```
exit-stats-end 2009-07-24 20:40:35 (86400 s)
exit-kibibytes-written 17=58902,23=9616,25=262579,40=9546,76=5789,
    80=681732,85=121859,143=7541,222=5133,300=9517,442=9634,443=12157,
    444=11692,690=5768,801=8100,850=9078,1000=6737,1015=57885,[...],
    other=15332199
exit-kibibytes-read 17=15,23=79,25=13221,40=7,76=2,80=1841879,85=926,
    143=1038,222=85,300=25,442=5,443=38435,444=94,690=8,801=9,850=12,
    1000=373,1015=68,[...],other=3035782
exit-streams-opened 17=12,23=88,25=141240,40=12,76=16,80=867896,
    85=2704,143=168,222=32,300=28,442=12,443=147348,444=92,690=4,
    801=16,850=16,1000=716,1015=56,[...],other=3165052
```

Fig. 3. Number of exiting bytes and opened streams as observed by an exit node

Statistics on traffic exiting the Tor network could be as sensitive as statistics on connecting client IP addresses. For one thing, the contents and targets of exiting traffic must not be disclosed, even without knowing which clients have sent or received these messages. After all, the majority of deployed application protocols do not encrypt traffic on the network. Similarly, the target address might reveal some information about the content and possible clients, especially if there are only few requests to that target. For another thing, exiting traffic, even in somewhat aggregated form, must not be usable to be combined with information on client IP addresses to correlate IP addresses to requests or responses. An adversary that runs an entry node or bridge should not gain additional information when combining her list of client IP addresses with exit traffic statistics.

Observations of exit traffic are processed in multiple steps to make them less useful for an adversary yet still useful for statistical analysis. In the first step, all information about the content of exiting traffic is discarded and only the meta data is preserved. Traffic content includes application headers and application content. While it is tempting from a statistical point of view to analyze at least the application headers, this analysis could cross the line from the pen register category (signaling and addressing) to the wiretap category (content) [3], so it is best avoided. Furthermore, the target address is discarded for statistics, as an adversary might draw conclusions about the content of requests. The remaining meta data that are used for statistical analysis are the target port and the number of outgoing and incoming bytes per connection.

In the next step, the exact times of observations are removed by accumulating observations over a measurement interval of 24 hours. Without this step, the information about an exiting connection including the target port number and number of transfered bytes might still give a hint on the content and/or client. Therefore, the number of written and read bytes as well as the number of opened streams are summed up per port. These sums not only make it impossible to restore timestamps, but they also hide single traffic patterns of incoming vs. outgoing bytes per connection. The intermediate result is a triple of written bytes, read bytes, and opened streams for every TCP port.

The third step of making these statistics less useful for an adversary is to report only the data for TCP ports that have seen a number of bytes exceeding a given threshold. All data for ports with data below this threshold are summed up and reported together.

Finally, in a fourth step, all observations are rounded up to conceal exact numbers of possibly only a few events. Bytes are rounded up to full KiB, and numbers of opened streams are rounded up to the next multiple of 4.

The results of the aggregation of exit traffic per port can be seen in Figure 3, which corresponds to the data shown in Table 1. The four lines describe when statistics were written and how long the measurement interval was, the number of written/read KiB, and the number of opened streams per port. For example, this exit node wrote 681732 KiB (666 MiB) and read 1841879 KiB (1.8 GiB) in 867896 streams on port 80. The threshold for a port being included in the statistics is 0.01% of all transfered bytes. All ports with fewer relayed bytes are summarized as port other. Again, the data format is described in the directory protocol specification document [12].

5.3   Guidelines

From these example cases as well as from earlier considerations we can derive a few guidelines. These guidelines shall apply to all future statistical analyses in the Tor network and hopefully to other anonymity systems as well.

Data minimalism. The first and most important guideline is that only the minimum amount of statistical data should be gathered to solve a given problem. The level of detail of measured data should be as small as possible.

Source aggregation. Possibly sensitive data should exist for as short a time as possible. Data should be aggregated at its source, including categorizing single events and memorizing category counts only, summing up event counts over large time frames, and being imprecise regarding exact event counts.

Transparency. All algorithms to gather statistical data need to be discussed publicly before deploying them. All measured statistical data should be made publicly available as a safeguard to not gather data that is too sensitive.

6   Discussion

This paper presents a case study of measuring two types of potentially sensitive data in the live Tor anonymity network: countries of connecting clients and exiting traffic by port. Both types of data have in common that they are sensitive in their raw form and need to be aggregated before being published and performing statistical analysis on them. We derived guidelines that can be useful for similar cases in the future when measuring sensitive data in anonymity networks. We hope that this paper starts a discussion on safely measuring network data in anonymity systems that serves both researchers studying anonymity networks and users relying on the protection that anonymity networks provide.

Acknowledgements

We thank Jacob Appelbaum and Jonathan Rippstein for measuring the presented statistics on their Tor relays.

References

1. Dingledine, R., Mathewson, N., Syverson, P.: Tor: The second-generation onion router. In: Proceedings of the 13th USENIX Security Symposium, August 2004, pp. 303–320 (2004)
2. Dwork, C.: Differential privacy. In: Bugliesi, M., Preneel, B., Sassone, V., Wegener, I. (eds.) ICALP 2006. LNCS, vol. 4052, pp. 1–12. Springer, Heidelberg (2006)
3. Electronic Frontier Foundation. Tor: Legal FAQ for Tor server operators, https://www.torproject.org/eff/tor-legal-faq.html
4. Lenhard, J., Loesing, K., Wirtz, G.: Performance measurements of Tor hidden services in low-bandwidth access networks. In: Abdalla, M., Pointcheval, D., Fouque, P.-A., Vergnaud, D. (eds.) ACNS 2009. LNCS, vol. 5536. Springer, Heidelberg (2009)
5. Loesing, K.: Measuring the Tor network from public directory information. Technical report, 2nd Hot Topics in Privacy Enhancing Technologies (HotPETs 2009), Seattle, WA, USA (August 2009)
6. Loesing, K., Sandmann, W., Wilms, C., Wirtz, G.: Performance measurements and statistics of Tor hidden services. In: Proceedings of the International Symposium on Applications and the Internet (SAINT 2008), Turku, Finland, July 2008. IEEE Computer Society, Los Alamitos (2008)
7. McCoy, D., Bauer, K., Grunwald, D., Kohno, T., Sicker, D.: Response to Tor study, http://systems.cs.colorado.edu/mediawiki/index.php/Response_To_Tor_Study
8. McCoy, D., Bauer, K., Grunwald, D., Kohno, T., Sicker, D.: Shining light in dark places: Understanding the Tor network. In: Borisov, N., Goldberg, I. (eds.) PETS 2008. LNCS, vol. 5134, pp. 63–76. Springer, Heidelberg (2008)
9. Murdoch, S.J., Zieliński, P.: Sampled traffic analysis by Internet-exchange-level adversaries. In: Borisov, N., Golle, P. (eds.) PET 2007. LNCS, vol. 4776, pp. 167–183. Springer, Heidelberg (2007)
10. Øverlier, L., Syverson, P.: Locating hidden servers. In: Proceedings of the 2006 IEEE Symposium on Security and Privacy, May 2006. IEEE CS, Los Alamitos (2006)
11. The Tor Project. Tor bridges specification (2009), https://git.torproject.org/checkout/tor/master/doc/spec/bridges-spec.txt
12. The Tor Project. Tor directory protocol, version 3 (2009), https://git.torproject.org/checkout/tor/master/doc/spec/dir-spec.txt
13. Wendolsky, R., Herrmann, D., Federrath, H.: Performance comparison of low-latency anonymisation services from a user perspective. In: Borisov, N., Golle, P. (eds.) PET 2007. LNCS, vol. 4776, pp. 233–253. Springer, Heidelberg (2007)

A Case Study in Ethical Decision Making Regarding Remote Mitigation of Botnets

David Dittrich[1], Felix Leder[2], and Tillmann Werner[2]

[1] University of Washington, Seattle WA 98195, USA
[2] Institute of Computer Science IV, University of Bonn, Germany

Abstract. It is becoming more common for researchers to find themselves in a position of being able to take over control of a malicious botnet. If this happens, should they use this knowledge to clean up all the infected hosts? How would this affect not only the owners and operators of the zombie computers, but also other researchers, law enforcement agents serving justice, or even the criminals themselves? What dire circumstances would change the calculus about what is or is not appropriate action to take? We review two case studies of long-lived malicious botnets that present serious challenges to researchers and responders and use them to illuminate many ethical issues regarding aggressive mitigation. We make no judgments about the questions raised, instead laying out the pros and cons of possible choices and allowing workshop attendees to consider how and where they would draw lines. By this, we hope to expose where there is clear community consensus as well as where controversy or uncertainty exists.

1 Introduction

The first distributed denial of service (DDoS) attacks occurred more than 10 years ago, in the summer of 1999 [7]. These were relatively small attack networks by today's standards, ranging from several hundred to more than two thousand computers. Even at those small sizes, these attack networks were capable of disrupting some of the largest educational and commercial service providers in existence for hours up to days at a time. The motivation for these attacks started out at the level of electronic *drive-by shootings* that were primarily over petty fights on Internet Relay Chat (IRC) channels. That soon shifted to extortion against online gambling sites as early as 2001 [26] and online pornography sites as early as 2003 [35], attacks against commercial competitors as early as 2003 [29], and politically-motivated attacks against national infrastructures in 2007 [2]. Perhaps just as frightening, if less apparent, are highly targeted attacks using small and subtle botnets used for less obvious attacks than brute-force denial of service [9].

Not only are malicious attack networks (or *botnets* as they are commonly known) capable of pure disruption of services, but they also cause harm to both companies and individuals through fraud, identity theft, abuse of computer and network resources and other violations of personal privacy. Some botnets remain

R. Sion et al. (Eds.): FC 2010 Workshops, LNCS 6054, pp. 216–230, 2010.
© IFCA/Springer-Verlag Berlin Heidelberg 2010

under hostile control for many months. This is driving researchers, security product and service vendors, and professionals in the security community to express growing frustration. While we focus in this paper on the former group – *researchers* – the same issues and challenges apply to the latter groups as well. Some in the general public perceieve a lack of visible action by law enforcement agencies or the private sector to stem malicious activity. Their frustration motivates calls for the right to fight back, as if this were an issue of *self-defense* against someone throwing punches.

We acknowledge that research of cybercriminal activity involves ethical choices, legal restrictions, liability concerns, as well as challenging political questions. We also acknowledge that each society and culture has its own norms and laws that must be considered when trying to deal with issues that are global in scope. Our primary goal in this work is to illuminate as many ethical issues as is possible surrounding alternatives for aggressively mitigating today's massive and highly robust distributed attack networks, allowing the reader to draw their own conclusions about what actions are or are not appropriate.

There are many different ethical codes and standards that apply to a greater or lesser degree to professional and academic activities, however that does not mean that any one of these codes or standards are sufficient to guide computer security researchers. [13] For example, Institutional Review Boards (IRBs) in the United States are commonly cited, however IRBs are focused on protection of human subjects of biomedical and behavioral research, only apply to research involving humans, and provide little in the way of guidance for developing new research protocols. Professional standards, industry standards, and the Internet Activities Board's best practices all have limitations. IRBs have a limited form of enforcement (in that they can refuse to approve applications and thus halt research they deem harmful), while the rest leave enforcement to unspecified authorities or membership-specific ethics boards.

Ethicists such as Markham suggest considering *ethic as method* and making conscious decisions about research methodology that reflect one's intentions and their source of, "consciousness, mindfulness, honesty, and sensitivity." [27] In discussing this topic Markham suggests researchers ask themselves self-reflective questions, perhaps along the lines of: "What is the intent in performing this research? Who is the stakeholder being served? How would this stakeholder view my actions and interpret my intent? Would they feel grateful, neutral or resentful?"

Proposing a complete new framework for designing ethical research protocols goes well beyond the scope of a case study. Rather than using a more formal method of analysis [12] and making judgments, we borrow and extend some analytic tools from other domains. By applying them to the specific area of computer security research involving *criminal botnets* we aim to get to the issues, not the answers.

We next review our cases, delve into the entities and ethical issues involved, then conclude with a call for a thoughtful dialog.

2   Storm, Conficker, and Beyond

2.1   Storm

In April 2007, Holz, et al, at the University of Mannheim [20], performed Storm botnet enumeration experiments in which they infiltrated the Storm botnet and used features of the distributed hash table (DHT) that is used by Storm to enumerate the bots. They were able to observe the effect of other researchers who were simultaneously doing their own enumeration experiments, and specifically noted UCSD and Georgia Tech (among other unnamed sites) as being observable participants in the Storm botnet. They discuss two attacks – eclipsing, or *Sybil attack*, and poisoning – that could be performed to degrade or render inoperable the Storm botnet. Both could be argued to be positive outcomes. While not stated by Holz, these two attacks would also not have negative effects on the owners of compromised computers. While potentially disabling the botnet, at least temporarily, these attacks do nothing to help mitigate the botnet by assisting in cleanup efforts of individually compromised hosts.

On December 29, 2008, researchers from the University of Bonn and the RWTH Aachen University presented a talk at the 25th Chaos Communication Congress (25C3) in Germany on "0wning the Storm botnet." This research was inspired by the Storm enumeration research at the University of Mannheim. The group demonstrated how knowledge gained from reverse engineering the Storm botnet's command and control (C&C) protocol allowed them to take control of Storm nodes. They showed how Storm bots could be commanded to download and replace Storm with *any chosen binary executable*. Such reverse engineering is required for comprehensive understanding of emerging malware threats [14,22,20,5,4]. Partial source code for their program that implements the counter-attack on the Storm botnet (named *Stormfucker*) was released on the `full-disclosure` mailing list. In their 25C3 presentation, and an interview following the conference [8], they caution that affecting compromised computers is illegal in many countries, but speculate that someone who resides in a country where there are no laws preventing such action might use the knowledge embodied in the released code to dismantle the Storm botnet, or complete their own working code and publish it. They reasoned that publication could have the positive effect of informing the owners of infected computers, who were likely unaware of these infections, could clean up their *zombie* computers. This work was not presented in an academic setting. Had it been, a program committee may have provided anonymous feedback and/or initiated more public discussion of the ethical principles that could justify attempting to clean up thousands of infected computers (e.g., offering guidance such as Denning [10] or Spafford [36] that could help guide those with access to the source code in deciding how to use it.)

Two of the Bonn researchers presented this research at a conference at the Cooperative Cyber Defence Centre of Excellence in Tallinn, Estonia, in June 2009. The abstract of their talk [25] "asks urgently for political discussions about authorization and legal feasibility" of taking offensive measures to clean computers without their owners' knowledge or consent, and argues that, "pro-actively fighting botnets requires immediate political and international consensus."

2.2 Conficker

Conficker (a.k.a. Downadup) version .A was first reported to have been found in the wild on November 21, 2008 [39]. Conficker.A exploits the Windows RPC vulnerability MS08-067 for propagation and uses a set of 250 randomly generated domain names as C&C rendezvous points. On December 29, 2008 (38 days later), version .B was released which added more propagation methods targeting hosts on the local and remote networks, as well as blocking access to Microsoft's patching servers, AV companies and other mitigation tool web sites. More notable was its switch from use of the SHA-1 hashing algorithm to MD-6, released on October 27, 2008 (64 days prior). A third version, .C[1], was observed on February 20, 2009 which also implemented a limited peer-to-peer (P2P) protocol for command and control and moved to random selection of a daily rotating subset of up to 50,000 domain names. 12 days later an updated .C release occurred that fixed a bug in MD-6 that was only publicly announced 16 days earlier. Another analysis of Conficker [24] was released on March 30, 2009, that described some weaknesses in Conficker that allowed for remote infection scanning. Again, a new release of Conficker.D on April 8, 2009 (8 days after [24]) rendered the first scanning method useless and required major changes to the scanners in order to stay effective. This shows ample evidence that the authors of Conficker are studying publications about Conficker and are capable of quickly responding when they wish. Furthermore, it illustrates the arms race that exists between open publication of defense methodologies and reactive counter-measures by attackers.

Conficker infected nodes have only been observed to attempt its HTTP-based update protocol via its domain generation algorithm (DGA). An active defense mechanism against those update attempts is the sinkholing of domains performed by the Conficker Working Group in cooperation with registrars all over the world. The power of this approach prompted Conficker's authors to add P2P functionality in order to be able to perform updates by another means. Eventually, the .D update was pushed using the new protocol showing researchers and defenders that sinkholing, while necessary, was not sufficient to completely stop updates. Again, this illustrates how information made public can degrade defensive mechanisms and hinder the ability of defenders to monitor malicious activity.

There have been no major releases of Conficker since the .D release, however millions of infected hosts remain active on the internet and DNS-based mitigation methods continue to be pursued and research into Conficker continues. A detailed analysis of Conficker.C's P2P algorithm was done by SRI and released on September 21, 2009 [33]. This analysis discusses several technical aspects of the design that have not been publicly discussed to date.

---

[1] Following the naming scheme in [24].

2.3   Alternative Countermeasures

In the examples just presented, there are several alternative means for trying to counter or mitigate these advanced threats. The encryption mechanisms in advanced bots like Nugache [14] and Conficker are sufficiently robust to prevent taking over the C&C channel and directly controlling the bots: the bots will ignore commands without proper signatures. Storm, on the other hand, was weak enough that someone could control the bots. It is likely that all three had programming vulnerabilities that could be exploited to attack via buffer overflow errors, etc., allowing the running bot to be hijacked.

Infected bots can be identified in one of several ways. One can passively monitor botnet activity to learn which peers are active; one might be able to write a crawler that can walk the botnet and enumerate all active bots; or one can scan for active bots that are listening for such connections. Of course NAT and firewalls can limit the ability to reach a subset of bots, which may limit the ability to communicate with bots to only using the in-band C&C channel (which may be hardened to the point that it is not usable). The fact that the entire infected population cannot be reached at any given moment means that there is no absolute *strike once* potential for completely taking the botnet out of the hands of the criminal.

There are two primary ways to attempt to remotely mitigate them (i.e., *clean up infected hosts or disable the malware* by exploiting weaknesses: some form of *targeted* attack that uses *hit lists*, or some form of *autonomous, self-propagating* mechanism like those used for other worms. The former method can be controlled very precisely, limiting its scope, rate, and timing. The latter method is typically less predictable, more prone to secondary side-effects on network infrastructure, and very indiscriminate. Staniford, et al [37] describe various methods to speed up worm propagation that could also be used to more precisely target and control worms (e.g., localized scanning, hit-list scanning, and topological scanning.) In terms of ethical principals, *proportionality* requires that actions be properly targeted (not indiscriminate) and the *Defense Principal* requires the actions be necessary for repel or prevent harm directed at the entity taking action. Once an anti-worm is spreading autonomously *in-the-wild*, the propagation effects may be impossible to predict or control.

An informal poll of university system administrators in 2003 [11] found 80% of the 76 respondents believed an autonomous *white worm* was unethical. When asked whether a more targeted (non-worm) method of worm mitigation used by Laurent Oudot to clean up Blaster infections within networks over which he had responsibility [31] was described, the response flipped and only 20% believed Oudot's method was unethical. This remaining hesitancy was partly due to the final command shown in the article (`shutdown -r -f -t 0 exit`) which immediately reboots the computer without the owner/operator's knowledge or consent.

At the less aggressive end of the spectrum are actions that researchers can take to try to identify those controlling malicious botnets. Crawling malicious P2P networks without leaving noticeable traces or at least attempting to conceal this activity, may allow identification of computers used to control the botnet without impacting law enforcement investigations or affecting enumeration activity of other researchers.

3   Ethical Questions Raised

As we have seen, today's sophisticated botnets pose a serious threat that is difficult to mitigate through end-user action alone, especially when those end-users do not possess the knowledge, skills, or tools to allow them to easily and effectively counter advanced malware. We have chosen to focus this case study on resilient botnets for several reasons.

First is the inability of the average computer user to either protect themselves against malware infection through social engineering attacks, or effectively respond when attacked. Even if it were possible to inform users that their computer was infected with resilient malware, it is extremely difficult for them to effectively cleanup the infection without resorting to wiping and re-installing the entire operating system, enlisting the help of costly expert assistance, and taking many hours or days of down-time to complete the task. This places the emphasis on finding ways of helping users who cannot help themselves.

The concept of the *Active Response Continuum* was developed to describe the problems resulting from differences in *capacity to respond* and in *aggressiveness of actions taken* to counter wide-spread malicious attack. [15,11] Both of these concepts are useful for this discussion and are adapted for use here in Tables 1 and 2. In terms of the ARC, most computer users operate at *Level 0* and a lesser number only operate at *Level 1* or higher. In addition, it must be mentioned that the use of protective software alone does not save users from getting infected because none of the known products has a detection rate of 100% [3]. They typically miss several hundreds of thousands of malware specimens.

The second interesting issue is that service providers and enterprises who manage computer systems for thousands or millions of users are capable of operating at higher ARC *Level 3*, but are often prevented (for various reasons, mostly non-technical) from being able to individually assist all infected users and/or cleanup the computers by hand. As malware gets more sophisticated and resilient to detection and mitigation, the problem grows.

Table 1. Levels of *Capacity*. (Original source: [15]).

Level	Victim Posture	Characteristic Actions
0	Unaware	No activity: passively rely on system to stay functional
1	Involved	Use and maintain protective software and hardware
2	Interactive	Modifies software and hardware in response to attacks
3	Cooperative	Implements joint traceback and investigation with other victims
4	Non-cooperative (Active Response)	Invasive tracebacks, controlling malware infected hosts, cease-and-desist measures, retaliatory counter-strike

Table 2. Levels of *Aggressiveness*. (Original source: [15]).

Level	Impacts	Characteristic Actions
Benign	Limited to victim's own systems	Sniffing, scanning, re-addressing hosts, honeypots
Intermediate	Impacts on remote systems, but not calculated to produce damage	Invasive tracebacks, remote evidence collection, interaction with (controlling) malware
Aggressive	Impacts calculated to alter function of remote system or affect integrity	Remote exploitation, corruption of data, patching, re-installation of software/malware, denial of service

Security researchers are also continuing to improve their skills, to the point where it is now common to obtain enough information to control a botnet and its infected hosts [28,18,38,20,22,32,23,8,9].

3.1   Who?

When engaged in what Markham calls "world-fixing," one needs to "[derive their methods] through constant, critical reflection on the goals of research and the research questions," understanding not only the problems to be solved, but the potential effects on all parties involved. [27] Before diving into our questions, let us first answer this question of, "who is involved with criminal botnets?"

The *Owners/Operators* of infected computers have responsibility for protecting the information and information systems that they own. When their systems are attacked, they have responsibility for taking actions to regain control of their assets. They are the least capable of detecting and responding to attacks. They have rights of privacy and autonomy of operation within their domain.

When botnets are used to perform secondary attacks, such as defrauding customers of specific banks through "phishing," distributed denial of service, spamming, etc., there are two kinds of *Victims*. Some may be entirely unrelated to the *Owner/Operators*, such as the banks and service providers suffering DDoS mentioned above. Alternatively, there are other *Victims* who are related only in terms of sharing the infected computing resources (e.g., friends, family, customers.) Actions taken to remove bots from the control of attackers benefit all *Victims*, but if the action harms the infected computers, the people sharing those computers are also harmed. *Victims* have little or no responsibility for the systems they use, or for the systems used to cause harm to them. They do not have authority to change those systems or to monitor network activity. They are similar to typical *Owners/Operators* in terms of capability to protect themselves, and have similar rights (e.g., to privacy.)

Service Providers provide network connectivity to the *Owners/Operators* of infected computers or *Victims*. In the case of enterprises these may also be the *Owners/Operators*, while in the case of home users these are Network Service Providers (NSPs), such as broadband, wireless, and DSL companies. *Service*

Providers are similar to *Owners/Operators* in terms of responsibility to protect their computer assets. In some cases, they are granted *provider exemptions* from various computer crime or privacy laws that allow certain activities, such as monitoring real-time communications, that would otherwise be an illegal wiretap. They may also have contractual terms extending their authority to the information systems of their customers (e.g., limited control of anti-malware software on customer computers.)

Researchers are the ones capable of reverse engineering today's advanced malware and developing methods to detect, cleanup, and possibly counter-attack the botnet via exploitation of design weaknesses. Their role is to help identify and analyze malicious software, deriving generalizable knowledge that can then be disseminated to corporations for improvement of their products and services, to service providers to improve the efficiency of their response, helping law enforcement understand computer crime tools and techniques, and helping the general public with awareness and training. They have an obligation to act responsibly. They are not exempt from computer crime statutes, and in academic settings may have legal obligations to submit their research protocols to institutional review boards for human subjects protection evaluation. They themselves have no authority to make changes to computer systems owned by others without the knowledge and consent of those owners, but they can work in consultative or advisory roles to those who do.

Since we are talking about criminal activity, two other classes of people involved are *Law Enforcement* and the *Criminals* themselves. *Law Enforcement*, as agents of sovereign governments, are the only other parties who have legitimate responsibilities to bring criminals to justice. They are bound to protect the legal rights of all others, while performing their duties with a minimum of negative impact on innocent or victimized parties. While they do some research, their role is not to provide generalizable knowledge and disseminate their research results to the public as is the case with *Researchers*, on whom they rely heavily for advanced applied and theoretical research. They also rely on *Owners/Operators*, *Service Providers*, and *Victims* to report crimes and provide evidence to further investigations. On the other side are the *Criminals*, who drive much of computer security research today. They act without regard for harm to anyone, may negatively impact the lives of millions, yet (arguably, to some) still have rights.

3.2   What, Where, Why, When, and How?

We now examine some of the most common and problematic ethical questions surrounding criminal botnet research.

[*Question 1*] **Is it ethical to perform research that alters an active crime scene without coordinating with law enforcement?**

[**YES**] Researchers in academia often value independence of thought, speech, and from involvement with investigative activities of the government. In some ways, there is a societal obligation for academics to be independent and to avoid the appearance of acting as unrestricted agents of law enforcement. It is not their role to collect and deliver evidence to the state, but to study the world and derive generalizable knowledge from their studies to enlighten the public. In certain situations where researchers are studying criminal behavior there are *certificates of confidentiality* limiting compelled disclosure of research data to the state, even under subpoena. Under the U.S. regulation governing the protection of human subjects in research (45 CFR 46, also know as "the Common Rule" [1]) there exists an exemption (§101(b)(2)) for, "Research involving [...] the observation of public behavior: unless: (i) information obtained is recorded in such a manner that human subjects can be identified, directly or through identifiers linked to the subjects; and (ii) any disclosure of the human subjects' responses outside the research could reasonably place the subjects at risk of criminal or civil liability or be damaging to the subjects' financial standing, employability, or reputation." Certainly identifying a criminal suspect to law enforcement could result in damage to their "financial standing, employability, or reputation," but is that the intent of this federal regulation?

In the case of the Storm worm, it was only possible to trace the origin of the network because researchers reverse engineered Storm's communication protocols and were actively collecting information about active nodes. Those behind Storm have not been identified, but commands originating from networks believed to be associated with criminal activity were clearly observed. It would be unlikely for law enforcement, unaided, to do the research necessary to learn these facts.

[**NO**] Let us assume that the researcher's goal is to maximize benefit to the public by learning about how criminal tools work and developing new detection mechanisms, better investigative capabilities, or new methods of protecting systems. How does protecting the privacy of criminals, or withholding research results for several months to fit conference publication cycles, impact law enforcement? Certificates of confidentiality were designed to (a) protect criminals who are *consenting research subjects*, and (b) are involved in biomedical research under the authority of the Department of Health and Human Services [30]. Even if such a certificate could be obtained, it may be difficult to argue that protection of the privacy rights of criminals results in a greater moral good than providing information to law enforcement officers protecting the public.

Beyond potentially identifying criminals to law enforcement officers, there are other potential impacts of certain research activities on active criminal investigations and thus a need for *deconfliction*. How do actions that fall into the *Aggressive* level in Table 2, which may introduce false evidence into an active crime scene as might result from a *Sybil* attack [16] on a P2P network, impact law enforcement? What may seem a joke – that the Storm botnet would "shrink to a handful of real bots [while] an army of rabid researchers [fight] with each other to measure whatever was left [17]" – has serious implications. What if researcher's actions divert law enforcement, causing them to issue one or more subpoenas before eventually learning they had "caught" a white hat instead of a black hat? Could this in some way even assist criminals? Should researchers even be allowed to perform such experiments without coordination, or some prior arrangement to work with security operators (who have legal exemptions and responsibility to protect information and information systems)? Is there a need for regulation limiting research to only non-criminal activities, or researching criminal botnet activity only under tightly controlled conditions similar to research into biological agents and toxins like anthrax, ricin, and smallpox (e.g., Public Law 107-188 in the United States)? Or is a government-mandated ethical review model like the Embryonic Stem Cell Research Oversight (ESCRO) [6] committees in the United States, which are separate from IRBs, necessary?

Cybercriminals today possess advanced technical expertise that demands constant study in order to keep up. This is hard enough for researchers, but it is impractical to expect law enforcement to be experts at *both* researching malware and performing complex investigations at the same time. For this reason, law enforcement relies heavily on private sector research. Cooperative efforts between law enforcement and the private sector are vastly improving the situation, but when does this close relationship risk the independence of researchers?

Finally, there arise questions related to *responsible conduct of research*. Should researchers be initiating experiments that alter cyber crime scenes without at least knowing how and when to contact law enforcement, reporting this activity before (or as soon as possible after) performing the experiment? What if the experiment uncovers evidence of very serious financial crime, industrial espionage, or possible national security espionage (e.g., as in the Ghostnet [9] investigation)? Shouldn't actions with potential risks to the researchers (or their institutions) require considering these issues in advance to minimize potential of loss of control of the experiment, or possibly being reported as suspects in criminal activity themselves? Again, the Storm worm is an example of of how actions by researchers alter an active crime scene. In 2008, researchers from different institutions all over the world were actively participating in the P2P network [17]. Research activity made up a large amount of the network traffic and complicated making a distinction between research machines, infected computers, and possible sources of actual malicious C&C traffic.

[*Question 2*] **Is it ethical to restrict researchers to only performing actions that are guaranteed to be risk-free, or avoid any potential ambiguity in laws?**

[**YES**] Since researching botnets necessitates interaction with the bots, which may alter data inside the botnet, there is always the chance of unpredictable side-effects. This is especially true because it is not always possible to know how communications with the botnet will influence the bots when analysis starts. Certain actions might affect or even break the systems of innocents. Simply introducing another zombie into the malicious botnet may result in that host becoming part of a DDoS attack, sending spam, or allowing a criminal to hide behind a proxied connection.

Running malware in sandboxes to observe behavior is now the standard investigation method for new malware. The risk of further spreading while doing so is high. Many researchers ran Conficker samples in order to investigate the exploitation mechanism. Limiting researchers to performing less dangerous analysis steps first (e.g., black-box analysis in closed lab environments, or using only static analysis techniques) reduces risk while often gathering the same information as *live infection*.

[**NO**] Limiting research to only that which is completely risk-free would result in "no research" at all. By not allowing any research the bot developers and criminals using the botnets would have a massive advantage. When no new analysis and mitigation tactics can be investigated, the botnet problem would grow. But where should we draw the line? Conficker, for example, does not appear to include any logic that does direct harm to infected computers (e.g., data destruction), nor has any such harm been observed. Without allowing interaction with the C&C server, it is impossible to know the malware's behavior *in the wild* and the threat it poses.

Attackers have learned to avoid simple means of detection, e.g., automated use of *sandbox* analysis of malware. Researchers must sometimes run malicious code for a long time in order to become a "trusted" node in the infrastructure and to see the heart of botnets. These nodes have to act "undercover" and must behave like regular infected machines. This includes sending spam and participating in DDoS attacks, which inflicts some amount of harm on third parties [21].

[*Question 3*] **Is it ethical to clean up infected computers owned by others without their knowledge and consent?**

[**YES**] Worm infected hosts can crash. They can disrupt networks and harm other hosts. Leaving them infected prolongs this harm. Worm infected hosts have been seen to disable medical facilities, prompting them to seek emergency active countermeasures against Conficker to restore network stability immediately. But how can one calculate the risk vs. benefit for *uncoordinated* cleanup?

[**NO**] It is hardly feasible to clean up only specific computers from remote locations because it is often not known whether commands are proxied to another machine or consumed right by the communication peer. Thus, a remote cleanup must be regarded similar to the actions of self-spreading worms that do not know the next victim machine in advance. There are no examples of *white worms* that were 100% effective and harmless at automatically cleaning up malicious worm infected hosts, but there are many examples of ones that caused more harm than good. The very first attempt at a helpful worm in 1978 left the entire Xerox Palo Alto Research Center (PARC) network useless for a couple of days while each computer had to be manually cleansed of a rampant worm. The *Code Green* worm and Linux *Cheese* worm in 2001, and the *Welchia (a.k.a., Nachi)* worm in 2003, all had problems that caused some systems to crash. There far were fewer systems connected to the internet in 2001-2003 than there are today, and vastly fewer systems involved in critical processes like patient care, emergency call routing, process control, etc.

Conficker arguably has infected several million computers (and is still spreading, one year after its first appearance.) At least two hospitals and one municipal government have reported hundreds of Conficker infected hosts involved in patient care and law enforcement activities. If someone were to release a *white worm* to clean up all Conficker infected hosts, without anyone knowing this was going to occur, there is no guarantee that patient care would not be disrupted or that a serious criminal might be let go on a minor traffic offense because a background check was not possible.

[*Question 4*] **Is it ethical to violate the ownership (privacy) rights of others in order to obtain information that helps mitigate a criminal botnet?**

[**YES**] Different studies, like [34], have been used to enumerate the groups of users affected by botnets. Holz, et al [19], have taken another step further and even investigated the private, mostly financial, information found in various drop zones. The data helps to understand the collection process of bots and can be useful to derive new preventive methods.

The Storm worm inflicted harm on users who, by themselves, would not have been able to handle it. The ability to perform remote disinfection would have been helpful for those with infected systems, removing the threat for all internet users.

[**NO**] These researchers looked at and used very private information, like credit-card numbers, banking data, and credentials for all kinds of web-sites, without the owners' knowledge. The point at which the benefit for potential future victims outweighs the violation of the privacy of victims in the present is hard to estimate, but it is not a binary function. When, if at all, is it ethical to violate the privacy rights of others in order to mitigate botnets?

4 Conclusion

We have seen how complicated it can be to develop effective countermeasures to today's advanced botnets. It is hard to calculate losses, estimate risks/benefits and achieve an acceptable balance. When an attack raises to the level of national impact – a reasonably predictable event, given past examples of financially and politically motivated attacks – policy makers will face decisions about taking control of computers owned by private citizens or corporations to limit further harm. We hope this work will help inform their discussion of options, how they weigh the potential benefits or harms and choose a series of actions to build into contingency plans. We also hope our peers will contribute additional questions, suggestions and their own opinions about where they believe the lines to be. Consensus is an important requirement for achieving ethical guidelines that are acceptable to the community and can be enforced as much through peers as through some official body.

The authors wish to thank the anonymous reviewers, and Aaron Burstein, for their valuable comments.

References

1. 45 CFR 46, http://www.hhs.gov/ohrp/humansubjects/guidance/45cfr46.htm
2. Estonia urges firm EU, NATO response to new form of warfare: cyber-attacks (May 2007),
   http://www.smh.com.au/news/Technology/Estonia-urges-firm-EU-NATO-response-to-new-form-of-warfarecyberattacks/2007/05/16/1178995207414.html
3. On-demand detection of malicious software. Technical Report No. 23, Anti-Virus Comparative (August 2009)
4. Bailey, M., Oberheide, J., Andersen, J., Mao, Z.M., Jahanian, F., Nazario, J.: Automated classification and analysis of internet malware. In: Kruegel, C., Lippmann, R., Clark, A. (eds.) RAID 2007. LNCS, vol. 4637, pp. 178–197. Springer, Heidelberg (2007)
5. Chiang, K., Lloyd, L.: A case study of the rustock rootkit and spam bot. In: HotBots 2007: Proceedings of the First USENIX Workshop on Hot Topics in Understanding Botnets (2007)
6. N. R. C. Committee on Guidelines for Human Embryonic Stem Cell Research. Guidelines for Human Embryonic Stem Cell Research. The National Academies Press, Washington (2005)
7. Criscuolo, P.J.: Distributed denial of service. Technical report, Department of Energy, Computer Incident Advisory Capability (CIAC) (February 2000)
8. Danchev, D.: Legal concerns stop researchers from disrupting the storm worm botnet (January 2009), http://blogs.zdnet.com/security/?p=2397
9. Deibert, R., Manchanda, A., Rohozinski, R., Villeneuve, N., Walton, G.: Tracking GhostNet: Investigating a cyber espionage network (March 2009),
   http://www.scribd.com/doc/13731776/Tracking-GhostNet-Investigating-a-Cyber-Espionage-Network
10. Denning, D.E.: The ethics of cyber conflict. In: The Handbook of Information and Computer Ethics, ch. 17 (June 2008)
11. Dittrich, D.: Second Agora workshop on Active Defense (Sponsored by Cisco Systems, Inc.) (September 2003),
    http://staff.washington.edu/dittrich/arc/AD-workshop-091203.pdf
12. Dittrich, D., Bailey, M., Dietrich, S.: Have we Crossed the Line? The Growing Ethical Debate in Modern Computer Security Research. Poster to be presented at the 16th ACM Conference on Computer and Communication Security (November 2009)
13. Dittrich, D., Bailey, M., Dietrich, S.: Towards Community Standards for Ethical Behavior in Computer Security Research. Technical Report CS 2009-01, Stevens Institute of Technology (April 2009)
14. Dittrich, D., Dietrich, S.: P2P as botnet command and control: a deeper insight. In: Proceedings of the 3rd International Conference on Malicious and Unwanted Software (Malware 2008), pp. 46–63 (October 2008)
15. Dittrich, D., Himma, K.E.: Active Response to Computer Intrusions. In: Handbook of Information Security, ch. 182, vol. III (2005),
    http://papers.ssrn.com/sol3/papers.cfm?abstract_id=790585
16. Douceur, J.R.: The sybil attack. In: Druschel, P., Kaashoek, M.F., Rowstron, A. (eds.) IPTPS 2002. LNCS, vol. 2429, pp. 251–260. Springer, Heidelberg (2002)
17. Enright, B., Voelker, G., Savage, S., Kanich, C., Levchenko, K.: Storm: When researchers collide. In: USENIX; login, vol. 33(4) (August 2008)

18. Holz, T., Engelberth, M., Freiling, F.: Learning more about the underground economy: A case-study of keyloggers and dropzones. Technical Report TR-2008-006, Department for Mathematics and Computer Science, University of Mannheim (December 2008)

19. Holz, T., Engelberth, M., Freiling, F.: Learning more about the underground economy: A case-study of keyloggers and dropzones. In: Reihe Informatik (2008)

20. Holz, T., Steiner, M., Dahl, F., Biersack, E.W., Freiling, F.: Measurements and mitigation of peer-to-peer-based botnets: a case study on storm worm. In: LEET 2008: First USENIX Workshop on Large-Scale Exploits and Emergent Threats (April 2008)

21. John, J.P., Moshchuk, A., Gribble, S.D., Krishnamurthy, A.: Studying Spamming Botnets Using Botlab. In: Proceedings of the 6th USENIX Symposium on Networked Systems Design and Implementation (NSDI 2009) (April 2009)

22. Kanich, C., Kreibich, C., Levchenko, K., Enright, B., Voelker, G.M., Paxson, V., Savage, S.: Spamalytics: an empirical analysis of spam marketing conversion. In: CCS 2008: Proceedings of the 15th ACM conference on Computer and communications security, pp. 3–14 (2008)

23. Kelly, S.: BBC team exposes cyber crime risk (March 2009), http://news.bbc.co.uk/2/hi/programmes/click_online/7932816.stm

24. Leder, F., Werner, T.: Know Your Enemy: Containing Conficker (April 2009), https://www.honeynet.org/papers/conficker/

25. Leder, F., Werner, T., Martini, P.: Proactive Botnet Countermeasures – An Offensive Approach. In: Cooperative Cyber Defence Centre of Excellence Tallinn, Estonia (March 2009)

26. Leyden, J.: DDoS protection racket targets online bookies (November 2001), http://www.theregister.co.uk/2001/11/26/ddos_protection_racket_targets_online/

27. Markham, A.: Method as ethic, ethic as method. Journal of Information Ethics 15(2), 37–55 (2006)

28. Naraine, R.: Kraken botnet infiltration triggers ethics debate (May 2008), http://www.eweek.com/c/a/Security/Kraken-Botnet-Infiltration-Triggers-Ethics-Debate/

29. Department of Justice. Criminal Complaint: United States of America v. Paul G. Ashley, Jonathan David Hall, Joshua James Schichtel, Richard Roby and Lee Graham Walker (2004), http://www.reverse.net/operationcyberslam.pdf

30. Office for Human Research Protections (OHRP). Guidance on Certificates of Confidentiality (February 2003), http://www.hhs.gov/ohrp/humansubjects/guidance/certconf.htm

31. Oudot, L.: Fighting Internet Worms With Honeypots (October 2003), http://www.securityfocus.com/infocus/1740

32. Phong, H.: Korean agency accuses BKIS of violating local and int'l. law (July 2007), http://english.vietnamnet.vn/reports/2009/07/859068/

33. Porras, P., Saidi, H., Yegneswaran, V.: Conficker C P2P Protocol and Implementation (September 2009)

34. Rajab, M.A., Zarfoss, J., Monrose, F., Terzis, A.: My Botnet Is Bigger Than Yours (Maybe, Better Than Yours): Why Size Estimates Remain Challenging (April 2007)

35. Shachtman, N.: Porn purveyors getting squeezed (July 2003), http://www.wired.com/news/print/0,1294,59574,00.html

36. Spafford, E.H.: Are computer hacker break-ins ethical. In: Johnson, D.G., Nissenbaum, H. (eds.) Computers, Ethics & Social Values, pp. 125–135. Oxford University Press, Oxford (1992)
37. Staniford, S., Paxson, V., Weaver, N.: How to own the internet in your spare time. In: Proceedings of the 11th USENIX Security Symposium, August 2002, pp. 149–170 (2002)
38. Stone-Gross, B., Cova, M., Cavallaro, L., Gilbert, B., Szydlowski, M., Kemmerer, R., Kruegel, C., Vigna, G.: Your Botnet is My Botnet: Analysis of a Botnet Takeover. Technical report, University of California (May 2009)
39. Symantec. The Downadup Codex: A comprehensive guide to the threat's mechanics Edition 2.0 (June 2009),
    http://www.symantec.com/content/en/us/enterprise/media/security_response/whitepapers/the_downadup_codex_ed2.pdf

Ethical Proactive Threat Research

John Aycock[1,*] and John Sullins[2]

[1] Department of Computer Science, University of Calgary,
2500 University Drive NW, Calgary, Alberta, Canada T2N 1N4
aycock@ucalgary.ca
[2] Department of Philosophy, Sonoma State University, 1801 East Cotati Ave.,
Rohnert Park, CA 94928
john.sullins@sonoma.edu

Abstract. Through a provocative examination of the positive effects of computer security research on regular users, we argue that traditional security research is insufficient. Instead, we turn to a largely untapped alternative, proactive threat research, a fruitful research area but an ethical minefield. We discuss practices for ethical research and dissemination of proactive research.

1   Introduction

Pity the poor user. Decades of computer security research undertaken in earnest and good faith have resulted in shockingly few dividends for regular users. The advice to users is little changed from five, ten, or even fifteen years ago: run anti-virus software and keep it up to date; keep your software patches up to date; use a firewall; don't run unknown programs or attachments. Everyone working in security is all too familiar with this litany. Security researchers are also all too aware that many regular users – picture the typical computer literacy level of friends and family – may not understand or act on this advice.

At the same time, the number of threats has grown exponentially. One large anti-virus vendor at the 2009 *Virus Bulletin* conference (the major anti-virus industry event) noted that they were seeing 20,000–40,000 new samples of malware *per day*. While this is almost certainly reflecting the effects of a smaller amount of malware being continuously, automatically repacked, rather than adversaries' prodigious output and admirable typing speeds,[3] the fact remains that current defensive techniques have not put a dent in the number of threats. It is also clear that human anti-virus analysts cannot keep up with the flood of new samples without computer assistance.

Or can they keep up at all? Once-anecdotal reports about anti-virus products' latency in terms of detecting new threats have now been shown quantitatively [1,2]. The anti-virus *modus operandi* of receiving a sample, analyzing the

---

* Research supported in part by a grant from the Natural Sciences and Engineering Research Council of Canada; thanks to the reviewers for their excellent comments.
[3] See Appendix A for definitions of the cast of characters.

R. Sion et al. (Eds.): FC 2010 Workshops, LNCS 6054, pp. 231–239, 2010.
© IFCA/Springer-Verlag Berlin Heidelberg 2010

sample, adding detection for the sample, performing quality assurance, creating an update, and finally sending the update to their users leaves a huge window of opportunity for the adversary... even assuming that anti-virus users update regularly. One of the key defenses regular users have is thus substantially flawed, despite the best efforts of smart, hard-working people in the anti-virus industry. Anti-virus vendors have responded by foisting work "into the cloud" [3,4] but this only addresses update time; tasks like analysis and quality assurance can only be short-circuited at the users' peril. In any case, the sad reality is that anti-virus has undertaken a Sisyphean task: Cohen proved over twenty years ago that detecting viruses by their appearance or behavior is undecidable [5].

The motivation of adversaries has shifted over the last decade too, also to the detriment of users' security. Where once adversaries might be hobbyists, fascinated by the creation and spread of malware, or fame-seekers awaiting their fifteen minutes on Symantec's "top ten" list, the overwhelming consensus is that the primary motivation for adversaries now is financial. There is lots of money [6] to be made by infecting users' computers and stealing their information, with a low risk of being caught compared to physical crime. Users' computers are no longer an incidental playground for the latest malware; users and their computers are now the target, yet they enjoy no substantially greater level of defense.

It is important to note that a number of the meager defenses regular users *do* have are primarily reactive in nature. Patches for software flaws, for example, can appear before or after a software flaw is actively exploited by adversaries, yet regardless they are reacting to a known, specific bug. Anti-virus software has moved beyond its early days as a glorified `grep` (see [7,8] for a full discussion of anti-virus techniques), yet still relies heavily on a reactive model responding to specific, known threats or minor variants thereof.

If we compare computer security to other adversarial situations, two striking differences become clear. First, defense is only part of a successful strategy; offense is also vital. Offense in computer security is fraught with legal, ethical, and technical challenges, and is an interesting topic but outside the scope of this paper. The second difference is our focus. It becomes readily apparent even to a child playing an adversarial board game that reacting to an opponent's moves is not sufficient: one must *anticipate* an opponent's possible moves.

This anticipation of the adversary, this proactive element, is sorely lacking in computer security research. We use the term *proactive threat research* to describe research that attempts to identify threats and appropriate defenses before the threats are seen in the wild.

We stress the difference between what we are calling proactive threat research and simply finding software exploits. The latter can be proactive, but is a subset of our proactive threat research. In fact, we are more interested in the identification of entirely new *types* of threat. The difference is finding an exploitable bug in Internet Explorer versus finding an entirely new attack technique; detecting a slight variant of a known virus versus devising and preventing an entirely new type of malware. In other words, anticipating the adversary in significant ways.

Proactive threat research is rife with ethical issues, and in the remainder of this paper we examine two of these: ethical research methods and ethical means to disseminate results. But first, we discuss what constitutes ethical standards for proactive threat research.

2   Ethical Standards for Proactive Threat Research

The primary difference between the malware research that we are proposing and what our adversaries do is that we will be ethically constrained. Mainstream computer ethics researchers have not addressed the ethics of the malware research we are proposing. If anything, there is widespread agreement that the creation and use of computer malware is unethical [9,10,11,12,13], and therefore by extension any research involving the discovery of unknown exploitable weaknesses in global information technologies must be suspect as well. This issue is not so easily resolved by the "hands off" approach to proactive threat research. If indeed, malware is a danger to global information technologies and if what we argue is true; that it is very likely that the only way to effectively mitigate malware is by undertaking proactive threat research, then we may conclude that it is ethical to begin developing proactive threat research. Or at the very least, that the research is not entirely suspect and that standards for this research can be set to ensure that this research is done in a responsible and ethical manner.

What will constitute these ethical standards depends on the means of analysis we use. A full ethical analysis of malware research is not possible here but we have begun that in other works [14,15]. What we will do here is look briefly at how we intend to justify our standards for ethical research in this area.

A strong argument in favor of our position can be obtained by taking a generally utilitarian approach and assuring that the greatest benefactors of any successful research be the users of global information technology taken as a whole. We need to ensure that the consequences of proactive threat research result in more useful and generally beneficial technologies for the largest group of people. There is an identifiable "largest" group involved: the general public as users and consumers of information and information technology as well as the companies that produce useful content and technologies for that public. Even with the digital divide in mind, the size of this group dwarfs all others we might consider. Therefore, if proactive threat research does not negatively impact the safety of these users' online lives, data, and property, then we would consider the research ethical. This gives us our first standard: proactive threat research must benefit the global information technology using community as a whole and not just propagate the interests of some smaller interest group, and the actions and consequences of proactive threat research must not compromise the safety of the general Internet-using public.

Our second standard is motivated by a more deontological approach[4] that takes seriously our reasonable moral duties towards other moral agents. This

---

[4] Space precludes us from fully reconciling the utilitarian and deontological roots of our standards, but we believe that they are not incompatible in this context.

imperative is expressed in the ACM Code of Ethics [16], which proposes that it is the researcher's duty to 'Contribute to society and human well-being' and 'Avoid harm to others.'[5] We recognize that these are broad commands that can be difficult to ascertain in specific situations. For instance, medical science has to occasionally harm the patient in the short run with painful procedures in order to help them in the long run. Since these situations can be so difficult to determine in isolation, it is important for any planned experiment to be presented openly to the community of researchers at large so that that its potential merits are fully vetted for any potential harm it may cause. It is surprising that institutions commonly require ethics approval for research involving animals, humans, or the environment, yet ethics approval is not required for research involving malware, which has the ability to impact all these. This leaves us with our second standard: proactive threat research must demonstrate in a responsible and open way that the products of its research will not harm others and ideally should improve their safety. At a minimum, this suggests that institutions' ethics boards may need a broader scope, or that a vetting process may be needed within the security research community itself.

The emerging field of information ethics also informs our thinking. The philosopher Luciano Floridi argues, 'because the informational revolution is causing an exponential growth in human powers to understand, shape, and control ever more aspects of reality, it is equally making us increasingly responsible, morally speaking, for the way the world is, will, and should be, and for the role we are playing as stewards of our future digital environment' [17]. Emerging global information technologies are best seen as a new environment where many of us spend an increasing amount of our lives. As we are collectively designing this environment we must work hard to not allow it to be irrevocably marred by malware. This results in our third standard: proactive threat research is necessary to the design of a functioning and moral digital environment.

3   Ethical Proactive Threat Research Methods

Proactive threat research must employ research methods chosen to uphold the ethical standards described in the last section. Specifically, research methods must not endanger the Internet-using public – creating a new type of malware and releasing it into the wild, for example, is obviously inappropriate.

We have identified five safe, suitable research methods for proactive threat research. Such a compilation of methods has not appeared in the literature before, to the best of our knowledge. We reiterate that the publication or other dissemination of this research is a separate issue and is discussed in Sect. 4.

---

[5] While we do not use the ACM Code as an unflinching guide (and cannot at the risk of ethical conventionalism), it is an established code that we use as a starting point. Ultimately, it is usable but too general for security research, just as general ethical theories are usable but too general for computer ethics, and a long-term goal is to develop a code of ethics more specific to security research.

Mathematical modeling. A purely mathematical, abstract formulation of a proactively identified threat poses no threat itself, because there is no code whatsoever. This method might be used to analyze the spread of a new threat by applying epidemiological models, for example (e.g., [18]).

Simulation. A simulation that abstracts out the malicious code is a safe method for much the same reason, the absence of actual code. For instance, a new threat whose interesting aspects lie in the communication between infected computers abstracts to a simulation of message-passing between nodes (infected computers) on a graph representing the network connections (e.g., [19]).

Component test. There are often ways of implementing components of a new threat that are not themselves malicious. This permits experiments with novel aspects of a threat while abstracting away harmful ones. In a new type of worm whose novelty lies in the method of finding targets, likely only implementation of the targeting mechanism is of interest; it is already well accepted that worms exist and can be created, so those aspects can be omitted. (See, for example, [20].)

Existence proof. Sometimes one example may be proof enough. This method is particularly useful when examining large-scale threats requiring a huge amount of computing power. An adversary may easily have this power in a botnet, whereas a researcher will not. Here, it may be sufficient for a researcher to perform a search for a single example, demonstrating that a threat is possible, even if it cannot be established in all cases. This method is safe because it can only be fully deployed by an adversary (e.g., [21]); a researcher can only create limited instances to study in the small and cannot pose a general threat.

***Gedanken* experiment.** Thought experiments are useful devices in proactive threat research, especially where the ability to implement a new threat is not in doubt, or where even limited threat testing would be illegal or require scale beyond a researcher's capacity. As in the case of mathematical modeling, this method is safe because no code is involved. The idea, the thought, is the valuable contribution, opening up the ability to discuss defenses to the new threat. For example, a new type of spam may obviously be implementable, yet present significant detection challenges, as in [22].

Some proactive research work (e.g., [23]) has involved the creation of full-blown malware, a research method not listed above. As a general research method, it cannot be supported according to the ethical standard unless the potential gain outweighs the risk of the malware escaping into the wild and causing damage (not to mention second-order effects for the researcher and their organization). The motivation for malware creation for research is often to support a claim along the lines of "this malware was not detected by current anti-virus products." However, this claim is fleeting – just because anti-virus does not detect something does not imply that it is not trivial to add detection. Therefore, malware creation is definitely not a safe endeavor, and is not always a net gain when the potential risk is considered. However, safe methods of handling created malware may reduce/eliminate the risk to the public (e.g., [24]) in specific cases; how to do this in general is a topic of future work.

The argument can be made that researchers have rights that include the right to free inquiry and (in terms of dissemination) free speech. We note, however, that the right to free speech is not absolute – one cannot yell "fire!" in a crowded theater – and similar arguments would apply to free inquiry. While ethical boundaries on researchers may give adversaries some small advantage, that may have to be the cost of performing ethical proactive threat research.

In addition to research methods, research problems to study must be carefully chosen. A full discussion is beyond this paper's scope, but the idea is to identify *likely* future threats using knowledge of trends and adversaries' capabilities. This way, the results will be of maximum benefit per our standards in Sect. 2.

4   Ethical Dissemination of Proactive Threat Research

How can the results of proactive threat research be published, if at all?[6] While critics of proactive research may dismiss it as simply giving ideas to the adversary, the ethical landscape is considerably more nuanced than that.

First, it is not ethically permissible to perform proactive research and *not* publish the result in a way that benefits the Internet-using public; this would conflict with the stated duties in the ACM Code, for instance. It is also not possible in general, because some technologies are dual-use, meaning they can be used for both "good" and "bad:" a new type of peer-to-peer system can be used for new types of botnets; new types of anti-spam techniques are also new types of censorship technology. The question is how best to publish the proactive threat results.

The key, we think, is to ensure that the threat information makes it to people who are able to act upon it defensively and thus benefit the Internet-using public. Of the defense mechanisms that are generally deployed, only two have the potential to protect vast numbers of users in a relatively short period of time: anti-virus software and automatic software patching. While the latency of anti-virus in *re*actively handling threats was noted in Sect. 1, we are leveraging its ubiquitous presence for *pro*active defenses, so the same timeliness issues do not apply. The people who must be notified of proactive threat research are thus those who work on anti-virus (more generally, security software) and deploy security patches; we refer to them collectively as *security personnel*.

Publication to a general audience, like an open mailing list, would potentially benefit both adversaries and security personnel, because both would find out about the new threat simultaneously. Similarly, presenting the proactive threat at a "hacker" conference like Black Hat or Defcon would reach a mixed audience. On the other hand, presentation at a specialized anti-virus security conference would reach security personnel with little risk of adversaries. Furthermore, attendees at such conferences often include law enforcement and security professionals

---

[6] Some of the ideas in this section appeared previously in [14].

in government and industry, who are also important consumers of threat information. A less-public method would be to notify security personnel using email or another relatively private channel, but while this has been done before [25], there are few researchers who have the reputation and contacts to succeed if many security personnel are involved. What this highlights is that, while there are some ethically permissible publication venues, a better dissemination mechanism for proactive threat research would be beneficial.

One final element we have not mentioned is time. All proactive threats are not equally urgent, and a threat that no adversary is able to take advantage of for some time may be published more widely without violating the safety principle of our ethical standard. On the other hand, the publication of an imminent threat that an adversary may easily take advantage of needs to be handled with more care, from an ethical standpoint. Dissemination must be tempered by knowledge of adversaries' capabilities. An imminent threat ethically requires that dissemination improves users' safety – this implies notification of security personnel, but also that a defense can be deployed in a timely fashion. Practically speaking, this means that any defense that can be enabled by a modest change to anti-virus software or by issuing a patch is fair game.

5   Conclusion

Identifying threats proactively, and ways to respond to those potential threats, is an important yet largely overlooked part of successful security. In order to perform such proactive research ethically, appropriate research methods and dissemination methods must be chosen. Our contribution is the identification of five such research methods, along with some practical guidelines as to the ethical publication of threats not yet in the wild.

References

1. Higgins, K.J.: Study: Antivirus software catches about half of malware, misses 15 percent altogether. Dark Reading (March 2, 2009)
2. Oberheide, J., Cooke, E., Jahanian, F.: CloudAV: N-version antivirus in the network cloud. In: 17th USENIX Security Symposium, pp. 91–106 (2008)
3. Nachenberg, C., Ramzan, Z., Seshadri, V.: Reputation: A new chapter in malware protection. In: 19th Virus Bulletin International Conference, pp. 185–191 (2009)
4. Yan, W., Arrott, A., McArdle, R., Roesler, M.: Volume of threat: The AV update deployment bottleneck. In: 19th Virus Bulletin International Conference, pp. 232–234 (2009)
5. Cohen, F.: Computer viruses: Theory and experiments. Computers & Security 6(1), 22–35 (1987)
6. Franklin, J., Paxson, V., Perrig, A., Savage, S.: An inquiry into the nature and causes of the wealth of Internet miscreants. In: 14th ACM Conference on Computer and Communications Security, pp. 375–388 (2007)
7. Aycock, J.: Computer Viruses and Malware. Springer, Heidelberg (2006)

8. Szor, P.: The Art of Computer Virus Research and Defense. Addison-Wesley, Reading (2005)
9. Edgar, S.L.: Morality and Machines. Jones and Bartlett, USA (2003)
10. Himma, K.E.: Internet Security. Jones and Bartlett, USA (2007)
11. Neumann, P.G.: Computer security and human values. In: Computer Ethics and Professional Responsibility. Blackwell, Malden (2004)
12. Spafford, E.H.: Are computer hacker break-ins ethical? In: Computer Ethics and Professional Responsibility. Blackwell, Malden (2004)
13. Spinello, R.: Cyberethics. Jones and Bartlett, USA (2006)
14. Aycock, J., Maurushat, A.: Future threats. In: 17th Virus Bulletin International Conference, pp. 275–281 (2007)
15. Sullins, J.P.: Artificial moral agency in technoethics. In: Luppicini, R., Adell, R. (eds.) Handbook of Research on Technoethics, pp. 205–221. Idea Group, USA (2008)
16. Association for Computing Machinery: ACM code of ethics and professional conduct (1992), http://www.acm.org/about/code-of-ethics
17. Floridi, L.: Understanding information ethics. The American Philosophical Association Newsletter on Computers and Society 7(1) (2007)
18. Staniford, S., Moore, D., Paxson, V., Weaver, N.: The top speed of flash worms. In: Proceedings of the 2004 ACM Workshop on Rapid Malcode, pp. 33–42 (2004)
19. Vogt, R.A.: The threat of biologically-inspired self-stopping worms. Master's thesis, University of Calgary (2008)
20. Szabo, J., Aycock, J., Acton, R., Denzinger, J.: The tale of the weather worm. In: ACM Symposium on Applied Computing, pp. 2097–2102 (2008)
21. Aycock, J., Gutiérrez Cárdenas, J.M., de Castro, D.M.N.: Code obfuscation using pseudo-random number generators. In: 1st International Workshop on Software Security Process., pp. 418–423 (2009)
22. Swimmer, M., Leiba, B., Whalley, I., Borenstein, N.: Breaking anti-spam systems with parasitic spam. In: Third Conference on Email and Anti-Spam (2006)
23. Borello, J.M., Filiol, É., Mé, L.: Are current antivirus programs able to detect complex metamorphic malware? An empirical evaluation. In: 18th Annual EICAR Conference, pp. 45–63 (2009)
24. Aycock, J., Barker, K.: Creating a secure computer virus laboratory. In: 13th Annual EICAR Conference, 13 pp. (2004)
25. Davis, J.: Secret geek A-team hacks back, defends worldwide web. Wired 16.12 (November 24, 2008)
26. Sullins, J.P.: Ethics and artificial life: From modeling to moral agents. Ethics and Information Technology 7, 139–148 (2005)
27. Sullins, J.P.: When is a robot a moral agent? International Review of Information Ethics 6 (December 2006)

A   Dramatis Personæ

Adversary. We use the term "adversary" generically to refer to a "bad guy," malware writer, or what other researchers have called "miscreants" [6].

Internet-using public. This is the largest group of people affected by proactive threat research. In general, this extends beyond the Internet to include all users/consumers of information technology, directly or indirectly.

Moral agent. Primarily moral agents will be other living humans but we also entertain the obligations we have to future humans, natural environments, non-human biological agents both natural and artificial, and perhaps even to autonomous information agents themselves (see [15,26,27]).

Researcher. We use a broad definition of the term "researcher," inclusive of traditional academic researchers as well as researchers within security companies (e.g., malware analysts within anti-virus companies who refer to themselves as researchers) and independent, unaffiliated researchers.

Security personnel. For completeness, we reiterate this definition from Sect. 4: this is the group of people who deploy software patches as well as those who work on anti-virus/security software.

A Framework for Understanding and Applying Ethical Principles in Network and Security Research

Erin Kenneally[1], Michael Bailey[2], and Douglas Maughan[3]

[1] The Cooperative Association for Internet Data Analysis
[2] University of Michigan
[3] US Department of Homeland Security

Abstract. Current information and communications technology poses a variety of ethical challenges for researchers. In this paper, we present an intellectual framework for understanding and applying ethical principles in networking and security research rooted in the guidance suggested by an ongoing Department of Homeland Security working group on ethics. By providing this prototype ethical impact assessment, we seek to encourage community feedback on the working group's nascent efforts and spur researchers to concretely evaluate the ethical impact of their work.

1 Introduction

Innovations in Information and Communications Technology (ICT) have revolutionized how we buy and sell products, how we record, store and playback media, how we communicate with each other, and many other aspects of our lives [4]. Studying the effects of these changes on human welfare, the properties of the enabling technologies themselves, and the ethical implications of the interaction between the two continues to be an active area of study [11,6]. Expectedly, as the research on impacts of ICT and the enabling technologies become increasingly complex and interconnected, scientists are often posed with moral dilemmas regarding the risks and benefits of such research [7].

One example of a current ICT research (IR) activity that raises novel ethical challenges are efforts to enhance accessibility of computer and network operational data for use in cyber defense research and development. This research acknowledges that the existing lack of practical and reproducible scientific results in ICT research stems in part from a gap between the producers of security-relevant network operations data and researchers who need this data. The PREDICT (Protected Repository for the Defense of Infrastructure against Cyber Threats) initiative of the Department of Homeland Security (DHS) [1] represents an effort to solve this problem. However, the collection and disclosure of networking and security data create a host of dilemmas for those participating in the project and more generally, to all ICT researchers, including: What are

R. Sion et al. (Eds.): FC 2010 Workshops, LNCS 6054, pp. 240–246, 2010.
© IFCA/Springer-Verlag Berlin Heidelberg 2010

user's current perceptions of privacy and confidentiality in network traffic? What are the legal prohibitions to collecting and disclosing network data for research purposes? Is it possible to receive consent by persons implicated in traffic traces? How does one identify a potentially at risk population in a network trace?

Acknowledging the need to resolve these ethical issues not only within its project, but to inform similar debates in other ICT research efforts, DHS hosted a two-day ethics workshop on May 26th-27th, 2009 in Washington, DC[12]. Inspired by the Belmont Report, the 1974 authoritative guide on ethical standards for human subject research[8] in social and behavioral sciences, the workshop brought together ethicists, institutional review boards, researchers, and lawyers to discuss these pressing issues. The primary anticipated outcome from this meeting is a set of ethical guidelines which, though anchored off of the original Belmont framework, reflects the unique questions facing ICT researchers. Subsequently in September and December of 2009, writers working groups met at UC San Diego and Menlo Park, respectively, to advance these guidelines with the intention of publishing them in the first half of 2010.

The goal of this document is to further refine these principles into a workable ethical impact assessment (EIA) that can be used as a framework to help ICT researchers think about the ethical impacts of their work. Unlike work which seeks to answer questions of who should enforce ethical behavior [3,9] or work that seeks to inform ethical policy debate through the use of case study analysis [7], this work is similar to that of [5,13] in that we seek to provide specific guidance on how to make ethical research decisions. As the DHS ethics group is a work-in-progress, a secondary goal of this paper is to inform a broader community of this effort and solicit feedback on how to improve the EIA[1].

2 Ethical Impact Assessment (EIA)

In this section, we offer an Ethical Impact Assessment (EIA) framework to more pragmatically assist researchers and evaluators in applying ethical principles in the context of ICT research. This EIA is an incipient prototype, modeled after the more established privacy risk management framework, the PIA (Privacy Impact Assessment) [14]. As such, the EIA offers non-exhaustive, yet directed, questions to guide compliance with the ethics principles that were put forth at the DHS ethics workshop. These ten principles fall into two categories: guidance on human subjects protection and guidance on professional ethics.

2.1 Human Subject Protections

What do the principles of Respect for Persons, Beneficence, and Justice means to ICT research stakeholders? Because these ethical mandates originated within the context of Human Subjects protection research [8], they have been evaluated and appropriately modified and clarified for ICT network and security context.

---

[1] The specific interpretations expressed in this paper are the authors and don't necessarily reflect that of other individual working group participants.

Respect for Persons. In the context of Human Subjects protection work, respect for persons encompasses at least two components: first, that individuals should be treated as autonomous agents, and second, that persons with diminished autonomy are entitled to protection [8]. These are often applied through the construct of *informed consent*, which in the context of ICT networking and security research, raises questions of identification, the appropriate level of disclosure of research methodology, comprehension by subjects via network modalities, and voluntariness. Resolving these questions can be vexing if not impracticable in network contexts, raising debate about whether these are suitable means to achieve informed consent, or even whether this construct itself is an appropriate mechanism to realize respect for persons.

1. In the cyber security context, respect for persons should include both individuals and society, and should consider organizations. Ethical challenges posed by privacy concerns can be vexing for ICT research because the underlying concept of identity in relation to network data artifacts is disjointed in both law and social convention. Unlike well-entrenched identifiers such as name or biometric markers, blanket characterizations of IPA or URLs as personally-identifying (or not) are misguided because they alone do not capture the range of privacy risks associated with network traffic which are referential and context-dependent. Furthermore, it may be difficult or impracticable to identify potentially at risk populations in a network trace, such as with juvenile subjects who may warrant greater protections, not to mention the ensuing challenges to obtaining valid consent. Question(s): Consider how data and computer systems may be tightly coupled with the entities to be respected. Can the IP address or URL be relatively easily linked to an identifiable person? Does the IP address map to an automated device, distinguish a human-operated host, or identify a home computer? Does the content of the collected data concern the substance, purport or meaning of a communication from an identifiable person? Does the data reveal behavioral information that could identify an individual? Researchers should be mindful that individuals' dignity, rights, and obligations are increasingly integrated with the data and IT systems within which they communicate, transact, and in general represent themselves in a cyber context.

2. Consent to use data and information systems for a specific purpose in research should be obtained. The challenging aspect of this precept is that *in vivo* Internet research may involve situations where individual consent is impracticable because it would be legally unwarranted or strategically or economically infeasible to identify persons implicated within network and security research data; or, failure to obtain consent would have no adverse impact on an identifiable person's rights and welfare. Since consent often presumes the existence of an underlying legal right, ambiguity over ownership and control of network traffic– e.g., is it public or subject to an expectation of privacy– may complicate consent obligations. Question(s): If the research involves identifiable individuals, have the individuals implicated in the network and security data consented to involvement? Can the individual decline participation in the research or in the uses of collected data? If the purpose of the data use has changed or is expanded, has renewed consent been obtained? If consent is impossible or directly impedes research goals, consider the risk-utility assessment guidance under Beneficence.

Beneficence. The Belmont Report [8] specifies two general rules under the obligation of beneficence: "(1) do not harm and (2) maximize possible benefits and minimize possible harms." Thus beneficence is applied as a *risk-benefit assessment*. The following EIA questions are intended to elicit what is meant by benefits and harm in the context of ICT networking and security research.

3. Researchers should systematically assess both risks and benefits of the research on privacy, civil rights, and the well-being of persons. Laws are enacted to secure the rights and well-being of individuals and they offer one systematic approach for evaluation. However, risk-benefit determinations can be challenging given gaps and grey areas in privacy and civil rights laws related to liability for actions undertaken in the interests of security research. Other enforcement mechanisms and systematic approaches have been challenged as inappropriate or incomplete including IRBs and professional codes [3,9]. This lack of concrete guidance, however, does not assuage the responsibility to perform more than a piecemeal or perfunctory ethical analysis of a study's impact. Question(s): What are the effects of network and security research on all the stakeholders: researchers, human subjects, and society (by way of how it may assist attackers)? In what circumstances will the benefits of the IR clearly outweigh any harmful impact on the stakeholders? Will the research result in no greater harm than what would have occurred in its absence? What checks and balances are in place to prevent both new harms and/or repeated historical abuses, including: violating the law and privacy interests; targeting and disrupting certain groups (based on politics, race, sex, etc.); chilling First Amendment rights (e.g., free speech, freedom of association); harming individuals (e.g., physical, financial, legal, reputational, mental); impairing data quality and integrity (e.g., distorting data that informs government policy or public perception); creating a high cost-to-effectiveness study; introducing surveillance harms (e.g., identity theft, disclosure of embarrassing information, government persecution, chilling or foregoing certain activities, introducing costs or altering behavior related to counter-surveillance); and, expanding network surveillance and perpetuating secrecy.

4. Research should be designed and conducted to maximize probable benefits and minimize harms to persons and organizations. Prominent application challenges here include the scale at which risk and benefits can occur, the ability to attribute research data and results to specific individuals and/or organizations, the increasing availability of data that are beyond the knowledge or control of the researcher (thereby challenging the effectiveness of disclosure controls), and the increasingly intertwined nature of the physical and virtual worlds. This principle seemingly imagines ex ante benefit maximization and risk minimization for research whose value may be conjectural and delayed and whose risk posture and mitigation may be speculative. As such, the following questions help to align expectations and capabilities into practical focus for researchers. Question(s): Does the research impact the integrity, confidentiality, and availability of information systems, including originating and transiting systems? Does the research design include controls to minimize harms and maximize benefits such as using test environments, anonymization techniques or other disclosure controls that limit the exposure of personal data? For example: What are possible unintended consequences of the IR? Are there exigent circumstances that should be factored into the evaluation of harm? Are there privacy-based harms from IR? What is the nature of the information collected by IR? What is the purpose for collecting the data? What is the intended use of information collected by IR? Will the research be disseminated to third parties and used consistent with its original purpose? What are the administrative and technical controls? In assessing the risk of re-identification, consider variables such as: triggers set by law or policy guidelines (e.g., highly probable, readily ascertainable, likely); the quantity of data that would be available; the threat perspective (e.g, a subjective person associated with the data, an objective member of the public, a motivated intruder); and, the level of time, effort and resources needed to re-identify a person.

5. *If research reveals or causes risk/harm to a person, including systems and data, the person should be notified.* ICT do not often require human interaction or human notification to cause harm or do good. As such, we have a special obligation to inform, where reasonable to do so, those individuals or organizations whose resources and welfare are affected by the phenomena we are measuring. Question(s): When notification of persons is not possible or appropriate, harm should be mitigated by notifying other appropriate parties.

6. *Researchers should consider the full spectrum of risks of harm to persons and information systems, including reputational, emotional, financial, and physical harms.* Significant here is our normative social immaturity regarding qualitative and quantitative assessment of damages and harms in the electronic realm, as opposed to the well-established and socially-embedded understanding of cause and effect harms resulting from physical interactions with human subjects. Question(s): What categories of activity have especially strong reasons for IR involving human subjects? Could the IR actually make the targeted problem (e.g., security) worse or undermine the research goal(s)?

Justice. In the context of human subjects research protection, Justice addresses fairness in determining who ought to receive the benefits of research and bear its burdens [8]. It is thus applied through the construct of *selection of subjects*. While most of these questions do not vary significantly for ICT networking and security research, their application, nonetheless, introduces previously addressed challenges related to identification of persons from referential network data, as well as difficulties in projecting results of research activities involving tightly coupled network systems.

7. *The benefits and burdens of research should be shared fairly between research target subjects and beneficiaries of the research results.* Question(s): Does the IR

raise fairness and discrimination concerns? Will the IR undermine cooperation from the community whose cooperation/participation is needed/targeted?

8. The selection of research subjects should be equitable, except when biased selection may be beneficial. Question(s): To what extent does the IR violate legal and ethical principles of equality? How can research design be altered to decrease the inequality or mitigate its effects?

2.2 Professional Ethical Guidance

Professional organizations such as IEEE and ACM offer professional codes of ethics for their members [10,2] and the primary difference between these codes and codes for protection of human subjects is that while these codes recognize an imperative for their member to do good, these codes focus on workplace and employment-related ethical situations rather than on the experimental subjects.

9. Research activities should not violate laws, operator agreements, contractual obligations, or other restrictions agreed to by private arrangements. This consideration ensures that researchers engage in legal due diligence for activities that occur outside of a closed, self-contained research setting and which are subject to laws or policies intended to protect individual and organizational rights. This provision may prove challenging in light of the uncertain application or interpretation of certain laws and regulations in the context of ICT research activities, including the heightened risk of unanticipated consequences or discoveries involved in *in vivo* ICT research. Question(s): If the IR is in conflict with law or policy, is there an exception or valid agreement otherwise permitting such research? Would the IR violate other countries' laws? If government is involved, will there be international and bilateral diplomatic ramifications? Should the IR methodology be modified or abandoned wholesale because of legal and other concerns?

10. Where possible, researchers should adhere to internationally accepted best practices and standards in conducting research and assessing risk. Similar to legal risk assessment involving domestic laws, international risk assessment may be even less clear given the discrepancies between nation-states on cyberlaws and rights. Again, the standard against which research should be measured is that of a reasonable researcher, and not a strict liability. Adherence to international standards or guidelines can often move researchers beyond ethical risks when laws are unclear or unsettled.

3 Conclusion

Increasingly, networking and security researchers are engaging in work that challenges our existing ethical frameworks. If we are to continue to occupy a moral high ground in which we claim the benefits of our work as necessary and the risks of our work minimal, we need to more explicitly justify this reasoning to other researchers and society as a whole. In this paper, we discuss an evolving Ethical Impact Assessment, based on the collaborative efforts of a DHS ethics working group, that seeks to define a set of imperatives for networking and security research. Used as an intellectual framework, it offers the promise of guiding researchers to ask the appropriate set of questions about their work and reason effectively about its ethical impact. As a living document, the authors and working group members actively solicit community feedback on this effort.

References

1. Protected repository for the defense of infrastructure against cyber threats (PREDICT), http://www.predict.org
2. ACM Council. Code of Ethics and Professional Conduct (October 1992), http://www.acm.org/about/code-of-ethics
3. Allman, M.: What ought a program committee to do? In: WOWCS 2008: Proceedings of the USENIX Workshop on Organizing Workshops, Conferences, and Symposia for Computer Systems, pp. 1–5 (2008)
4. Baase, S.: A Gift of Fire: Social, Legal, and Ethical Issues in Computing. Prentice Hall PTR, Upper Saddle River (2002)
5. Burstein, A.J.: Conducting cybersecurity research legally and ethically. In: LEET 2008: Proceedings of the 1st Usenix Workshop on Large-Scale Exploits and Emergent Threats, pp. 1–8 (2008)
6. Bynum, T.W., Rogerson, S.: Computer Ethics and Professional Responsibility: Introductory Text and Readings. Blackwell Publishers, Inc., Cambridge (2003)
7. Dittrich, D., Bailey, M.D., Dietrich, S.: Towards community standards for ethical behavior in computer security research. Technical Report 2009-01, Stevens Institute of Technology, Hoboken, NJ, USA (April 2009)
8. National Commission for the Protection of Human Subjects of Biomedical and Behavioral Research. The belmont report - ethical principles and guidelines for the protection of human subjects of research, http://ohsr.od.nih.gov/guidelines/belmont.html
9. Garfinkel, S.L.: IRBs and security research: Myths, facts and mission creep. In: Proceedings of UPSEC 2008 (Usability, Psychology and Security) (April 2008)
10. IEEE Board of Directors. IEEE Code of Ethics (February 2006), http://www.ieee.org/portal/pages/iportals/aboutus/ethics/code.html
11. Johnson, D.G., Miller, K.W. (eds.): Computers Ethics. Prentice-Hall, Inc., Upper Saddle River (2009)
12. Kenneally, E.: What's belmont got to do with it?, http://blog.caida.org/best_available_data/2009/06/12/whatelmont-got-to-do-with-it/
13. Kenneally, E., Claffy, K.: An internet sharing framework for balancing privacy and utility. In: Engaging Data: First International Forum on the Application and Management of Personal Electronic Information. MIT, IEEE (October 2009)
14. DHS Privacy Office. DHS official privacy impact assessment guidance, http://www.dhs.gov/files/publications/gc_1209396374339.shtm

Ethical Concerns in Computer Security and Privacy Research Involving Human Subjects

Lorrie Faith Cranor

Carnegie Mellon University, Pittsburgh, PA
lorrie@cmu.edu

Abstract. In this panel statement I highlight four specific types of ethical concerns I've encountered when designing security and privacy human subjects studies.

Increasingly, computer security researchers are employing human subjects studies, which raise additional ethical concerns that go beyond the typical concerns associated with vulnerability research, publishing security holes, and the double-edged sword of anonymity tools. Here I highlight four specific types of ethical concerns I've encountered when designing security and privacy human subjects studies.

For government-funded researchers in the United States, human subjects studies require approval by an Institutional Review Board (IRB). Similar requirements exist in some other countries and some companies have internal review processes for human subjects studies. IRB review helps ensure that most ethical issues associated with security and privacy human subjects studies are appropriately addressed, for example, by minimizing data collection and quickly de-identifying data, obtaining informed consent from study participants, and debriefing study participants at the end of the study. However, computer security researchers are not always aware of the need to seek IRB approval, and IRBs do not always have the expertise to provide adequate review.

1 Detailed Personal Data Collection

Human subjects studies sometimes involve collection of large amounts of personal data about participants—this is not unique to security and privacy research. However, for some security and privacy research, the data collected may be particularly sensitive. For example, some privacy research involves putting participants in situations where their privacy is potentially at risk to observe the steps they take to protect their privacy or the types of controls they use to limit data disclosure. Thus, participants may be exposing to researchers data that they would not wish to have exposed more widely. For example, some of my research involves tracking users' location information and providing them with tools to specify the conditions under which that information may be shared (based on who wants to see it, time of day, where they are located, etc.). As a result we have detailed "location trails" for all of our study participants [1].

R. Sion et al. (Eds.): FC 2010 Workshops, LNCS 6054, pp. 247–249, 2010.
© Springer-Verlag Berlin Heidelberg 2010

2 Exposing Personal Data

Sometimes studies go a step beyond collecting personal data, and expose data to parties beyond the study researchers. For example, in a study on privacy policies in which we asked participants to purchase a privacy-sensitive item (a sex toy) from a website, participants' contact information was exposed to the vendors. In addition, if the items were shipped to participants' homes, the fact that they purchased these items could be exposed to other members of their household. We addressed the second concern by allowing participants to ship the items to our laboratory [2].

In another study, designed to explore the use of a peripheral display to help users understand the privacy risks of unencrypted wireless networks, we eavesdropped on our university's wireless network and projected selected words typed by participants on a nearby wall. We mitigated privacy concerns by situating the eavesdropping system and display in a non-public workspace and obtaining consent for our data collection from the occupants of that workspace. Furthermore, we filtered out proper nouns and non-dictionary words to reduce the risk that personal information would be exposed to the other occupants of the workspace [3].

3 Observation of Login Credentials

Security user studies sometimes require participants to login to an account under the observation of an experimenter. This may occur in studies of authentication mechanisms, as well as in other studies in which the details of the authentication process may be incidental. For example, my students conducted a laboratory study to determine participant's behavior when a web browser displayed an SSL certificate warning. Unbeknownst to participants, we had removed the root certificate from the browser on our lab computer so that certificate warnings would be triggered at websites that use SSL. In order to provide a situation where participants would actually have something at risk, we included a task in which participants were asked to login to their online bank accounts. Often when we conduct laboratory studies, we employ screen capture software to record all of a user's interactions with the computer and allow us to gather detailed data about the steps users take to complete a task and how long each step takes. For this study we decided to forgo the screen capture because of concerns about collecting users' account credentials [4]. The presence of the experimenter in the laboratory could have potentially been a concern as well, as that person might have been able to observe a participant's account number and their keystrokes as they typed their password. This can be mitigated somewhat by the position of the experimenter relative to the participant in the room or by providing a privacy shield for the keyboard.

Authentication studies sometimes require participants to generate and use passwords that are necessarily exposed to the experimenter. In one such study we emphasized to participants that they should create a new password that was different form the ones they used for their real accounts [5]. In some cases the experimenter may be able to ask users questions about their password to collect data needed for experimental analysis, without requiring users to expose the passwords themselves. However, with such an approach it is important to consider the likelihood that passwords could be guessed based on the information revealed.

4 Attacks and Deception

Observing how users behave in the presence of an attack can be difficult because attacks are relatively rare events and computers are not usually instrumented to collect data that would allow us to observe these events in the wild. Thus, in order to observe users under attack, researchers may need to conduct real or simulated attacks themselves. Attacks, even when conducted in a laboratory, may violate applicable laws if not carefully designed. Setting up the attack without arousing participant suspicion may require some deception or diversionary tactics. For example, in order to study user reactions to browser phishing warnings, we invited participants to our laboratory for an online shopping study. After they made a purchase we had them fill out a survey about online shopping while we sent them a simulated phishing message that spoofed the store from which they had just purchased. We asked them to check their email to get their receipt for reimbursement. Almost all of them found our phishing message and fell for it, triggering the warning and allowing us to observe their behavior [6]. In a field study we sent simulated phishing messages spoofing various university departments to students, faculty, and staff at our university. In this case we had recruited participants to opt-in to receiving emails from us as part of a study (but did not tell them the emails would be spoofed), and sent all participants a debriefing email after the study was over. In addition, we notified all of the campus help desks about the study and engaged their cooperation so that participants who contacted them with concerns about our spoofed emails would be assured that their accounts were not actually at risk [7].

References

1. Tsai, J., Kelley, P., Drielsma, P., Cranor, L., Hong, J., Sadeh, N.: Who's Viewed You? The Impact of Feedback in a Mobile-location System. In: CHI 2009 (2009)
2. Egelman, S., Tsai, J., Cranor, L., Acquisti, A.: Timing Is Everything? The Effects of Timing and Placement of Online Privacy Indicators. In: CHI 2009 (2009)
3. Kowitz, B., Cranor, L.: Peripheral Privacy Notifications for Wireless Networks. In: Proceedings of the 2005 Workshop on Privacy in the Electronic Society (2005)
4. Sunshine, J., Egelman, S., Almuhimedi, H., Atri, N., Cranor, L.: Crying Wolf: An Empirical Study of SSL Warning Effectiveness. In: USENIX Security 2009 (2009)
5. Kuo, C., Romanosky, S., Cranor, L.: Human Selection of Mnemonic Phrase-Based Passwords. In: Proceedings of the 2006 Symposium on Usable Privacy and Security (2006)
6. Egelman, S., Cranor, L., Hong, J.: You've Been Warned: An Empirical Study of the Effectiveness of Web Browser Phishing Warnings. In: CHI 2008 (2008)
7. Kumaraguru, P., Cranshaw, J., Acquisti, A., Cranor, L., Hong, J., Blair, M.A., Pham, T.: School of Phish: A Real-Word Evaluation of Anti-Phishing Training. In: Proceedings of the 2009 Symposium on Usable Privacy and Security (2009)

Ethical Guidelines for Computer Security Researchers: "Be Reasonable"

Len Sassaman*

Katholieke Universiteit Leuven
len.sassaman@esat.kuleuven.be

1 Introduction

For most of its existence, the field of computer science has been lucky enough to avoid ethical dilemmas by virtue of its relatively benign nature. The sub-disciplines of programming methodology research, microprocessor design, and so forth have little room for the greater questions of human harm. Other, more recently developed sub-disciplines, such as data mining, social network analysis, behavioral profiling, and general computer security, however, open the door to abuse of users by practitioners and researchers. It is therefore the duty of the men and women who chart the course of these fields to set rules for themselves regarding what sorts of actions on their part are to be considered acceptable and what should be avoided or handled with caution out of ethical concerns. This paper deals solely with the issues faced by computer security researchers, be they vulnerability analysts, privacy system designers, malware experts, or reverse engineers.

The computer security researcher can do well to take a cue from the Hippocratic oath: first, do no harm. Of course, were the matter as simple as that, we would not as a community have discussed these issues for the past twenty-five years.

2 What Is Harm?

Questions surrounding the nature of acceptable research activities in the computer security field have been a persistent feature of the field almost since its inception. Examples of well-intentioned breaches of ethics can be found throughout the early literature, perhaps none more notorious than the Morris worm of the 1980s [14]. While it is easy to see the lack of malice intended by Morris with his experiment, modern researchers would almost unanimously agree that releasing malware onto the public network, intended to exploit unpatched security vulnerabilities on systems not controlled by the experimenter, without the authorization or knowledge of the affected network operators, is itself unethical.

Despite that, there remains a significant, though minority, group of opinion-makers who propose effectively the same sort of conduct when it comes to fighting

* Supported in part by the Concerted Research Action (GOA) Ambiorics 2005/11 of the Flemish Government, by the IBBT (Flemish Government), and the IAP Programme P6/26 BCRYPT of the Belgian State (Belgian Science Policy).

the present scourge of botnets, arguing that the Internet would benefit from the release of "benign worms" to patch the security holes being exploited by botnet authors; or from uninstall instructions issued from botnet command and control servers that have been seized by network administrators. When researcher Julia Wolf gained control of the command-and-control server domains for the largest spam botnet of 2008, Srizbi, many people asked why she did not use the botnet for "good" purposes [16]. Most commonly proposed uses involved removing the Srizbi bot from the affected clients with an update and patching the vulnerabilities that allowed those machines to become infected in the first place [15].

Similarly, when the Code Red worm infected over 359,000 machines on the Internet in 2001 [9], it was a matter of days before a programmer released a software package called "Code Green" – intended to "infect" already-infected Code Red nodes with a program that removed Code Red and patched the exploit [5]. Many network operators and security experts were quick to decry this approach both on ethical grounds, for it involved the installation of outside software without the consent of the administrators of the target machines, and for practical concerns, since it would necessitate a reboot of potentially critical systems with no means for the Code Green operators to address errors should they occur (or even identify "critical machines" so that they could avoid targeting them). Nevertheless, the idea of "killer worms" persists on certain Internet mailing lists and in academic communities. A paper on this topic by Wu et al. of Zhongshan University supporting this approach dismisses concerns about the potential criminal nature of such a worm by proposing a "centralized administrative power" with the authority to unleash "helpful" worms on systems without the necessity of consent [17]. The potential for unexpected behavior to cause damage is not acknowledged or discussed in that paper.

The Western legal doctrine of property rights has come to play a key role in guiding the actions of computer security professionals in cases like this — network operators are free to cease routing packets from worm-infested machines, dropping them from the net, but once an individual takes it upon himself to modify the restricted-access state of another party's system, he is in breach of ethical standards, as well as cyber-crime laws in many jurisdictions.

3   Software Vulnerability Analysis

For over a decade, a debate in the computer security community raged: what was the ethical course of action for a vulnerability researcher to take upon discovering an exploitable flaw in a piece of software? Many researchers espoused the doctrine of "full disclosure" — publication of their findings, including the necessary information to reproduce them, in accordance with the traditions of scientific research. Other parties, notably software vendors whose code these researchers were evaluating, argued that dissemination of knowledge on performing exploits put the general public at risk and helped facilitate criminal action[1].

---

[1] As recently as 2003, a Microsoft representative took the stance that vulnerability disclosure was reckless and irresponsible [3].

Our field has, in recent years, come to a happy medium, where responsible disclosure is considered to be the publication of reproducible vulnerability analysis after a "vendor notification period", sufficient to allow the affected software author time to verify, patch, and test fixes to their software's flaws. Details of exploits are then released after a patch has become available, and serve to encourage adoption of the bugfix.

The relatively straightforward process of responsible full disclosure has become more complicated in recent years, however. Web-based applications are more prevalent, meaning the act of vulnerability discovery is no longer conducted against an instance of code contained on a machine owned by the researcher, but often performed against a live server operated by a web service provider. In cases such as this, the researcher must tread lightly, for the simple act of discovering an exploit may mean performing that exploit on another party's system.

One of the first widely publicized cases of this problem involved a man popularly referred to as "the homeless hacker", Adrian Lamo, who took it upon himself to penetrate the computer systems of high-profile websites and companies, with the stated intent of improving their security [12]. By performing basic SQL injection attacks and other relatively simple techniques against websites such as that of the New York Times and Microsoft, he was able to gain access to information such as Social Security numbers and other confidential data. Lamo was initially unapologetic for his actions, insisting he was performing a public service. Popular opinion was mixed, with some members of the press going so far as to defend his theft of multiple Lexis/Nexis database logins, which he used to perform vanity searches [11]. The opinion of this author, however, is that Lamo knowingly and with premeditation conducted unethical and illegal intrusions into private computer systems, stole the resources of other parties for his own personal gain, and regardless of any security enhancements he may have performed on the systems he attacked, his actions did not render a service to his victims, who were left to audit the compromised systems, pay the usage fees he accrued, and engage in time-consuming legal proceedings[2] resulting as a direct consequence of Lamo's crooked moral compass. Regardless of motive, behavior such as this should be condemned.

Numerous individuals have run afoul of the law during the course of their investigations of website security. The technology media routinely reports stories of well-intentioned individuals stumbling upon (or seeking out) a security flaw in a website, reporting the problem to its administrators, and then facing prosecution for bypassing the website's security. Similarly, research into physical security that relies on computer science has its risks; after publishing a proof-of-concept that demonstrated weaknesses in airport checkpoint security, graduate student Christopher Soghoian had his house raided by the FBI, his computers seized, and was subject of an investigation after a congressman called for his arrest [6,2]. While that case was dropped, this and similar cases illustrate that caution when

---

[2] As Lamo's actions violated criminal statutes, the victims were not in a position to choose whether to sue or not — they could simply have been called as witnesses for the prosecution, leaving them little option but to comply.

conducting evaluations of information security is not only important from an ethical standpoint, but also prudent from a legal perspective.

4   Responsible Data Handling

The simple line between "my system" and "another party's system" is not the end of the matter, however. Operators of services that process user data, or have the ability to collect information on usage patterns for specific users, have an obligation to those users. Examples of well-intentioned mismanagement of private user data include the notorious "Netflix Challenge", where online video rental site Netflix published a large data set containing user commerce logs with the intent that researchers would develop a better recommendation system for the service. The company removed the obvious identifying information prior to releasing the data, but researchers were able to cross-correlate the user preferences in that dataset with other information and deanonymize the user data [10]. AOL made a similar mistake when it released logs of queries to its search engine [4].

Other recent incidents involve the willful violation of user privacy in the name of research. Swedish independent researcher Dan Egerstad operated a server for the popular anonymity network Tor during 2007. His intent, rather than to provide a service to his users, as would be reasonable to expect, was instead to use his server as a surveillance mechanism. He published user login credentials he gathered by listening to the cleartext network traffic exiting from his server. His experiment added little to the literature, for the attack he performed was generally common sense, had already been published [13], and his publication of the actual login information (rather than, for example, collated statistics on usage of insecure protocols over Tor, without identifying the victims of his attack or their passwords) was highly ethically unsound.

5   Summary

In this paper, we have discussed some of the ethical conflicts researchers and other members of the software and network security communities have encountered in recent years. We have drawn attention to specific instances of ethical failings, as a means of illustrating the problems that can arise when the ethical course of action is not perfectly clear, or the community neglects its responsibility to enforce ethical standards for itself and its members. Despite the obvious impropriety of some of the examples given, it is almost certainly the case that the people involved in ethically improper actions, or who have proposed ethically questionable schemes, were not engaging in a conscious, willful breach of ethics when doing so. It is essential that we as a community hold debates and discussions concerning the ethics of the choices before us, for they are rarely black and white, and it is through such critical examination that we develop the standards by which we hold ourselves and each other accountable to the collective conscience of our field. Dilemmas by their nature are not easily resolved, and thus such self-examination is a necessary part of our development as a community respectful of others. In her 1988 paper, Campbell suggests that a major cause of ethical lapses is a lack of this type of introspection [1]. Whether researchers choose to adhere to a specific set of ethical guidelines set forth by their peers, institutions, or professional organizations[3], or simply look inward to answer the question "Is what I am doing *good?*", the question must be asked, if for no other reason than the sake of the questioner's own happiness. To paraphrase Leibniz, perhaps the first computer scientist to ponder questions of ethics, the more a man desires to know virtue in his quest for knowledge, and the more inspired he is to incorporate virtue in his life, the happier his life will be.[4].

As computer security researchers, we have a duty to advance the state of the art of secure systems, encourage their adoption, and identify weaknesses in currently deployed software, protocols and systems. We must do so in a manner that balances overall improvement in system security, correction of specific security concerns, and advances in the general foundation of our discipline without endangering current users or putting existing deployed systems at unnecessary risk of attack. Sometimes it is not clear where to strike such a balance, but a responsible researcher will respect the need for open discussion of security issues (including offensive techniques) while attempting to accommodate the needs of at-risk services and vulnerable software vendors, as well as the users reliant upon their software for their security, privacy, industry, and peace of mind.

This discourse on ethical conduct in computer security research is critical, and must be revisited frequently as threats change and technology advances. We must answer our calling as scientists, to pursue knowledge for its own sake, which is justification enough to seek new methods and techniques for uncovering attacks on computer systems, or applying known attacks to systems whose flaws have not yet been fully excavated, upon which the light of understanding has not yet shined brightly enough to illuminate all of their unintended operation potential.

As scientists, we have a duty to preserve academic freedom — but with care, we can exercise that freedom in a responsible manner, and (if we believe Leibniz) by conducting ourselves virtuously, find happiness through our quest for knowledge in this tiny slice of all that, which awaits our knowing it.

Acknowledgements

The author would like to thank the people, too numerous to list, who have helped shape his views on ethical conduct, both in the field of computer security, and as a human being. *Duplicatur autem jucunditas reflexione, qvoties contemplamur*

---

[3] Examples of formal ethical guidelines can be found in [1]; additional such treatises have been authored in the twenty-two years since the publication of that paper, but they share a common goal: the codification of standards of conduct compatible with ethical action for the purpose of informing and guiding the individual's conscience.

[4] "Il faut tenir pour asseuré que plus un esprit desire de connoitre l'ordre, la raison, la beauté des choses que Dieu a produites et plus il est porté à imiter cet ordre dans les choses que Dieu a abandonnées à sa conduite, plus il sera heureux." [7].

pulchritudinem ipsi nostram, qvod fit conscientia tacita virtutis nostrae. Sed qve-
madmodum duplex in visu refractio contingere potest, altera in lente oculi, altera
in lente tubi, qvarum haec illam auget, ita duplex in cogitando reflexio est, cum
enim omnis mens habeat speculi instar, alterum erit in mente nostra, alterum
in aliena, et si plura sint specula, id est plures mentes bonorum nostrorum ag-
nitrices, major lux erit, miscentisbus speculis non tantum in oculo lucem, sed et
inter se, splendor collectus gloriam facit [8].

References

1. Campbell, M.: Ethics and Computer Security: Cause and Effect. In: CSC 1988: Proceedings of the 1988 ACM Sixteenth Annual Conference on Computer Science, pp. 384–390. ACM, New York (1988)
2. Carmack, J.: IU Student, Focus of FBI Probe, Speaks Out (2006)
3. Stanford Cyberlaw Clinic. CyberSecurity, Research and Disclosure (2003)
4. Hafner, K.: Researchers Yearn to Use AOL Logs, but They Hesitate. The New York Times (2006)
5. HexXer, H.: CodeGreen Beta Release (September 2001), http://archives.neohapsis.com/archives/vuln-dev/2001-q3/0575.html
6. Krebs, B.: Student Unleashes Uproar with Bogus Airline Boarding Passes. The Washington Post (2006)
7. Leibniz, G.W.: La Félicité. In: Textes Inédits D'après les Manuscrits de la Bibliothèque Provinciale de Hanovre. Presses Universitaires de France (1948)
8. Leibniz, G.W.: Elementa Juris Naturalis. In: Philosophische Schriften. Akademie Verlag GmbH (2006)
9. Moore, D., Shannon, C.: The Spread of the Code Red worm (2008), http://www.caida.org/research/security/code-red/coderedv2_analysis.xml
10. Narayanan, A., Shmatikov, V.: How To Break Anonymity of the Netflix Prize Dataset (2006)
11. Newitz, A.: TECHSPLOITATION: Subpoena Me, Too! San Francisco Bay Guardian (October 2003)
12. Poulsen, K.: Feds say Lamo Inspired Other Hackers. The Register (2004), http://www.theregister.co.uk/2004/09/16/feds_on_lamo/
13. Sassaman, L.: The Faithless Endpoint: How Tor puts certain users at greater risk. Technical Report ESAT-COSIC 2007-003, Katholieke Universiteit Leuven (2007)
14. Spafford, E.H.: The Internet Worm Program: an Analysis. SIGCOMM Computer Communication Review 19(1), 17–57 (1989)
15. Wolf, J.: Technical Details of Srizbi's Domain Generation Algorithm (2008), http://blog.fireeye.com/research/2008/11/technical-details-of-srizbis-domain-generation-algorithm.html
16. Wolf, J., Sassaman, L.: Unpublished manuscript (December 2008)
17. Wu, D., Long, D., Wang, C., Guan, Z.: Modeling and Analysis of Worm and Killer-Worm Propagation Using the Divide-and-Conquer Strategy. In: Hobbs, M., Goscinski, A.M., Zhou, W. (eds.) ICA3PP 2005. LNCS, vol. 3719, pp. 370–375. Springer, Heidelberg (2005)

Author Index

Androulaki, Elli   123
Auletta, Vincenzo   94
Aycock, John   231
Azuara, Guillermo   57

Bailey, Michael   240
Basin, David   182
Bellovin, Steven M.   123
Blundo, Carlo   94

Canard, Sébastien   19
Coisel, Iwen   19
Coron, Jean-Sébastien   107
Cranor, Lorrie Faith   247

De Caro, Angelo   94
De Cristofaro, Emiliano   94
Dietrich, Sven   195
Dingledine, Roger   203
Dittrich, David   216

Engels, Daniel   3
Etrog, Jonathan   19

Fan, Xinxin   3
Fathi, Hanane   47
Fleischmann, Kenneth R.   197

Garcia-Alfaro, J.   34
Gong, Guang   3
Gouget, Aline   107

Herrera-Joancomarti, J.   34
Hu, Honggang   3

Imai, Hideki   47

Kamara, Seny   136
Kenneally, Erin   240
Kiayias, Aggelos   105
Kobara, Kazukuni   47
Kravitz, David William   166

Lauter, Kristin   136
Leder, Felix   216
Loesing, Karsten   203

Martínez, Santi   80
Matsuo, Shin'ichiro   182
Maughan, Douglas   240
Melia-Segui, J.   34
Miret, Josep M.   1
Miyazaki, Kunihiko   182
Moradi, Amir   68
Murdoch, Steven J.   203

Otsuka, Akira   182

Paillier, Pascal   107
Persiano, Giuseppe   94
Piles, Joan J.   57
Poschmann, Axel   68

Roig, Concepció   80

Sadeghi, Ahmad-Reza   150
Sako, Kazue   105
Salazar, José L.   57
Sassaman, Len   250
Schulz, Steffen   150
Sebé, Francesc   1
Smith, Eric M.   3
Sullins, John   231

Tamura, Jin   47
Tornos, José L.   57

Valls, Magda   80
Villegas, Karine   107
Visconti, Ivan   94

Werner, Tillmann   216

Printed in the United States
By Bookmasters